Web App Development Made Simple with Streamlit

A web developer's guide to effortless web app development, deployment, and scalability

Rosario Moscato

‹packt›

Web App Development Made Simple with Streamlit

Copyright © 2024 Packt Publishing

All rights reserved. No part of this book may be reproduced, stored in a retrieval system, or transmitted in any form or by any means, without the prior written permission of the publisher, except in the case of brief quotations embedded in critical articles or reviews.

Every effort has been made in the preparation of this book to ensure the accuracy of the information presented. However, the information contained in this book is sold without warranty, either express or implied. Neither the author, nor Packt Publishing or its dealers and distributors, will be held liable for any damages caused or alleged to have been caused directly or indirectly by this book.

Packt Publishing has endeavored to provide trademark information about all of the companies and products mentioned in this book by the appropriate use of capitals. However, Packt Publishing cannot guarantee the accuracy of this information.

Group Product Manager: Rohit Rajkumar

Publishing Product Manager: Chayan Majumdar

Book Project Manager: Sonam Pandey

Senior Editor: Anuradha Joglekar

Technical Editor: K Bimala Singha and Simran Haresh Udasi

Copy Editor: Safis Editing

Proofreader: Safis Editing

Indexer: Pratik Shirodkar

Production Designer: Jyoti Kadam

DevRel Marketing Coordinators: Namita Velgekar and Nivedita Pandey

Publication date: February 2024

Production reference: 1110124

Published by Packt Publishing Ltd.

Grosvenor House

11 St Paul's Square

Birmingham

B3 1RB, UK

ISBN 978-1-83508-631-5

www.packtpub.com

This book was in progress for a long time, and I would like to thank all my e-students for supporting me and pushing me to turn video lessons into pages. I would also to thank my kids, Liv and Giu, for motivating me to be a role model, and my parents for inspiring me to do great things and keep moving forward toward a noble target, come what may!

- Rosario Moscato

Contributors

About the author

Rosario Moscato has a master's degree in electronic engineering (Federico II University, Naples) as well as a master's degree in internet software design (CEFRIEL, Milan). He also has a diploma in apologetics (Pontifical Athenaeum Regina Apostolorum, Rome) and a master's degree in science and faith (Pontifical Athenaeum Regina Apostolorum, Rome). Rosario has gained about 25 years of experience, always focusing his attention on the development and fine-tuning of the most innovative technologies in various international companies in Europe and Asia, covering various highly technical, commercial, and business development roles.

In recent years, his interest has focused exclusively on artificial intelligence and data science, pursuing, on the one hand, the goal of enhancing and making every business extremely competitive by introducing and supporting machine and deep learning technologies, and on the other hand, analyzing the ethical-philosophical implications deriving from the new scenarios that these disciplines open up. Rosario has authored two books, and he is a speaker at international research centers and conferences as well as a trainer and technical/scientific consultant on the huge and changing world of AI. Currently, he is working as a CTO with one of the oldest AI companies in Italy.

About the reviewers

Alessio Ligios is a dynamic data scientist, renowned for his proficiency in data analysis and machine learning. With a solid foundation in science and engineering, Alessio excels in transforming intricate data into practical business solutions. In his current role at Live Tech - Amplify your Data, Alessio has demonstrated his expertise by developing and implementing advanced textual content classification models. He excels in predictive modeling, leveraging machine learning (ML) and deep learning (DL) algorithms for accurate trend forecasting. Educationally, Alessio holds a master's degree in computer science from Università degli Studi "Roma Tre" with a distinguished vote of 110/110.

Corrado Silvestri is a computer engineer. He earned a master's degree from "Roma Tre" University with a GPA of 100/110. Passionate about the realm of AI and ML, he has produced models and projects of many types, such as forecasting, NLP, and computer vision, establishing the groundwork for his present position as a data scientist at a company that is verticalized in AI. An expert in the analytical phase and data manipulation, he has implemented AI models and solutions, expanding his technical experience and excelling in this field. He is a specialist at finding the perfect compromise by combining engineering expertise, data manipulation, and AI to build cutting-edge solutions for businesses in a variety of industries.

Table of Contents

Preface   xiii

Part 1: Getting Started with Streamlit

1

Getting to Know Streamlit – A Brief Overview   3

The importance of turning an idea into a prototype – the changing scenario in computing methods	4	Python libraries for web applications (Flask and Django)	8
		Examples of Streamlit's capabilities	10
The importance of a full Python web framework	5	The importance of turning an idea into a prototype	11
Local versus the cloud	7	Summary	12

2

Setting Up the Python Coding Environment   13

Technical requirements	13	What is a virtual environment?	22
Setting up the OS	14	Summary	29
IDE selection	20		

3

Exploring Streamlit's Features and Functionality   31

Technical requirements	31	Colored textboxes	39
Installing and launching Streamlit	32	Images, audio, and video	40
Streamlit features and widgets	36	Inputting text and numbers	47

Slider	50	DataFrames, plots, and visualizations	51
Balloons	51	Date, time, and more	57
		Summary	63

Part 2: Building a Basic Web App for Essential Streamlit Skills

4

Streamlit Essentials – Configuring the Environment, Managing Packages, and More   67

Technical requirements	68	Building the menu and adding decorations	79
Configuring our environment	68		
Installing and importing packages	70	Summary	86
App skeleton building	73		

5

Organizing and Displaying Content with Columns, Expanders, and NLP Techniques   87

Technical requirements	88	Adding the two basic functions	99
Organizing and arranging content in a web app	88	Adding a wordcloud	105
		Introducing NLP concepts – tokens and lemmas	107
Adding decorations	89		
Adding the Text Analysis part	90	Adding the summarization function	107
Hiding and showing parts depending on importance	95	Tokens and lemmas	110
		Using the text_analysis function	112
Adding columns, expanders, and a textbox	95	Summary	118

6

Implementing NLP Techniques for Text Analysis and Processing in Streamlit 119

Technical requirements	120	Performing the translation task	124
Deep-diving into NLP techniques	120	Diving deep into sentiment analysis	129
What is translation?	121	Recap of our first web application	135
What is sentiment analysis?	122	Summary	135
Deep-diving into language translation	122		
Adding a text area	122		

7

Sharing and Deploying Your Apps on the Cloud Using Streamlit Share 145

Technical requirements	146	What are Streamlit Share and Streamlit Cloud?	148
Understanding the importance of deployment	146	A quick introduction to GitHub	148
Best practices in web application deployment	147	Getting familiar with the Streamlit Share service	150
Additional benefits of web application deployment	147	Summary	161

Part 3: Developing Advanced Skills with a Covid-19 Detection Tool

8

Advanced Environment Setup and Package Management for Building an AI-Powered Web App 165

Technical requirements	166	Building the menu and adding decorations	175
Configuring our environment	166	Summary	175
Installing and importing packages	167		
Building the app skeleton	172		

9

Optimizing Streamlit Web App UX with Customization and UI Features   179

Technical requirements	180	Brightness	188
Dealing with more advanced web app features	180	Original	190
		Adding the Disclaimer and Info section	192
Adding the Image Enhancement section using the Pillow library	184	Summary	196
Contrast	186		

10

Utilizing Pretrained Models to Create Specialized and Personalized Web Applications   199

Technical requirements	200	Creating customized web apps to improve user experience	202
Understanding the benefits of pretrained ML models	200	Utilizing predictions from ML	206
		Summary	215

11

Deploying and Managing Complex Libraries on Streamlit Share   217

Technical requirements	217	Creating a GitHub repository	221
Consolidating cloud deployment skills	218	Avoiding runtime errors	222
		Managing difficult libraries	224
Avoiding bad behavior	220	Deploying the app on Streamlit Cloud	228
Creating a list of all the packages that were installed and used to develop the Python code	220	Summary	232

Part 4: Advanced Techniques for Secure and Customizable Web Applications

12

Smart File Uploading – Advanced Techniques for Professional Web Applications — 235

Technical requirements	235	Creating a suitable file uploader for web apps	243
Understanding the customized features of the file uploader	236	Simplifying web apps with smart components	250
Creating a new virtual environment	236	Summary	250
Building the app skeleton	237		
Creating a radio button for the app menu	239		

13

Creating a Secure Login and Signup Process for Web Applications — 251

Technical requirements	252	Creating the Login menu	259
Understanding the logic behind the login and signup page	252	Creating the Sign Up menu	261
		Running the app	262
What is SHA-256 and why should we use it?	253	Adding a graphical user interface	264
Connecting to a relational database and interacting with it	257	Retrieving or saving credentials from and to the database	266
		Summary	274

14

Customizing Pages, Personalizing Themes, and Implementing Multi-Pages — 275

Technical requirements	275	Understanding theming and .toml files	285
Understanding new features related to deep customization	276	Exploring the multi-pages feature	286
Creating deeply customized pages	281	Creating multi-pages	287
		Passing a variable from one page to another	292
		Summary	298

15

Enhancing Web Apps with Forms, Session State, and Customizable Subdomains — 299

Technical requirements	300	What is Session State and when do we use it?	306
What are forms and when and why do we use them?	300	What are customizable subdomains and what possibilities do they offer?	311
The context manager approach	301	Summary	313
The classic approach	305		

16

Takeaways and Conclusion — 315

How and when to use our web app working template	316	How to deploy web applications on the cloud	319
How and when to use databases and advanced skills	317	Farewell!	320

Index — 321

Other Books You May Enjoy — 328

Preface

In the swiftly evolving landscape of web application development, the desire to transform innovative ideas into functional web apps has never been more pressing. *Web App Development Made Simple with Streamlit* is a book that emerges as a beacon for those who seek to navigate this dynamic domain with ease and confidence. This book is meticulously crafted for a diverse range of professionals who share a common goal – the rapid transformation of code into working web applications.

At its core, *Web App Development Made Simple with Streamlit* is more than just a guide; it's a journey. It takes you from the fundamentals of Streamlit, a powerful tool that simplifies web app development, to the intricate processes of deploying your solutions on cloud services. This journey is designed to be accessible, empowering you to make your applications available to a vast, global audience with minimal hassle.

Throughout the book, you'll find a harmonious blend of theoretical knowledge and practical application. The chapters are structured to provide a clear, step-by-step guide, ensuring that even those new to web development can follow along with ease. Moreover, the book is peppered with real-world examples and case studies, providing you with a tangible understanding of how Streamlit can be leveraged in various scenarios.

As you delve into the pages of this book, expect to embark on a transformative learning experience. You'll gain not just the skills to develop web applications but also the vision to see the potential of your code in the digital world. This book is your companion in unlocking the power of Streamlit, simplifying web app development, and bringing your ideas to the global stage.

Who this book is for

This book is tailored for Python programmers looking to transform their scripts into interactive web applications. It's an essential resource for web developers seeking to streamline their prototyping process using Streamlit's intuitive framework. Computer science students will find this book a practical guide for applying their theoretical knowledge to real-world web app development. IT professionals and enthusiasts eager to explore the realm of web app creation, especially those keen on deploying applications quickly and efficiently, will discover invaluable insights within these pages. Essentially, this book is a comprehensive toolkit for anyone passionate about bringing web app ideas to life with simplicity and speed.

What this book covers

Chapter 1, *Getting to Know Streamlit – A Brief Overview*, introduces Streamlit's role in web app development. The chapter offers an overview of Streamlit's user-friendly features and capabilities, as well as insight into rapid development with Streamlit.

Chapter 2, *Setting Up the Python Coding Environment*, includes a step-by-step guide for Python environment setup. The chapter includes tips for efficient Streamlit integration and focuses on creating a streamlined development workflow.

Chapter 3, *Exploring Streamlit's Features and Functionality*, explores Streamlit's functionalities in detail. Practical examples showcasing its versatility are included. The chapter also offers insights into Streamlit's unique feature set.

Chapter 4, *Streamlit Essentials – Configuring the Environment, Managing Packages, and More*, describes key techniques for Streamlit environment configuration as well as best practices for efficient package management. Tips for optimizing the Streamlit setup are included.

Chapter 5, *Organizing and Displaying Content with Columns, Expanders, and NLP Techniques*, explores strategies for content organization using Streamlit's tools. The chapter introduces **natural language processing** (**NLP**) techniques for enhanced content management and describes methods for effective data presentation.

Chapter 6, *Implementing NLP Techniques for Text Analysis and Processing in Streamlit*, teaches you how to apply NLP for text analysis within Streamlit. A step-by-step guide for NLP integration and case studies showcasing NLP in web app development are included.

Chapter 7, *Sharing and Deploying Your Apps on the Cloud Using Streamlit Share*, describes instructions for cloud deployment using Streamlit Share. Tips for making apps accessible globally are included. The chapter also offers insights into cloud-based app sharing.

Chapter 8, *Advanced Environment Setup and Package Management for Building an AI-Powered Web App*, teaches you advanced setup techniques for AI-driven web apps. Package management for AI integration and strategies for setting up an efficient AI web app environment are explained in detail.

Chapter 9, *Optimizing Streamlit Web App UX with Customization and UI Features*, explains how to enhance user experience through Streamlit customization. The chapter also explores UI features for functional aesthetics. Techniques for UI-driven app optimization are described.

Chapter 10, *Utilizing Pretrained Models to Create Specialized and Personalized Web Applications*, delves into the integration of pretrained models in web apps. The chapter explains how to create specialized, user-centric applications. Personalization strategies using AI models are described.

Chapter 11, *Deploying and Managing Complex Libraries on Streamlit Share*, explores techniques for deploying complex libraries on Streamlit Share. Strategies for managing robust app performance and complex library integration are included.

Chapter 12, *Smart File Uploading – Advanced Techniques for Professional Web Applications*, explains advanced file uploading methods for professionalism. The chapter teaches you how to streamline file uploads for user ease and enhance web apps with efficient file management.

Chapter 13, *Creating a Secure Login and Signup Process for Web Applications*, shows you how to design secure authentication processes, ensure user data protection, and implement robust login/signup systems in web apps.

Chapter 14, *Customizing Pages, Personalizing Themes, and Implementing Multi-Pages*, describes techniques for unique page customization. The chapter teaches you how to personalize themes for brand identity and utilize multi-page layouts for complex apps.

Chapter 15, *Enhancing Web Apps with Forms, Session State, and Customizable Subdomains*, teaches you how to utilize forms and session states for dynamic content. The chapter also describes how to implement customizable subdomains for branding. Strategies for enhancing web apps with advanced features are explored.

Chapter 16, *Takeaways and Conclusion*, summarizes the book's essential insights and what you have learned, reflecting on Streamlit's impact on web app development and offering concluding thoughts on future trends.

To get the most out of this book

You will need an understanding of the basics of Python programming and the Linux Terminal.

Software/hardware covered in the book	Operating system requirements
Python 3.X	The Linux Terminal

If you are using the digital version of this book, we advise you to type the code yourself or access the code from the book's GitHub repository (a link is available in the next section). Doing so will help you avoid any potential errors related to the copying and pasting of code.

Download the example code files

You can download the example code files for this book from GitHub at `https://github.com/PacktPublishing/Web-App-Development-Made-Simple-with-Streamlit`. If there's an update to the code, it will be updated in the GitHub repository.

We also have other code bundles from our rich catalog of books and videos available at `https://github.com/PacktPublishing/`. Check them out!

Conventions used

There are a number of text conventions used throughout this book.

`Code in text`: Indicates code words in text, database table names, folder names, filenames, file extensions, pathnames, dummy URLs, user input, and Twitter handles. Here is an example: "Let's check whether `pip` is installed in our Ubuntu box."

A block of code is set as follows:

```
st.header("This is a header")
st.subheader("This is a subheader")
st.text("This is a simple text")
st.write("This is a write dimension")
```

Any command-line input or output is written as follows:

```
pip --version (or pip3 --version)
```

Bold: Indicates a new term, an important word, or words that you see on screen. For instance, words in menus or dialog boxes appear in **bold**. Here is an example: "We have also completed the **Text Analysis** and **About** sections of the menu."

> **Tips or important notes**
> Appear like this.

Get in touch

Feedback from our readers is always welcome.

General feedback: If you have questions about any aspect of this book, email us at `customercare@packtpub.com` and mention the book title in the subject of your message.

Errata: Although we have taken every care to ensure the accuracy of our content, mistakes do happen. If you have found a mistake in this book, we would be grateful if you would report this to us. Please visit `www.packtpub.com/support/errata` and fill in the form.

Piracy: If you come across any illegal copies of our works in any form on the internet, we would be grateful if you would provide us with the location address or website name. Please contact us at `copyright@packtpub.com` with a link to the material.

If you are interested in becoming an author: If there is a topic that you have expertise in and you are interested in either writing or contributing to a book, please visit `authors.packtpub.com`.

Share Your Thoughts

Once you've read *Web App Development Made Simple with Streamlit*, we'd love to hear your thoughts! Scan the QR code below to go straight to the Amazon review page for this book and share your feedback.

`https://packt.link/r/1835086314`

Your review is important to us and the tech community and will help us make sure we're delivering excellent quality content.

Download a free PDF copy of this book

Thanks for purchasing this book!

Do you like to read on the go but are unable to carry your print books everywhere?

Is your eBook purchase not compatible with the device of your choice?

Don't worry, now with every Packt book you get a DRM-free PDF version of that book at no cost.

Read anywhere, any place, on any device. Search, copy, and paste code from your favorite technical books directly into your application.

The perks don't stop there, you can get exclusive access to discounts, newsletters, and great free content in your inbox daily

Follow these simple steps to get the benefits:

1. Scan the QR code or visit the link below

https://packt.link/free-ebook/9781835086315

2. Submit your proof of purchase
3. That's it! We'll send your free PDF and other benefits to your email directly

Part 1: Getting Started with Streamlit

Part 1 serves as the foundation for your journey into Streamlit. It begins with a comprehensive introduction to Streamlit, highlighting its significance in the realm of web app development. You are then guided through setting up the necessary Python coding environment, ensuring a smooth start. The part culminates with an in-depth exploration of Streamlit's diverse features and functionalities, providing a solid base of understanding for you to start building your own web application. This part is crucial for establishing the knowledge and skills needed for the more advanced concepts covered in later sections of the book.

This part contains the following chapters:

- *Chapter 1, Getting to Know Streamlit – A Brief Overview*
- *Chapter 2, Setting Up the Python Coding Environment*
- *Chapter 3, Exploring Streamlit's Features and Functionality*

1
Getting to Know Streamlit – A Brief Overview

Streamlit is a Python library that allows developers to quickly create interactive web applications with plottings, widgets, themes, and more. It provides an intuitive and easy-to-use interface that makes it simple to create custom web apps with minimal coding effort. It offers a range of built-in widgets and components, such as sliders, dropdowns, and text inputs, that can be used to create interactive visualizations and dashboards. The library also supports real-time data updates and even integrates with popular data science tools, such as pandas, Matplotlib, and TensorFlow.

Compared to other Python libraries for creating web apps, such as Flask and Django, Streamlit focuses on providing an intuitive interface for creating interactive visualizations and dashboards in a very simple and fast way. Flask and Django are more general-purpose web frameworks that can be used for a wider range of web applications, but they require more coding effort to set up and customize. Streamlit is designed to be used primarily for prototyping and creating small to medium-sized web apps and makes it possible to speed up the development process, enabling programmers to share their results with others in a user-friendly and engaging way.

In this chapter, we will first understand the changing scenario in computing methods and cover some key benefits of web applications. Next, we will understand the importance of a Python web framework. After that, we will focus on understanding when to use a local approach and when to work on the cloud. Then, we will learn about some very interesting capabilities of Streamlit. Finally, we will emphasize the importance of turning ideas into prototypes.

In this chapter, we're going to cover the following main topics:

- The changing scenario in computing methods
- The importance of a full Python web framework
- Local versus the cloud

- Python libraries for web applications (Flask and Django)
- Examples of Streamlit's capabilities

The importance of turning an idea into a prototype – the changing scenario in computing methods

Computing has advanced dramatically over the past few decades. Earlier systems relied on programs that were installed and run on individual personal computers. Users would purchase software licenses, install the programs themselves, and then access those applications from their desktops. If you wanted to use an application on another computer, you had to install it there as well.

This model dominated computing for many years but was limited and static. It lacked interconnectivity and did not facilitate true collaboration or data sharing across machines. Users were confined to the specific software they installed locally and had to manage separate copies of files and settings on each computer they used.

The rise of networks, improved connectivity, and the early internet started to change this. New possibilities emerged for distributed software, real-time collaboration, and synchronized information across devices. Users no longer had to install and manage many duplicate software installations. Applications could be accessed from anywhere with an internet connection.

Web-based services fueled this transition and accelerated the move to more cloud-centric and mobile-friendly computing. Apps began to launch directly in web browsers instead of requiring installation. Data and files could be stored in central cloud platforms instead of locally, and new devices such as smartphones, tablets, and laptops made the cloud and web even more compelling.

People now live their digital lives in the cloud through web-based services, mobile apps, and cloud platforms. Everything from business software, media, productivity tools, educational resources, and more now have predominantly cloud-based and web-centered counterparts. The cloud provides ubiquitous access across any connected device, constant integration and interoperability between services, automatic updates, scalable resources, collaboration features, mobile optimization, and cost benefits.

Local software is still used in some contexts but is increasingly viewed as limited or outdated. The transition to the cloud and web computing has been rapid and enormously impactful. It has reshaped how we work, learn, play, communicate, consume media, and more. And this transformation will likely only accelerate as enhanced AI technologies, IoT devices, VR/AR systems, and other innovations integrate more deeply into web-based services and cloud platforms.

We have come far from the software installations of yesterday, but the potential is hugely promising. Cloud computing is reimagining technology to fit our modern highly connected and increasingly mobile lifestyles. And this new era of ubiquitous, web-first computing is here to stay.

But considering that we are dealing with web applications in this book, what exactly is a web app?

A web application is a software application that runs within a **web browser**.

It is accessed via a network and delivers an interactive user experience through a web browser.

The purpose of a web application is to provide access to software capabilities and data over a network using standard web technologies. They allow users to access features and content from any internet-connected device with a web browser.

Web applications are useful when you want to provide access to software and data for a large number of users, potentially within an organization or to external customers and partners. They provide a convenient, consistent interface that works across devices and locations.

Here are some of the key benefits of web applications:

- **Accessibility**: Available anywhere with an internet connection and web browser.
- **Consistency**: The same interface and features are available on any device. The look and feel translate across platforms (desktop, mobile, tablet, and more).
- **Centralized management**: It's easy to update web applications for all users simultaneously. New features and enhancements automatically propagate to all users.
- **Integration**: Can integrate with other web services, databases, APIs, and more using standard web technologies.
- **Scalability**: Can scale to support a large number of simultaneous users with minimal additional overhead. Additional computing resources can be allocated as needed.
- **Cost-effective**: Often, it's more affordable and economical to develop and deploy web applications versus standalone software applications.

To summarize, use web applications when you need to provide an application and its data to a large number of users over a network, with the benefits of accessibility, consistency, integration, and scalability that web applications offer. They are a very effective and popular type of software solution.

Now that we know the benefits of web applications, we can move on to the next section, where we will understand the importance of a full Python-based framework.

The importance of a full Python web framework

Building and publishing web applications on the cloud today relies on several key frameworks, languages, and techniques. Some of the most important are as follows:

- **Web frameworks**: Frameworks such as React, Angular, and Node.js make developing web apps easier and more efficient. They handle key tasks such as routing, state management, building components, and handling events. Developers can focus on writing code for their specific applications instead of building infrastructure.

- **Server-side languages**: Languages such as PHP, Ruby on Rails, Python, Java, and C# are used on the server side to handle requests, access databases, build APIs, and generate dynamic web content. Node.js, which uses JavaScript, has also become very popular for server-side development.
- **JavaScript**: JavaScript is the primary language of the frontend web. It is used to build client-side interfaces, animate and create interactive content, handle user input, request data via HTTP requests, and more. Modern JavaScript frameworks have also enabled the rise of single-page applications.
- **Version control**: Tools such as Git help developers collaborate and keep a project's code and file history synchronized. They enable useful features such as branching, merging, committing, pushing to remote repositories, and rolling back changes.
- **Deployment:** There are several options for deploying web applications, including server management services such as AWS EC2, managed services such as Firebase, **virtual private servers** (**VPS**), and bare-metal servers. Continuous integration and deployment help get new features and code live as quickly and seamlessly as possible.
- **Containerization**: Docker containers package web applications and all their dependencies into isolated, portable, lightweight environments. They help keep development, staging, and production environments consistent and optimized. Containers simplify deploying and scaling web apps.
- **Application programming interfaces** (**APIs**): These allow web applications to integrate with external services and pass data back and forth seamlessly. APIs power features such as user authentication, payment handling, location services, social networking, and much more without requiring multiple web apps to share code bases.

As we can see, there are many tools and techniques we can use to build, deploy, scale, and integrate web applications professionally and efficiently today. When combined effectively, they enable fast, robust development cycles, optimized performance, and seamless connectivity between services. Moreover, as technologies continue to evolve, these best practices and stacks will adapt to meet new demands.

This great variety of frameworks, languages, and techniques is a strong weapon in our hands that can make it possible to develop more or less any idea we could have. However, this requires continuous learning and huge know-how of too many different topics.

For this reason, it would be great if a unique framework fully available in **Python**, a simplistic programming language, could help us develop our web applications quickly, making their deployment simple and smooth. The answer to this problem is **Streamlit**.

So, in a few words, Streamlit is something that makes it much easier for us to develop, implement, and deploy our ideas and turn them into wonderful web apps. But should the product be made available on our local machines or in the cloud?

Local versus the cloud

There are some key differences to keep in mind when developing software applications versus cloud-based web applications:

- **Installation**: Traditional software needs to be installed on local machines or servers. This includes copying files, setting permissions, possibly configuring settings, and other setup steps. Web apps hosted on cloud platforms such as AWS, GCP, and Azure are deployed and managed by the cloud provider. No local installation is required.
- **Updates**: Software updates typically require manual installation on all machines where the application is installed. Web apps hosted on the cloud are automatically updated when developers push new code deployments. Users always get the latest version without any manual work.
- **Scalability**: Servers hosting traditional software applications would require manual configuration to scale resources up or down as needed. Cloud infrastructure is infinitely scalable on demand through API calls or automatic scaling policies. More or less CPU, memory, disk space, and more can be allocated programmatically.
- **Availability**: Uptime depends on local infrastructure for traditional software. Downtime can occur due to issues with individual servers, networking equipment, database servers, and more. Web apps benefit from the high availability of scalable cloud infrastructure. Regions, availability zones, and replication help minimize outages.
- **Mobility**: Traditional software is accessed through dedicated desktop or mobile applications. Web apps are accessible through any modern browser on any internet-connected device. This includes laptops, phones, tablets, TVs, watches, and more.
- **Collaboration**: Multiple developers can work together simultaneously, editing code and deploying updates to web apps hosted on version control repositories and cloud hosting services. Edits to code bases are easily synced through source version control systems such as Git. Concurrent editing exposes opportunities for conflicts in traditional development workflows.
- **Costs**: Significant upfront costs are typically associated with purchasing and maintaining hardware and software licenses for traditional infrastructure. Cloud computing is based on a pay-per-use model with costs that can be reduced by scaling down or turning off unused resources. No large capital expenses are required. Resources can be scaled on-demand as needs evolve.

To summarize, developing web applications on cloud platforms differs from building traditional software installations in key ways. Web apps are often easier to deploy, update, scale, and make highly available and mobile, involve more concurrent collaboration, and have lower upfront costs and more adjustable pricing models.

As we can see, cloud platforms have a lot of advantages and should be our first choice. Now, let's delve a little bit deeper and look at the differences and specific features of the most popular Python libraries for web applications.

Python libraries for web applications (Flask and Django)

Here's an overview of some popular Python libraries for building web applications:

- **Flask**: A lightweight and flexible web framework. It's great for building small to mid-sized apps. Some of its main features are as follows:

  - It has a minimal and intuitive core that can be easily extended. This makes it suitable for anyone looking to create web applications.
  - It supports extensions and integrates with many Python libraries. This allows you to easily expand its functionality.
  - It has built-in support for routing, templates, file uploading, and more, which means it's quite easy to build APIs and render HTML templates.
  - It's suited for both small and large-scale projects. Many big companies such as Airbnb and Pinterest use Flask.

  Let's look at some situations when we should use Flask:

  - Building a small to mid-sized website or web app
  - When we need more flexibility and control than what a microframework provides
  - The need to support extensions and integrations with other libraries
  - When we're familiar with Python and want a framework that's easy to get started with

- **Django**: A high-level Python web framework that encourages rapid development and clean design. It's suited for large projects and applications. Some of its main features are as follows:

  - It has an **object-relational mapper** (**ORM**) that supports multiple databases.
  - It has a permission system and built-in support for users, groups, permissions, and more.
  - It scales well and is used by huge companies such as Instagram, Netflix, Spotify, and others.
  - It has a lot of add-on libraries and integrations available.
  - It enforces a certain structure and best practices. This can be good for newcomers but can also be restrictive.

  Let's look at some situations when we should use Django:

  - For building a large and complex website or web application
  - When we need a structured and scalable framework
  - When we require advanced features such as authentication, permissions, administrators, and more out of the box

- When we want a framework that scales well and can support a lot of traffic and load
- When we prefer a rigid structure and enforceable best practices

In summary, choose Flask for small to mid-sized web apps and Django for large, complex web applications with advanced features.

If you want to write web applications with beautiful and useful dashboards easily, choose Streamlit. This, among all the tools and solutions we've described so far, is an important Python web application framework for several key reasons:

- **Convenience and ease of use**: Streamlit simplifies building web apps in Python dramatically. It handles complex tasks such as setting up servers, routing, templating, databases, and more under the hood so that developers can focus on their application logic. This makes the development process faster and more accessible.
- **Integrated Python support**: Streamlit allows you to build entire web applications using only Python code. No additional templates, routing setup, or database configuration is required. Developers can utilize all of Python's libraries and features, and there is no need to learn additional languages or frameworks.
- **Rapid prototyping**: Streamlit's convenient and lightweight nature makes it ideal for quickly building prototypes, dashboards, demos, and minimum viable products. New ideas can be converted into shareable web applications very quickly.
- **Reusable components**: Streamlit has a library of pre-built reusable frontend and backend components such as dropdowns, file uploaders, search bars, pagination, and more. These help speed up development and ensure a consistent user experience.
- **Cloud deployment**: Streamlit web apps can be deployed on major cloud providers, including AWS, GCP, Azure, and Docker. This provides scalable infrastructure, global reach, and the flexibility to adapt resource usage as an application grows. Deployment is simplified through seamless integration.
- **Interactive dashboards**: Streamlit specializes in interactive applications and dashboards. It is used by data scientists and analysts to create insightful exploratory data analysis tools and reports. Users can filter, sort, pivot, search, select features, and examine data from multiple angles.
- **Community and support**: Streamlit has an active community and team behind it that supports usage questions, contributes to documentation, accepts pull requests, and addresses security issues promptly. The project is also backed by major tech companies and researchers.

In summary, Streamlit provides an easy-to-use, integrated, and scalable framework for building and deploying full web applications in Python. It allows you to convert ideas into apps faster, enables shortcutting low-level setup, facilitates prototyping and experimentation, enables interactive visualizations and dashboards, and supports customization and contribution from an open community. Overall, Streamlit makes web development in Python more accessible, productive, and impactful.

So far, we've covered the main Python web application libraries and their specificities. Since we'll be focusing on Streamlit in this book, let's see what it's capable of.

Examples of Streamlit's capabilities

Here are some useful examples of Streamlit's capabilities:

- **Interactive data exploration**: Streamlit is great for building dashboards that allow users to explore datasets interactively. Users can filter, sort, pivot, search, select features, and analyze data from multiple perspectives.
- **Prototyping minimum viable products** (**MVPs**): Streamlit's ease of use makes it perfect for building quick prototypes and MVPs. New ideas can be converted into shareable web apps in no time without any complex setup. This "code-first" approach speeds up iteration and feedback.
- **Model deployment**: Streamlit apps can expose trained **machine learning** (**ML**) models as web services. This allows other apps, scripts, or users to interact with and make predictions from the models. Apps become deployable, productive ML applications and platforms.
- **Embeddings**: Streamlit code and widgets can be embedded into Jupyter notebooks, JupyterLab, and the Jupyter Notebook interface. This close integration with the data science ecosystem streamlines the process of building apps from notebooks and vice versa.
- **Collaborative editing**: Streamlit streams edits in real time, enabling the co-editing of code bases seamlessly. Multiple developers can work together simultaneously on one Streamlit app, with changes appearing instantly. Conflicts are avoided, and productive collaboration is possible.
- **Automated testing**: Streamlit includes tools for writing automated tests in the form of test suites, individual test functions, fixtures, stubs, mocks, and more. Test coverage reports ensure new features do not break existing functionality. Continuous integration workflows run tests on each commit, leading to stable, high-quality code.
- **User interfaces** (**UIs**) **as code**: The Streamlit syntax is based on Python, treating UIs as code. This "UI as code" approach provides many benefits over graphical tools, including version control, reproducibility, collaboration, and integration with the rest of an application's code base. Streamlit UIs are flexible, programmatic, and build-time optimized.
- **Reproducible research**: Streamlit's apps are executed line by line, building up a complete, interactive, and shareable environment. All inputs, code, outputs, and widget values are recorded, allowing anyone to reproduce analysis and results. Apps can be packaged and archived, then re-opened and resumed later. Streamlit facilitates transparent and reproducible data science.
- **Automating experiments**: Streamlit's support for modular functions, classes, loops, conditionals, and more allows you to automate experiment workflows. Infrastructure can be scaled up and down programmatically, different models and hyperparameters can be tested systematically, and A/B testing of features and UX elements becomes possible. Automation reduces manual effort and leads to discovering the combinations that work best faster.

Streamlit is incredibly versatile and can help us create more or less any kind of application we have in mind in quite a short time and with an affordable effort. Considering this enormous point of strength, let's understand why turning our ideas into working prototypes in a short time can be the most useful weapon in our hands.

The importance of turning an idea into a prototype

The faster an idea can be turned into a tangible prototype, the greater the opportunities and advantages. There are several key benefits to building rough prototypes as quickly as possible:

- **Get customer feedback early**: By creating prototypes that embody an idea, even in a basic form, you can get real user feedback much sooner. Customers can experience the idea, comment on what they like and don't like, and suggest important changes to make the final product more useful and appealing. Incorporating feedback early avoids wasting time and resources developing features or designs that don't resonate with customers.

- **Discover flaws and issues early**: Early prototypes highlight any problems with how an idea might work in practice. Issues that are hard to identify conceptually become immediately obvious when developing a prototype. These issues can then be addressed, and alternative approaches can be explored before a massive amount of time has been invested. It's far easier to change course with a prototype than with a nearly finished product.

- **Gauge viability and enthusiasm**: By demonstrating prototypes for others, including team members, managers, mentors, and investors, you can get a sense of how compelling and exciting they seem. Enthusiasm and validation at early stages provide confidence that an idea has real potential and traction. A lack of enthusiasm shows that an idea may not be as promising as what people first thought.

- **Iterate and improve rapidly**: Prototyping, by its nature, enables an iterative approach. You build, get feedback, make changes, build again, and continue refining. Each iteration improves the prototype, making it more attractive and useful. What starts as a basic mockup can quickly evolve into an engaging product concept through ongoing feedback and development.

Turning ideas into prototypes as rapidly and as frequently as possible leads to better products, happier customers, higher enthusiasm within teams and partners, and a greater likelihood of building something that ultimately succeeds in the market. Early and iterative prototyping opens up opportunities and advantages at every stage of development and product design. With quick prototypes, you can pivot, improve, and innovate your way to success.

Summary

In this chapter, we introduced Streamlit from a theoretical point of view and looked at several reasons that make this framework an incredible tool for creating web applications and prototypes quickly and easily. Turning an idea into a prototype – or even better, into a working web application – quickly, easily, and painlessly is a terrific weapon in our hands. The power of such a library can only be fully expressed by using it, so let's not wait any longer and start setting up our coding environment!

To start coding, we still need some things: a good operating system with a Python installation, an **integrated development environment** (IDE), virtual environments, and more.

In the next chapter, we are going to ensure that everything we need will be available and fully functioning. Don't worry – this installation will act as the foundation for all our future developments!

2
Setting Up the Python Coding Environment

Before we start coding with Streamlit, we need to prepare our environment. Setting up a Python coding environment, especially in Linux (for example, Ubuntu), can be done in a few simple steps: update (or install) Python, install a code editor or IDE (maybe something free, such as **Sublime Text**), set up a virtual environment (in the book, we are using **pipenv**, but any other would be good), and install dependencies. After these steps, we should have a fully functional Python coding environment (in Ubuntu or any other **operating system** (**OS**)) that's ready to use for our web application's development.

This chapter is all about the environment setup. We need to prepare all the tools needed to make our developments with Streamlit smooth and productive. So, first of all, we are dealing with the choice of OS, which can be real or virtual, and either Windows, macOS, or Linux (our preferred solution). Next, we have to decide what kind of editor or **integrated development environment** (**IDE**) to use for coding. Some of them are very advanced and expensive, and some others are a little bit simpler but free. Finally, we'll talk about virtual environments and the advantages of using them.

In this chapter, we're going to cover the following main topics:

- Setting up the OS
- IDE selection
- What is a virtual environment?

Technical requirements

In this chapter, we will be using the following libraries, packages, and tools:

- VirtualBox
- Ubuntu
- Python 3

- Sublime Text
- `pipenv`
- `pipenv-pipes`

Setting up the OS

It's extremely important to have a very well-working environment. The OS is the place where everything is supposed to run. Even if the first choice we are asked to make is in regard to the OS to be used, we can say that from this point of view, we are lucky, because Streamlit is a framework in Python. This programming language works more or less on any OS, so we are really free to select what we want – for example, macOS, Windows, any Linux distribution, or, if you like, even any BSD flavor.

For several reasons that we are going to explain shortly, we prefer Ubuntu, and if you are concerned about its usage or about installing it, take it easy because first of all, it's really easy to use. And, if you don't want to, you don't need to install it on your machine as an exclusive and unique OS as you can use virtualization software, a very useful tool that makes it possible to run an OS inside another OS! Moreover, knowing how to manage a virtualization tool and install on it any kind of OS can be a very useful skill for the future!

Since we need not only the OS but, among other tools, an IDE, the best choice may be to adopt free tools in order to keep our costs very low. So, in order to minimize our expenses, I suggest you use Ubuntu, a very user-friendly and easy-to-use-and-install Linux distribution. You can download it from Ubuntu's official website (`https://ubuntu.com/`) and install it on your machine:

Figure 2.1: Ubuntu home page

Consider using virtualization software if you prefer not to install Ubuntu alongside your primary OS in a "dual boot mode" and avoid the need to choose between Linux distributions when starting your computer. The choice of which valid solution to use ultimately depends on your preferences. The main objective is to enable you to run Ubuntu within your primary OS, treating it as a regular software program. A very valid solution, once again free, is Oracle VirtualBox, which works for any kind of OS:

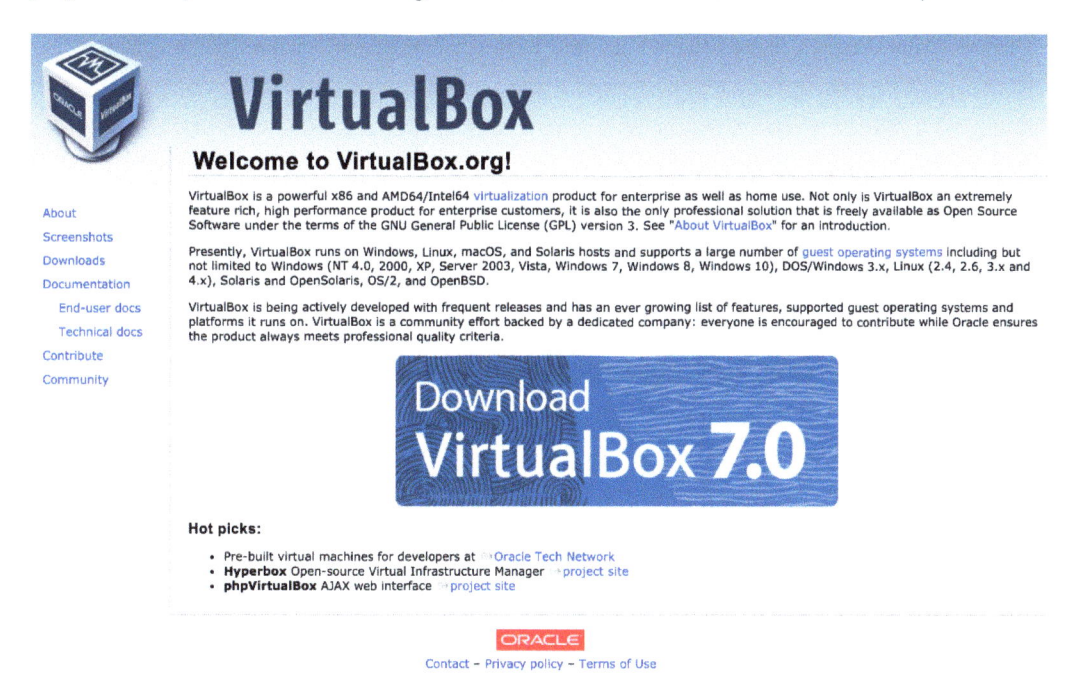

Figure 2.2: VirtualBox home page

It doesn't matter whether you have a real Ubuntu OS or a virtualized version of it; it's just important that you are able to start and use it. When you run your freshly installed Linux Ubuntu, please update it by typing the following command in the terminal:

```
sudo apt update
```

Now, it's time to check whether Python is installed on the system, so open the terminal and simply type the following:

```
python3
```

You should get some content such as that in the following picture:

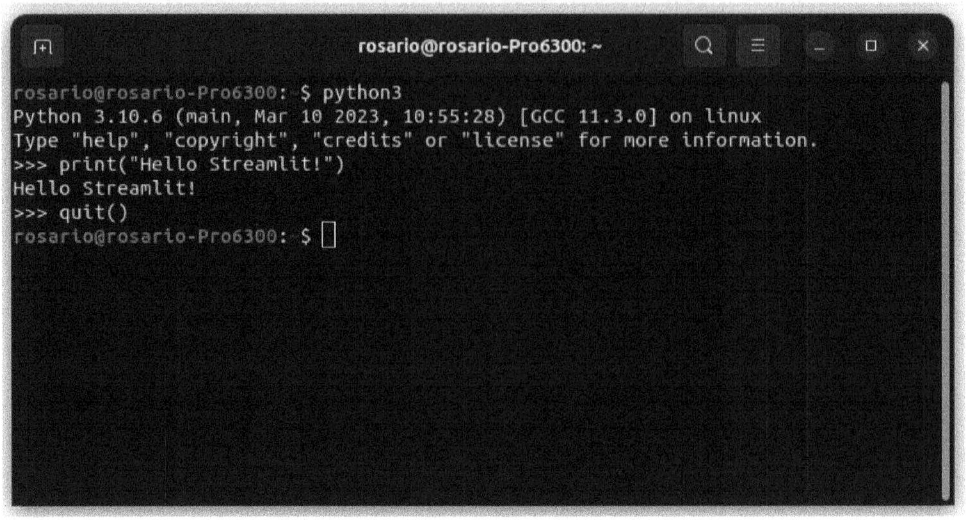
rosario@rosario-Pro6300: ~
rosario@rosario-Pro6300: $ python3
Python 3.10.6 (main, Mar 10 2023, 10:55:28) [GCC 11.3.0] on linux
Type "help", "copyright", "credits" or "license" for more information.
>>> print("Hello Streamlit!")
Hello Streamlit!
>>> quit()
rosario@rosario-Pro6300: $

Figure 2.3: Python 3 in Ubuntu's terminal

As we can see, Python 3 is already installed in Ubuntu, and when we type `python3`, we can enter Python and start coding. In *Figure 2.3*, we just printed a nice `Hello Streamlit!` message and then quit.

If you encounter an error while typing `python3`, it is possible that your system has Python available as `python` without the `3`. In such cases, you should use `python` instead of `python3`.

Let's check whether `pip` is installed in our Ubuntu box. Type in the following command:

```
pip --version (or pip3 --version)
```

If `pip` is not installed, we can install it by typing in the following command:

```
sudo apt install python3-pip
```

In the following figure, we can see how easy the `pip` installation is:

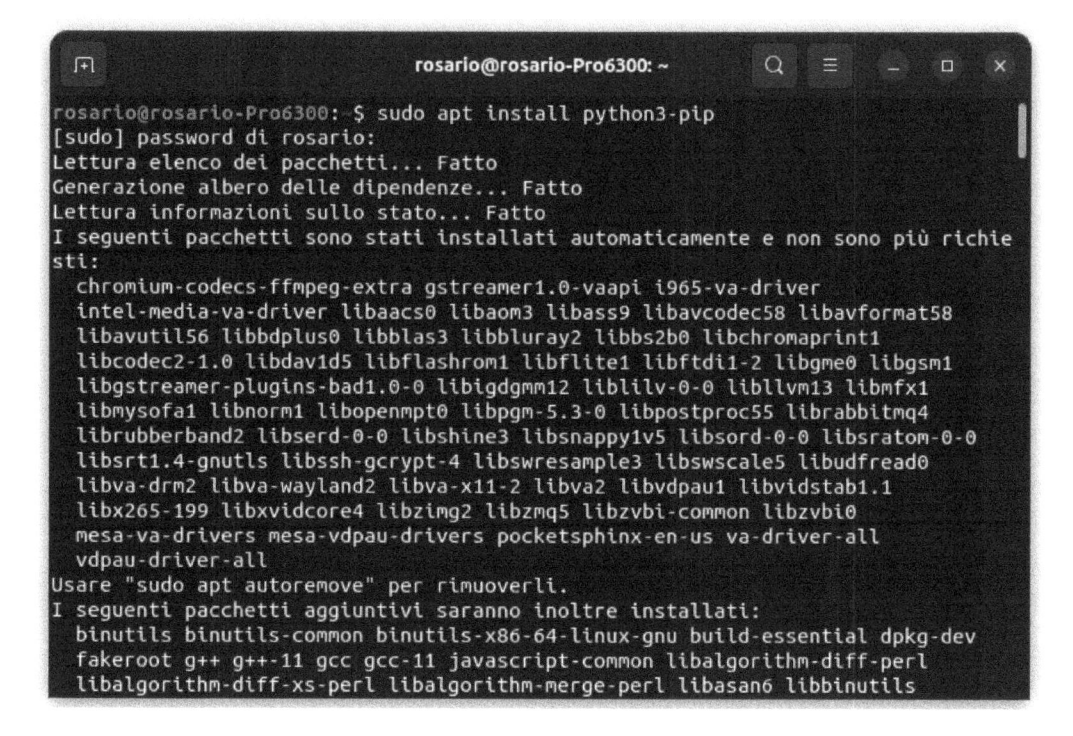

Figure 2.4: pip3 installation

Now, just to get familiar with `pip`, we will install a couple of tools that will be quite useful in the future: `tree` and `terminator`.

`tree` is a simple tool to visualize files and folders in the terminal as trees. We can install it by typing the following command:

```
sudo apt install tree
```

And once the installation is completed, just type `tree` and you will have a nice tree view of the working directory, as shown in the following figure:

Setting Up the Python Coding Environment

Figure 2.5: The "tree" command

`terminator` is an alternative terminal that has some advanced features, such as horizontal and vertical splits, focus shifting, and zooming and preferences settings, but the most important one for sure is the possibility of splitting the screen into tiles as many times as we want. Let's install it by typing the following command:

```
sudo apt install terminator
```

Then, once the installation is finished, just type `terminator`. As you can see in the following figure, by just right-clicking, you can create as many tiles with new terminals as you want, both vertically and horizontally:

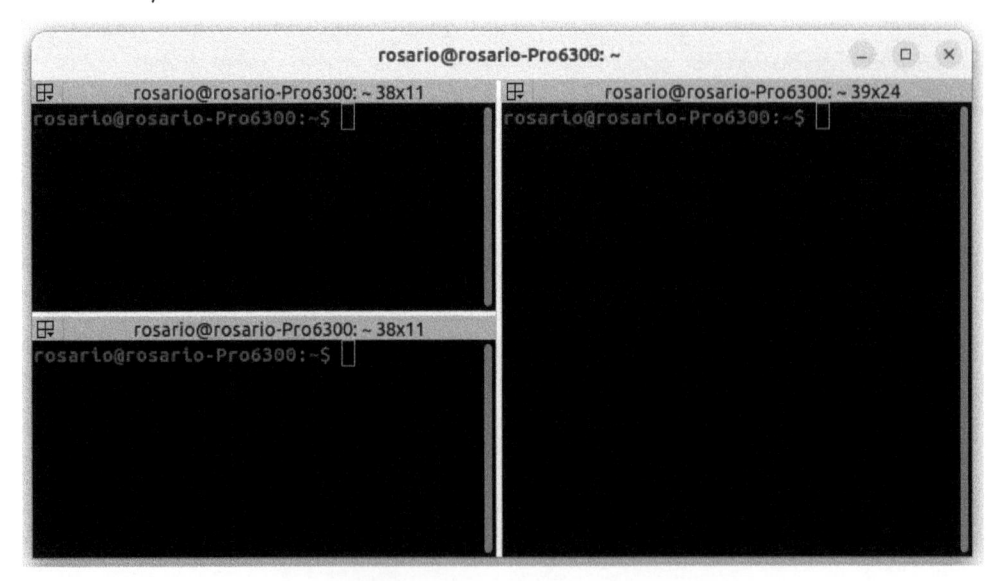

Figure 2.6: Terminator and its tiles

Finally, what is important is having Python running. We prefer running it on Ubuntu just to keep things cheap and simple, but if you want to use your own OS it's no problem at all. Just double-check whether you have the Python 3 version installed and if not, please download it from Python's official website (https://www.python.org/) and then install it (please get the version specific to your OS):

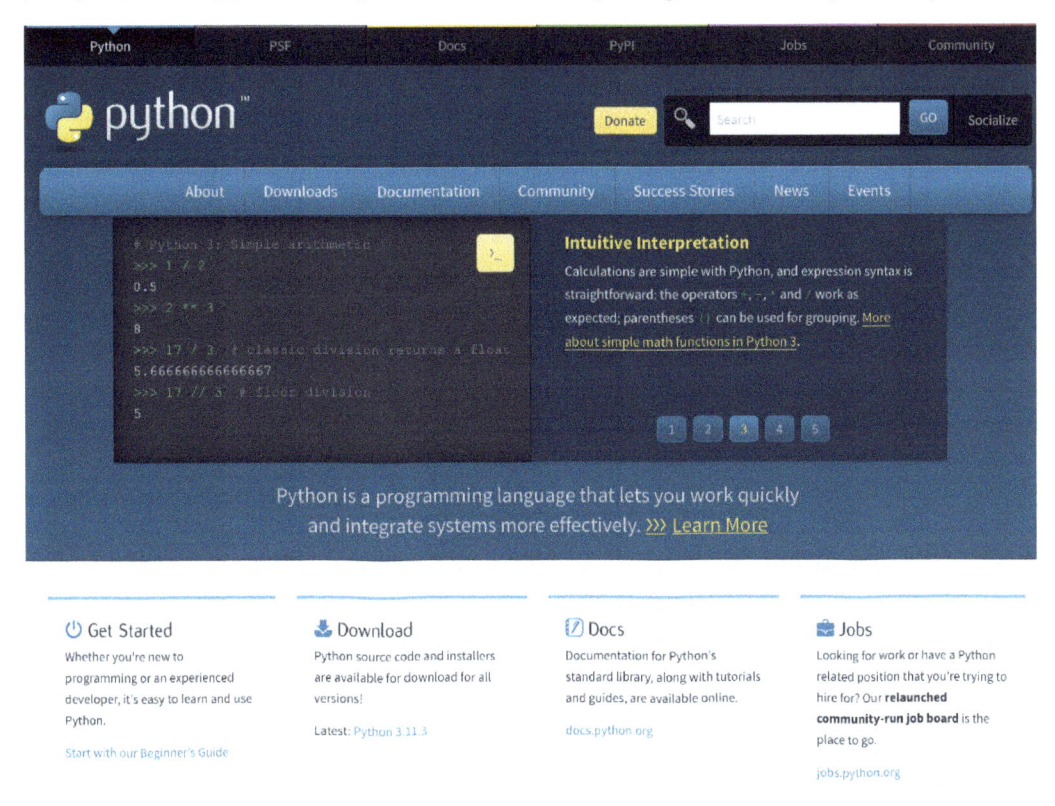

Figure 2.7: Python website

At this point, we have done more or less 50% of the job, since we have a fresh OS with Python and the `pip` installation, together with a couple of nice tools such as terminator and tree. What we are still missing is a beautiful editor, so let's get one!

IDE selection

Having a good IDE is very important for coding in Python. It provides many useful features that help you write code faster and with fewer errors, and keeps your code clean and well organized. For example, the autocomplete feature saves a lot of time by suggesting code completions as you type. This reduces typing errors. Syntax highlighting makes the code easier to read by coloring different elements. Powerful debugging tools in the IDE make debugging easier and faster. Refactoring features help keep the code organized and readable. Linting checks your code for stylistic issues, improving the quality.

On the market, there are several excellent tools such as PyCharm and VSCode, but these tools are usually heavy and a little bit expensive. For the sake of our coding sessions, we can use a quite light application that, at least at the beginning, can be installed and used at no cost: Sublime Text.

Sublime Text has many nice features that you can explore by yourself, including programming language recognition and syntax highlighting. You can install it directly from its home page (https://www.sublimetext.com/) by carefully following the instructions:

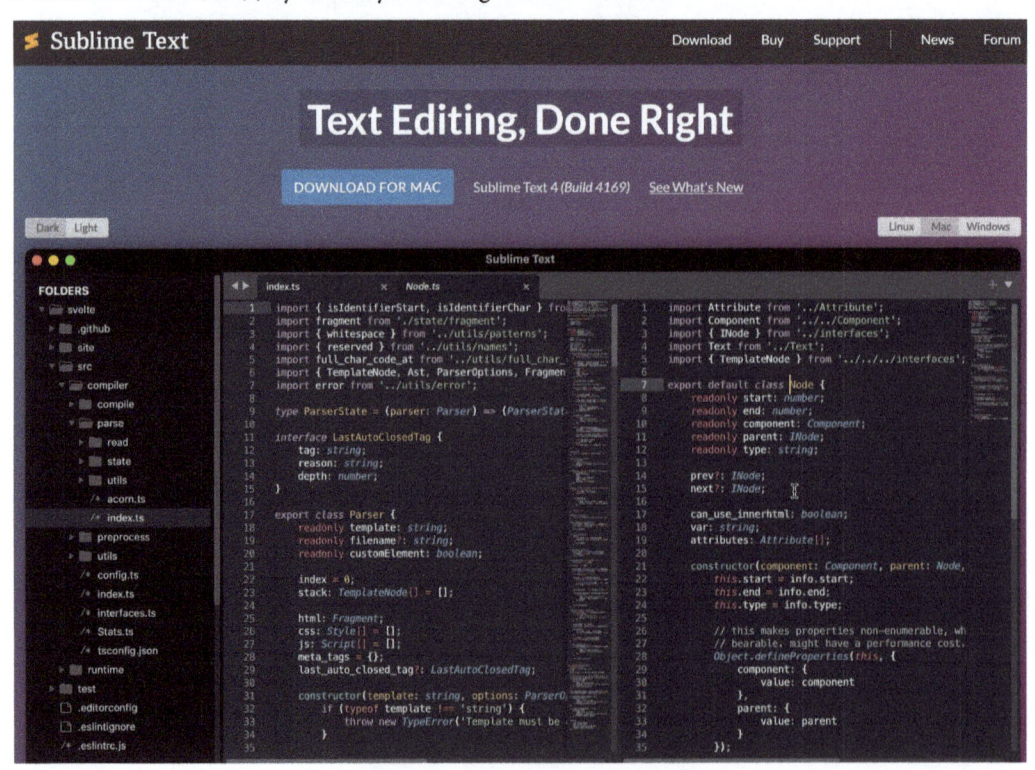

Figure 2.8: Sublime Text home page

Now, from your working directory in Terminator, just type `subl .` and Sublime Text will open up. Please select **Python** in the extension list in the bottom-right corner:

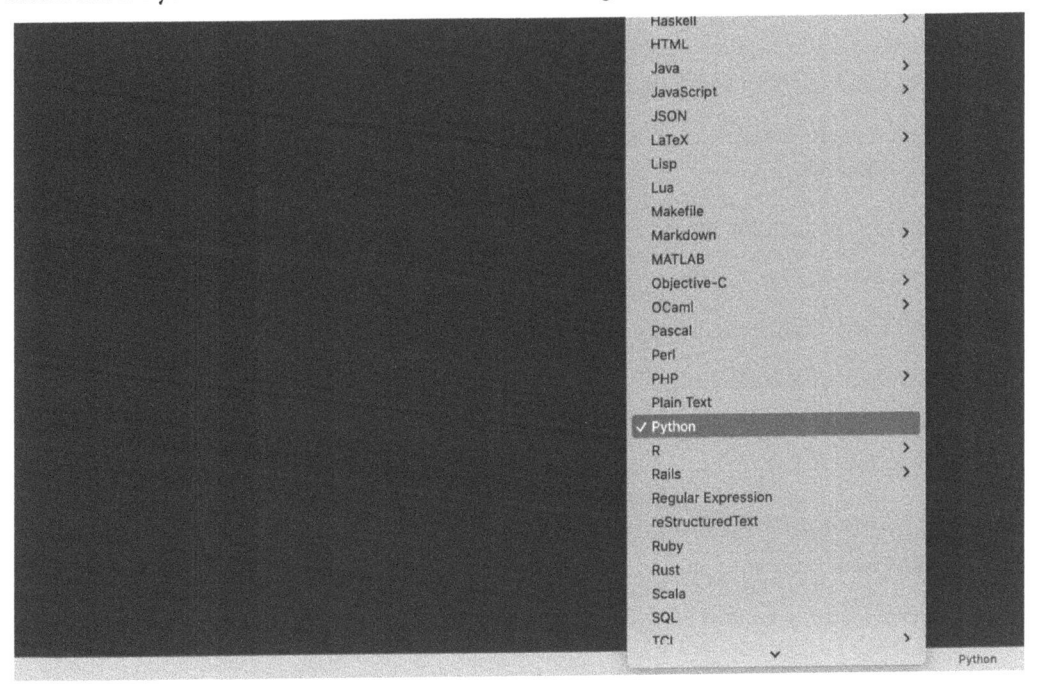

Figure 2.9: Python syntax selection in Sublime Text

Considering that Python is available and Sublime Text is installed, we could start coding with Streamlit immediately, but this is not the best option. In Python, every time we start a new project, we tend to install some specific new packages and libraries, and if we install this new stuff every time into the same basic environment, sooner or later, our environment will be a total mess. A very clean way to avoid this potential mess is the usage of virtual environments, so let's see what they are.

What is a virtual environment?

Virtual environments are useful tools in Python development that allow you to isolate package installations related to a specific project from the main system's Python installation. This means you can have separate environments with different package dependencies for different projects.

Creating a virtual environment is easy using the `venv` module in the Python standard library. The basic steps are as follows:

1. Create the virtual environment by running the following command:

   ```
   python3 -m venv venv
   ```

   This will create a `venv` folder that contains the isolated environment.

2. Activate the virtual environment.

   On Unix/Linux systems, run the following command:

   ```
   source venv/bin/activate
   ```

   On Windows, run the following command:

   ```
   venv\Scripts\activate
   ```

   Your command prompt will now show the virtual environment name enclosed in parentheses. Any package installations will now be isolated in this environment.

3. You can install any packages needed for your project using `pip`:

   ```
   pip install package-name
   ```

4. When you are done, you can deactivate the environment and switch back to the global Python install with the following command:

   ```
   deactivate
   ```

Virtual environments make it easy to try out different package combinations for your projects without interfering with the global Python install or other virtual environments.

In order to have a complete view of virtual environments in Python, please check the Real Python website (https://realpython.com/python-virtual-environments-a-primer/#use-third-party-tools):

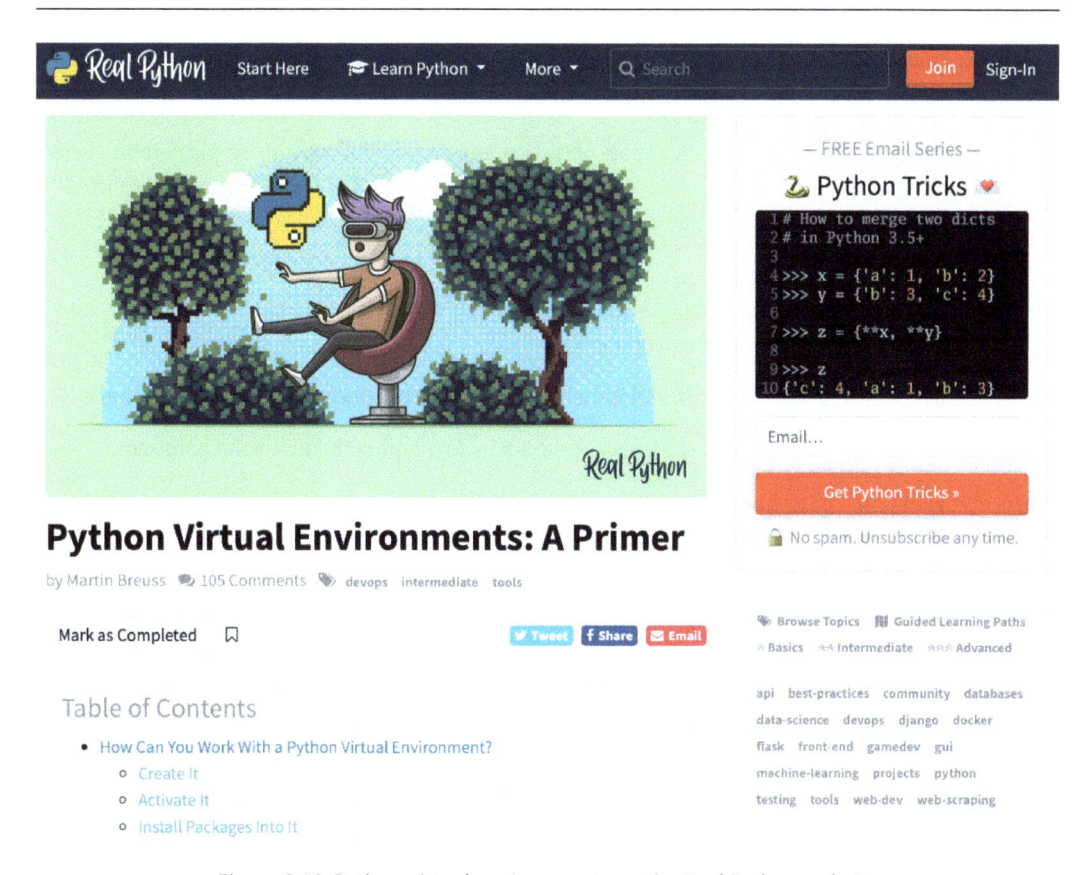

Figure 2.10: Python virtual environments on the Real Python website

Apart from the built-in `venv` module, there are several third-party tools such as `virtualenv` and `pipenv` for managing virtual environments in Python. The following bullets list the various benefits of using these third-party tools:

- **Easier to use**: The `virtualenv` and `pipenv` tools come with some additional convenience features that make them easier to use than the `venv` module. For example, `pipenv` automatically creates a **Pipfile** to track package dependencies and versions.

- **More features**: These tools offer some additional features beyond just isolating package installations: for example, `pipenv` manages both the environment and package dependencies, making your setup fully reproducible.

- **More flexibility**: Some projects prefer these tools over `venv` as `pipenv` has features to help manage development dependencies separately from production dependencies.

- **Better compatibility**: These tools work on all major platforms and have been around for longer, so they tend to have fewer quirks and compatibility issues. The `venv` module is a newer addition to the Python standard library.

- **Independent of Python version**: Since `virtualenv` and `pipenv` are third-party tools, they can work with different Python versions, unlike `venv`, which is tied to a specific Python installation.

So, in summary, while the `venv` module is part of the Python standard library, third-party tools such as `poetry` and `pipenv` offer more features, flexibility, and compatibility for managing your virtual environments. But for simple needs, the `venv` module works well and has the benefit of being built into Python itself.

All the reasons mentioned in the preceding list are enough to make `pipenv` our choice for the management and creation of virtual environments.

Now, we'll proceed with the `pipenv` installation and with the description of its main commands.

We can install `pipenv` together with `pipenv-pipes` by just typing the following command:

```
sudo python3 -m pip install pipenv pipenv-pipes
```

Next, let's create a testing directory named `pipenvtest1`:

```
mkdir pipenvtest1 && cd pipenvtest1
```

With list or tree, we can check whether this folder is empty:

```
pipenv --venv
```

We will get the output shown in *Figure 2.11*. It tells us that, at the moment, there are no virtual environments:

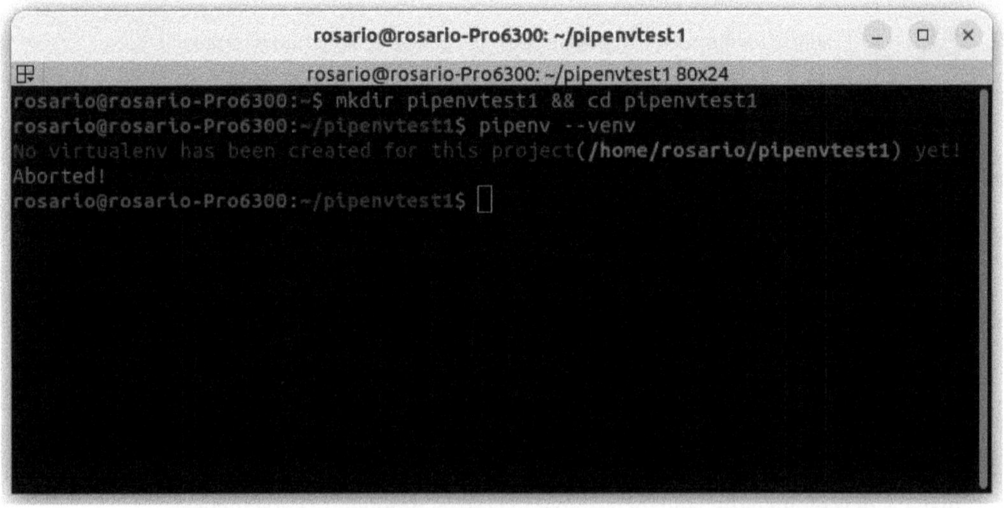

Figure 2.11: pipenv --venv

When executing the `pipenv shell` command at this point, `pipenv` will search for a file called `Pipfile` in the present directory. This file is needed for the creation of the virtual environment. If there is no Pipfile, it will be created together with the virtual environment and we will get a successfully created virtual environment message on the screen:

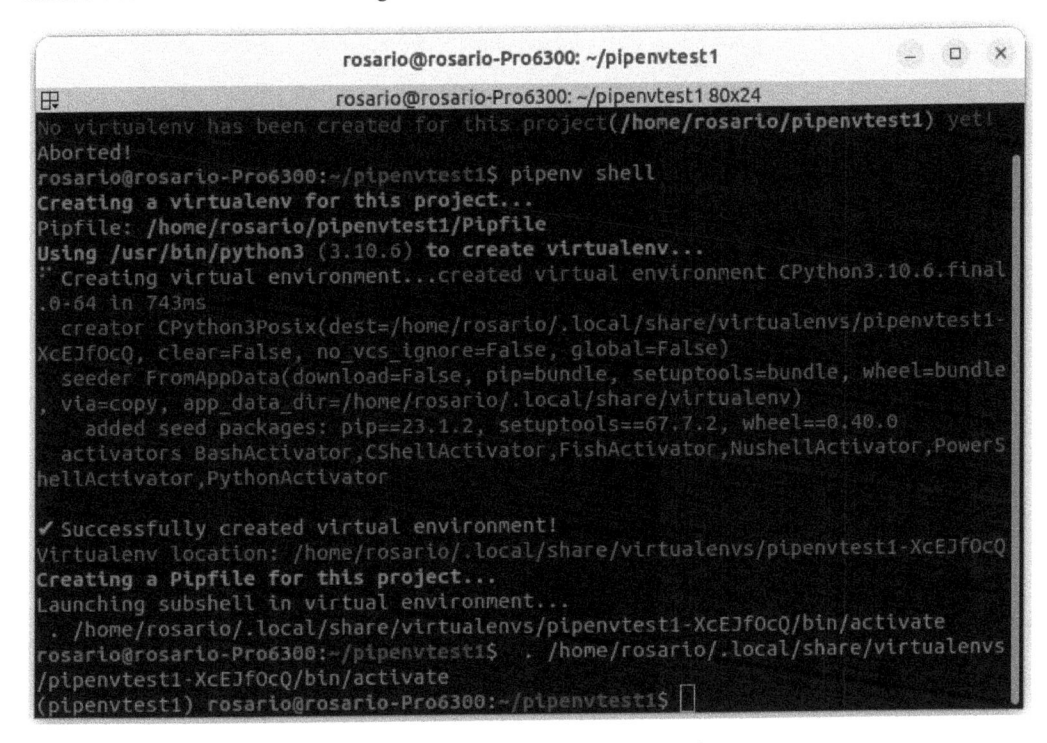

Figure 2.12: Virtual environment creation

Now, by launching Sublime Text from the working directory, we can see that a `Pipfile` has been created and we can explore its content. It contains all the information about the virtual environment such as the Python version, installed packages (empty at the moment), and dev packages (empty as well):

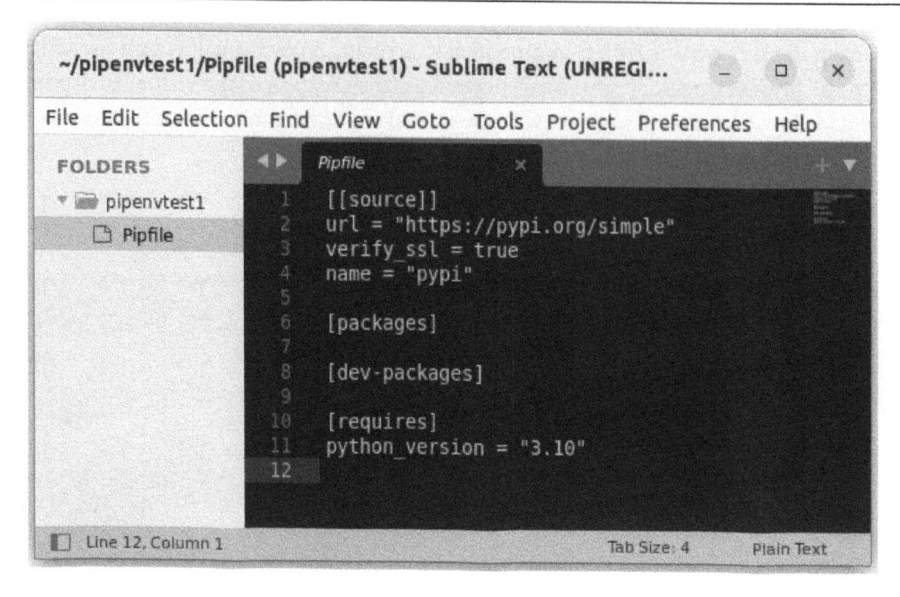

Figure 2.13: The Pipfile content

To install any package in our new virtual environment, we just have to type the following:

```
pipenv install <package_name>
```

For example, we can try with numpy:

Figure 2.14: Packages installation

As we can read on the screen, the package has been successfully installed, the `Pipfile` has been updated, it now contains `numpy`, and a new `Pipfile.lock` file, containing the list of all the hashes and dependencies, has been created and updated. Let's see it in Sublime Text:

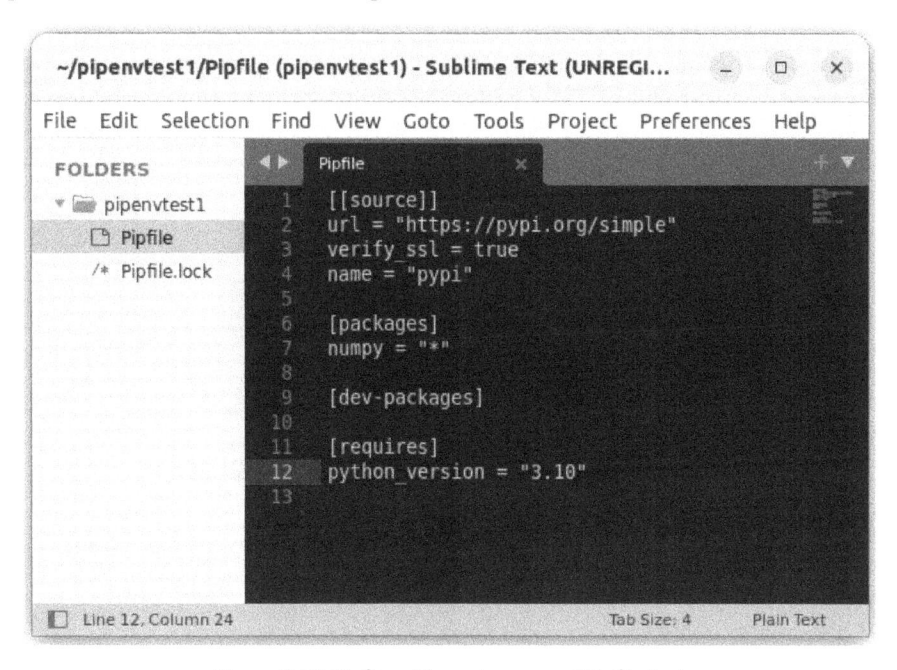

Figure 2.15: Pipfile with packages and Pipfile.lock

Another very interesting option is to create a requirements file in the `Pipfile.lock` file that will be very useful when we deploy our web applications. So, to create a `requirements.txt` file, we can simply type the following:

```
pipenv lock -r > requirements.txt
```

Please note that starting from `pipenv` version 2022.8.13, the previous command has been replaced with the following:

```
pipenv requirements > requirements.txt
```

Inside `pipenv`, we can run any kind of command just by using the `run` instruction. So, if we want to run, let's say Python, we can just type the following:

```
pipenv run python
```

By running the `pipenv check` command, you can examine package updates, and if any are found the updates will be executed accordingly.

Uninstalling a package (and removing it from the Pipfile) is very simple. In fact, we just have to type the following:

```
pipenv uninstall <package_name>
```

In addition to `pipenv`, we have also installed `pipenv-pipes`, which is an intriguing tool. By typing `pipes` in the terminal, we can obtain a list of the installed virtual environments. We can then navigate through the list using the cursor to select the desired virtual environment for activation, as shown in the following figure:

Figure 2.16: Pipes

When we are in a virtual environment and want to close it to come back to the original status, we just have to type `exit` in the terminal.

To remove a virtual environment, we can navigate to its directory and execute the following command:

```
pipenv --rm
```

This command removes the virtual environment without deleting the files in the directory:

Figure 2.17: Virtual environment deletion

If we want to remove the directory with all its files, we have to do it manually.

Summary

In this chapter, we prepared the ground for our next activities. We learned how to create a developing environment while keeping costs very low (almost free). So, we decided to use Ubuntu as our main OS. After that, we made sure to have Python already available and installed `pip`. The selection of the IDE was quite straightforward since we chose Sublime Text, a quite light, powerful, and advanced text editor.

After that, we focused on Python's virtual environment. In this case, our choice was `pipenv` because it is quite powerful, easy to use, and full of advanced features. We spent some time on a quite complete overview of this tool and its main features and instructions.

Now, everything is ready, so finally, in the next chapter, we are going to take a kind of crash course on the basic features of Streamlit. Are you ready?

3
Exploring Streamlit's Features and Functionality

This chapter is a beginner-friendly tutorial that introduces you to the core features and functionalities of the Streamlit Python framework, aiming to help you get started with the library quickly and easily. This chapter covers the basic concepts of Streamlit, such as creating and customizing widgets, laying out the user interface, and adding visualizations and charts.

By the end of this chapter, you should be able to create and run Streamlit apps and have a solid understanding of the library's features and capabilities. This is the first hands-on step of our exciting journey together!

In this chapter, we're going to cover the following main topics:

- Installing and launching Streamlit
- Streamlit features and widgets
- DataFrames, plots, and visualizations
- Date, time, and more

Technical requirements

- In this chapter, we will use the following libraries, packages, and tools:
    - Sublime Text
    - Python 3
    - `pipenv`
    - `streamlit`
    - CSV files

- The code for this chapter can be found in this book's GitHub repository: https://github.com/PacktPublishing/Web-App-Development-Made-Simple-with-Streamlit/tree/fcb2bd740a2df7263b4470164805926fee3157a1/Chapter03

Installing and launching Streamlit

Finally, we are ready to write our code to create beautiful web applications! Where do we start? The first thing we must do is install Streamlit.

So, let's create a new directory – we will call it `streamlit_course`. Once you're inside it, prepare a new virtual environment by typing the well-known `pipenv shell` command. Once you are done running the `pipenv shell` command, you will get the following output:

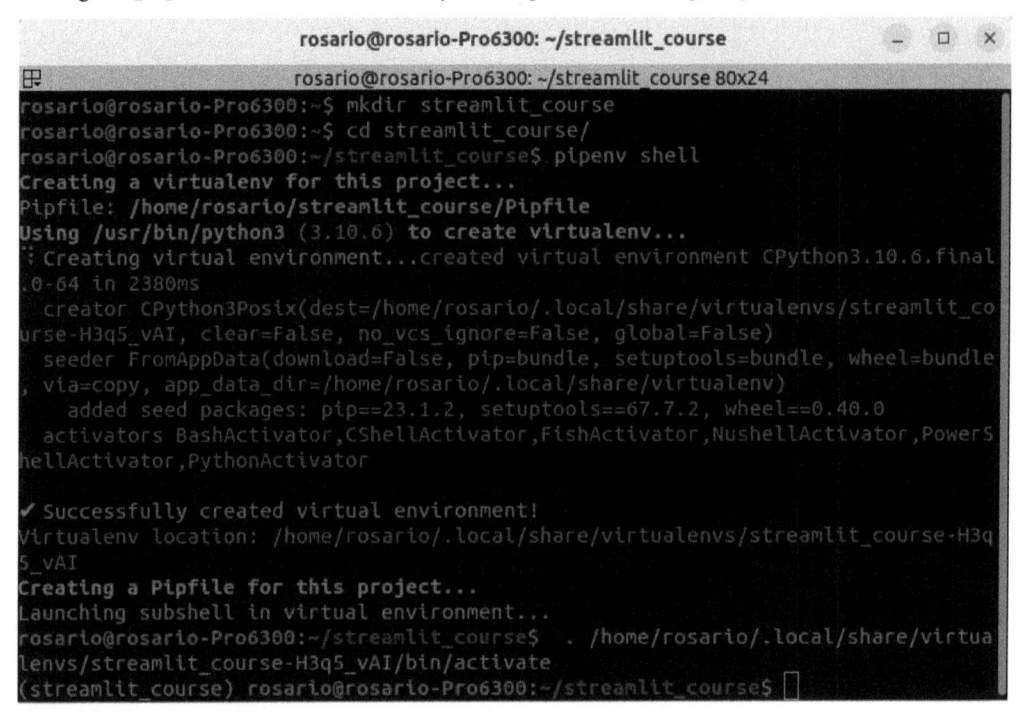

Figure 3.1: The streamlit_course virtual environment creation

Installing Streamlit is very easy – it's a matter of using a simple instruction, as indicated on its official website (www.streamlit.io):

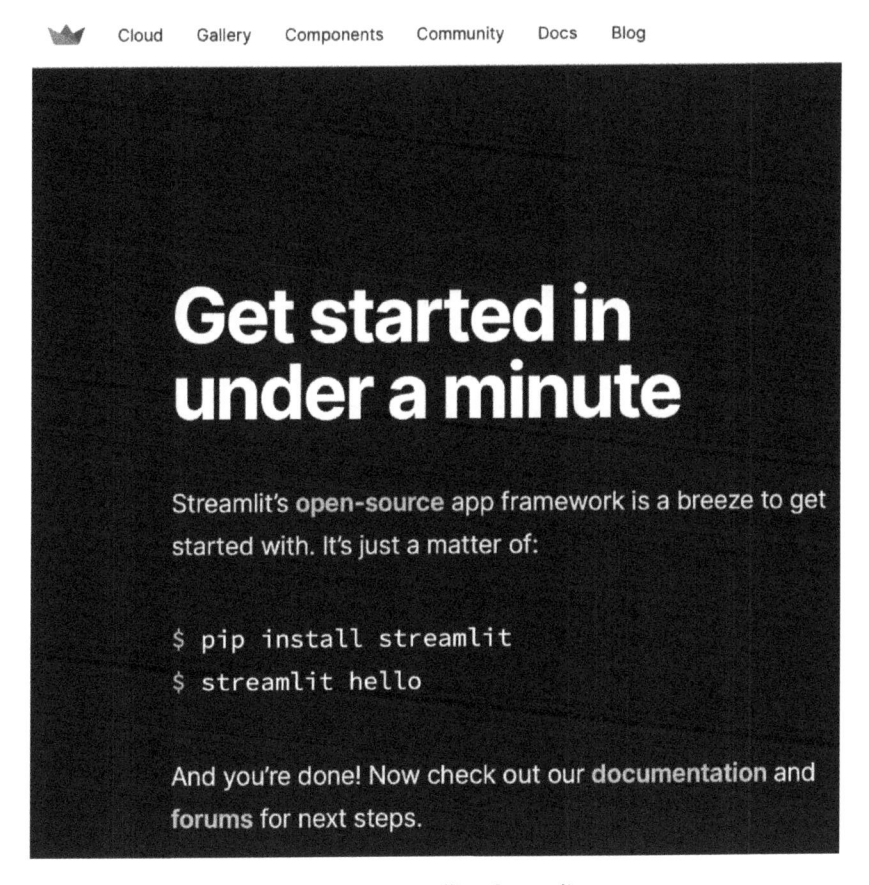

Figure 3.2: Installing Streamlit

Since we are using `pipenv` and the `streamlit_course` virtual environment that we just created, we have to modify the instruction suggested in *Figure 3.2* slightly, like so:

```
pipenv install streamlit
```

You will get the following result:

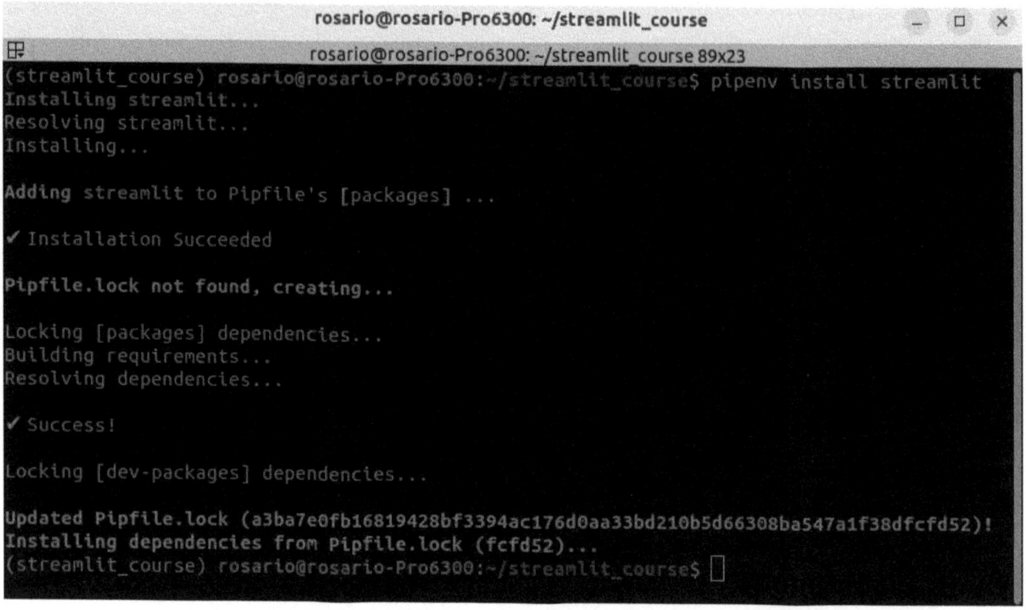

Figure 3.3: Streamlit installation with pipenv

In this way, Streamlit will be easily installed and `Pipfile` will be updated.

Now, let's create an empty file to be used as our Python script by typing the following:

```
touch app.py
```

As we can see, in our `streamlit_course` directory, we have three files:

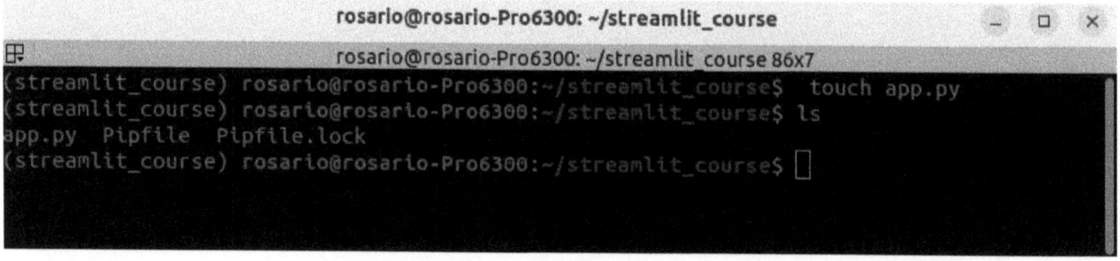

Figure 3.4: The files in the streamlit_course directory

So far, we have installed Streamlit and we have an empty Python file. Although this isn't much, we are ready to launch our first web application!

The instruction to launch Streamlit is very simple – just type `streamlit run <python_file_name.py>`, where the Python file in our case is the empty `app.py` file we just created. However, since we are in a `pipenv` virtual environment, we have to tell `pipenv` that we want to launch something. So, let's write the following:

```
pipenv run streamlit run app.py
```

In this way, `pipenv` launches Streamlit, which runs the `app.py` file. Our browser will open on an empty page, but if we check the address bar carefully, we will see that something is running on `localhost:8501`. Our Streamlit web app is alive and running on our local machine on its standard 8501 port (if you are asked to write your email in the terminal, just press *Enter*):

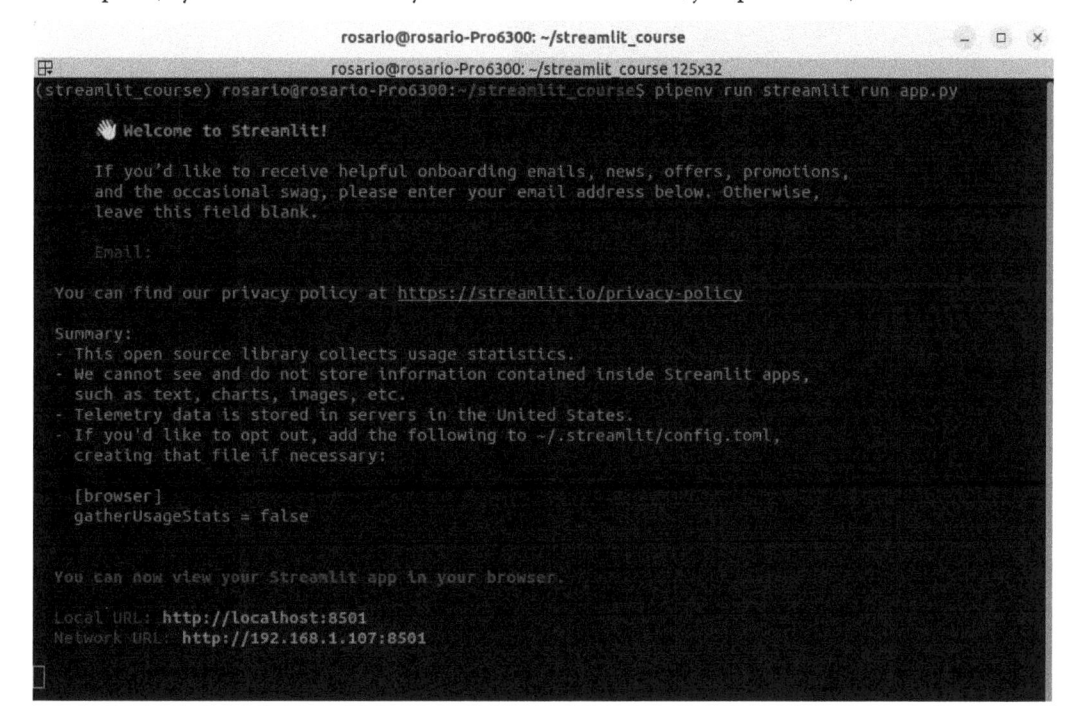

Figure 3.5: Streamlit running on localhost:8501

At this point, our web app can be improved by adding widgets and elements. Open another terminal in our terminator (another tile), enter our virtual environment, and run our Sublime Text editor with `"subl ."`.

Streamlit features and widgets

The very first step has been completed: Streamlit is up and running. What we need to do now is add text, widgets, elements, and more to make something beautiful that also works correctly.

To start populating our web app with nice and useful widgets, we need to write some Python code. The best way to do this is to put Sublime Text and our browser side by side, as shown in the following screenshot:

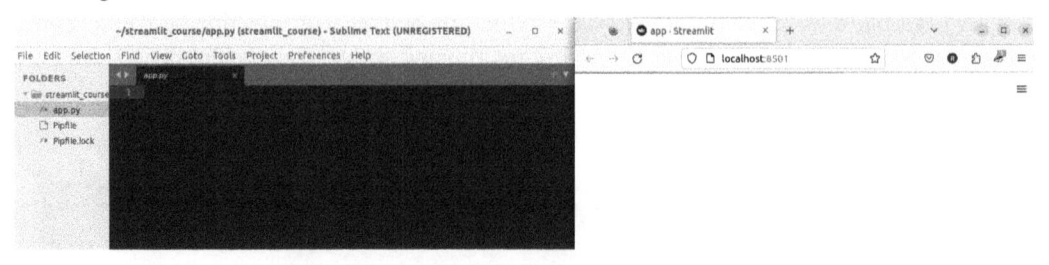

Figure 3.6: Sublime Text and a browser side by side

This kind of visualization is very convenient because we can immediately see any change we make to the code (in real time, as soon as we save our code changes), in our editor directly, in the browser by just selecting **Always Rerun** from the top-right menu of our web application:

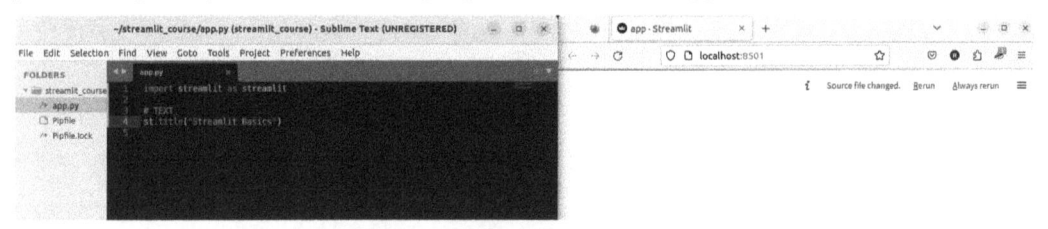

Figure 3.7: Code changes and Always Rerun

So, let's import Streamlit (with `st` as the alias) and start dealing with some text. We can write the following:

```
import streamlit as st
st.title("Streamlit Basics")
```

The result is shown in *Figure 3.8*:

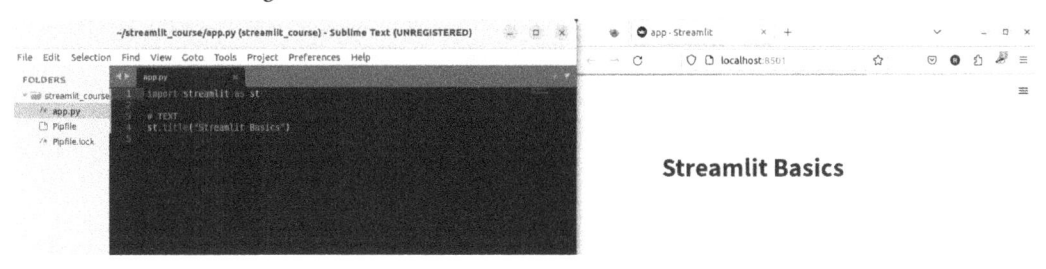

Figure 3.8: Code changes and their effect on the web app

`st.title` gives back a long string of text. We can use many other text dimensions in Sublime Text. For example, we can write and save the following code:

```
st.header("This is a header")
st.subheader("This is a subheader")
st.text("This is a simple text")
st.write("This is a write dimension")
```

Since we've already selected **Always Rerun**, we'll immediately see that our web app changes in the browser, introducing the header, subheader, text, and write text dimensions we wish to visualize:

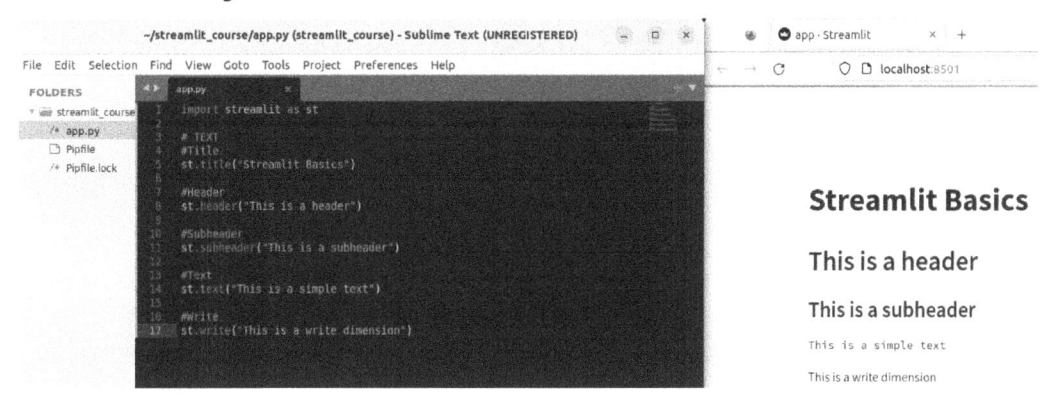

Figure 3.9: Different text dimensions

Streamlit can even directly manage the markdown. This is quite simple since we just have to use `markdown` and pass the text inside the parenthesis. For example, we can write the following:

```
st.markdown("[Streamlit](https://www.streamlit.io)")
```

In this way, we write the word "Streamlit" on the screen as a hyperlink to the official Streamlit website. If we wish to put the link directly on the screen, to make the URL visible, we can write the following:

```
st.markdown("https://www.streamlit.io")
```

In Streamlit, we can use HTML in a very simple way – we just need to create a variable containing all our HTML code, then put it inside a markdown instruction together with the `unsafe_allow_html` argument set to `True`. Let's take a look:

```
html_page = """
<div style="background-color:blue;padding:50px">
<p style="color:yellow;font-size:50px">Enjoy Streamlit!</p>
</div>
"""
st.markdown(html_page, unsafe_allow_html=True)
```

This is the result we get:

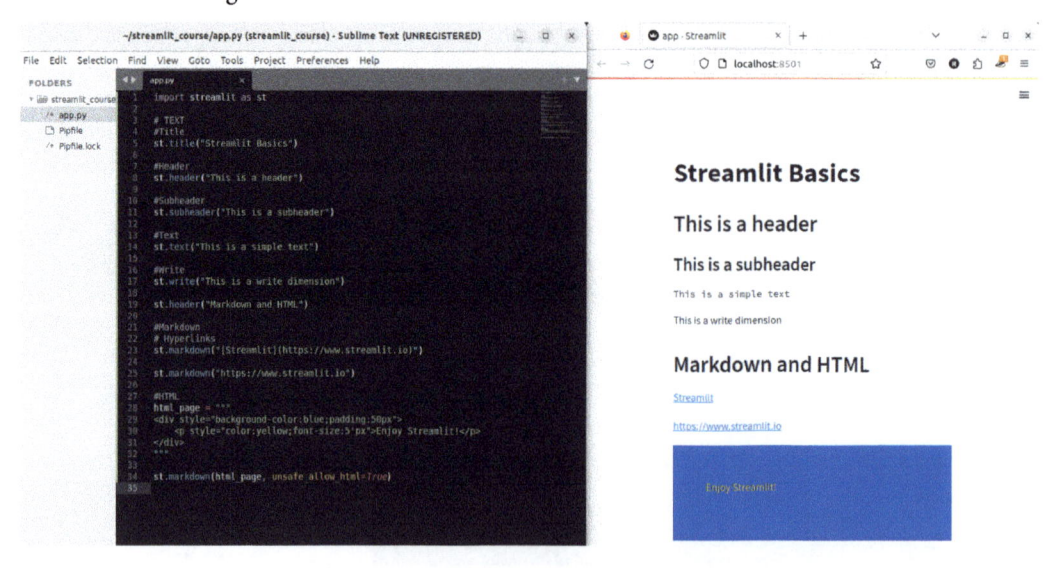

Figure 3.10: Markdown and HTML

See what happens when you set `unsafe_allow_html` to `False`.

Colored textboxes

In terms of text, we can have beautiful textboxes consisting of different colors to indicate a warning, an error, and so on. This kind of color code can be very useful when we're building our web application. Let's take a look at the code:

```
st.success("Success!")
st.info("Information")
st.warning("This is a warning!")
st.error("This is an error!")
```

The first piece of code returns a green box with some text, the second a light blue box with text, the third a yellowish box containing text, and the last a red box containing the error message:

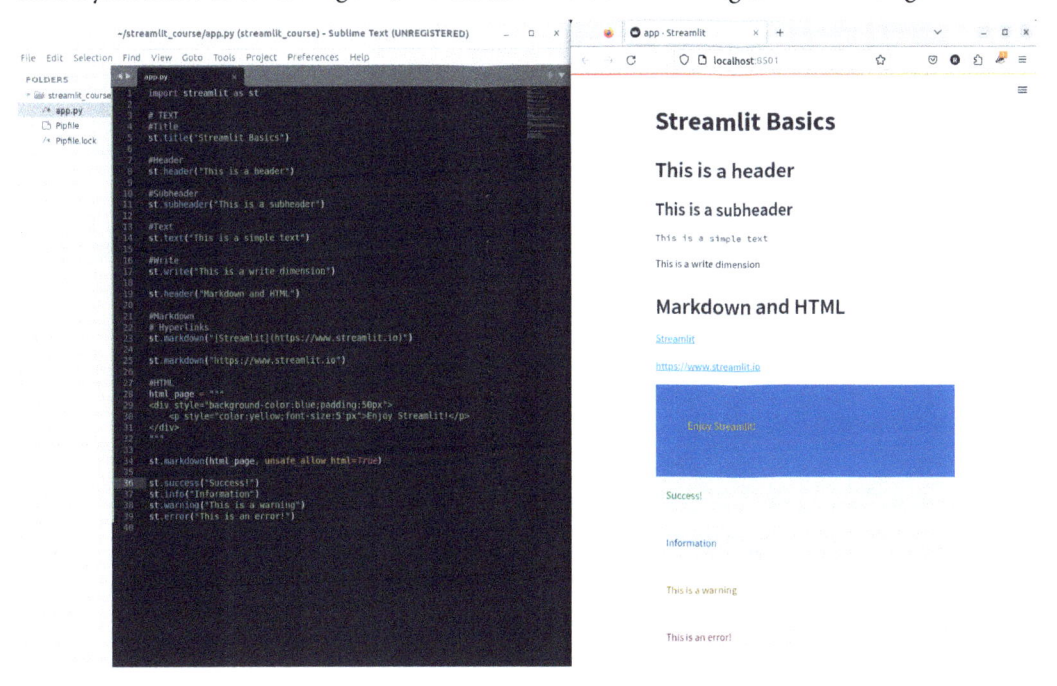

Figure 3.11: Colored textboxes

Colored textboxes are something really interesting since we can use them to advise about something wrong, such as an issue, using the reddish tone, or something very good, such as a success case, using a greenish tone. Moreover, we can use this feature to give a little vivacity to our text.

Images, audio, and video

In Streamlit, it's extremely easy to manage multimedia, such as images, audio, and video. Starting with images, we need to import the PIL library and then add a couple of lines of code:

```
from PIL import Image
img = Image.open("packt.jpeg")
st.image(img, width=300, caption="Packt Logo")
```

Here's the output:

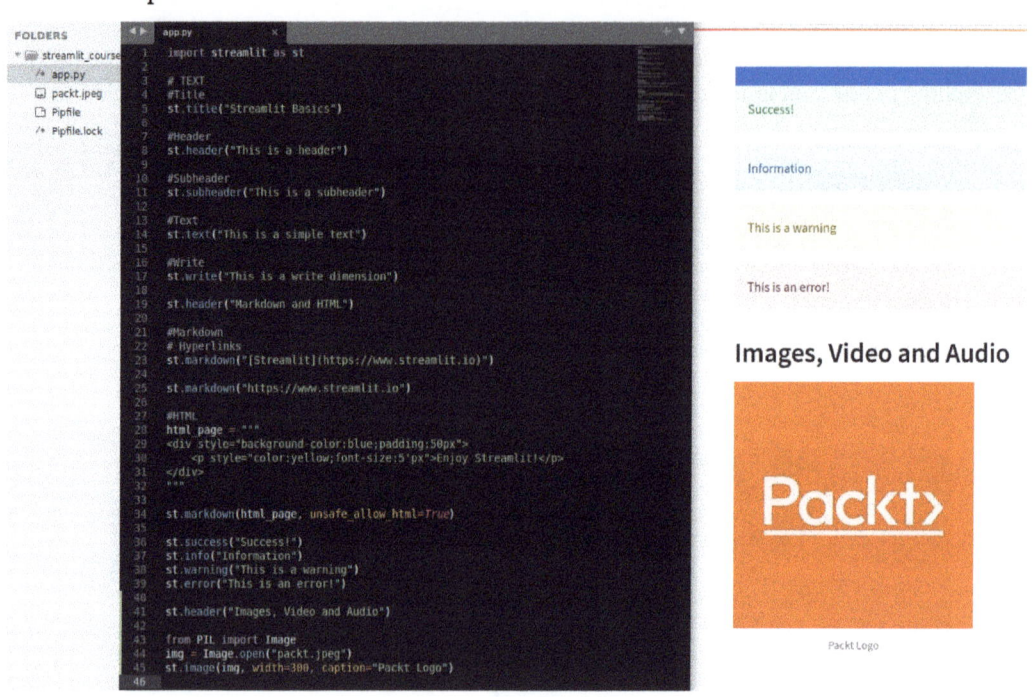

Figure 3.12: The st.image

Please note that the JPEG image is in the same directory as our `app.py` file. If we want, we can change the width and the caption of the image.

Working with video is not very different – we can put a video file in the same directory as our `app.py` file and open it:

```
video_file = open("SampleVideo_1280x720_1mb.mp4","rb")
video_bytes = video_file.read()
st.video(video_bytes)
```

In the box, there are buttons for play/pause, volume control, and fullscreen:

Figure 3.13: The st.video widget from a file

We can also open videos directly from the web by using a URL with the `st.video` widget. For example, we can write the following:

```
st.video("https://www.youtube.com/watch?v=q2EqJW8VzJo")
```

The result is shown in the following screenshot:

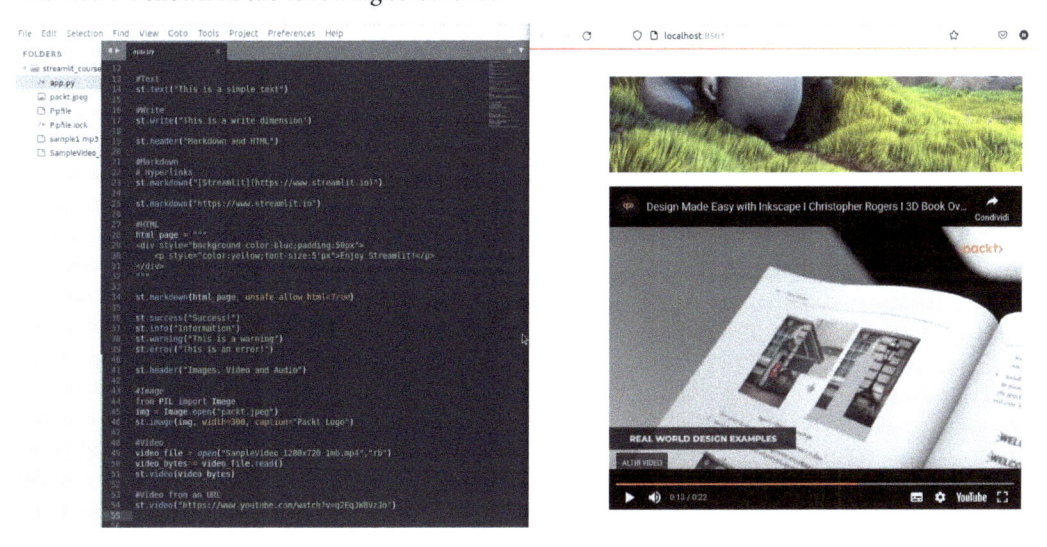

Figure 3.14: The st.video widget from a URL

For audio files, we can do more or less the same. We can write the following:

```
audio_file = open("sample1.mp3", "rb")
audio_bytes = audio_file.read()
st.audio(audio_bytes, format="audio/mp3")
```

Please note that this time, we have to specify the format. Once again, out of the box, we get the play/pause button and volume control:

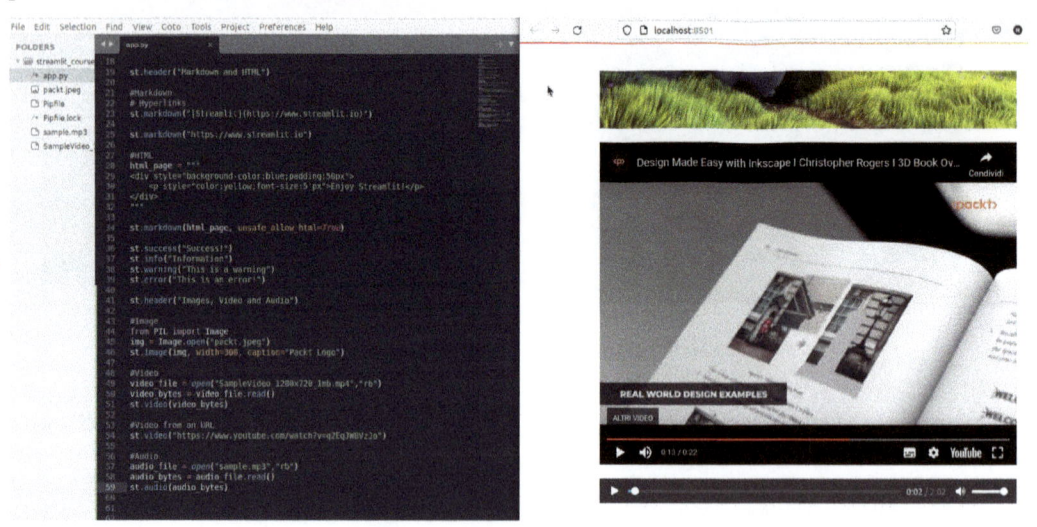

Figure 3.15: The st.audio widget

Now, let's look at another widget that will be very useful in the next few chapters. First up is the "button" widget. So, please comment all the code we've written so far (we can create a comment by putting # at the beginning of the line of code we want to ignore), excluding the instruction that imports Streamlit, and continue. We can start by writing a simple instruction:

```
st.button("Play")
```

This instruction gives us a beautiful button with a caption stating **Play**. However, when we click on it, nothing happens!

Figure 3.16: The st.button widget

Nothing happens because there is no code related to the button, so things will change if we slightly change the previous line of code in the following way:

```
if st.button("Play"):
    st.text("Hello world!")
```

As we can see, when the **Play** button is clicked, a beautiful piece of text stating **Hello World!** will appear:

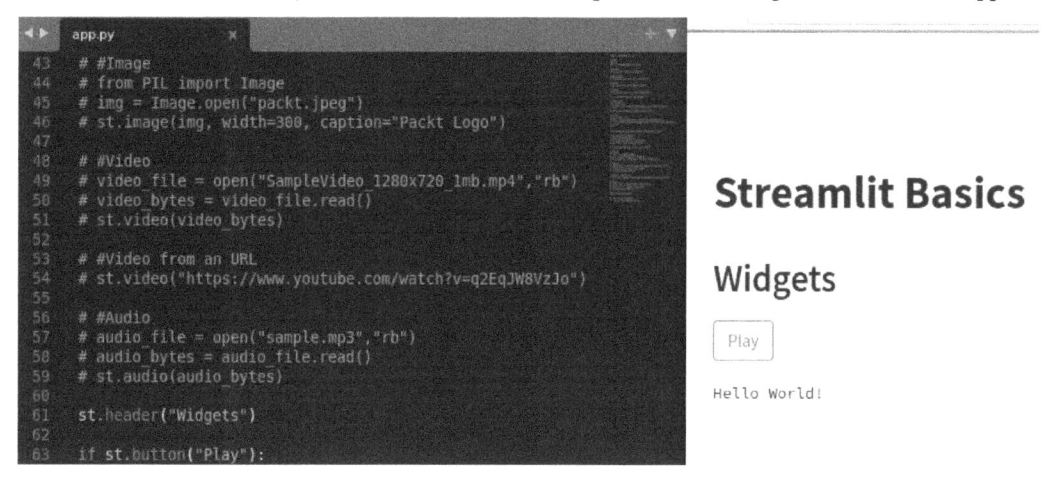

Figure 3.17: Event associated with st.button

Many other widgets work in the same way, such as `"Checkbox"`. Let's say we write the following code:

```
if st.checkbox("Checkbox"):
    st.text("Checkbox selected")
```

We will get the result shown in *Figure 3.18*:

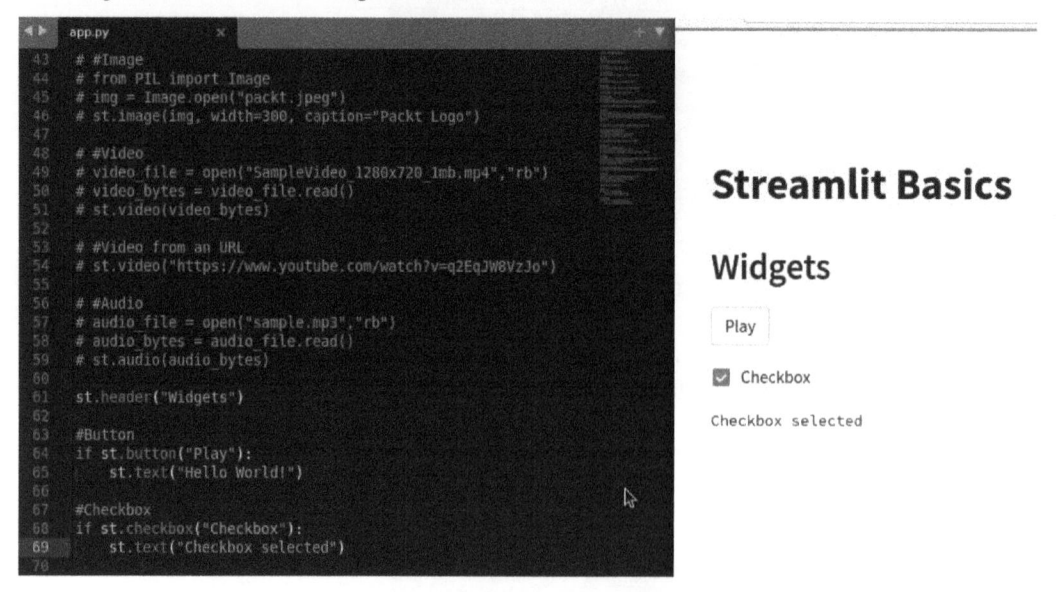

Figure 3.18: The st.checkbox widget

The radio button works a little differently – we have to specify a list of options and then decide what happens when we select each of them:

```
radio_but = st.radio("Your Selection", ["A", "B"])
if radio_but == "A":
    st.info("You selected A")
else:
    st.info("You selected B")
```

The preceding code will give us the following result:

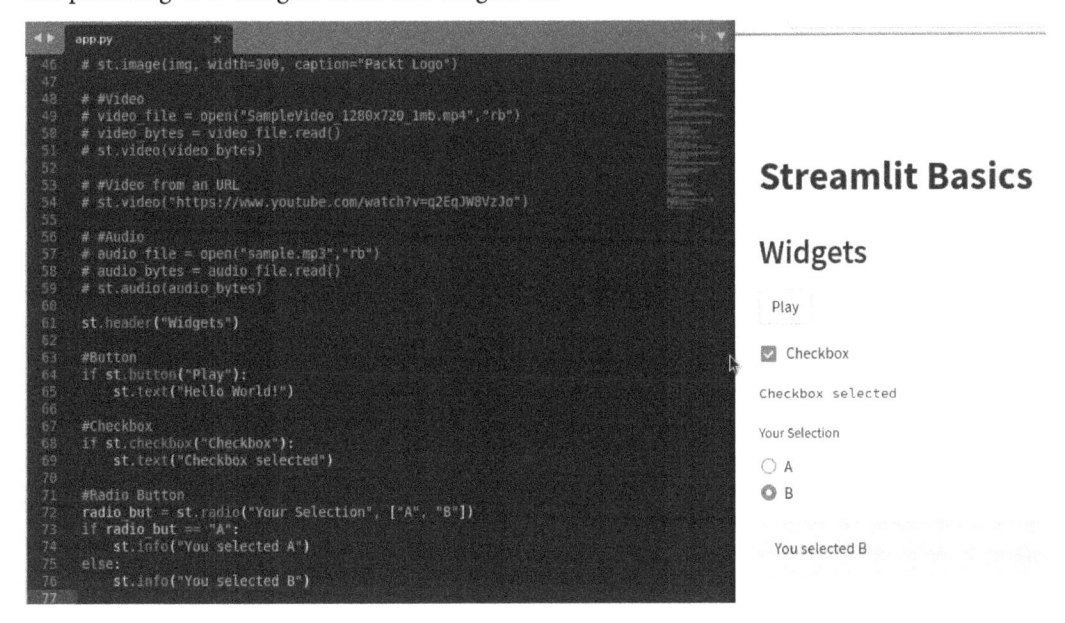

Figure 3.19: The st.radio widget

Also, in the selectbox, we need to specify a list of options:

```
city = st.selectbox("Your City", ["Napoli", "Palermo", "Catania"])
```

We select one of the options (in this case, an Italian city) that will be saved in the `city` variable:

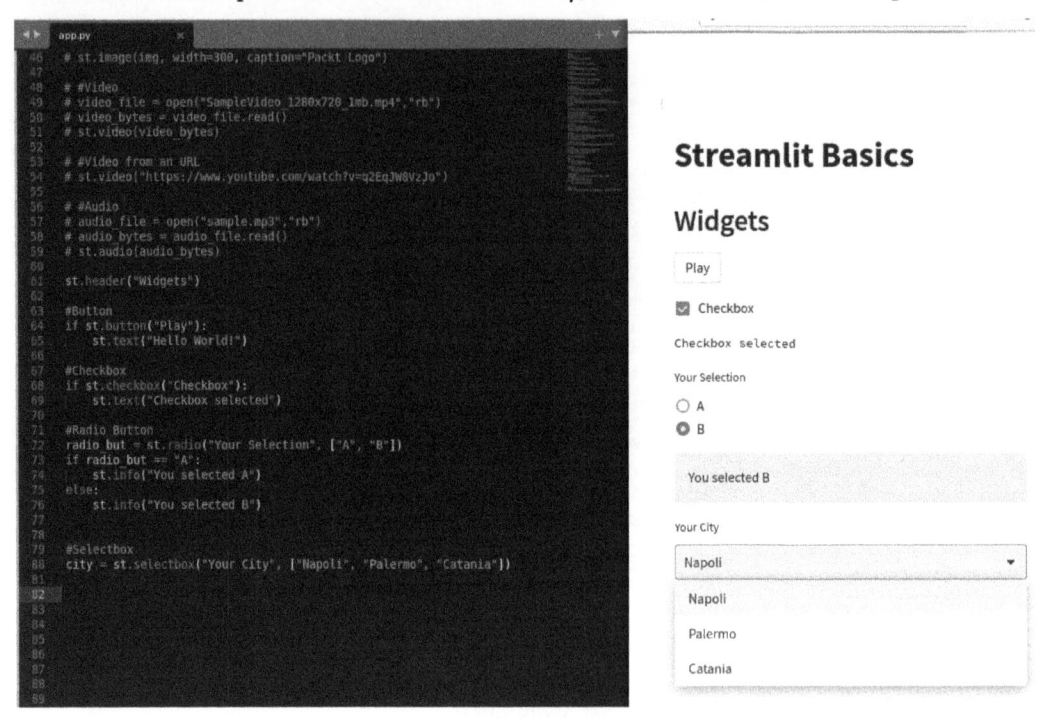

Figure 3.20: The st.selectbox widget

In this case, we want to have a multi-selection. We can use the `multiselect` widget in the following way:

```
occupation = st.multiselect("Your Occupation", ["Programmer", "Data 
Scientist", "IT Consultant", "DBA"])
```

The coding is very similar to the previous one but this time, we can select more than one option. This can be seen in the following figure, where we selected two jobs (if we want, we can click on the **x** button to cancel a selected option):

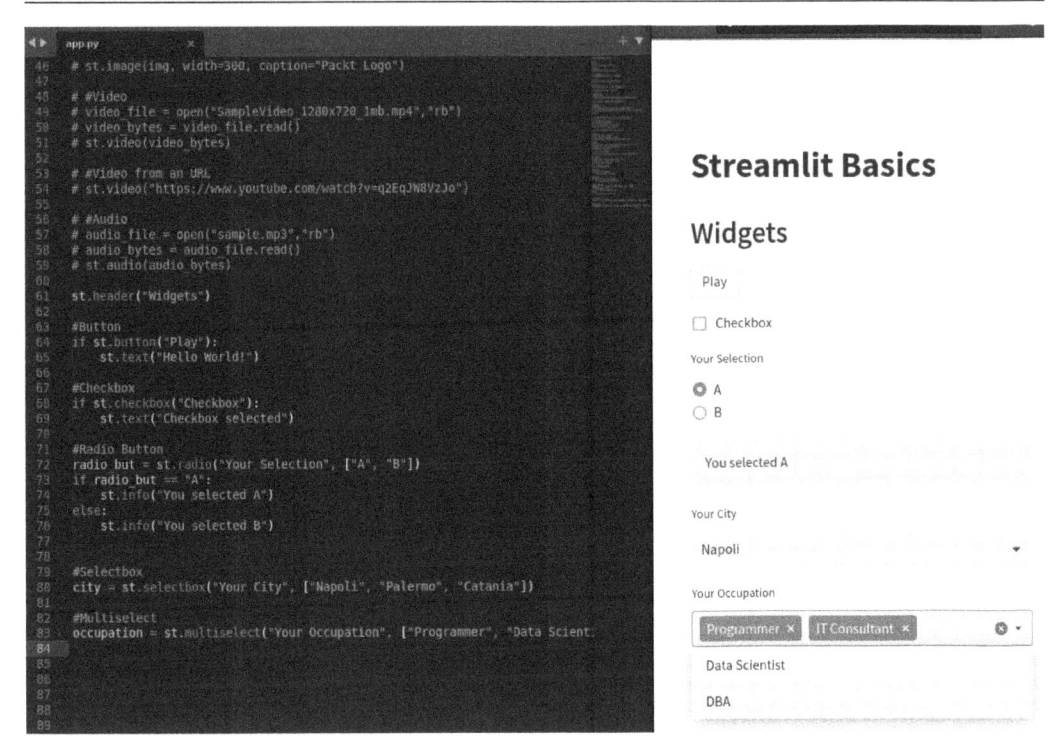

Figure 3.21: The st.multiselect widget

Multiselect is a very elegant way to make multiple selections, keeping the screen clean and functional.

Inputting text and numbers

Another extremely useful function in our web application is *inputting*, which is the process of entering some information. In this case, we have many widgets available out of the box.

In the `text_input` widget, we only have to specify a label or caption and a placeholder – very easy!

```
Name = st.text_input("Your Name", "Write something…")
st.text(name)
```

Everything we write will be saved in the `name` variable and printed on the screen thanks to `st.text()`:

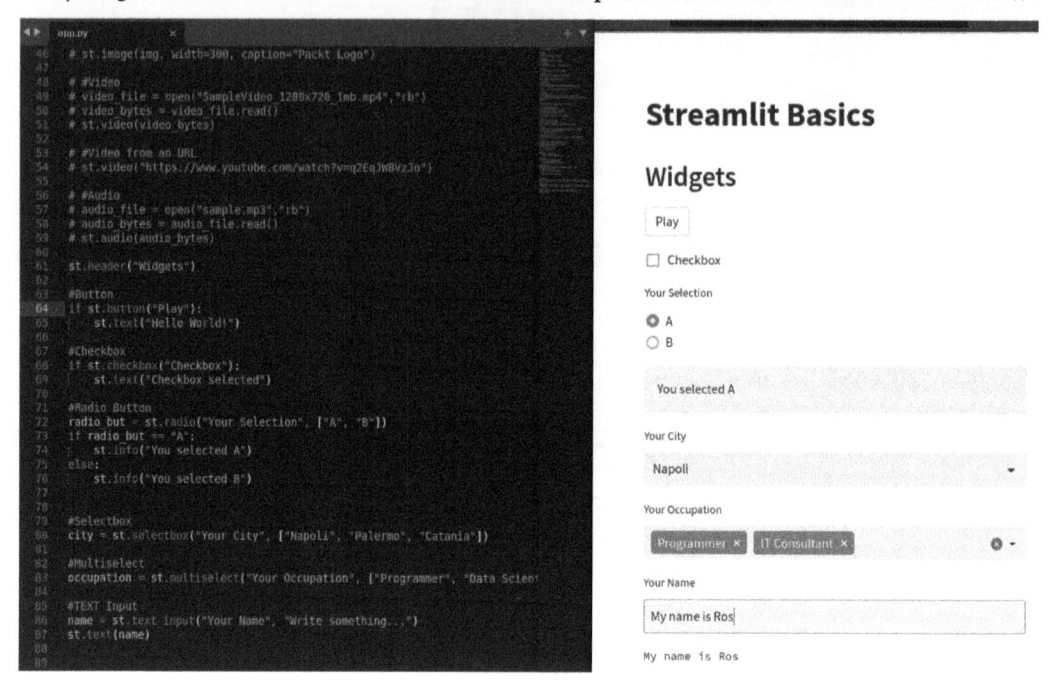

Figure 3.22: The st.text_input widget

In the same easy way, we can also input numbers. This time, it's possible to write a number directly or use the + and - icons to increase or decrease it just using `st.number_input`:

```
Age = st.number_input("Input a number")
```

Here's the output:

Figure 3.23: The st.number_input widget

Moving back to text, to input text on more than one line, we can use the `text_area` widget, like so:

```
message = st.text_area("Your Message", "Write something...")
```

As we can see, this time, a wider text area will be displayed:

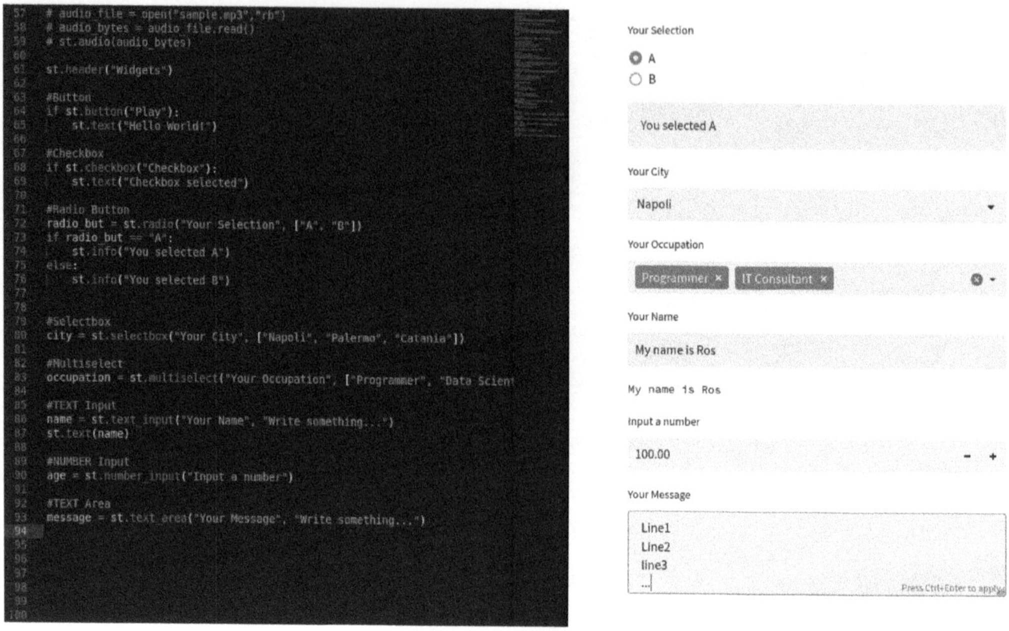

Figure 3.24: The st.text_area widget

`text_area` is the perfect tool when we need to input long text, and it can be configured according to our needs.

Slider

Another wonderful input widget is the slider, where we just need to specify a starting and an ending value to have a nice selector on the screen. The syntax is extremely easy:

```
select_val = st.slider("Select a Value", 1, 10)
```

Here's the output:

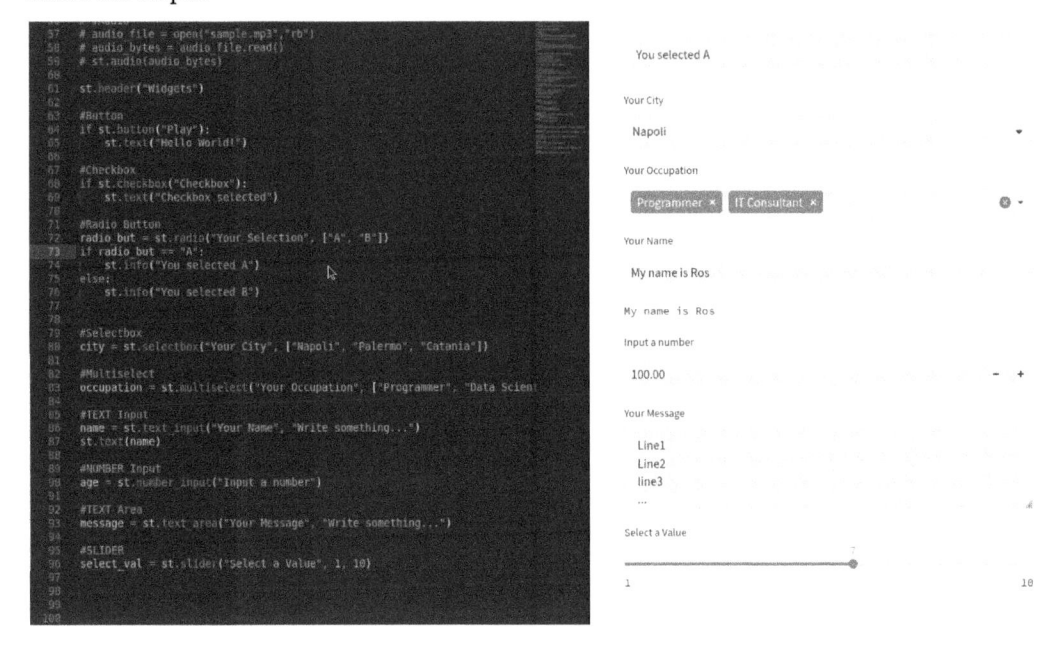

Figure 3.25: The st.slider widget

The slider is quite nice to see and very effective in pursuing its task.

Balloons

A very nice widget is `balloons`. Think of a situation where you want to show happiness after something good hashappened. In this case, you can use it by clicking on a button, as shown in the following code:

```
if st.button("Balloons"):
    st.balloons()
```

See what happens after clicking the button!

DataFrames, plots, and visualizations

Now, it's time to deal with DataFrames, so let's comment on something and continue exploring widgets.

DataFrame is the name that the pandas library gives to its data. When a file, such as a CSV file, is imported into pandas, the result will be a DataFrame. We can think of a DataFrame as an Excel or Google Sheets table – that is, a piece of data made up of columns and rows. Columns are the features or variables and rows are the records or cases. So, to keep things simple, we can say that a DataFrame is a data structure made up of columns and rows.

52 Exploring Streamlit's Features and Functionality

First, we need to install pandas, with the following command:

```
pipenv install pandas
```

If you followed our suggestion and are using `pipenv` for virtual environments, run the following command:

```
pip install pandas
```

If you are using a plain, standard Python installation, then write the following code:

```
st.header("Dataframes and Tables")
import pandas as pd
df = pd.read_csv("auto.csv")
st.dataframe(df.head(10))
```

First of all, please consider that all the files used in this book are available in its GitHub repository, including the `auto.csv` file. Now, let's comment on the code.

First, we import pandas, a powerful library for data/datasets management, with the `pd` alias. After that, we load the `auto.csv` file into a variable named `df` (which stands for DataFrame), and then we visualize the first 10 rows of the DataFrame (its head) with the `dataframe` widget.

The result is shown in the following figure:

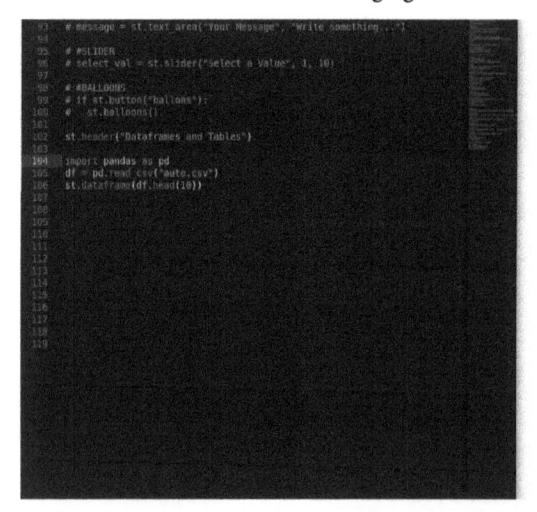

Figure 3.26: The st.dataframe widget

As we can see, thanks to `st.dataframe`, we can visualize the CSV file in a very nice format, with all the columns and rows similar to a Microsoft Excel sheet. If we go to the bottom or the right part of it, we can scroll left/right and up/down. Moreover, we have the opportunity to maximize the DataFrame!

DataFrames, plots, and visualizations

If we prefer, we can visualize the DataFrame in the *table* format since, out of the box, we also have a nice `table` widget. Unfortunately, in this case, it's not possible to scroll our data.

So, let's say we write the following:

```
st.table(df.head(10))
```

Then, we'll get the following table:

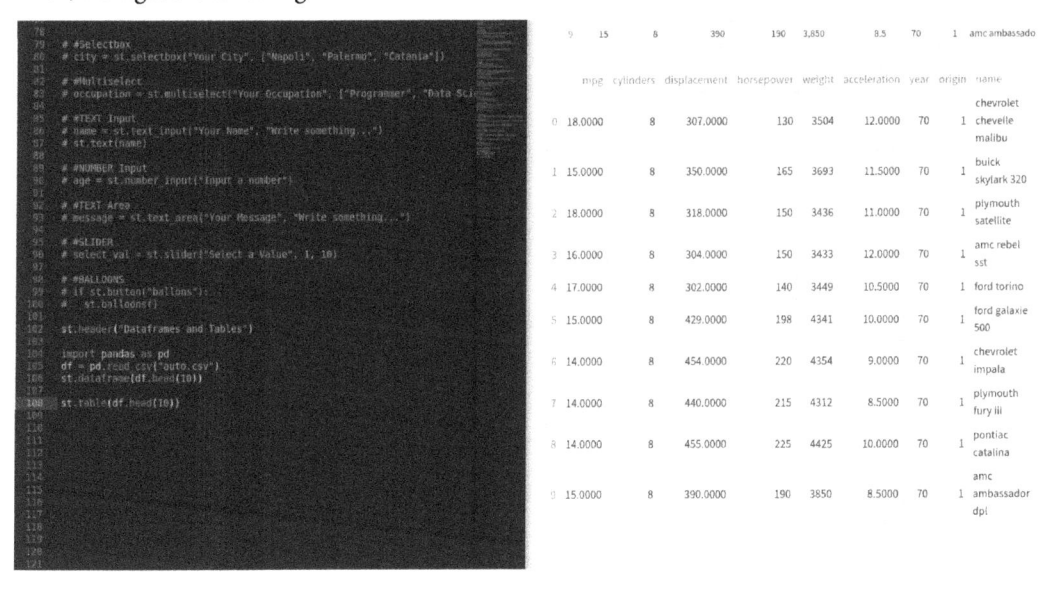

Figure 3.27: The st.table widget

Out of the box, Streamlit can also manage plottings – for example, we can show area, bar, and line charts. All we need is a DataFrame.

Streamlit, together with the plottings, automatically displays the list (in different colors) of all the visualized variables (please note we are using just "mpg" and "cylinders").

Here, we can use the DataFrames we loaded in the previous example.

So, let's write the following:

```
st.area_chart(df[["mpg","cylinders"]])
```

We'll get the following area chart:

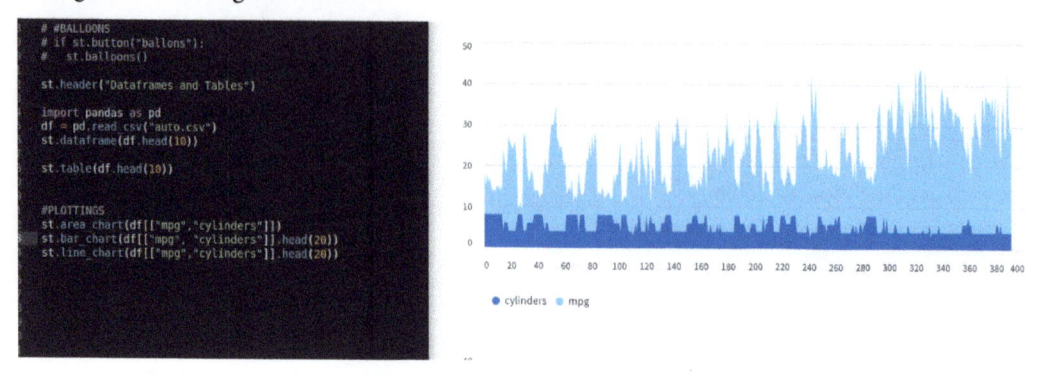

Figure 3.28: The st.area_chart widget

Let's write the following:

```
st.bar_chart(df[["mpg","cylinders"]].head(20))
```

Then, we'll get the following bar chart:

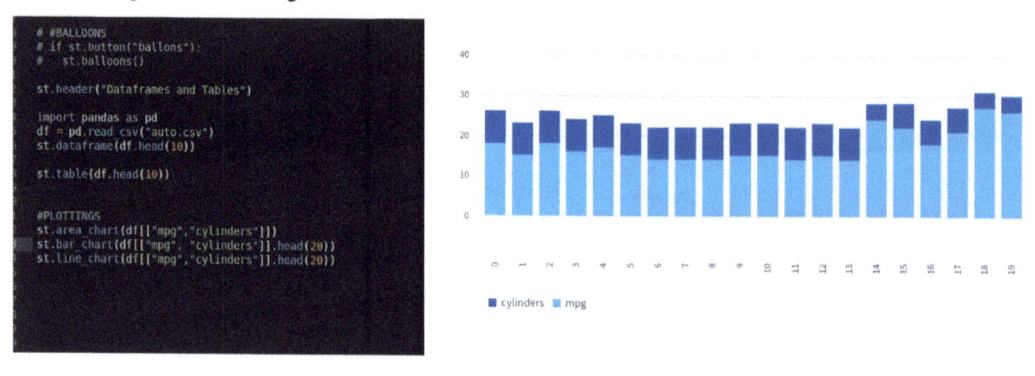

Figure 3.29: The st.bar_chart widget

Let's write the following:

```
st.line_chart(df[["mpg","cylinders"]].head(20))
```

Then, we'll get the following line chart:

Figure 3.30: The st.line_chart widget

If we enter the charts, we can zoom in and out. By clicking on the three dots at the top right of each plotting, we can save the charts as PNG files, view the source, and perform some other operations:

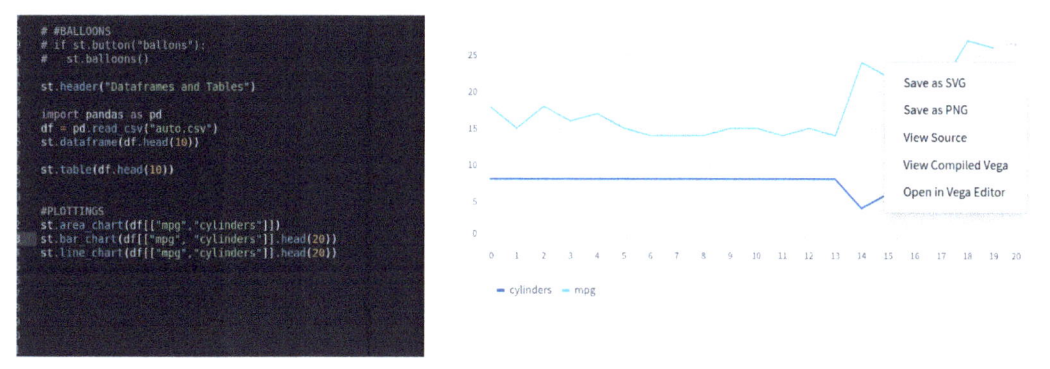

Figure 3.31: Out-of-the-box plotting functions

Finally, as we saw with DataFrames, we can maximize all the charts to see them fullscreen:

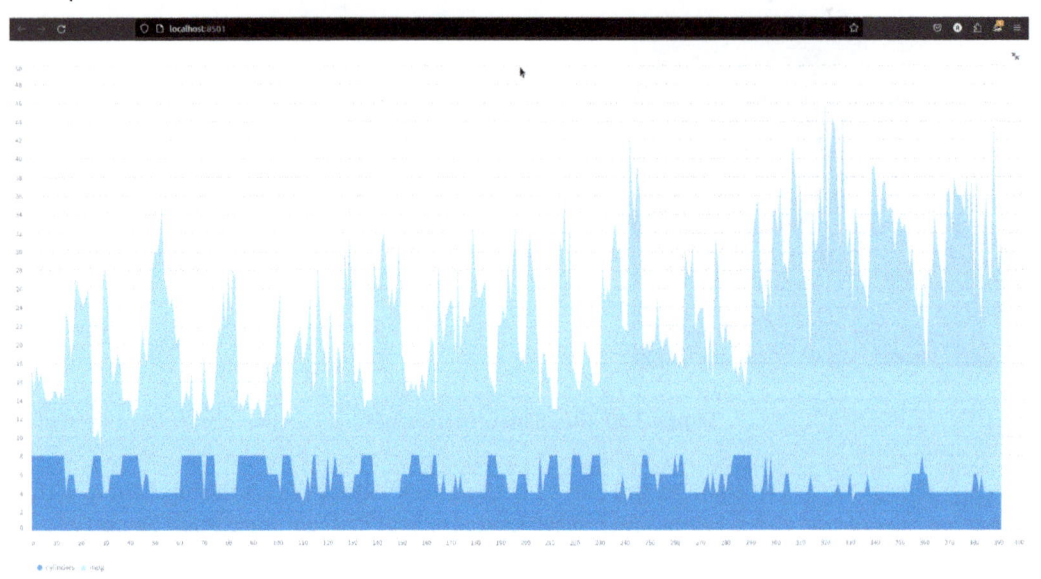

Figure 3.32: Fullscreen plotting

With Streamlit, we can plot much more beautiful graphs using the `matplotlib` and `seaborn` Python packages. So, first of all, let's install these packages:

```
pipenv install matplotlib seaborn
```

If we are in a pure Python environment, we can run the following code:

```
pip install matplotlib seaborn
```

At this point, we can import these packages, like so:

```
import matplotlib.pyplot as plt
import seaborn as sns
```

Now, we are ready to start plotting. Here, we're plotting a heatmap of the correlation matrix of our DataFrame:

```
fig, ax = plt.subplots()
corr_plot = sns.heatmap(df[["mpg","cylinders", "displacement"]].corr(), annot= True)
st.pyplot(fig)
```

The first instruction creates an empty figure. The second line, leveraging `seaborn`, creates a heatmap plotting (with annotations) of the correlation matrix coming from the variables in the `df` DataFrame. Finally, the third command plots our figure using `matplotlib.pyplot`, which is directly managed by Streamlit. Here is the result:

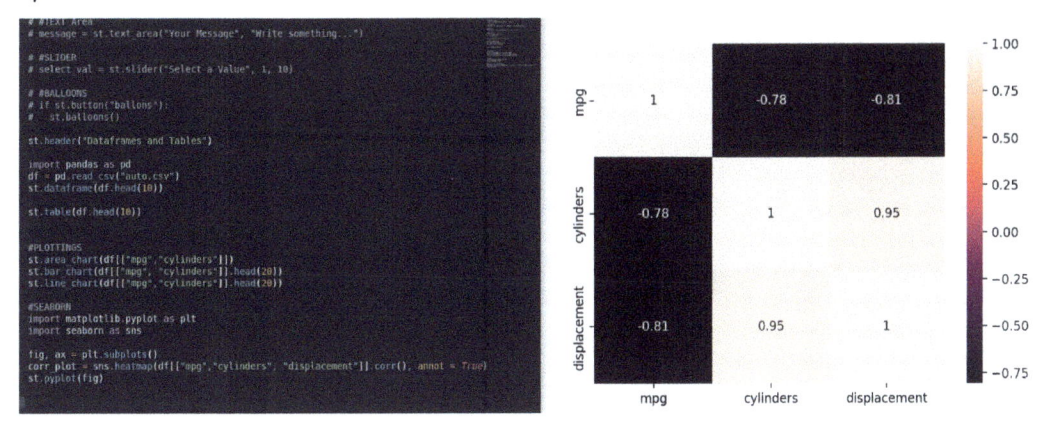

Figure 3.33: Heatmap plotting with Seaborn

Please note that we have displayed the correlation plot with labels and the heatmap with colors and annotations.

Date, time, and more

Another very useful element that we can manage out of the box in Streamlit is date and time – that is, dates, hours, and so on.

For example, to print today's date on the screen, we just have to write the following:

```
import datetime
today = st.date_input("Today is",datetime.datetime.now())
```

Here, the first line simply imports the `datetime` package while the second, using Streamlit's `date_input`, asks the user to select a date. This date will be saved in the `today` variable:

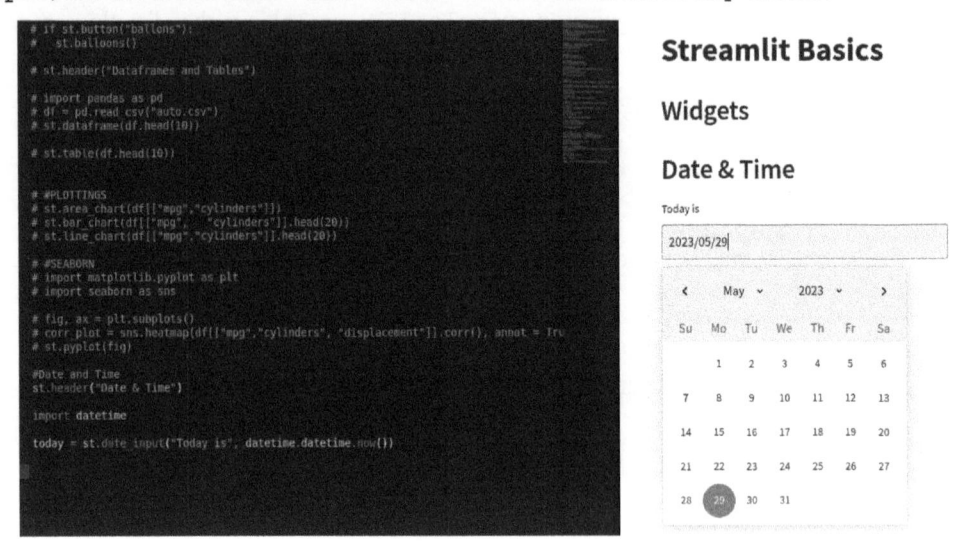

Figure 3.34: The st.date_input widget

Continuing with date and time, we can do the same with time, as follows:

```
import time
hour = st.time_input("The time is",datetime.time(12,30))
```

This time, we are importing `time` and using `time_input`, where we specify that the time is 12:30. On the screen, we can select any time we want:

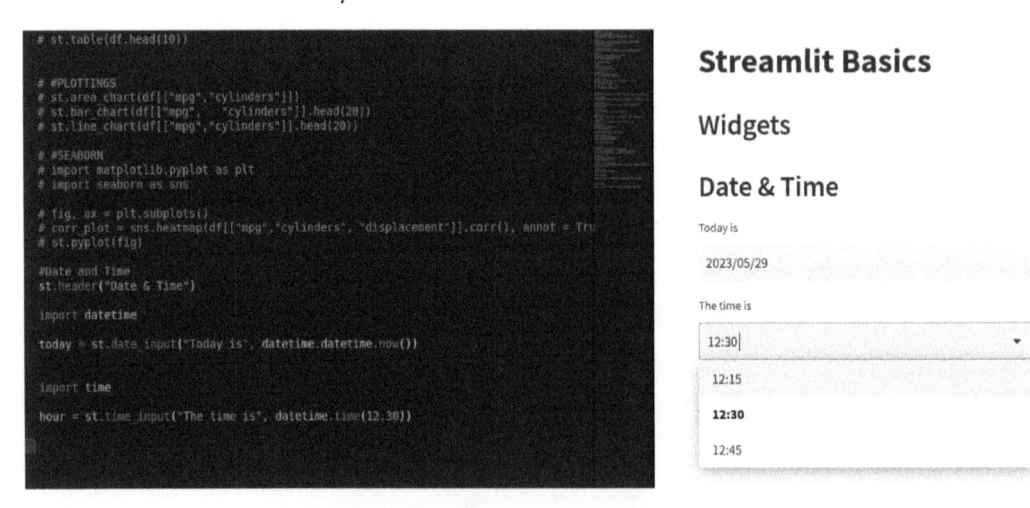

Figure 3.35: The st.time_input widget

Streamlit is powerful and easy to use, and we can even manage text in JSON or programming language formats such as Julia or Python.

Let's type the following:

```
data = {"name":"John","surname":"Wick"}
st.json(data)
```

Here, we've created a variable called `data` that contains two key-value pairs that are displayed on the screen in JSON format using the `st.json` widget – easy and clean:

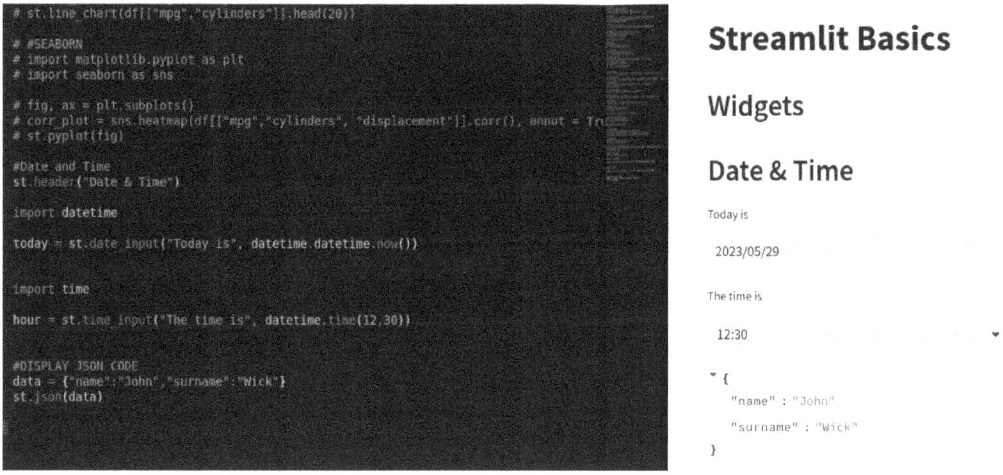

Figure 3.36: The st.json widget

If we click on the arrow, we can close/minimize the JSON.

Displaying code is also very easy – we simply use `st.code` while specifying the programming language as an argument (for Python, this is not necessary since it is the default). Here's an example:

```
st.code("import pandas as pd")
```

We'll see the following output:

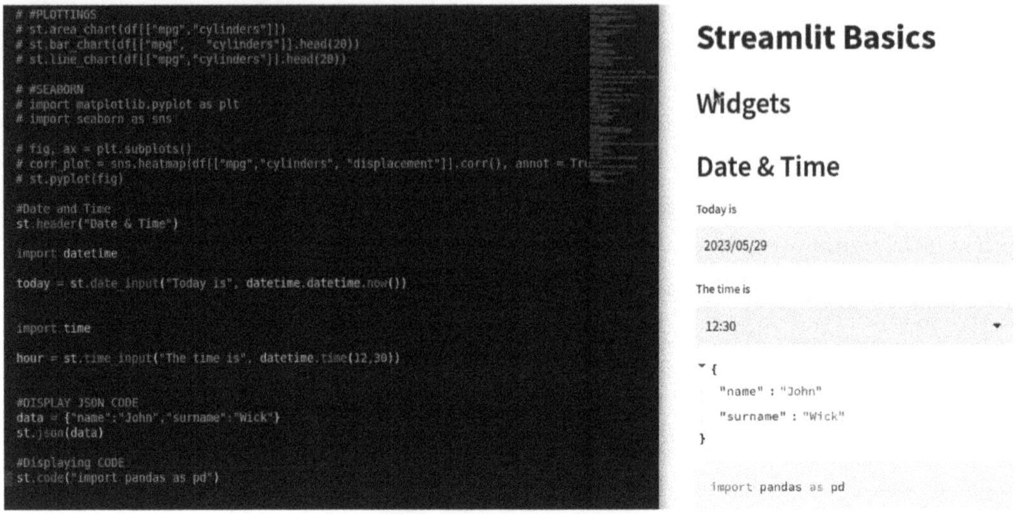

Figure 3.37: The st.code widget for Python

In the case of Julia, we must specify the programming language, so we can write the following:

```
julia_code = """
function doit(num::int)
        println(num)
end
"""
st.code(julia_code, language='julia')
```

This is the result:

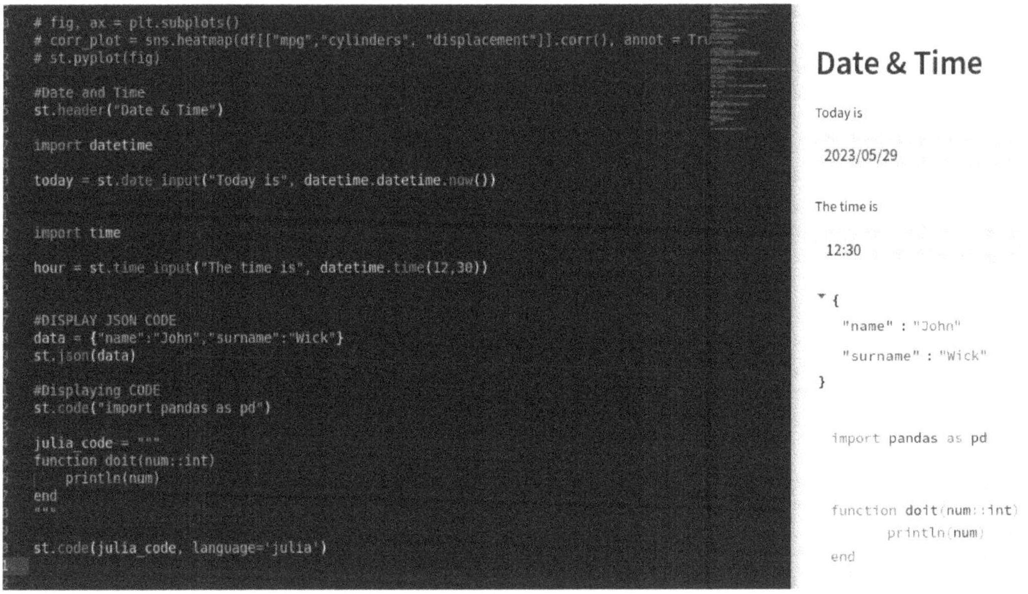

Figure 3.38: The st.code widget for Julia

We can use also progress bars and spinners as standard widgets. Let's see how they work.

For example, to create a progress bar that goes from 0 to 100, increasing its value by 1 every 0.1 seconds, we can write the following:

```
import time
my_bar = st.progress(0)
for value in range(100):
    time.sleep(0.1)
    my_bar.progress(value+1)
```

The result is very nice. For a faster bar, we can use `time.sleep(0.01)`, while for a slower bar, we can use `time.sleep(1)`. This is the result:

Figure 3.39: The st.progress widget

The spinner works more or less in the same way as the progress bar, so we can write the following:

```
import time

with st.spinner("Please wait..."):
    time.sleep(10)
st.success("Done!")
```

Very easily, we can set a starting message of *wait for 10 seconds*, like so:

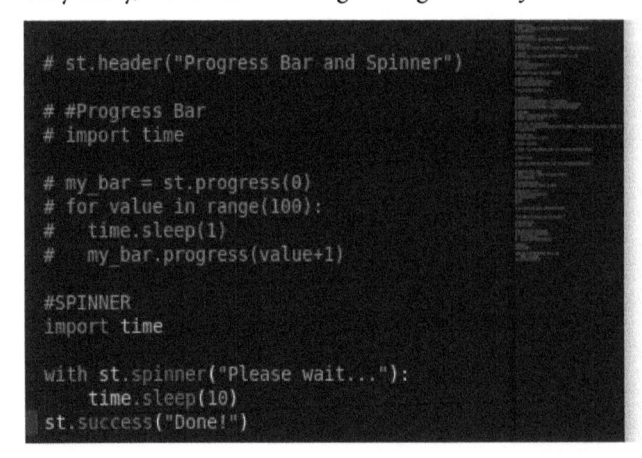

Figure 3.40: The st.spinner widget during the waiting time

Finally, we can print *Done!* in green (success), like so:

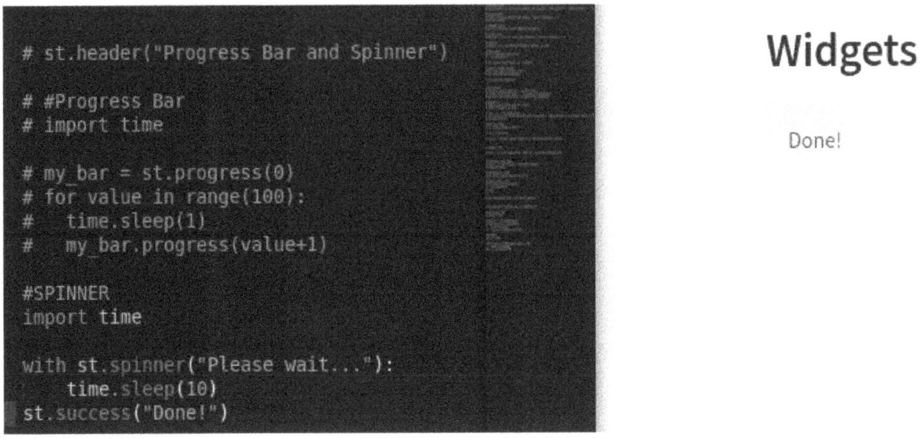

```
# st.header("Progress Bar and Spinner")

# #Progress Bar
# import time

# my_bar = st.progress(0)
# for value in range(100):
#     time.sleep(1)
#     my_bar.progress(value+1)

#SPINNER
import time

with st.spinner("Please wait..."):
    time.sleep(10)
st.success("Done!")
```

Widgets

Done!

Figure 3.41: The st.spinner widget after completion

Very nice!

Now that we've covered progress bars and spinners, we can close this quick introduction to Streamlit's main functions and widgets, which acted as a crash course for full immersion.

Summary

In this chapter, we explored Streamlit's main out-of-the-box features and widgets. We started by creating an empty Python file and launching Streamlit, where we saw how to manage its web interface using the "rerun" feature and leverage its real-time updating functionality.

Then, we learned how to deal with text in various ways, in terms of size, colors, and format. We also explored multimedia widgets, such as images, audio, and video.

A lot of elements, such as buttons, checkboxes, radio buttons, and others, were also explained and utilized.

Many different kinds of inputs are supported natively – it's very easy to input text, numbers, dates, time, and so on. Widgets such as text areas or sliders are also ready to be used out of the box.

As we saw, data plots are extremely easy to create – we can use DataFrames and plot bar, line, or area charts with one line of code. Even heatmaps are a clean and neat option.

Even formatting text in a programming language style, such as Python or Julia, is just a matter of a couple of lines of code.

Finally, we saw that if we need to wait for some calculation or activity in charge of our application, we can use progress bars or spinners to create a nice "wait please..." effect on the screen.

All these components are the basic elements that make up the toolbox that we are going to use, starting from the next chapter, to build up our real web applications. By doing so, we'll extend our knowledge of Streamlit's more advanced features!

Part 2: Building a Basic Web App for Essential Streamlit Skills

Part 2 delves into the hands-on aspect of Streamlit, focusing on building a basic yet robust web application. It starts with the essentials of configuring the Streamlit environment and managing packages, laying a practical foundation for app development. The section progresses to demonstrate how to effectively organize and display content, incorporating advanced elements such as columns, expanders, and **natural language processing** (**NLP**) techniques. You will then explore the implementation of NLP for text analysis and processing, applying these skills to enhance your web application. The part concludes with a comprehensive guide on sharing and deploying these applications on the cloud using Streamlit Share, equipping you with the skills to make your apps accessible to a wider audience. This part is designed to boost your confidence in your Streamlit skills, preparing you for more complex app development in the subsequent parts.

This part has the following chapters:

- *Chapter 4, Streamlit Essentials – Configuring the Environment, Managing Packages, and More*
- *Chapter 5, Organizing and Displaying Content with Columns, Expanders, and NLP Techniques*
- *Chapter 6, Implementing NLP Techniques for Text Analysis and Processing in Streamlit*
- *Chapter 7, Sharing and Deploying Your Apps on the Cloud Using Streamlit Share*

4

Streamlit Essentials – Configuring the Environment, Managing Packages, and More

This chapter covers the basics of building a Python web application using the Streamlit framework. It is designed for beginners who want to learn how to develop a web application from scratch and covers several important topics, including setting up a virtual environment, installing and managing packages, creating an app skeleton, and adding a menu and decoration to the app.

This chapter is the first of a section consisting of four more chapters. In these chapters, we will learn how to build basic web applications while developing essential Streamlit skills. We are adopting a *learning-by-doing* approach, so we are going to build, test, and deploy a real working web app – a **natural language processing** (**NLP**) app – from scratch. So, let's make it!

This chapter starts by recalling the concept of virtual environments and explains why they are important for Python development. Once the development environment has been set up, the focus moves on to creating the application skeleton, which involves defining the structure and layout of the app. This kind of skeleton is a very valuable resource to be used for future web app development. After that, we'll cover how to add a menu and decoration to the app to create a nice, good-looking, and user-friendly web interface.

By the end of this chapter, you should have a basic understanding of how to build a Python web application using Streamlit and be able to create an app with custom menus and decorations while leveraging the skeleton that you've created.

In this chapter, we're going to cover the following main topics:

- Configuring our environment
- Installing and importing packages
- App skeleton building
- Building the menu and adding decorations

Technical requirements

- In this chapter, we will use the following libraries, packages, and tools:
    - Sublime Text
    - Python 3
    - `pipenv`
    - `streamlit`
    - `textblob`
    - `spacy`
    - `neattext`
    - `matplotlib`
    - `wordcloud`
- The code for this chapter can be found in this book's GitHub repository: https://github.com/PacktPublishing/Web-App-Development-Made-Simple-with-Streamlit/tree/4306036e2ddf9a714f2f058f76363aac5b402d5b/Chapter04

Configuring our environment

We are finally here and building our first web application from scratch! From scratch means working from the beginning, even before an empty Python file. The approach is easy – we start by sitting and coding together. Let's start by creating our virtual environment, which is dedicated exclusively to this new app we will develop:

1. As we've already learned in previous chapters, we must fire up our Terminator terminal and create an empty directory named `web_app1` with the following instructions:

    ```
    mkdir web_app1
    ```

2. Then, we must enter the following instruction in the terminal:

    `cd web_app1`

3. Finally, we must write the following:

    `pipenv shell`

The last instruction, as we saw previously and already know, will create the virtual environment with `pipenv`, as shown in *Figure 4.1*:

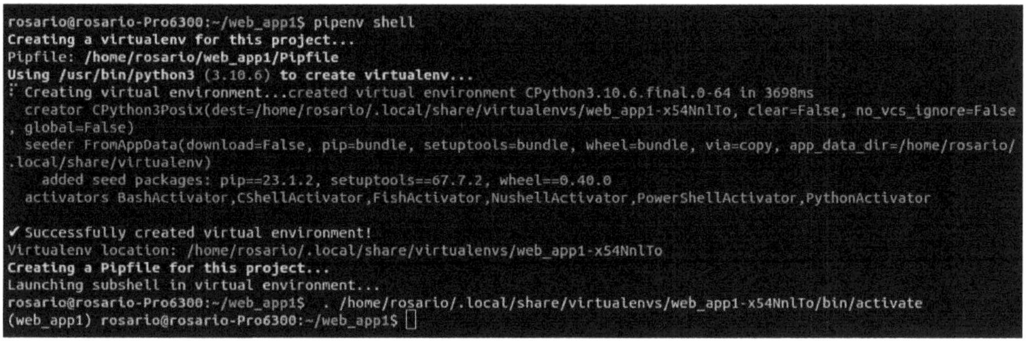

Figure 4.1: Creating a virtual environment in pipenv

Since it will help us a lot in managing code and Streamlit's execution, let's divide our Terminator terminal into two parts, splitting it horizontally.

1. Write the following line in the lower tile:

    `pipes`

    As shown in *Figure 4.2*, the list of available virtual environments will appear.

2. Select `web_app1` by moving the cursor up or down, then hitting *Enter*:

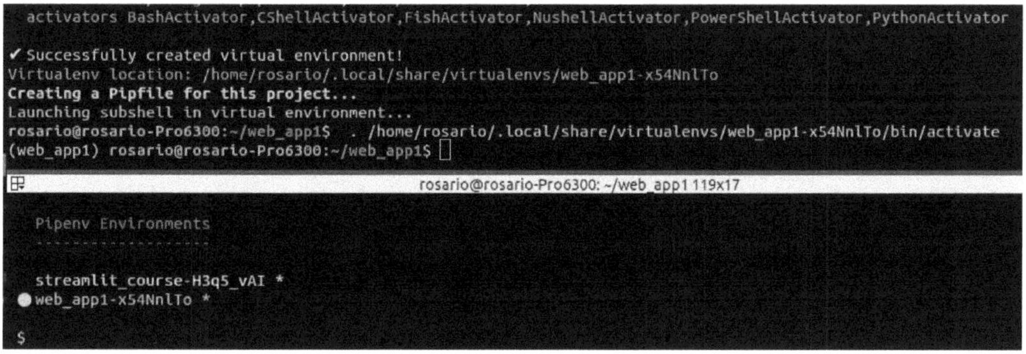

Figure 4.2: Selecting a virtual environment

Once you are inside the virtual environment, in your terminal prompt, you will see its name in parentheses (in our case, web_app1).

3. We are inside web_app1, so we can open our editor, Sublime Text, by typing the following:

    subl .

> **Note**
> Please be aware of the point (.) after the blank space; in other words, there is a blank space between subl and the point (.).

By doing this, Sublime Text will fire up from our working folder:

```
rosario@rosario-Pro6300:~/web_app1$ pipes
Project directory: '/home/rosario/web_app1'
Environment: '/home/rosario/.local/share/virtualenvs/web_app1-x54NnlTo'
Launching subshell in virtual environment...
rosario@rosario-Pro6300:~/web_app1$  . /home/rosario/.local/share/virtualenvs/web_app1-x54NnlTo/bin/activate
(web_app1) rosario@rosario-Pro6300:~/web_app1$ subl .
(web_app1) rosario@rosario-Pro6300:~/web_app1$
```

Figure 4.3: Launching Sublime Text from the virtual environment

With that, our virtual environment is working, and our editor is ready. This means that it's time to deal with all the packages that are required by the web application. We need to install these packages to make the web app work correctly.

Installing and importing packages

To make our web application work properly, we need the following Python packages:

- streamlit: This is the core – that is, the framework that makes the magic happen
- textblob: This is a nice package for basic sentiment analysis and some other basic NLP tasks (NLP is how computers understand human language, its meaning, its syntax, and so on)
- spacy: This is quite an advanced package; it's state of the art and can be used for almost any NLP task
- neattext: A very simple package for text cleaning
- matplotlib: Python's most famous package for plotting graphs, diagrams, and so on
- wordcloud: A package dedicated to nice word cloud creation and visualizations

We can install all these packages in our virtual environment (so we must already be inside the virtual environment) by typing the following unique instruction:

`pipenv install streamlit textblob spacy neattext matplotlib wordcloud`

Please note that this operation can take a few minutes to run:

Figure 4.4: Package installation

If you check the Pipfile from Sublime Text, you will see that all the packages have been installed correctly, as reported in *Figure 4.5*:

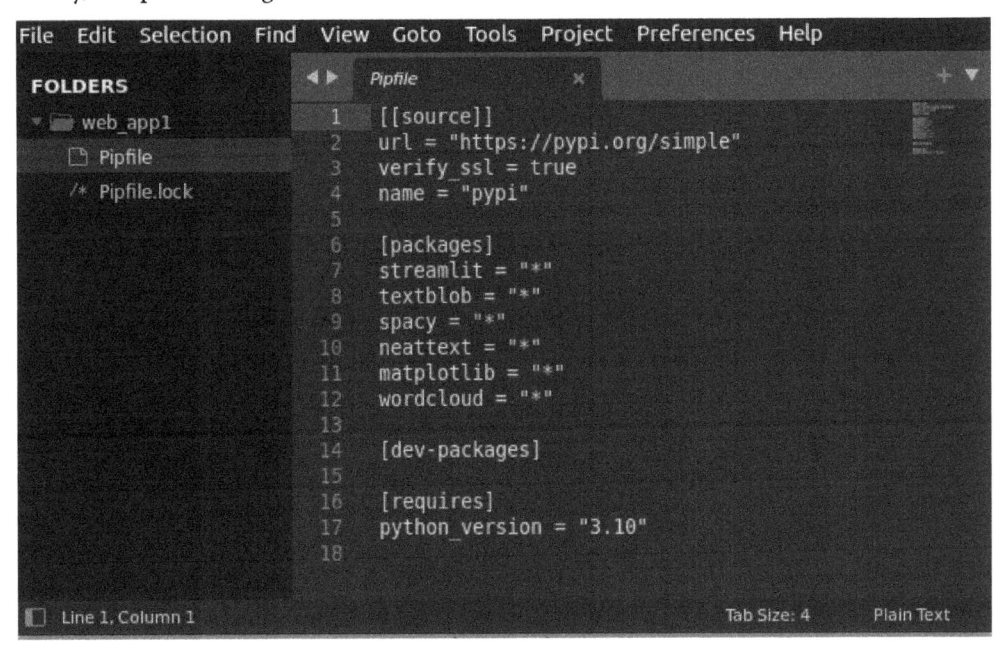

Figure 4.5: Pipfile with the installed packages

spaCy is a very powerful package for NLP and requires a dedicated language model for each language we want to manage. So, before we start coding, we need to download the English language model. Let's write the following instruction in our terminal:

`pipenv run python -m spacy download en_core_web_sm`

This instruction will download the `en_core_web_sm` English language model, whose size is 12.8 MB. The file's name is quite self-explanatory: `en` means English, `core_web` means that the model has been trained on a dataset containing text coming from the web, and `sm` stands for small (if you want to get an idea of all languages, models, and their size, you can check spaCy's official website):

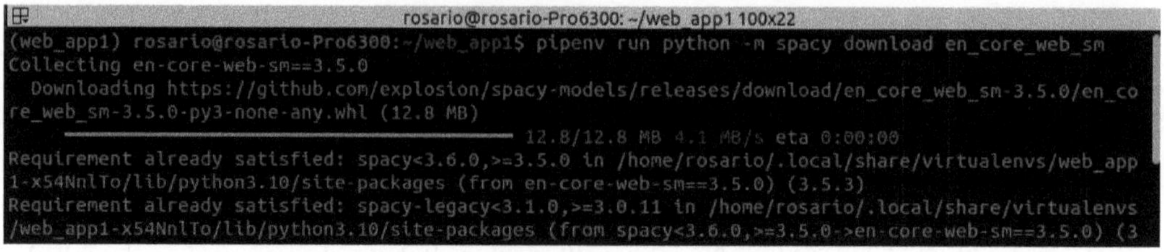
rosario@rosario-Pro6300: ~/web_app1 100x22
(web_app1) rosario@rosario-Pro6300:~/web_app1$ pipenv run python -m spacy download en_core_web_sm
Collecting en-core-web-sm==3.5.0
Downloading https://github.com/explosion/spacy-models/releases/download/en_core_web_sm-3.5.0/en_core_web_sm-3.5.0-py3-none-any.whl (12.8 MB)
12.8/12.8 MB 4.1 MB/s eta 0:00:00
Requirement already satisfied: spacy<3.6.0,>=3.5.0 in /home/rosario/.local/share/virtualenvs/web_app1-x54NnlTo/lib/python3.10/site-packages (from en-core-web-sm==3.5.0) (3.5.3)
Requirement already satisfied: spacy-legacy<3.1.0,>=3.0.11 in /home/rosario/.local/share/virtualenvs/web_app1-x54NnlTo/lib/python3.10/site-packages (from spacy<3.6.0,>=3.5.0->en-core-web-sm==3.5.0) (3

Figure 4.6: Downloading the spaCy language model

Now, we have everything we need to start coding. There's just one thing missing: the Python file! Without it, we cannot code. Let's create it by typing a simple instruction:

```
touch app.py
```

Here's the output:

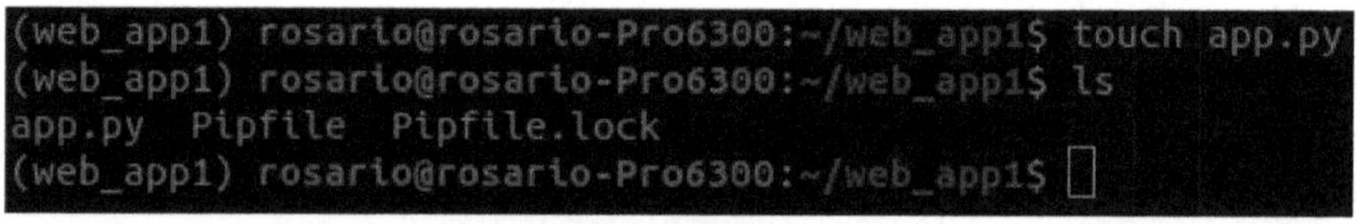
(web_app1) rosario@rosario-Pro6300:~/web_app1$ touch app.py
(web_app1) rosario@rosario-Pro6300:~/web_app1$ ls
app.py Pipfile Pipfile.lock
(web_app1) rosario@rosario-Pro6300:~/web_app1$

Figure 4.7: The app.py file

So far, everything is ready: our environment is OK, our packages have been installed, and our empty `app.py` file is there.

We are now ready to start writing the code for our first working web application.

The first step is to open the app.py file in Sublime Text and import all the libraries we have installed so that we can write the code, as shown in *Figure 4.8*:

```
# Core Pkgs
import streamlit as st

# NLP Pkgs
from textblob import TextBlob
import spacy
import neattext as nt

# Viz Pkgs
import matplotlib.pyplot as plt
import matplotlib
matplotlib.use("Agg")
from wordcloud import WordCloud
```

Figure 4.8: Importing the necessary libraries

The preceding code imports streamlit with the st alias and imports all NLP packages (textblob, spacy, and neattext) and all the visualization libraries. Please note that for matplotlib, we are using the Agg engine since, with Streamlit, it works better than the default one.

After importing, we are finally ready to write all the code for our first real web application. Let's do it right now!

App skeleton building

First of all, we need a main function – a function that contains all the business logic of our app and the frontend too. This is the power of Streamlit – building the frontend directly inside Python code. There's no need for different programming languages, files, and so on; everything is in one place using the same language. Writing this function is very easy – we can add the code shown in *Figure 4.9*:

```
1   # Core Pkgs
2   import streamlit as st
3
4   # NLP Pkgs
5   from textblob import TextBlob
6   import spacy
7   import neattext as nt
8
9   # Viz Pkgs
10  import matplotlib.pyplot as plt
11  import matplotlib
12  matplotlib.use("Agg")
13  from wordcloud import WordCloud
14
15
16  def main():
17      """NLP web app with Streamlit"""
18
19      st.title("NLP Web App")
20
21
22  if __name__ == "__main__":
23      main()
```

Figure 4.9: Importing the necessary libraries and the main function

The first part of the code is quite self-explanatory – we are just importing all the libraries that were introduced a couple of pages before. Just note that when we import `matplotlib` (the library needed for plotting), we are specifying that we wish to use the `Agg` engine (without this instruction, `matplotlib` would use its default engine). With Streamlit's initial versions, this `Agg` engine used to work better, but with the very recent versions, `matplotlib`'s standard engine performs well too. So, the suggestion is to try with and without this instruction and to use it only in the case of a real improvement.

So, thanks to `def`, we can create a function named `main`. At the moment, this function just prints a title on the screen (`st.title`): *NLP Web App*.

That's it – we are ready to launch the web application we've made with Streamlit. In our browser, we'll see our beautiful title: *NLP Web App*.

To run the app in our terminal, we should write `streamlit run app.py`. However, since we are inside a `pipenv` environment, we have to type the following:

```
pipenv run streamlit run app.py
```

This instruction starts a web server that runs our Streamlit app on port `8501`. Our Streamlit app is the code contained in the `app.py` file.

Immediately, the browser will open up on `localhost port 8501` and we will see the web app, as shown in *Figure 4.10*:

NLP Web App

Figure 4.10: Web app running on localhost:8501

At the moment, the web application is doing nothing but showing the *NLP Web App* title, together with the *hamburger menu* at the top right. Please explore all the options contained in this menu.

What is important to understand now is that usually, all applications perform a set of tasks, let's say three or four or *N* (any number), and for this reason, all applications have the same *skeleton*, a common structure or backbone that enables each task. These tasks can be included in an application menu and built up by a *selectbox*, allowing the user to choose what to do. We can put this selectbox on the left-hand side of our app. So, assuming that the tasks of *NLP Web App* will be **Text Analysis**, **Translation**, **Sentiment Analysis**, and **About**, we can create a *list* of them and a selectbox that works on this list by adding the following code in the main function just after the `st.title` line:

```
activity = ["Text Analysis", "Translation", "Sentiment Analysis", "About"]
choice = st.sidebar.selectbox("Menu", activity)
```

Now, save the `app.py` file and click on **Always rerun** in the web app (in the top-right corner); in this way, all the new lines of code will be immediately executed as soon as we save them. As shown in *Figure 4.11*, we have added the menu on the left-hand side of our web app. This menu contains the four tasks we included in the *activity* list. If you want, you can click on the **x** button to minimize the left-hand side column:

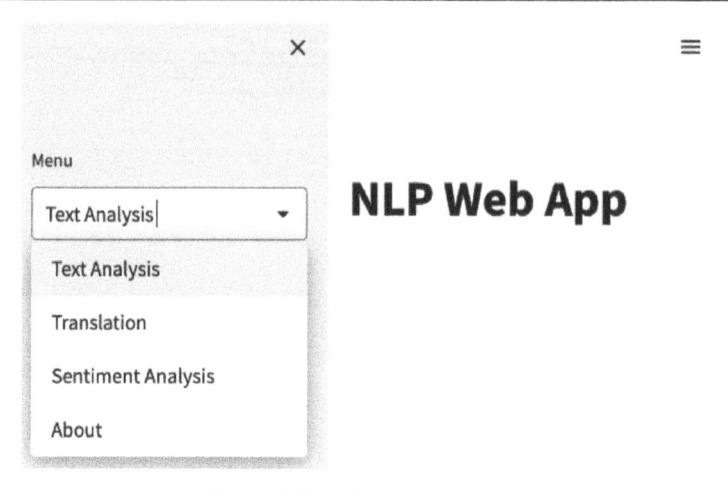

Figure 4.11: Left-hand side menu

To let our menu do something, we have to add some logic for each of its items. We can do this by adding the following code in the main function. At the moment, we are just displaying some sub-headers any time we select a specific option on the menu:

```python
def main():
    """NLP web app with Streamlit"""

    st.title("NLP Web App")

    activity = ["Text Analysis", "Translation", "Sentiment Analysis", "About"]
    choice = st.sidebar.selectbox("Menu", activity)

    if choice == "Text Analysis":
        st.subheader("Text Analysis")
        st.write("")

    if choice == "Translation":
        st.subheader("Translation")
        st.write("")

    if choice == "Sentiment Analysis":
        st.subheader("Sentiment Analysis")
        st.write("")

    if choice == "About":
        st.subheader("About")
        st.write("")


if __name__ == "__main__":
    main()
```

Figure 4.12: Adding some logic to the main menu

The code in *Figure 4.12* is quite easy: we create a list of four items (the `activity` variable) and use it to populate a *selectbox* on the sidebar. This means that this selectbox will show only four options. When we select one of these options (for example, **Sentiment Analysis**, as shown in *Figure 4.13*), we need to perform a related action. This logic is valid for all four different options, so we need some `if`s (four ifs because we have four options) to understand the value of the selection in the selectbox. Simply put, we check `if` our selection in the selectbox is *equal to* any of the items in the menu; if so, we just print a subheader (for now, the related action is only printing a subheader; we'll write a more complex action in the future) with the item's name and a blank line. So, if we select **Sentiment Analysis**, we print a **Sentiment Analysis** subheader on the screen, as displayed in *Figure 4.13*:

Figure 4.13: "Sentiment Analysis" selection from the left-hand side menu

At this point, it should be clear that any kind of logic has to be applied in the `main` function inside its specific `if` clause. For example, if we want the **About** section to do something more than just display a subheader containing the **About** text, we can write the code for its business logic in the following way:

```python
if choice == "About":
    st.subheader("About")
    st.write("")

    st.markdown("""
    ### NLP Web App made with Streamlit

    for info:
    - [streamlit](https://streamlit.io)
    """)


if __name__ == "__main__":
    main()
```

Figure 4.14: Business logic inside the "About" section

To summarize, when the `choice` variable is *equal to* **About**, we display a subheader on the screen containing the **About** text, followed by an empty line (`st.write("")`), and then some text formatted with the Markdown language.

The code we wrote with the `st.markdown` instruction is quite self-explanatory; we are just printing (using the Markdown format) some information on the screen about our web application and a clickable link to Streamlit's website, considering that the `[streamlit](https://streamlit.io)` instruction is just the Markdown syntax to include hyperlinks in the text:

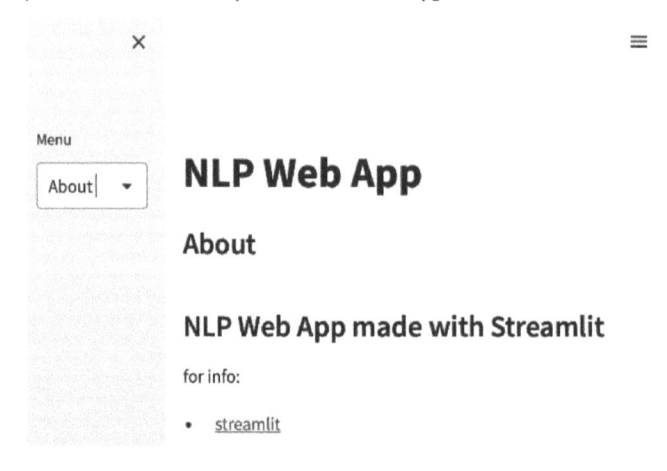

Figure 4.15: The "About" section of our web app

So far, we've created a very neat skeleton (that is, a structure) for our web application, imported all the libraries we are going to use, created a main function where we created a menu (..., which will be displayed on the left-hand side of the app and is collapsible) containing all the tasks our web application is going to cover, and created the **About** section of the app, putting some business logic inside its `if` clause.

It's incredible, but this simple skeleton can be applied to all the web applications we are going to build from now on. All we need to change or adapt is the list of tasks (the list inside the menu on the left-hand side) and the business logic for each of these items.

The point is that, even if the web app is working well now, it is not very appealing. So, let's try adding some decorations.

Building the menu and adding decorations

NLP Web App might be a good title for our application, but to be honest, it's just some black text on a white background, so it's not very appealing at the moment.

One of the greatest features of Streamlit is that we can use HTML very easily. So, let's add some simple HTML code to our `main` function just to make everything much more stylish! We can change the old `st.title("NLP Web App")` first line of code that sits after the main function declaration with the following one:

```
def main():
    """NLP web app with Streamlit"""

    title_template = """
    <div style="background-color:blue; padding:8px;">
    <h1 style="color:cyan">NLP Web App</h1>
    </div>
    """

    st.markdown(title_template, unsafe_allow_html=True)

    activity = ["Text Analysis", "Translation", "Sentiment Analysis", "About"]
    choice = st.sidebar.selectbox("Menu", activity)
```

Figure 4.16: Adding some HTML to our title

In `title_template`, we are specifying the *background color* (blue), the *padding size*, and the *text style* (h1) and its *color* (cyan). With the `st.markdown` instruction, as we learned previously, we are just visualizing the HTML; you can play around and customize it as you want by changing the background and text color, padding, text, and more. This is the result:

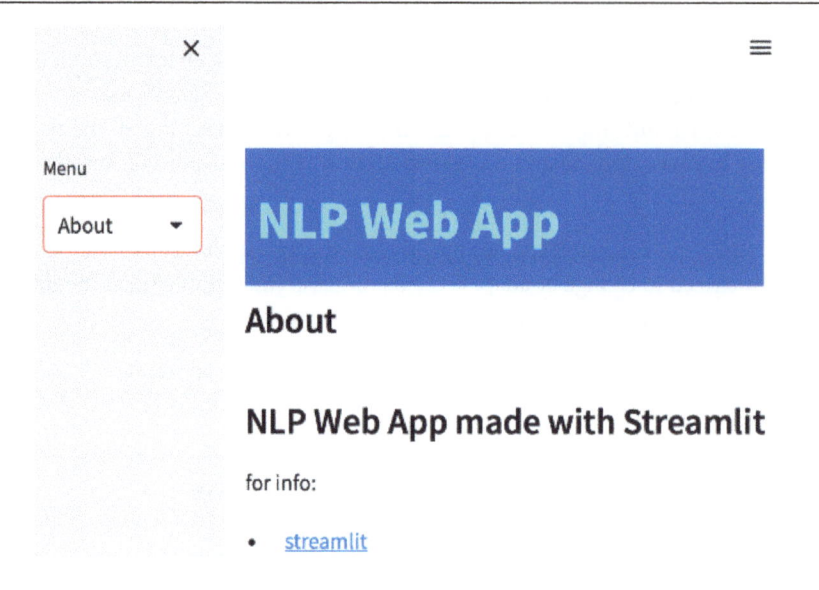

Figure 4.17: A colored title for our app

The effect is very nice.

Now, let's create a subtitle. To do this, we can use a subheader and use more or less the same HTML code. We just need to add another couple of lines of code, as shown in the following figure:

```python
def main():
    """NLP web app with Streamlit"""

    title_template = """
    <div style="background-color:blue; padding:8px;">
    <h1 style="color:cyan">NLP Web App</h1>
    </div>
    """

    st.markdown(title_template, unsafe_allow_html=True)


    subheader_template = """
    <div style="background-color:cyan; padding:8px;">
    <h3 style="color:blue">Powered by Streamlit</h1>
    </div>
    """

    st.markdown(subheader_template, unsafe_allow_html=True)
```

Figure 4.18: The final code for the title and subheader

We approached this the same way we approached `title_template` in *Figure 4.16*: we defined some HTML in a variable (in this case, `subheader_template`) and then visualized it using `st.markdown` and by setting the `unsafe_allow_html` argument to `True`.

As mentioned previously, everything is fully customizable according to your ideas. This is the final result:

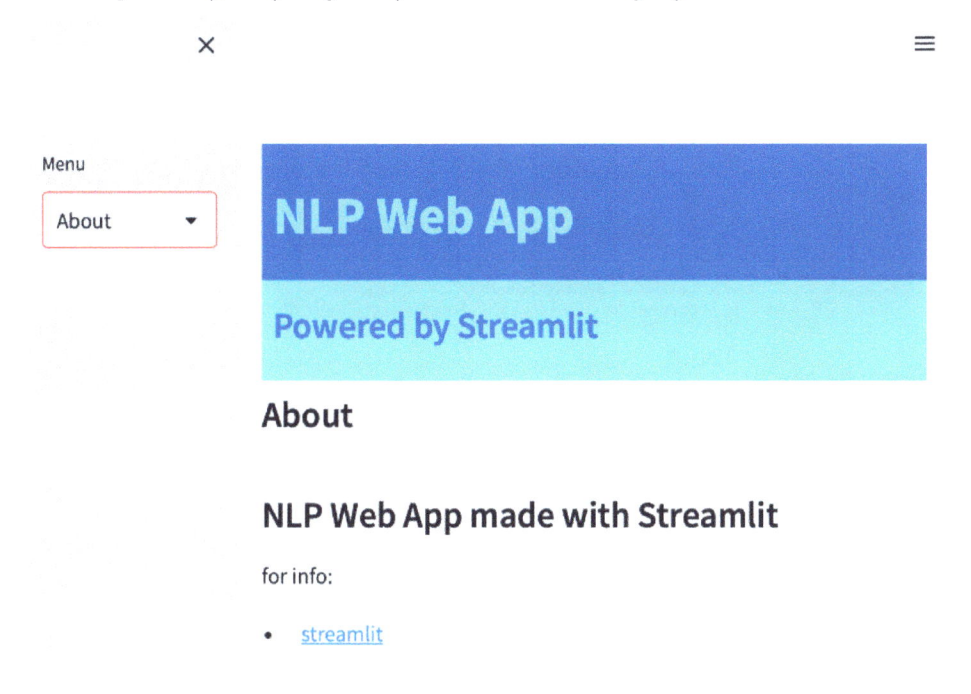

Figure 4.19: The final colored title and subheader

Since we put these decorations at the very beginning of the main function – that is, before creating the left-hand side menu and the `if` clauses that are in charge of selecting various tasks – the colored HTML title and header will not change when we switch the various menu items since they are fixed on the top of the screen and give our web application a very good *style consistency*. In short, since we put this HTML code at the beginning of the main function, it will be applied to the entire web application and not to any specific task – everything will be affected by this title. The title will be a fixed element of our web application.

If we look at our web application's panel in the browser, we will see that the icon and the title are the default ones since the icon is Streamlit's, and the title is just the name of our Python file (`app.py`):

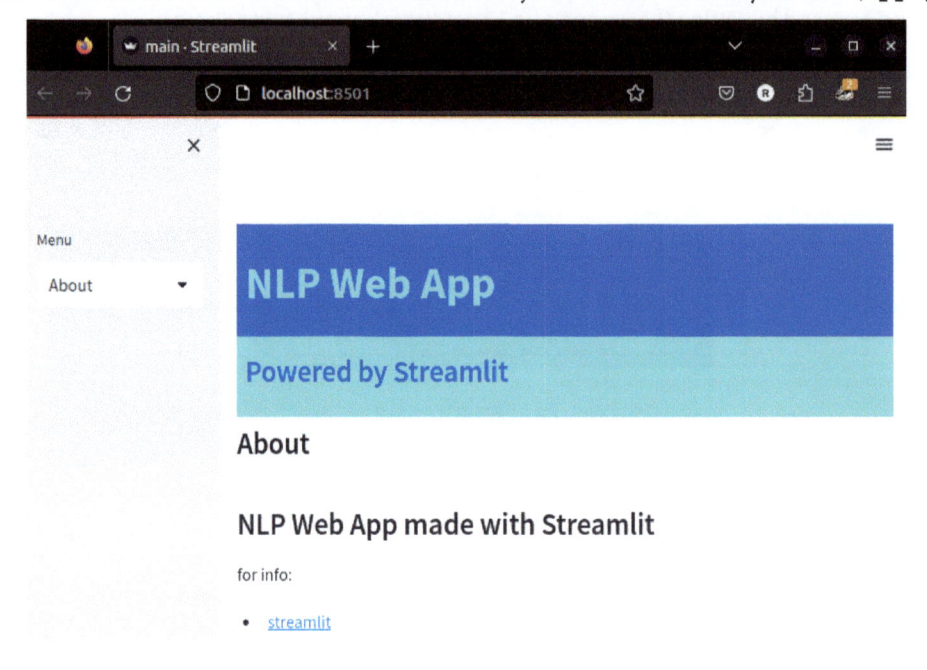

Figure 4.20: The web app's default icon and title in the browser

Let's customize these two very important features. In Streamlit, there is an instruction dedicated exactly to this purpose, but – and this is very important – it has to be placed immediately after the `streamlit import` line. This instruction is `set_page_config`. Let's add it to our `app.py` file and then explain how it works:

```python
# Core Pkgs
import streamlit as st
st.set_page_config(page_title="NLP Web App", page_icon="👍", layout="centered", initial_sidebar_state="auto")

# NLP Pkgs
from textblob import TextBlob
```

Figure 4.21: The set_page_config instruction

`set_page_config` accepts a certain number of arguments, as follows:

- `page_title`: The title of our page; this is a string
- `page_icon`: An icon (an image file) or an emoji (the emoji itself or its code)
- `layout`: This can be `centered` or `wide`
- `initial_sidebar_state`: This can be `wide`, `expanded`, or `collapsed`

You can experiment with different configurations and easily find information on how to use each instruction in Streamlit's **Documentation** section, which includes input arguments and output results.

The following screenshot explains the `set_page_config()` instruction. As you can see, there are several different configurations that we didn't explore, and it's possible to combine them to fully customize your web application. So, please don't forget to carefully check the official Streamlit documentation to get the most value out of this incredible framework:

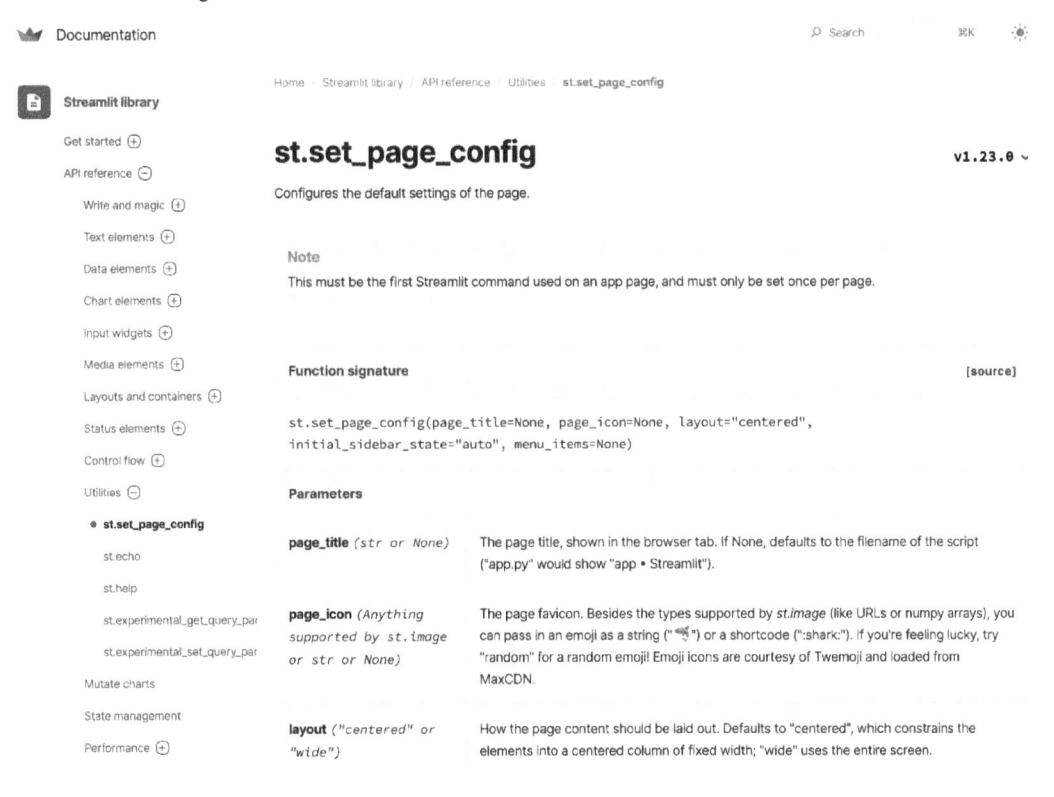

Figure 4.22: Streamlit's official documentation

Now that we've looked at Streamlit's official documentation, let's have a look at our web application with the new page title and icon:

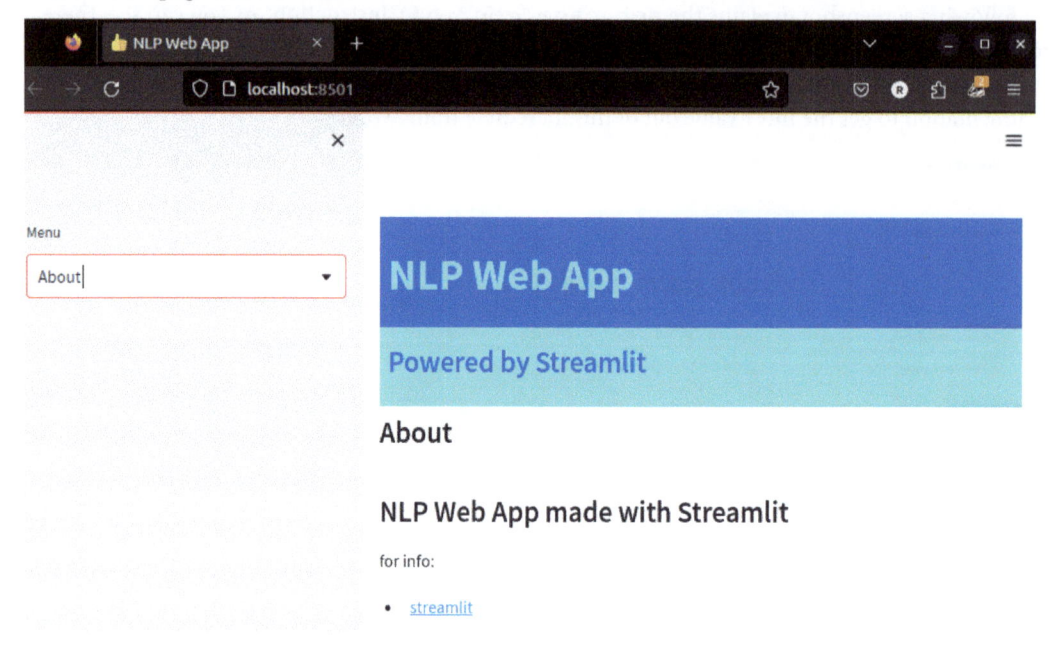

Figure 4.23: Icon and title customization in the browser panel

As you can see, in the browser tile related to our web application, we have a full set of customizations: an icon representing a thumb and a personalized title stating *NLP Web App*. This is the result of the code we saw in *Figure 4.21*.

If you want to, you can see what happens upon changing the 👍 emoji we used as an icon with an image, such as a PNG file that you like. You can also check how the web application behaves when we set `initial_sidebar_state` to `wide`, `expanded`, or `collapsed` and `layout` to `wide`.

The decorations we added to our web app skeleton are clean, neat, and good-looking but up until now, excluding the **About** section, which can be considered closed, the rest need to be completed with some business logic to make the various **Text Analysis**, **Translation**, and **Sentiment Analysis** tasks work properly. This is exactly what we are going to do in the next chapter.

The following figure shows all the code we wrote. It's quite interesting to point out how, in only 64 lines of code, including empty lines and comments, we have built up a working web application that lives on the web and can be used by a browser and that contains a menu, some sections, HTML, titles, and decorations:

```python
# Core Pkgs
import streamlit as st
st.set_page_config(page_title="NLP Web App", page_icon="👍", layout="centered", initial_sidebar_state="auto")

# NLP Pkgs
from textblob import TextBlob
import spacy
import neattext as nt

# Viz Pkgs
import matplotlib.pyplot as plt
import matplotlib
matplotlib.use("Agg")
from wordcloud import WordCloud


def main():
    """NLP Web app with Streamlit"""

    title_template = """
    <div style="background-color:blue; padding:8px;">
    <h1 style="color:cyan">NLP Web App</h1>
    </div>
    """

    st.markdown(title_template, unsafe_allow_html=True)

    subheader_template = """
    <div style="background-color:cyan; padding:8px;">
    <h3 style="color:blue">Powered by Streamlit</h1>
    </div>
    """

    st.markdown(subheader_template, unsafe_allow_html=True)

    activity = ["Text Analysis", "Translation", "Sentiment Analysis", "About"]
    choice = st.sidebar.selectbox("Menu", activity)

    if choice == "Text Analysis":
        st.subheader("Text Analysis")
        st.write("")

    if choice == "Translation":
        st.subheader("Translation")
        st.write("")

    if choice == "Sentiment Analysis":
        st.subheader("Sentiment Analysis")
        st.write("")

    if choice == "About":
        st.subheader("About")
        st.write("")

        st.markdown("""
        ### NLP Web App made with Streamlit

        for info:
        - [streamlit](https://streamlit.io)
        """)

if __name__ == "__main__":
    main()
```

Figure 4.24: The app.py file

The best part is that you can reuse it as you wish!

Summary

In this chapter, we began from scratch. First of all, we prepared our `pipenv` environment, installed all packages needed for the web application, and finally created an empty Python file.

After that, we built up a *skeleton* that can be reused any time we want to develop a new web application. This skeleton is made up of an initial part where we import all the packages we need and a *main* function that is dedicated to containing all the business logic of our web app.

In the first part of the main function, some features must be applied to the entire web application, such as its title and subtitle, which we created with very beautiful and colorful HTML, and the web browser's panel icon and title.

In the second part of the main function, we created a menu that will be shown on the left-hand side of our web application and that lets the user choose from the various tasks our web application can perform. Upon selecting one of the tasks in the menu, the web application will show its specific section performing its specific task. We implemented this because we wanted to start with a very easy case. The **About** section now performs well, showing the name/title of the web application and some useful information – in this case, the working link to Streamlit's website.

Everything is working well and has been customized according to our willingness and future needs. This shows that this skeleton is a great weapon in our developer's toolkit!

In the next chapter, we'll start building the complete business logic of our application by using and learning about some very powerful widgets such as columns and expanders, as well as some NLP techniques!

5
Organizing and Displaying Content with Columns, Expanders, and NLP Techniques

In this chapter, we will develop all the business logic required for the skeleton app we implemented in *Chapter 4*. We are going to learn about some extremely important features of Streamlit.

Columns and expanders are two layout features in the Streamlit framework that allow for more flexible and organized display of content in a web application.

Columns allow for dividing the screen horizontally into multiple sections, each with its own content. This is useful for displaying multiple visualizations or data tables side by side, or for separating different parts of the app's interface. Expanders, on the other hand, allow for collapsing and expanding sections of content within a column. This is useful for hiding less important or less frequently used parts of the app's interface, and allowing users to expand them only when needed.

In NLP, tokens are individual text units segmented by white space or punctuation. Lemmas, on the other hand, are the base or dictionary form of a word, which may differ from the inflected or derived form found in the text.

By the end of the chapter, our first web application should appear much more complete and you should have a wider understanding of how to build a Python web application using Streamlit.

In this chapter, we're going to cover the following main topics:

- Organizing and arranging content in a web app
- Hiding and showing parts depending on importance
- Introducing NLP concepts – tokens and lemmas

Technical requirements

- In this chapter, we will use the following libraries, packages, and tools:
  - Sublime Text
  - Python 3
  - `pipenv`
  - Streamlit
  - Spacy
  - `neattext`
  - `matplotlib`

- Code in the chapter can be accessed through the following GitHub link: https://github.com/PacktPublishing/Web-App-Development-Made-Simple-with-Streamlit/tree/bd70c6ee45d046134e71c3c8a93c3d97172bf3f9/Chapter05

Organizing and arranging content in a web app

In *Chapter 4*, we built the foundations of our first web application and wrote some Python code that, once executed, gives us the following result:

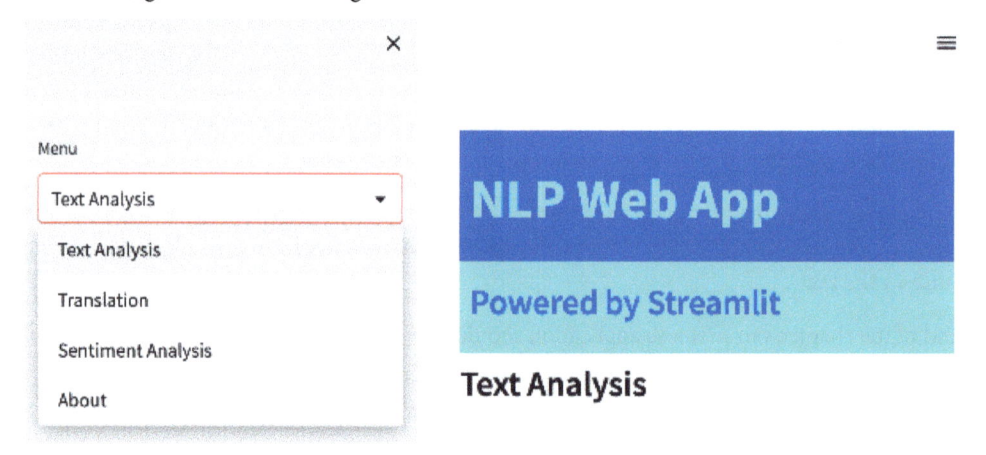

Figure 5.1: Chapter 5 starting point

We completed the **About** section, made some decorations in terms of colors, and added an icon (the so-called *favicon*) and a title to the web browser page.

It's time to complete the three remaining voices of the menu: **Text Analysis**, **Translation**, and **Sentiment Analysis**.

Adding decorations

Before completing the three voices of the menu, however, let's add a nice decoration to the sidebar of our web app. So, once again, open the Sublime Text editor and restart coding.

We need to add an image to the sidebar immediately after the second HTML of the title on *lines 35-36* of our code. This is an easy coding task, and it is shown in the following figure:

```
28    subheader_template = """
29    <div style="background-color:cyan; padding:8px;">
30    <h3 style="color:blue">Powered by Streamlit</h1>
31    </div>
32    """
33
34    st.markdown(subheader_template, unsafe_allow_html=True)
35
36    st.sidebar.image("nlp.jpg", use_column_width=True)
37
38    activity = ["Text Analysis", "Translation", "Sentiment Analysis", "About"]
39    choice = st.sidebar.selectbox("Menu", activity)
40
41    if choice == "Text Analysis":
```

Figure 5.2: st.sidebar.image

The process is extremely easy: we are adding to the sidebar (`st.sidebar`) an image. We just wrote NLP in Google and downloaded an image, saving it as `nlp.jpg` in the same folder as our Python script. Since we are setting the `unsafe_allow_width` argument to `True`, the width of our image will be exactly the same as that of all other elements in the sidebar. If you want, instead of `unsafe_allow_width`, you can use the `width` one in the following way:

```
width = 200
```

You can try with different widths (100, 300, etc.) and observe the different results.

In *Figure 5.3*, we can see the result of the last decoration:

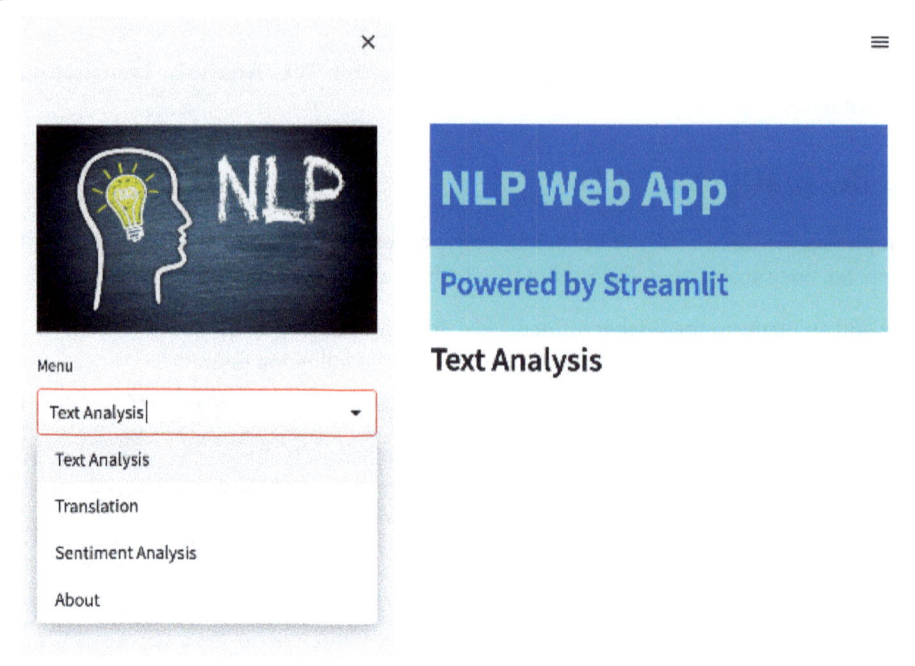

Figure 5.3: A picture in the sidebar

Our web application is starting to look appealing! Now we can move on to the text analysis part.

Adding the Text Analysis part

In this part, we will use `textblob`, a Python library for processing textual data. It provides a simple API for diving into common NLP tasks such as part-of-speech tagging, sentiment analysis, classification, and more. For more details, visit `pypi.org` (the famous Python Package Index).

As usual, we need to install the package in our virtual environment by just typing the following command:

```
pipenv install textblob
```

And then, we import it into our Python script, adding the following line at the very beginning in the `importing libraries` part:

```
from textblob import TextBlob
```

Anyway, if you followed *Chapter 4* carefully, you have already done this, but it's better to repeat it just in case.

Let's jump to the *Text Analysis* part of our script and finally add its specific business logic. *Text Analysis*, as we will see during the coding, is a function focused on text stats (length, number of words, etc.), wordstopping, lemmas and tokens, and so on. We will quickly explain these concepts one by one in the next pages. Besides NLP concepts, what is very important here is to understand how to use the various Streamlit widgets, functions, and technicalities in order to create and build up solid and well-performing web applications.

Adding a text area

Currently, in this part, we just have a header and a subheader. In order to perform text analysis, for sure we need some text, so as the very first operation, let's add a text area where we can input all the text we want:

```
38    activity = ["Text Analysis", "Translation", "Sentiment Analysis", "About"]
39    choice = st.sidebar.selectbox("Menu", activity)
40
41    if choice == "Text Analysis":
42        st.subheader("Text Analysis")
43        st.write("")
44
45        raw_text = st.text_area("Write something", "Enter a text in English...", height=300)
46
47    if choice == "Translation":
```

Figure 5.4: st.text_area

We are using `text_area` to get some text and put it in a variable named `raw_text`. Try to play with `st.text_area` arguments a little, and especially try to discover what happens if you don't use *height*.

Adding the Analyze button

We want to do something with the text typed in this `text_area` so, just to understand better how it works, let's add a button named **Analyze** that, when pushed, writes our text on the screen. The code is quite simple, as shown in the following figure:

```
41    if choice == "Text Analysis":
42        st.subheader("Text Analysis")
43        st.write("")
44
45        raw_text = st.text_area("Write something", "Enter a text in English...", height=300)
46
47        if st.button("Analyze"):
48            st.write(raw_text)
49
50    if choice == "Translation":
```

Figure 5.5: A button to show our text

To keep it very neat and clean, we write something in the text area – for example, `Hello everybody!` – click on the button, and see what we wrote on the screen. This is the result:

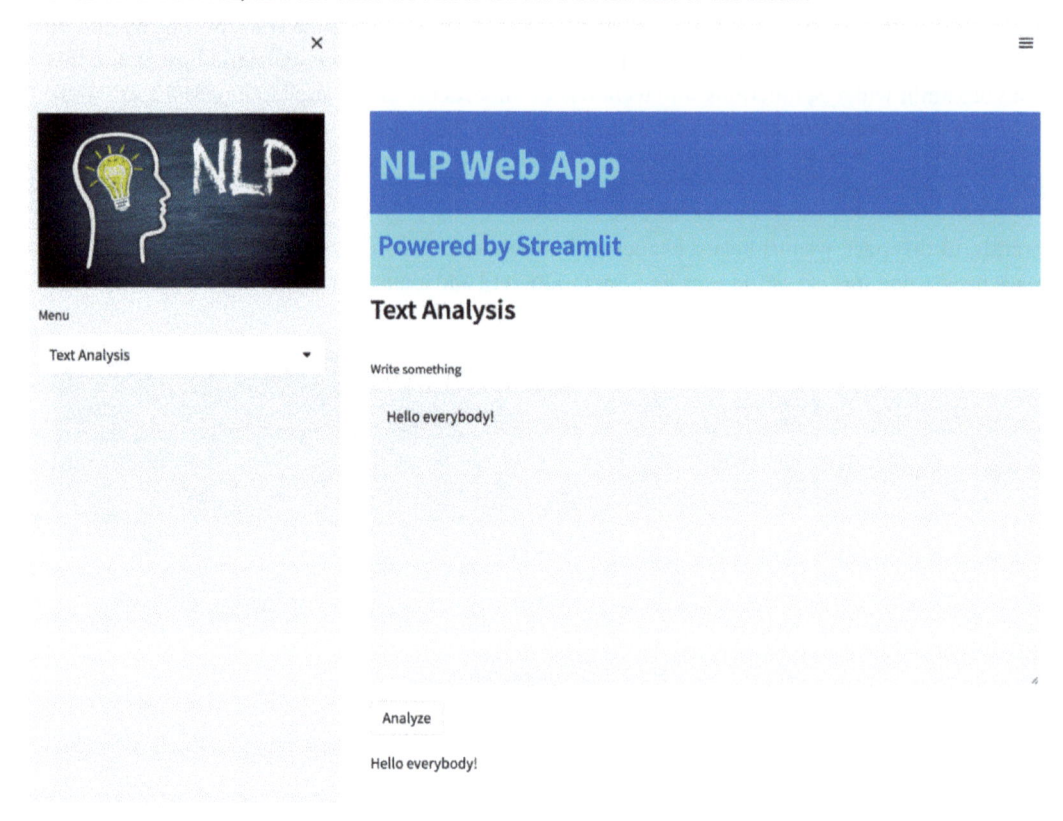

Figure 5.6: Hello everybody!

To perform any NLP task, TextBlob needs to convert any text into a `Blob` object, something specific to this nice package. Let us see how.

Creating the Blob object

To perform all our NLP tasks with TextBlob, we have to be sure that this Blob can be created, and it can be created only if the text area contains some text – in other words, if the text area is not empty.

Let's modify the preceding code a bit, just to be sure that the text area is not empty and that the `Blob` object will be created without issues:

```
41    if choice == "Text Analysis":
42        st.subheader("Text Analysis")
43        st.write("")
44
45        raw_text = st.text_area("Write something", "Enter a text in English...", height=300)
46
47        if st.button("Analyze"):
48            if len(raw_text) == 0:
49                st.warning("Enter a text...")
50            else:
51                blob = TextBlob(raw_text)
52                st.write("OK")
53
54    if choice == "Translation":
```

Figure 5.7: TextBlob in action

So, *if* there is no text in the `text_area`, its length (`len`) is equal to zero and we display a warning message; otherwise (`else`) we create a `TextBlob` object, save it as a variable named `blob`, and display a confirmation message (`OK`).

And now, we have our `TextBlob` object working.

Adding basic functions

Up to now, we have edited all code properly and we are ready to implement some real text analysis functions. In fact, we will be using `TextBlob` later on for the sentiment analysis function. Now, we just use it to check that the application runs correctly, so if you want, you can comment on the following line of code, like this:

```
#blob = TextBlob(raw_text)
```

Let's get started with **Basic Functions**, so replace the `st.write("OK")` line with the following:

```
st.info("Basic Function")
```

So far, we are at the stage shown in the following screenshot:

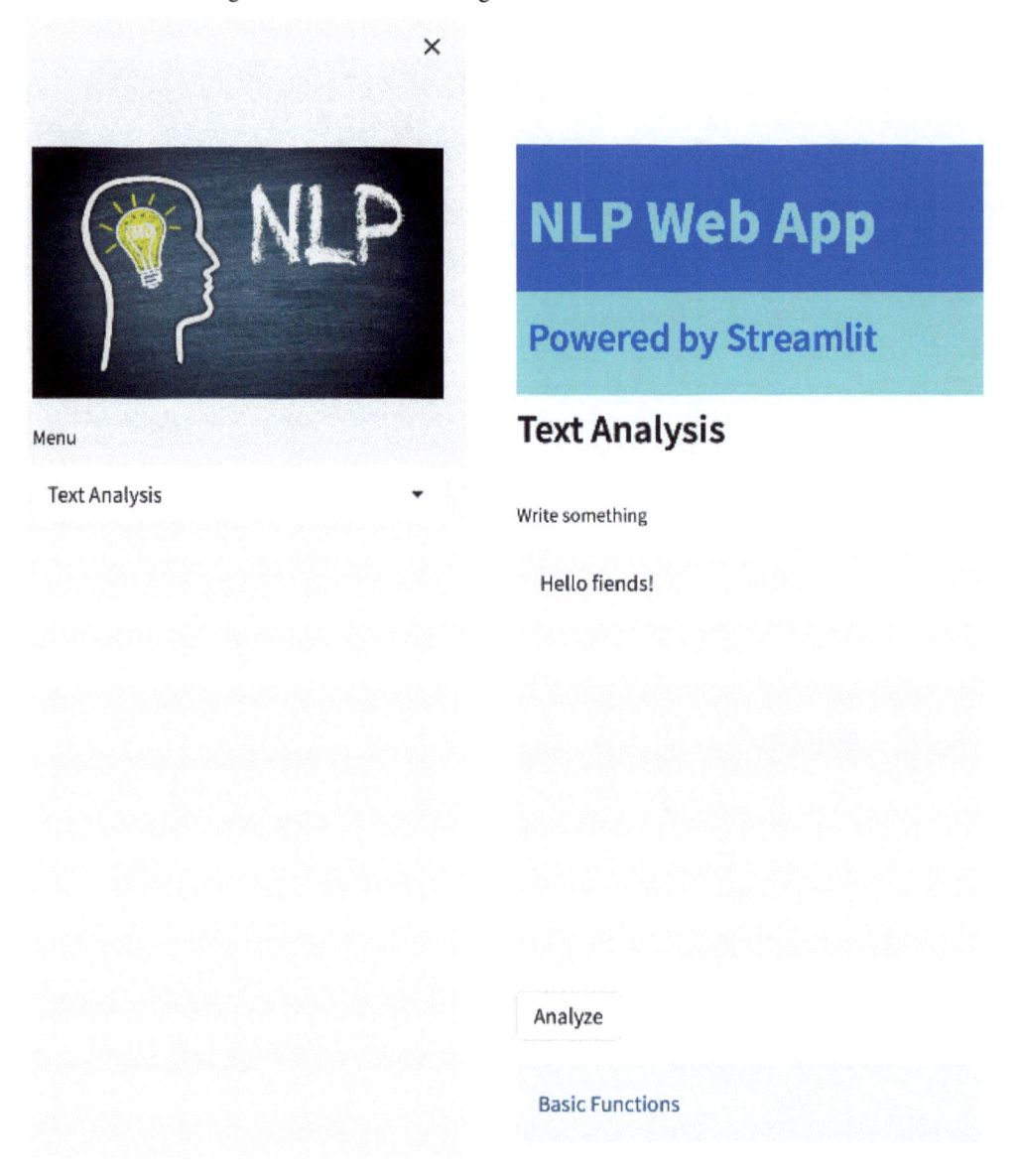

Figure 5.8: Basic functions

It's time to understand how to show and hide information on the screen using columns, expanders, and more advanced coding.

Hiding and showing parts depending on importance

From a very broad point of view, an application is just a way to visualize, transform, and save information. Not always showing all the available information at the same time is a winning idea. For example, having all the information on a unique screen could make our app very crowded. In other cases, we are not interested in visualizing all the information simultaneously because we want to see only a specific piece of information that is of our interest. So, hiding and properly showing information in our web application is a very valuable skill to acquire.

Adding columns, expanders, and a textbox

Columns are very useful because they allow us to create some *layers* or *different parts*. This means that by using columns, we can divide the screen into as many vertical sections as we want and use these sections (or columns) for any kind of specific purpose we think should be in a specific – or let's say dedicated – container. All we need to do is create or declare these widgets.

We start using them by adopting the `with` instruction. Let's see it in detail:

```
40
41    if choice == "Text Analysis":
42        st.subheader("Text Analysis")
43        st.write("")
44
45        raw_text = st.text_area("Write something", "Enter a text in English...", height=300)
46
47        if st.button("Analyze"):
48            if len(raw_text) == 0:
49                st.warning("Enter a text...")
50            else:
51                blob = TextBlob(raw_text)
52                st.info("Basic Functions")
53
54                col1, col2 = st.columns(2)
55
56                with col1:
57                    with st.expander("Basic Info"):
58                        st.write("Text Stats")
59
60                with col2:
61                    with st.expander("Processed Text"):
62                        st.success("Stopwords Excluded Text")
63
64
65
66
67    if choice == "Translation":
```

Figure 5.9: Columns and expanders

The `col1, col2 = st.columns(2)` line just creates two columns named `col1` and `col2`. In the two `with` lines, we use these columns. In each of the columns, we create an *expander*; any expander has its own label (`Basic Info` and `Processed Text`). Expanders are clickable since they have an *up arrow* and *down arrow* symbol. Clicking on these symbols, we *expand* or *collapse* these widgets to reveal their content – in our example, just `st.write` and `st.success` instructions. The effect in the browser is very beautiful:

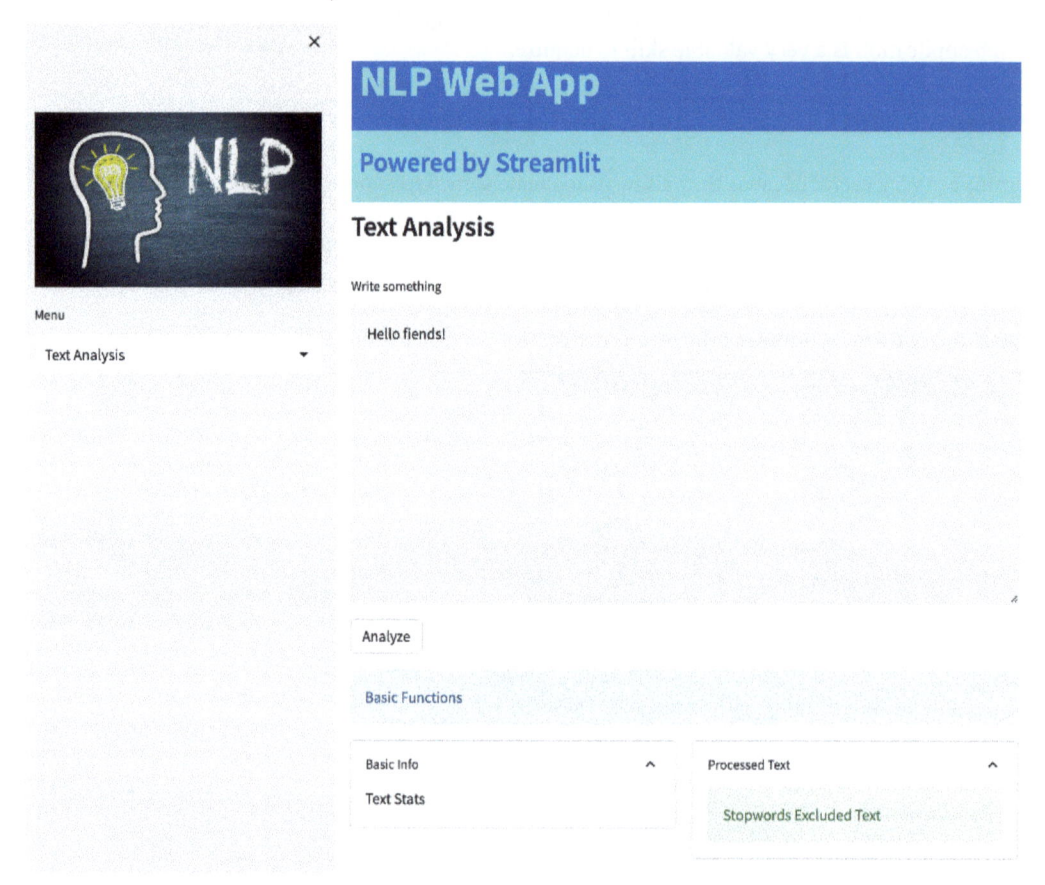

Figure 5.10: Columns and expanders in our web application

Since we want to also include a couple of *Advanced Features* in our web app, let's copy the latest part of the code in order to create another couple of columns and expanders, plus an `info` text box:

```
40
41    if choice == "Text Analysis":
42        st.subheader("Text Analysis")
43        st.write("")
44
45        raw_text = st.text_area("Write something", "Enter a text in English...", height=300)
46
47        if st.button("Analyze"):
48            if len(raw_text) == 0:
49                st.warning("Enter a text...")
50            else:
51                blob = TextBlob(raw_text)
52                st.info("Basic Functions")
53
54                col1, col2 = st.columns(2)
55
56                with col1:
57                    with st.expander("Basic Info"):
58                        st.write("Text Stats")
59
60                with col2:
61                    with st.expander("Processed Text"):
62                        st.success("Stopwords Excluded Text")
63
64                st.write("")
65                st.write("")
66                st.info("Advanced Features")
67
68                col3, col4 = st.columns(2)
69
70                with col3:
71                    with st.expander("Tokens&Lemmas"):
72                        st.write("T&K")
73
74                with col4:
75                    with st.expander("Summarize"):
76                        st.success("Summarize")
```

Figure 5.11: New columns and expanders

98   Organizing and Displaying Content with Columns, Expanders, and NLP Techniques

The code we added is the same as we already commented previously. Its impact on the web application is the following:

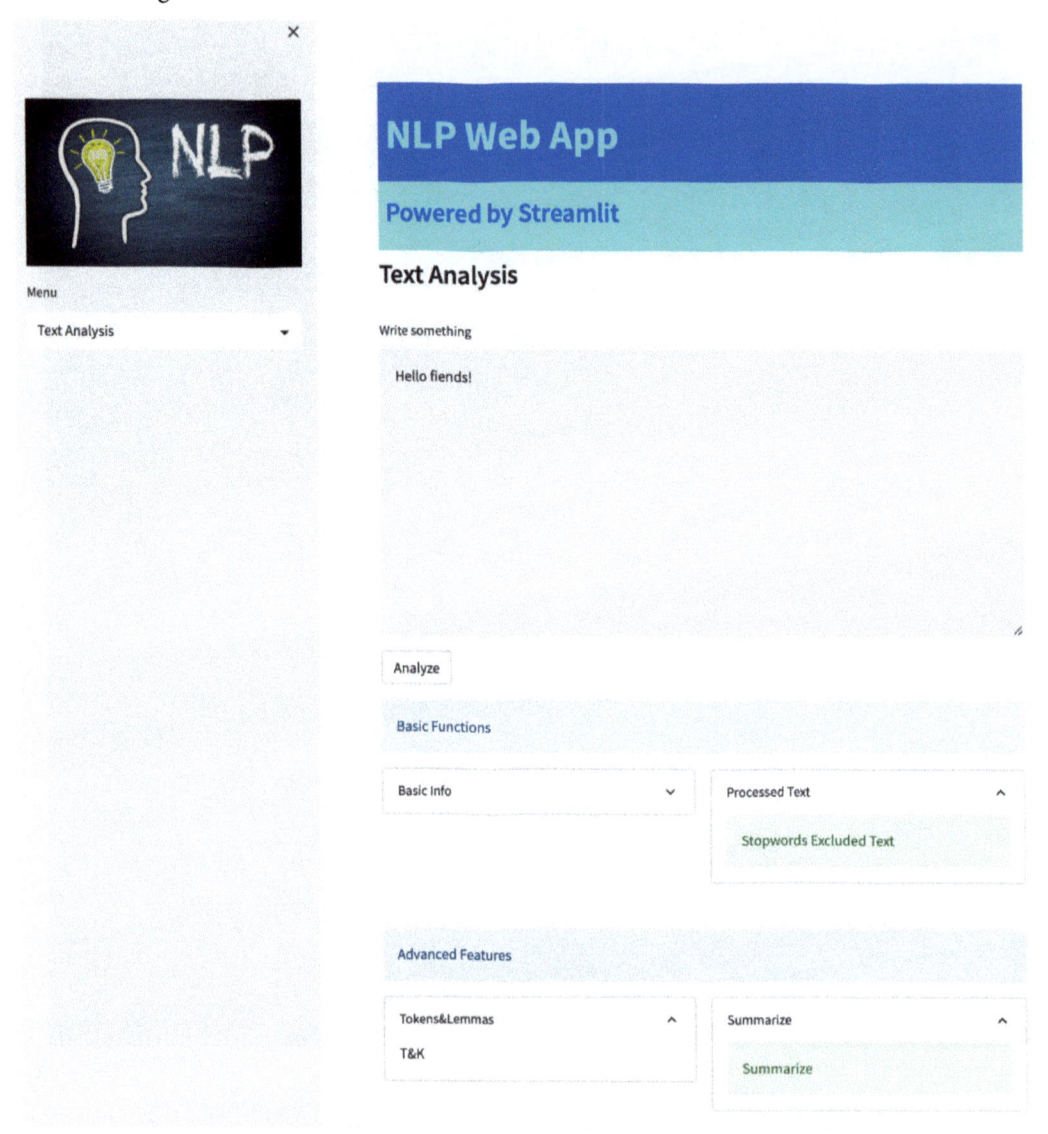

Figure 5.12: Our application layout is going to be completed

To summarize, up to now we have two layers, two expanders, and two columns for every layer; the effect is very clean and well-balanced. Now we can take care of the four functions: two basic and two advanced.

Adding the two basic functions

Let's start with the first basic function: **Basic Info**. Expanding **Basic Info**, we get **Text Stats**. In *Chapter 4*, among others, we imported the `neattext` package, which is very useful for our statistics as it has a function named `word_stats`. If you haven't already imported it, it's time to do so.

`word_stats` returns a dictionary, so a `key:value` data structure; all we need to do is to get the information from it (putting in the `word_desc` variable), then write everything on the screen in the proper column. The following screenshot shows the code that obviously is part of `col1`:

```
54          col1, col2 = st.columns(2)
55
56      with col1:
57          with st.expander("Basic Info"):
58              st.info("Text Stats")
59              word_desc = nt.TextFrame(raw_text).word_stats()
60              result_desc = {"Length of Text":word_desc['Length of Text'],
61                              "Num of Vowels":word_desc['Num of Vowels'],
62                              "Num of Consonants":word_desc['Num of Consonants'],
63                              "Num of Stopwords":word_desc['Num of Stopwords']}
64              st.write(result_desc)
65
66      with col2:
67          with st.expander("Processed Text"):
```

Figure 5.13: Text Stats

We can access the stats using a simple key:value combination. However, the logic of the required code is outside the scope of this book, which focuses on Streamlit. The important thing to understand is that any specific function must be coded in the correct column section. This is what we see in our web application:

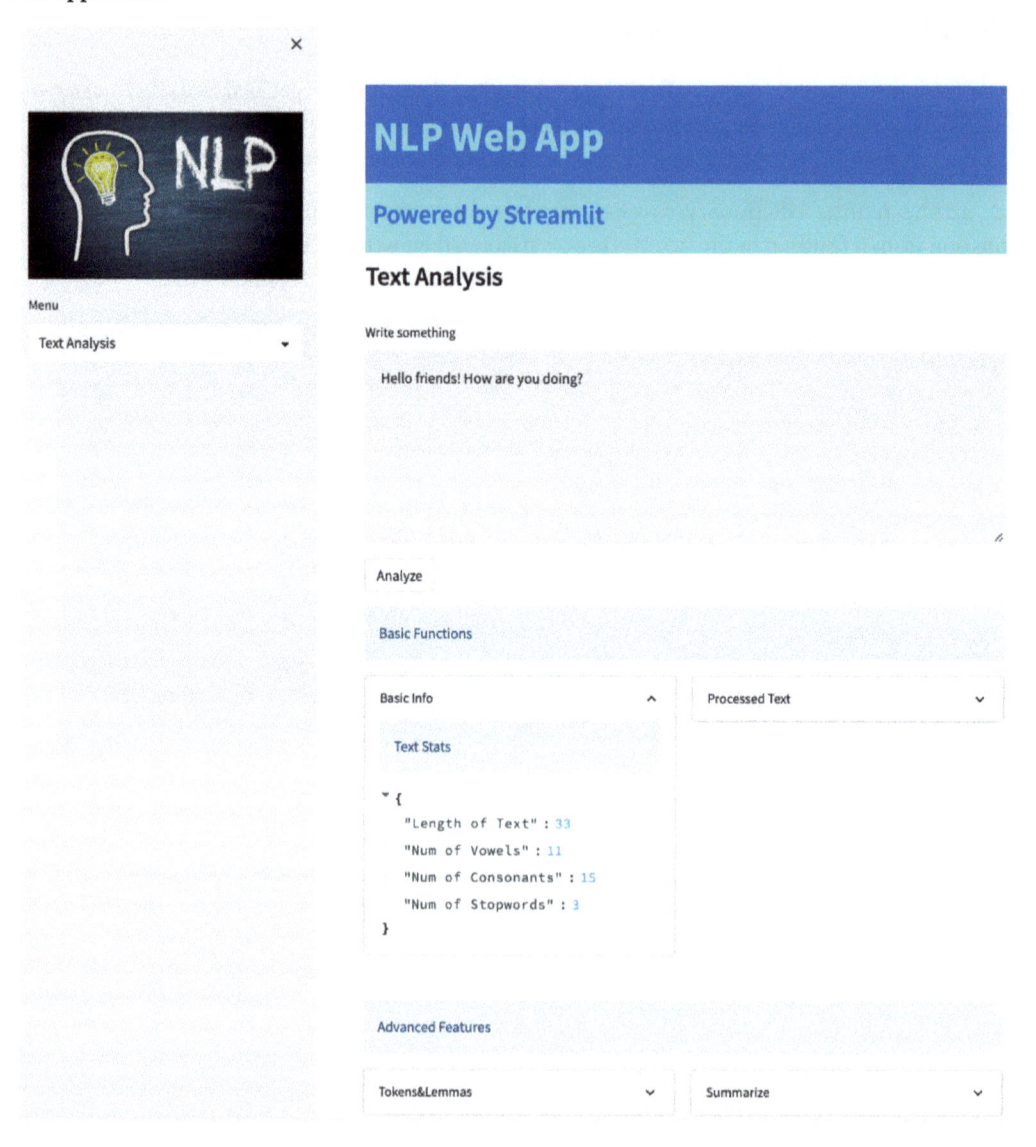

Figure 5.14: Text Stats function effect on the screen

Now, let's add the second basic function: **Processed Text**. The `neattext` library is also very useful for **Processed Text** and this task is quite easy. We can jump to the **Processed Text** part of the code and add a very simple instruction, as illustrated in the following figure:

```
with col1:
  with st.expander("Basic Info"):
    st.info("Text Stats")
    word_desc = nt.TextFrame(raw_text).word_stats()
    result_desc = {"Length of Text":word_desc['Length of Text'],
                   "Num of Vowels":word_desc['Num of Vowels'],
                   "Num of Consonants":word_desc['Num of Consonants'],
                   "Num of Stopwords":word_desc['Num of Stopwords']}
    st.write(result_desc)

with col2:
  with st.expander("Processed Text"):
    st.success("Stopwords Excluded Text")
    processed_text = str(nt.TextFrame(raw_text).remove_stopwords())
    st.write(processed_text)

st.write("")
st.write("")
st.info("Advanced Features")
```

Figure 5.15: The Processed Text expander

We can use `neattext`'s `remove_stopwords()` to get the text we input without the stopwords, then cast it to a string (`str`), and save it in a variable named `processed_text`; finally, we write the processed text on the screen. This is the result:

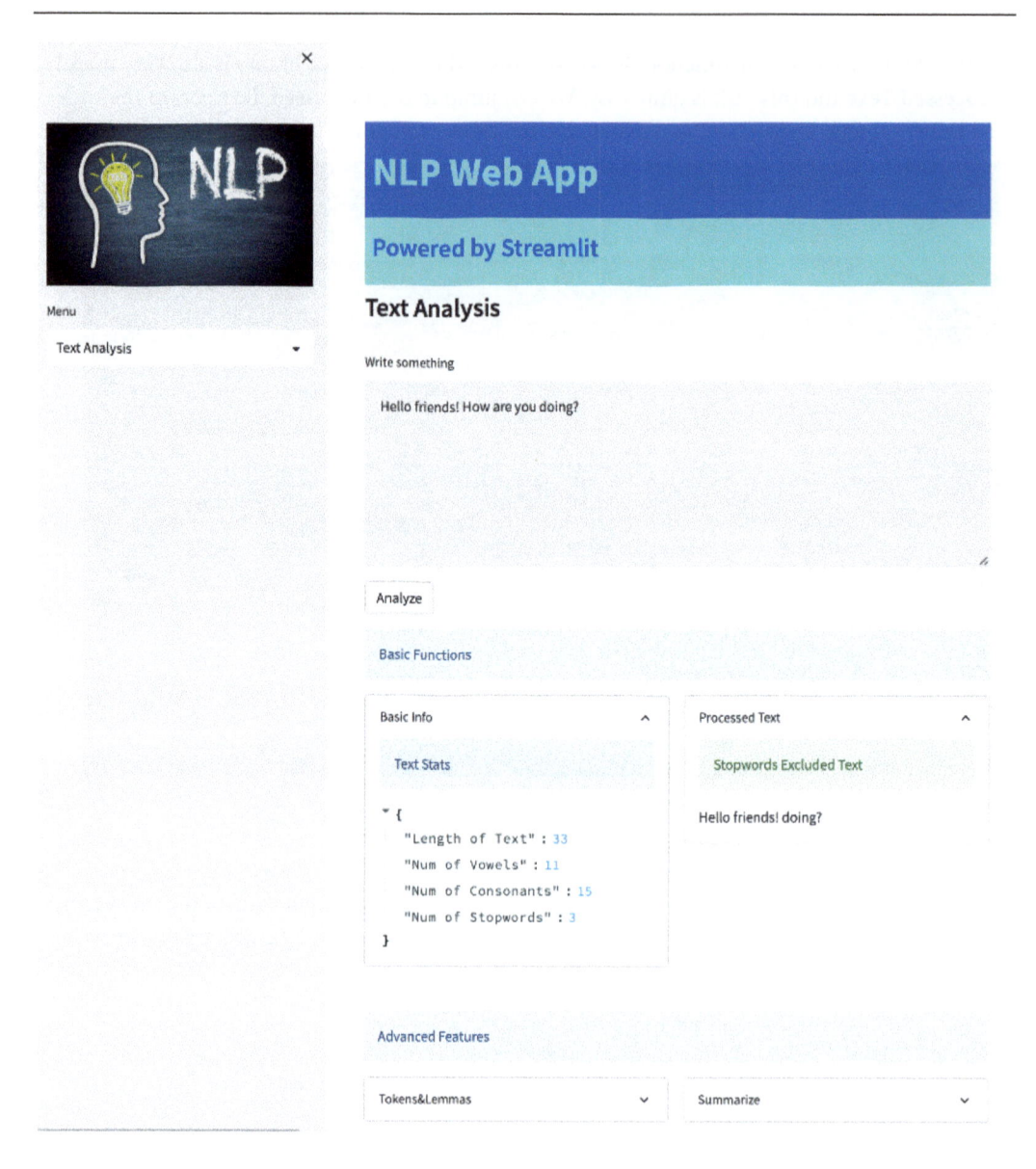

Figure 5.16: The Processed Text function effect on the screen

The result is nice, but we can do even better – for example, writing on the screen the list of the stopwords we removed from the text. Please note that stopwords are, let's say, *common words* that don't add any information to our original text.

We can add this list into the first column, adding to it a second expander exactly below the first one; this is the code:

```
56      with col1:
57          with st.expander("Basic Info"):
58              st.info("Text Stats")
59              word_desc = nt.TextFrame(raw_text).word_stats()
60              result_desc = {"Length of Text":word_desc['Length of Text'],
61                             "Num of Vowels":word_desc['Num of Vowels'],
62                             "Num of Consonants":word_desc['Num of Consonants'],
63                             "Num of Stopwords":word_desc['Num of Stopwords']}
64              st.write(result_desc)
65
66          with st.expander("Stopwords"):
67              st.success("Stop Words List")
68              stop_w = nt.TextExtractor(raw_text).extract_stopwords()
69              st.error(stop_w)
70
71      with col2:
72          with st.expander("Processed Text"):
73              st.success("Stopwords Excluded Text")
```

Figure 5.17: The code to extract the stopwords

So, we add a second expander (`st.expander() "Stopwords"`) and, once again using `neattext`, we extract `stopwords (extract_stopwords)` and put them into a variable (`stop_w`), then print this variable on the screen, this time using `st.error`. Here is the result:

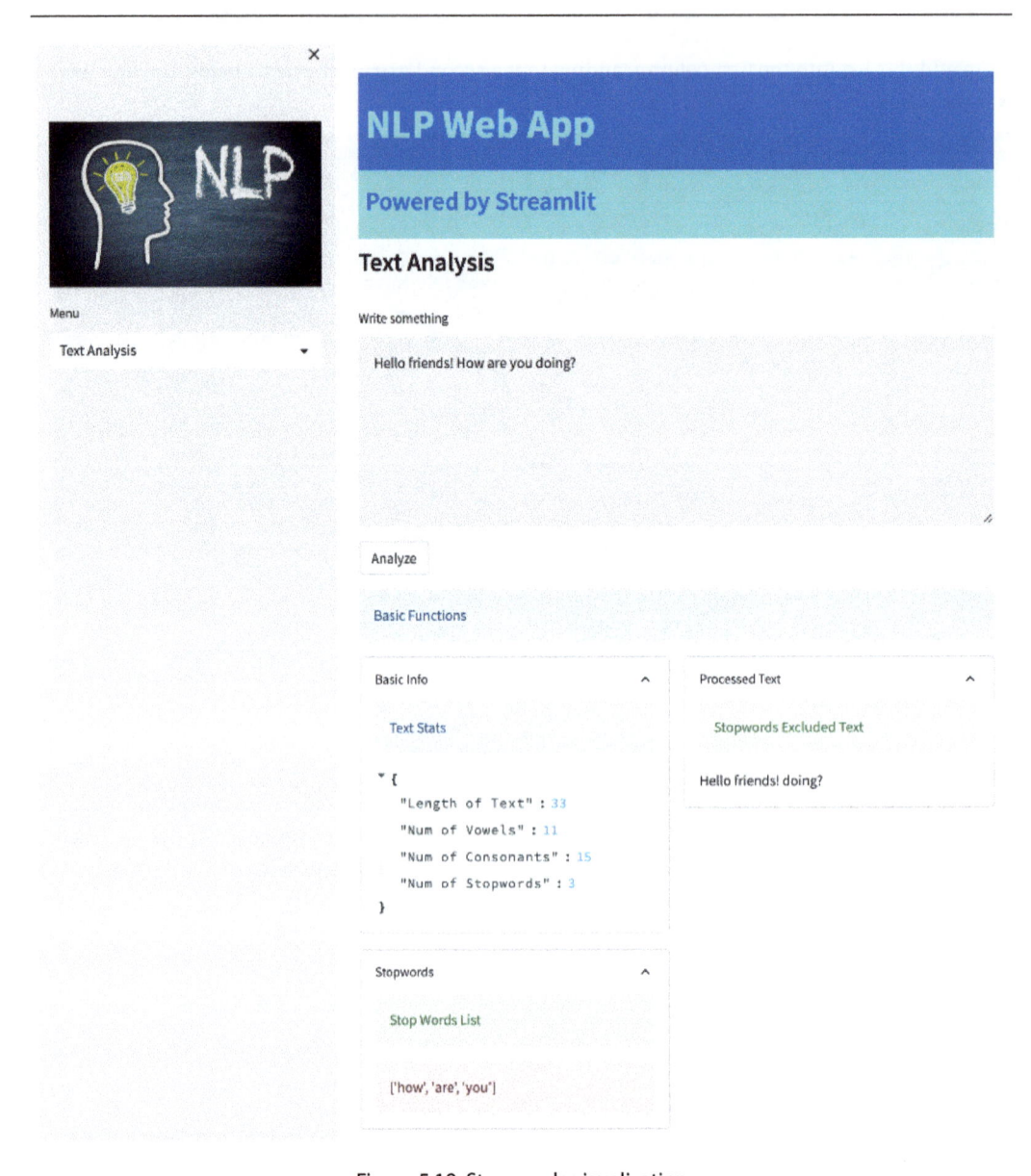

Figure 5.18: Stopwords visualization

Everything is working fine: **Text Stats** tells us how many stopwords we have, **Stop Words List** shows us those stopwords in a list, and **Processed Text** shows the text without these items.

Adding a wordcloud

Since the **Basic Functions** layer is now unbalanced, let's add a beautiful *wordcloud* on the right, just to make everything much more symmetric. Please double-check that you already imported the `Wordcloud` library, as suggested in *Chapter 4*. This time, we can add another expander into the second column and write a few lines of code, as illustrated in the following figure:

```
69              st.error(stop_w)
70
71      with col2:
72          with st.expander("Processed Text"):
73              st.success("Stopwords Excluded Text")
74              processed_text = str(nt.TextFrame(raw_text).remove_stopwords())
75              st.write(processed_text)
76
77          with st.expander("Plot Wordcloud"):
78              st.success("Wordcloud")
79              wordcloud = WordCloud().generate(processed_text)
80              fig = plt.figure(1, figsize=(20,10))
81              plt.imshow(wordcloud, interpolation = 'bilinear')
82              plt.axis('off')
83              st.pyplot(fig)
84
```

Figure 5.19: Wordcloud plotting code

A few lines of code and a wordcloud will appear! So, we add another expander, then create a wordcloud from the original text using the `generate` method, and then define a figure with its size. Finally, use `plt` (we already imported `pyplot`) to plot the wordcloud without `axis`. We used a longer original text for a richer wordcloud. The bigger the words appear, the more often they occur in the text. This is the result:

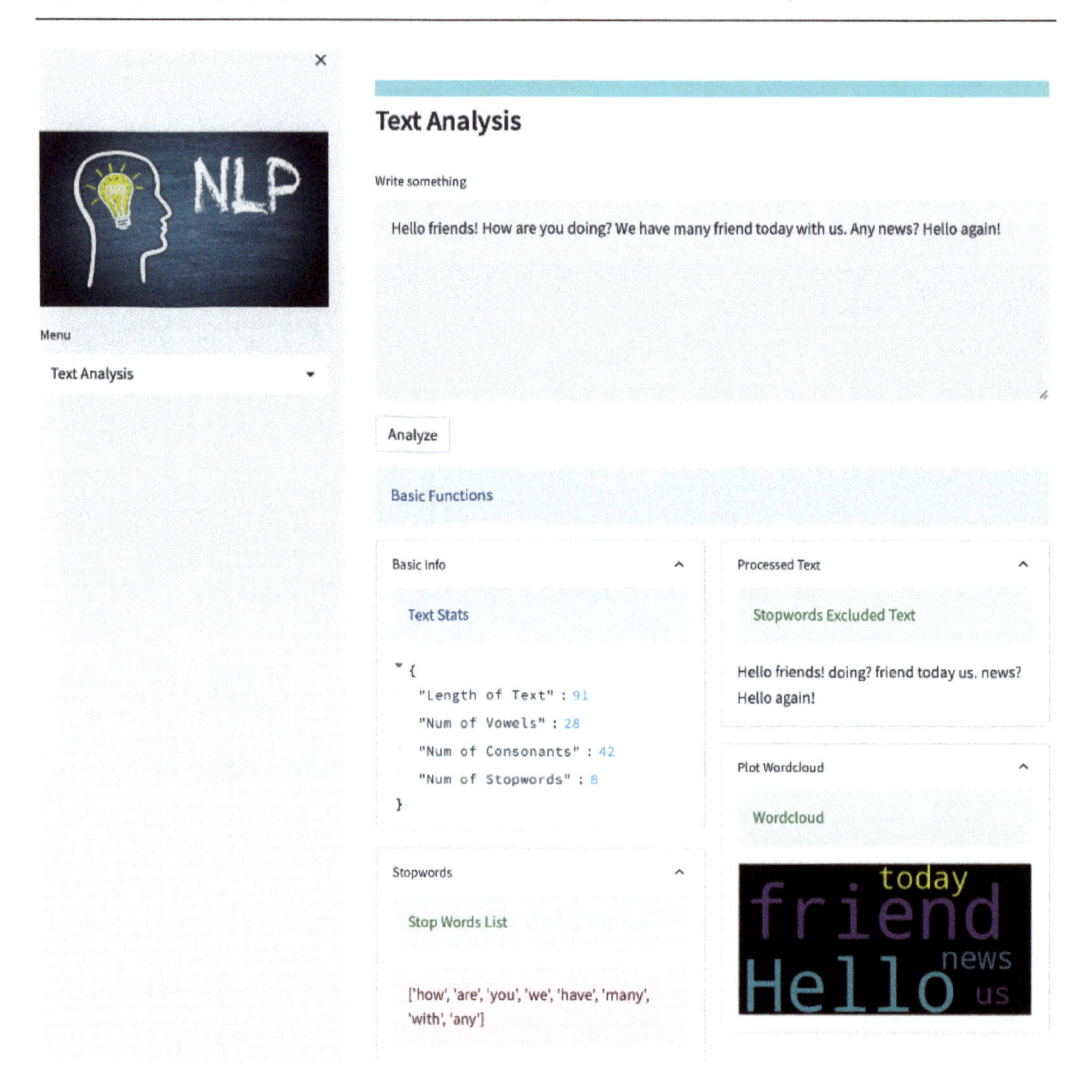

Figure 5.20: Wordcloud on the screen

Now our **Basic Functions** part really is finished. We have a beautiful text that shows the beginning of the section and two columns, and in each of them, two expanders, with everything working well and fluidly. It's time to address the advanced features, such as handling tokens, lemmas, and summarization. We will discuss these in detail further in this chapter.

Introducing NLP concepts – tokens and lemmas

Let's begin exploring **Advanced Features** by creating a simple summarization function in Python and Streamlit. Although many packages and libraries offer powerful summarization capabilities, this book focuses on web application development rather than NLP or summarization.

Adding the summarization function

Though the name is self-explanatory, a `summarization` function is a piece of code that summarizes a sentence or a text, extracting only the most important part of it. This task can be achieved in many ways – some very easy, like the one we are proposing just to show how to develop complex web applications with Streamlit, and some very sophisticated, leveraging artificial intelligence and neural networks. *Figure 5.21* shows the code where we add the `summarize_text` function:

```python
# NLP Pkgs
from textblob import TextBlob
import neattext as nt
#import spacy

from collections import Counter
import re

def summarize_text(text, num_sentences=3):
    # Remove special characters and convert text to lowercase
    clean_text = re.sub('[^a-zA-Z]', ' ', text).lower()

    # Split the text into words
    words = clean_text.split()

    # Calculate the frequency of each word
    word_freq = Counter(words)

    # Sort the words based on their frequency in descending order
    sorted_words = sorted(word_freq, key=word_freq.get, reverse=True)

    # Extract the top `num_sentences` most frequent words
    top_words = sorted_words[:num_sentences]

    # Create the summary by joining the top words
    summary = ' '.join(top_words)

    return summary

def main():
```

Figure 5.21: The summarize_text function

An attention point is that after the NLP packages, we imported two new libraries:

```
from collections import Counter
import re
```

Both of them are Python standard packages; the first one is a set of collections that includes a counter and the second is the regular expressions package.

After this import activity, we defined the `summarize_text` function by writing the following code:

```
def summarize_text(text, num_sentences=3):
```

This function is very simple: it takes text as input, cleans the text by lowercasing it, splits everything into words, calculates the frequency of each word (that's why we need the counter), sorts the words according to their frequency, extracts the most frequent, and then creates a summary just by joining the top words.

This function can be used inside the expander of the summarization as follows:

```
108
109         st.write("")
110         st.write("")
111         st.info("Advanced Features")
112
113         col3, col4 = st.columns(2)
114
115         with col3:
116             with st.expander("Tokens&Lemmas"):
117                 st.write("T&K")
118
119         with col4:
120             with st.expander("Summarize"):
121                 st.success("Summarize")
122                 summary = summarize_text(raw_text)
123                 st.success(summary)
124
```

Figure 5.22: The Summarize expander

Introducing NLP concepts – tokens and lemmas   109

In the expander of `col4`, we are just using the `summarize_text` function with the input text (`raw_text`) and showing the result on the screen, as follows:

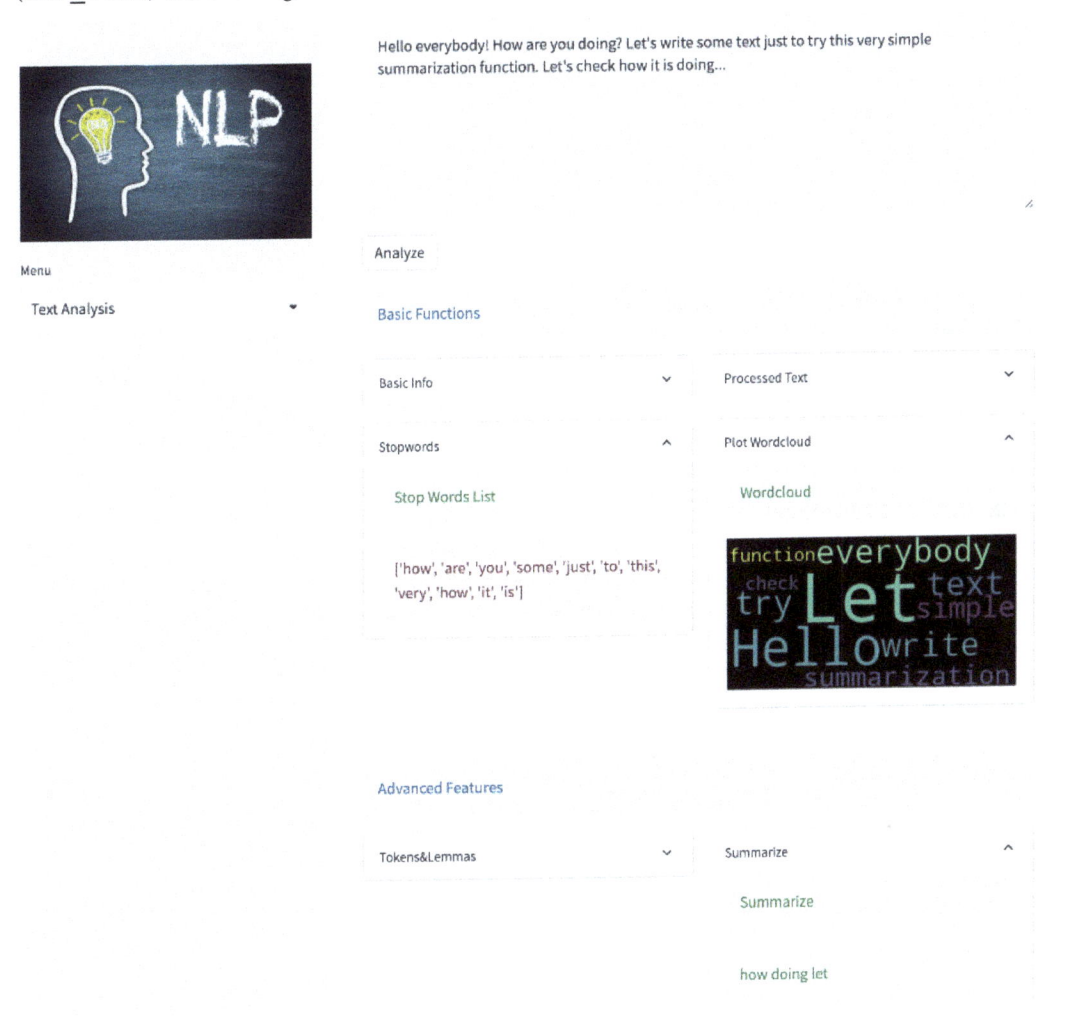

Figure 5.23: Summarize in action

OK, this feature is not the best, but why don't you try to improve it by yourself? For example, you could add some advanced summarization features offered online by many companies via API calls.

Next, let us learn what tokens and lemmas are.

Tokens and lemmas

Tokens and **lemmas** are quite classical concepts of NLP. Tokens are the smallest *units* of a text and are usually identified with words. So, if we say *I write code*, we have three tokens: *I*, *write*, and *code*. Depending on the granularity level, things can get more complex because sometimes tokens can be identified with single letters. We don't consider the letters, just the words. Please note that even with words, tokenization can be challenging; for example, in the sentence *I'm writing code*, we have many tokens – three or four. In the first case, *I'm* is a unique token, while in the second case, we can consider *I'm* as two words, with two different tokens.

There is no right or wrong approach but everything depends on the language and the use case to be considered. Lemmas are made of so-called *plain text*, so if we say *code*, *coding*, or *coder*, we can assume that for all these three words, the lemma is just *code*.

For *Tokens&Lemmas*, we can use `spacy`, a very powerful NLP package we imported in *Chapter 4*. Maybe you remember that, in *Chapter 4*, we also downloaded the English model used by spaCy (`en_core_web_sm`). Now we are using both the library and the model.

As we did for summarization, let's write a function that takes care of tokens and lemmas. We can write, immediately after the summarization function, something like this:

```
39      return summary
40
41  @st.cache_data
42  # Lemma and Tokens Function
43  def text_analyzer(text):
44      # import English library
45      nlp = spacy.load('en_core_web_sm')
46      # create an nlp object
47      doc = nlp(text)
48      #extract tokens and lemmas
49      allData = [('"Token":{},\n"Lemma":{}'.format(token.text, token.lemma_)) for token in doc]
50      return allData
51
```

Figure 5.24: Lemmas and tokens function

First of all, we load in spaCy the English model, then create an `nlp` object (an object specific to the `spacy` library) from a text (`doc=nlp(text)`), and thanks to this object, we can extract tokens and lemmas (`token.text and token.lemma_`), saving them into a dictionary (a key:value data structure) named `allData`. At the very end, we return this `allData` variable.

Please note the strange `@st.cache_data` at the beginning of our function. It's a *decorator* that tells Streamlit to save in a cache the data managed by this function, so unless the function's input doesn't change, any time we select the function, the response will be very fast.

Please check Streamlit's official documentation about caching (`https://docs.streamlit.io/library/advanced-features/caching`) because it's really something that can help a lot with response time:

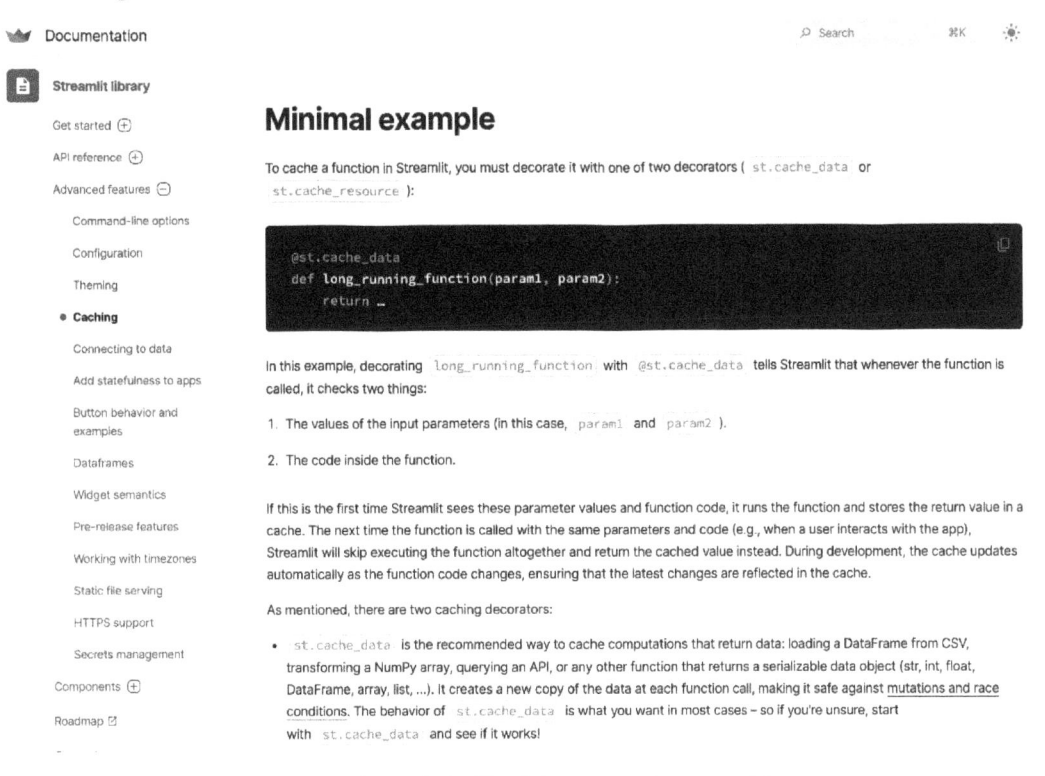

Figure 5.25: Streamlit's official documentation on caching

Our *Tokens&Lemmas* function is ready so we can use it inside our final expander.

Using the text_analysis function

Before using the *Tokens&Lemmas* function, we will clean the text a little bit; let's see how to do it:

```
124
125          col3, col4 = st.columns(2)
126
127          with col3:
128            with st.expander("Tokens&Lemmas"):
129              st.write("T&K")
130              processed_text_mid = str(nt.TextFrame(raw_text).remove_stopwords())
131              processed_text_mid = str(nt.TextFrame(processed_text_mid).remove_puncts())
132              processed_text_fin = str(nt.TextFrame(processed_text_mid).remove_special_characters())
133              tandl = text_analyzer(processed_text_fin)
134              st.json(tandl)
135
136          with col4:
137            with st.expander("Summarize"):
138              st.success("Summarize")
139              summary = summarize_text(raw_text)
140              st.success(summary)
```

Figure 5.26: Tokens&Lemmas expander

Before using the `text_analysis` function we just discussed, we will clean the text with `neattext`. First of all, we will remove stopwords from it, then we will remove the punctuation, and finally, we will remove special characters such as `"@"`, `"#"`, and so on.

We will pass this cleaned text to `text_analyzer` and then print the result on the screen.

Please note that, since the `text_analyzer` function returns a dictionary – or better, a list of dictionaries – we are printing it in the JSON format (`st.json(tandl)`); this is the result:

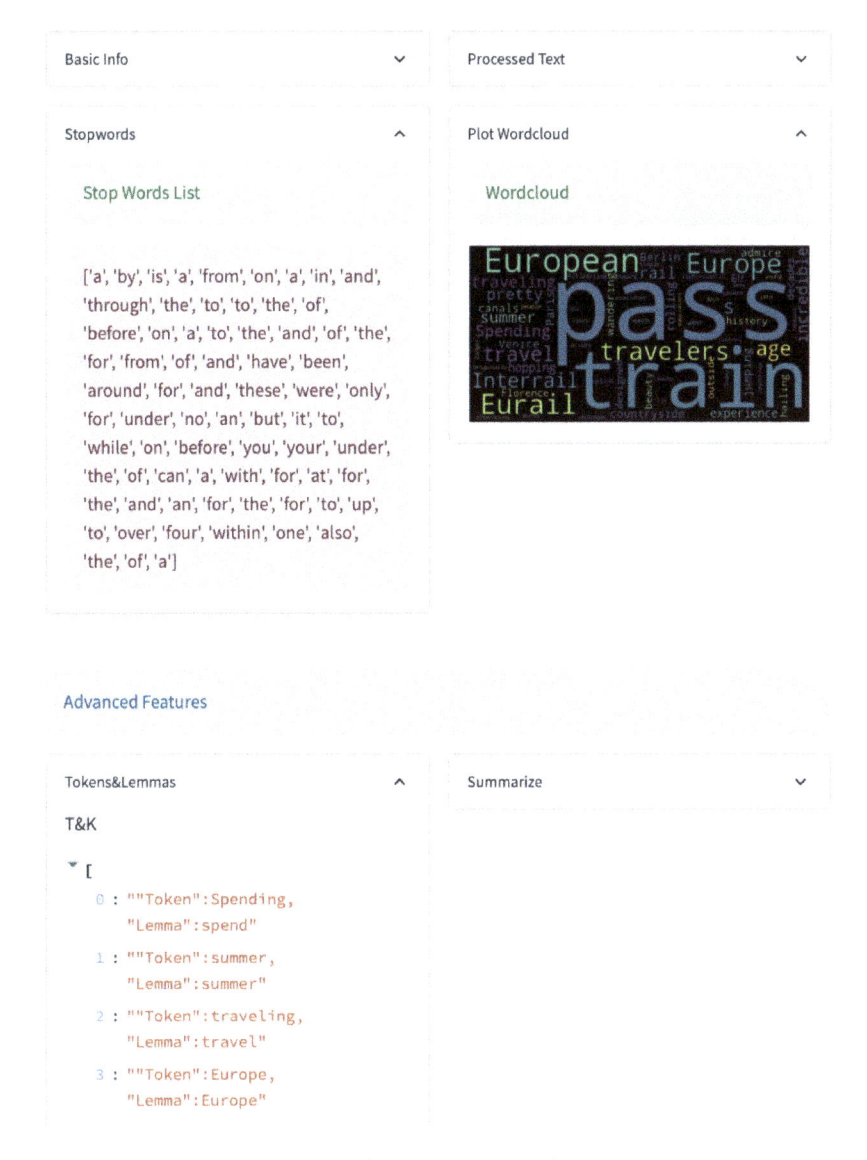

Introducing NLP concepts – tokens and lemmas   113

Figure 5.27: Tokens&Lemmas on the screen

To make it very clear, tokens are the words of our text after we clean it, while lemmas are something called *the normal shape* of the words; for example, we can see that the word *spending* has *spend* as a lemma, the token *traveling* has *travel* as a lemma, and so on.

Finally, to test that everything works properly, we can copy some text from the web – for example, an extract from some article from the CNN website – and put it in our web application. This is the result in the case of an article about traveling and journeys:

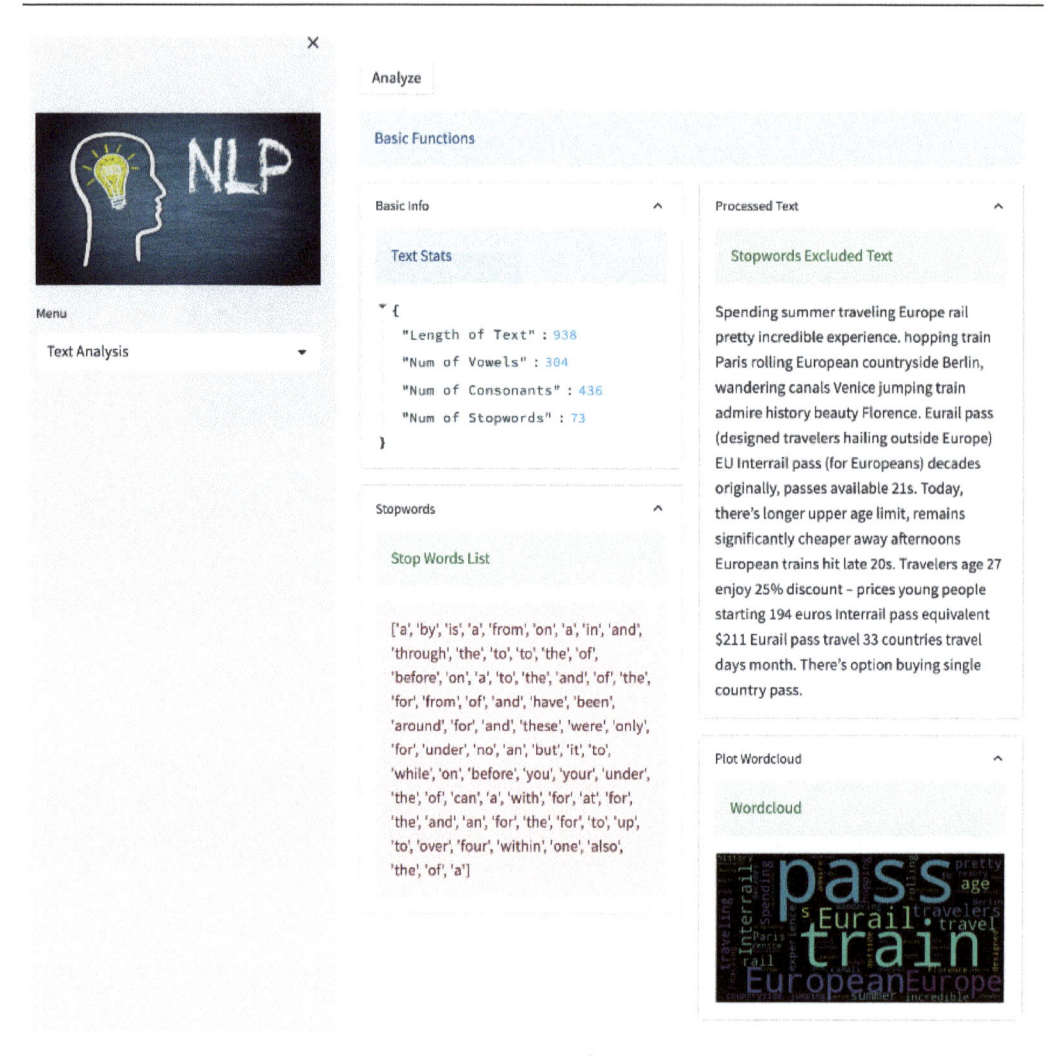

Figure 5.28: Text Analysis test

The result is quite impressive; please consider that by using only Python, Streamlit, and some libraries, we've already got a very good-looking, working web application that can be used directly online. All we need is a browser!

If possible, try to use the application from a device – for example, a tablet or smartphone – that is on the same (Wi-Fi) network as the computer from which you are coding. This is the great point of these web applications: immediately accessible from everywhere! We write code once and can use it from everywhere, with no need to install locally, manage patches, manage new versions, and so on. Everything stays in one place and it's accessed by a web browser. In case of changes or new versions, we only need to update the code *server*-side, meaning no pain for users. Smooth, clean, and easy!

Introducing NLP concepts – tokens and lemmas   115

As usual, here are the screenshots of the code produced up to now:

```python
1   # Core Pkgs
2   import streamlit as st
3   st.set_page_config(page_title="NLP Web App", page_icon="👍", layout="centered", initial_sidebar_state="auto")
4
5   # Viz Pkgs
6   import matplotlib.pyplot as plt
7   import matplotlib
8   matplotlib.use("Agg")
9   from wordcloud import WordCloud
10
11  # NLP Pkgs
12  from textblob import TextBlob
13  import neattext as nt
14  import spacy
15
16  from collections import Counter
17  import re
18
19  # Sumarization Function
20  def summarize_text(text, num_sentences=3):
21      # Remove special characters and convert text to lowercase
22      clean_text = re.sub('[^a-zA-Z]', ' ', text).lower()
23
24      # Split the text into words
25      words = clean_text.split()
26
27      # Calculate the frequency of each word
28      word_freq = Counter(words)
29
30      # Sort the words based on their frequency in descending order
31      sorted_words = sorted(word_freq, key=word_freq.get, reverse=True)
32
33      # Extract the top `num_sentences` most frequent words
34      top_words = sorted_words[:num_sentences]
35
36      # Create the summary by joining the top words
37      summary = ' '.join(top_words)
38
39      return summary
40
41  @st.cache_data
42  # Lemma and Tokens Function
43  def text_analyzer(text):
44      # import English library
45      nlp = spacy.load('en_core_web_sm')
46      # create an nlp object
47      doc = nlp(text)
48      #extract tokens and lemmas
49      allData = [('"Token":{},\n"Lemma":{}'.format(token.text, token.lemma_)) for token in doc]
50      return allData
51
52
53  def main():
54      """NLP web app with Streamlit"""
55
56      title_template = """
57      <div style="background-color:blue; padding:8px;">
58      <h1 style="color:cyan">NLP Web App</h1>
59      </div>
60      """
```

Figure 5.29: Code – part 1

In part 1, we imported the packages, set the page configuration, and defined the `"summarize_text"` and `"text_analyzer"` functions.

```python
62    st.markdown(title_template, unsafe_allow_html=True)
63
64    subheader_template = """
65    <div style="background-color:cyan; padding:8px;">
66    <h3 style="color:blue">Powered by Streamlit</h1>
67    </div>
68    """
69
70    st.markdown(subheader_template, unsafe_allow_html=True)
71
72    st.sidebar.image("nlp.jpg", use_column_width=True)
73
74    activity = ["Text Analysis", "Translation", "Sentiment Analysis", "About"]
75    choice = st.sidebar.selectbox("Menu", activity)
76
77    if choice == "Text Analysis":
78      st.subheader("Text Analysis")
79      st.write("")
80
81      raw_text = st.text_area("Write something", "Enter a text in English...", height=350)
82
83      if st.button("Analyze"):
84        if len(raw_text) == 0:
85          st.warning("Enter a text...")
86        else:
87          #blob = TextBlob(raw_text)
88          st.info("Basic Functions")
89
90          col1, col2 = st.columns(2)
91
92          with col1:
93            with st.expander("Basic Info"):
94              st.info("Text Stats")
95              word_desc = nt.TextFrame(raw_text).word_stats()
96              result_desc = {"Length of Text":word_desc['Length of Text'],
97                             "Num of Vowels":word_desc['Num of Vowels'],
98                             "Num of Consonants":word_desc['Num of Consonants'],
99                             "Num of Stopwords":word_desc['Num of Stopwords']}
100             st.write(result_desc)
101
102           with st.expander("Stopwords"):
103             st.success("Stop Words List")
104             stop_w = nt.TextExtractor(raw_text).extract_stopwords()
105             st.error(stop_w)
106
107         with col2:
108           with st.expander("Processed Text"):
109             st.success("Stopwords Excluded Text")
110             processed_text = str(nt.TextFrame(raw_text).remove_stopwords())
111             st.write(processed_text)
112
113           with st.expander("Plot Wordcloud"):
114             st.success("Wordcloud")
115             wordcloud = WordCloud().generate(processed_text)
116             fig = plt.figure(1, figsize=(20,10))
117             plt.imshow(wordcloud, interpolation = 'bilinear')
118             plt.axis('off')
119             st.pyplot(fig)
120
```

Figure 5.30: Code – part 2

Introducing NLP concepts – tokens and lemmas   117

In part 2, we wrote the `"main"` function that visualizes the main title of the application, the menu in the sidebar that uses an `IF` clause to make the menu's voices selection possible, and used some interesting widgets such as columns and expanders.

```python
        st.write("")
        st.write("")
        st.info("Advanced Features")

        col3, col4 = st.columns(2)

        with col3:
          with st.expander("Tokens&Lemmas"):
            st.write("T&K")
            processed_text_mid = str(nt.TextFrame(raw_text).remove_stopwords())
            processed_text_mid = str(nt.TextFrame(processed_text_mid).remove_puncts())
            processed_text_fin = str(nt.TextFrame(processed_text_mid).remove_special_characters())
            tandl = text_analyzer(processed_text_fin)
            st.json(tandl)

        with col4:
          with st.expander("Summarize"):
            st.success("Summarize")
            summary = summarize_text(raw_text)
            st.success(summary)




  if choice == "Translation":
    st.subheader("Translation")
    st.write("")

  if choice == "Sentiment Analysis":
    st.subheader("Sentiment Analysis")
    st.write("")

  if choice == "About":
    st.subheader("About")
    st.write("")

    st.markdown("""
    ### NLP Web App made with Streamlit

    for info:
    - [streamlit](https://streamlit.io)
    """)



if __name__ == "__main__":
    main()
```

Figure 5.31: Code – part 3

In part 3, we completed the `"main"` function, then created placeholders for the **Translation** and **Sentiment Analysis** features, and finally, created a beautiful **About** section, leveraging simple markdown.

Let's underline once again how powerful Streamlit can be, since with a few lines of code, we are able to create a complete web application made of both back and frontend parts.

Summary

In this chapter, we started completing the decorations by adding a beautiful picture in the sidebar. The application should always work correctly but giving it a quite beautiful *shape* is always a good idea.

After decoration, we focused on the first voice of the menu: **Text Analysis**. **Text Analysis** is a quite complex section and in order to make it clear, good-looking, and well-performing, we decided to arrange our web application into different sections that cover different topics. The best solution to make this possible is to learn how to use columns and expanders. The **Text Analysis** section we created has two layers, one for **Basic Functions** and another for **Advanced Features**, and by using columns and expanders, we can manage both layers in a very effective and elegant way.

Columns allow us to place everything we want into pillars, while expanders allow us to *expand* or *collapse* anything we want to show or hide.

Having good-looking sections and well-arranged topics in our application is very important, but an extremely important point is having very well-performing code.

Code should run in a fast and smooth way, without taking a long time to load and show information on the screen. This is the reason why we also had a first look at caching in Streamlit.

In the next chapter, we are going to complete the two remaining voices of our menu: **Translation** and **Sentiment Analysis**.

6
Implementing NLP Techniques for Text Analysis and Processing in Streamlit

Translation and sentiment analysis are very important techniques used in **natural language processing** (**NLP**) for analyzing and processing text data.

Translation is the process of converting text from one language to another. Sentiment analysis is the process of identifying the emotional tone or sentiment of a piece of text. It is used to analyze customer feedback, social media sentiment, and product reviews.

Both of them are powerful techniques that enable NLP applications to process and analyze text data and extract valuable insights from it. In this chapter, we will continue our exploration of web app creation with Streamlit while learning more about the techniques. In the previous chapter, we completed the **Text Analysis** voice of our web application's menu, and now, finally, we are ready to finish all the parts of this application.

By the end of the chapter, our first web application will be more or less completed, and you will have a good understanding of how to build a Python web application step by step using Streamlit, in a very easy way.

In this chapter, we're going to cover the following main topics:

- Deep-diving into NLP techniques
- Learning more about language translation
- An in-depth look at sentiment analysis
- Recap of our first web application

Technical requirements

- In this chapter, we will use the following libraries, packages, and tools:

    - Sublime Text
    - Python 3
    - `pipenv`
    - Streamlit
    - `spacy`
    - `textblob`
    - `neattext`
    - `deep_translator`

- The code in the chapter can be accessed through the following GitHub link: https://github.com/PacktPublishing/Web-App-Development-Made-Simple-with-Streamlit/tree/c51973f13b69b94065544c4a33057412986e9b99/Chapter06

Deep-diving into NLP techniques

Our web application already has a well-structured skeleton that can be applied to future applications, which is very important. Additionally, our app offers a high level of customization, such as the ability to set a title and icon in the browser. We have also completed the **Text Analysis** and **About** sections of the menu. To see the current status of our developments, please refer to *Figure 6.1*.

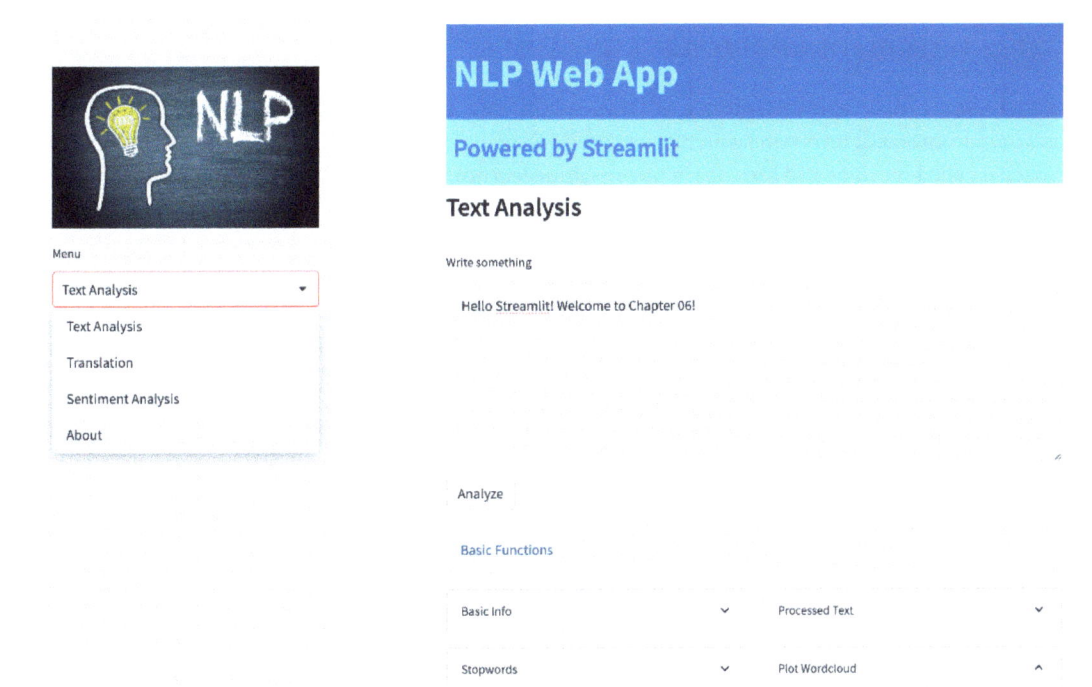

Figure 6.1: Starting point of Chapter 6

When we click on **Translation** or **Sentiment Analysis**, we just get, in the main part of our web app, a subheading reminding us of the section we are in, and nothing else. So, it's now time to code these two functions.

Before delving into the code, let's try to understand exactly what translation and sentiment analysis are.

What is translation?

Translation in NLP is the task of automatically converting text or speech from one language to another. It helps break down language barriers and facilitates global communication. Advances in **machine translation** (**MT**) have revolutionized the field, with **statistical machine translation** (**SMT**) and **neural machine translation** (**NMT**) playing key roles. NMT, powered by deep learning and transformer models, captures context and generates more fluent translations. Challenges include preserving style, handling idioms, and adapting to specific domains. The future holds promise for further advancements in accurate and culturally sensitive translation systems, promoting cross-cultural understanding.

What is sentiment analysis?

Sentiment analysis, or **opinion mining**, is a task in NLP that aims to extract emotions or subjective information from text. It involves classifying text into *positive*, *negative*, or *neutral* sentiments. Traditional approaches relied on rules and lexicons, while machine learning techniques, including deep learning and pre-trained models such as BERT, have revolutionized sentiment analysis. Challenges include fine-grained analysis and aspect-based sentiment. The future holds advancements in accuracy, language coverage, and ethical considerations. Sentiment analysis provides valuable insights for decision-making in various applications.

Sentiment analysis provides insights into opinions and emotions expressed in text. It helps businesses understand customer feedback, market trends, and public sentiment. By analyzing sentiment, companies can improve products, tailor marketing strategies, and make data-driven decisions. Sentiment analysis also finds applications in social media monitoring, reputation management, and public opinion analysis.

Together, translation and sentiment analysis offer enhanced customer understanding. Businesses can analyze sentiment across languages, gaining insights from multilingual sources. This integration enables comprehensive views of customer sentiment across markets, aiding in identifying patterns, areas for improvement, and cultural context adaptation.

These tools also contribute to social and political analysis. By analyzing sentiment across languages, researchers and policymakers gain a broader understanding of public sentiment on various topics, policies, and social movements. This facilitates effective communication and informed decision-making.

Let's begin by checking out the **Translation** option on our menu.

Deep-diving into language translation

Translation breaks language barriers, facilitating global communication and cross-cultural understanding. It enables businesses to expand internationally, connect with diverse audiences, and foster cultural exchange. MT advancements make accurate and accessible translation services widely available, transforming the way we communicate in our interconnected world.

To add the translation function to our web app, we must add some lines of code in a very precise sequence.

Adding a text area

As you can imagine, the first thing to do to perform translation is to introduce a text area where we can write the text that needs to be translated. As we know very well, this operation is extremely easy since it needs just a line of code. So, the first step is to place our code in the appropriate section of the menu, as shown in *Figure 6.2*:

Deep-diving into language translation   123

```
140            st.success(summary)
141
142
143
144 v  if choice == "Translation":
145        st.subheader("Translation")
146        st.write("")
147
148
149
```

Figure 6.2: Translation section

Then, add `text_area`, as shown in *Figure 6.3*:

```
143
144 v  if choice == "Translation":
145        st.subheader("Translation")
146        st.write("")
147        st.write("")
148        raw_text = st.text_area("Original Text", "Write something to be translated...", height=200)
149
150
151
```

Figure 6.3: A new text area

Now, by rerunning our web application in the browser, the new text area will be displayed. The text we put in this new `text_area` is stored in a variable named `raw_text`. When dealing with text, it's always a good idea to check whether we really have some text to process or whether our content is empty, so let's add a simple `if` clause to our code, as follows:

```
144 v  if choice == "Translation":
145        st.subheader("Translation")
146        st.write("")
147        st.write("")
148        raw_text = st.text_area("Original Text", "Write something to be translated...", height=200)
149 v      if len(raw_text) < 3:
150            st.warning("Please provide a text with at least 3 characters...")
151
```

Figure 6.4: Text length check

Now, we would want to print a warning message if the text length is shorter than three characters. This is because many translation libraries need a minimum number of characters in order to process the text. So, if we write, for example, `hi`, we get the following result:

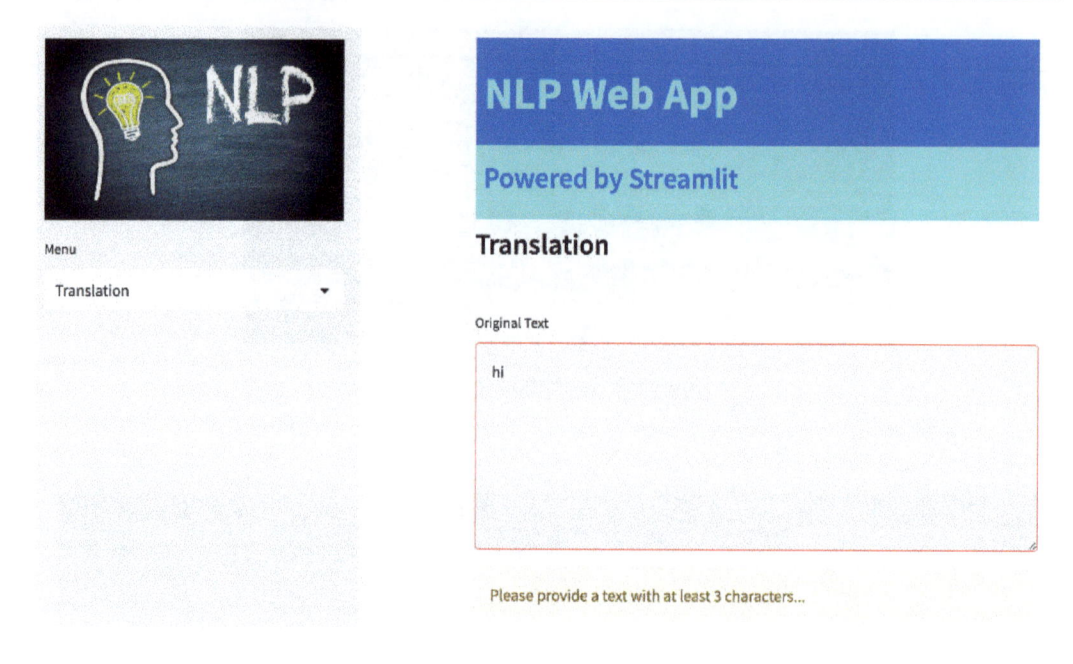

Figure 6.5: Text length check on the browser side

Now that the text to be translated is ready, we need to deal with the translation itself.

Performing the translation task

To perform the translation task, we will use a new library named `deep_translator`. So, first of all, let's install it by simply typing the following command:

```
pipenv install deep_translator
```

After that, let's import this library by typing the following:

```
from deep_translator import GoogleTranslator
```

As you can see, we are leveraging `GoogleTranslator` services.

If you want to get more information about `deep_translator`, please check its dedicated space on PyPI (https://pypi.org/project/deep-translator/). You really will find out about a lot of extremely valuable features to explore.

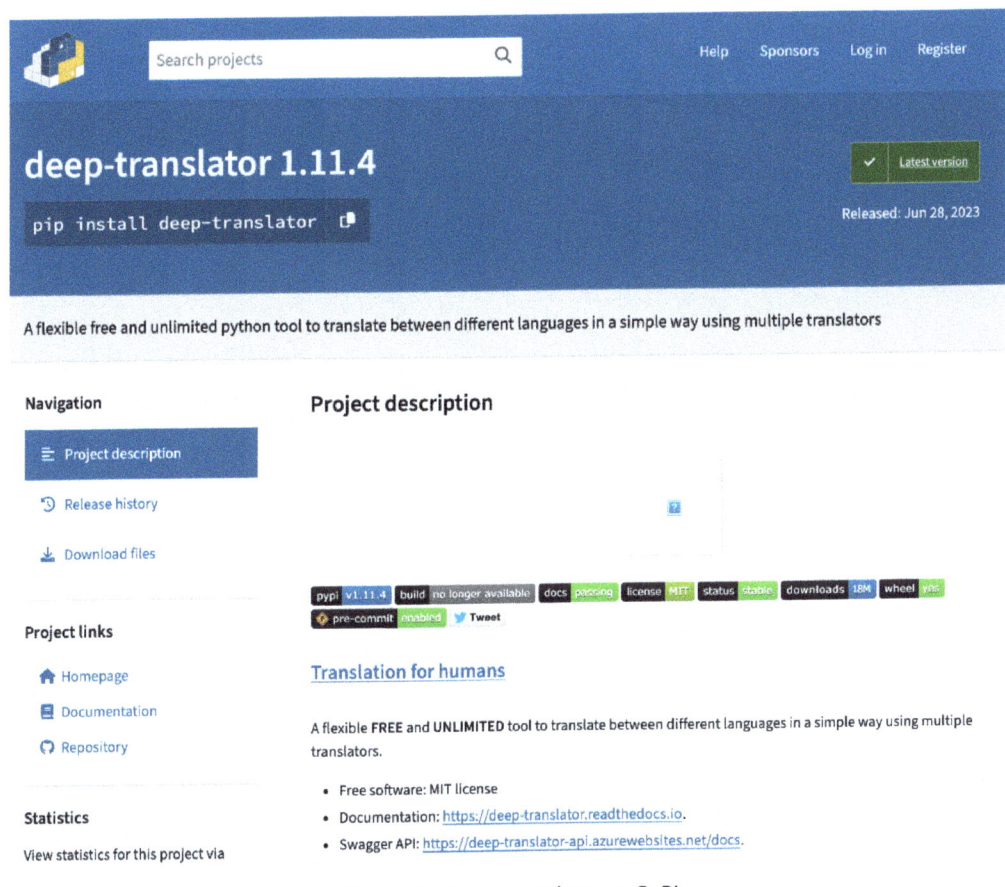

Figure 6.6: Deep-translator on PyPI

It is very important to define the language of the translation. So, let's create a `select_box` that will enable users to choose a specific language:

```
145
146   if choice == "Translation":
147       st.subheader("Translation")
148       st.write("")
149       st.write("")
150       raw_text = st.text_area("Original Text", "Write something to be translated...", height=200)
151       if len(raw_text) < 3:
152           st.warning("Please provide a text with at least 3 characters...")
153       else:
154           target_lang = st.selectbox("Target Language", ["German", "Spanish", "French", "Italian"])
155           if target_lang == "German":
156               target_lang = "de"
157           elif target_lang == "Spanish":
158               target_lang = "es"
159           elif target_lang == "French":
160               target_lang = "fr"
161           else:
162               target_lang = "it"
```

Figure 6.7: Text language selection

This code is very simple: we are just selecting a language from among a little subset (actually, a list) and assigning the proper code to it (`de` for German, `es` for Spanish, etc.).

Finally, now that we have the target language, we just need to execute the translation and we can perform it, for example, by clicking on the **Translate** button; this is the complete code:

```
146   if choice == "Translation":
147       st.subheader("Translation")
148       st.write("")
149       st.write("")
150       raw_text = st.text_area("Original Text", "Write something to be translated...", height=200)
151       if len(raw_text) < 3:
152           st.warning("Please provide a text with at least 3 characters...")
153       else:
154           target_lang = st.selectbox("Target Language", ["German", "Spanish", "French", "Italian"])
155           if target_lang == "German":
156               target_lang = "de"
157           elif target_lang == "Spanish":
158               target_lang = "es"
159           elif target_lang == "French":
160               target_lang = "fr"
161           else:
162               target_lang = "it"
163
164           if st.button("Translate"):
165               translator = GoogleTranslator(source='auto', target=target_lang)  # set source and target languages
166               translated_text = translator.translate(raw_text)
167               st.write(translated_text)
168
```

Figure 6.8: The Translation function code

So, when the **Translate** button is pressed, we call the `GoogleTranslator` function of the `deep_translator` package (already imported previously), put the result into a `translated_text` variable, and then write it on the screen.

This is the result on the browser side:

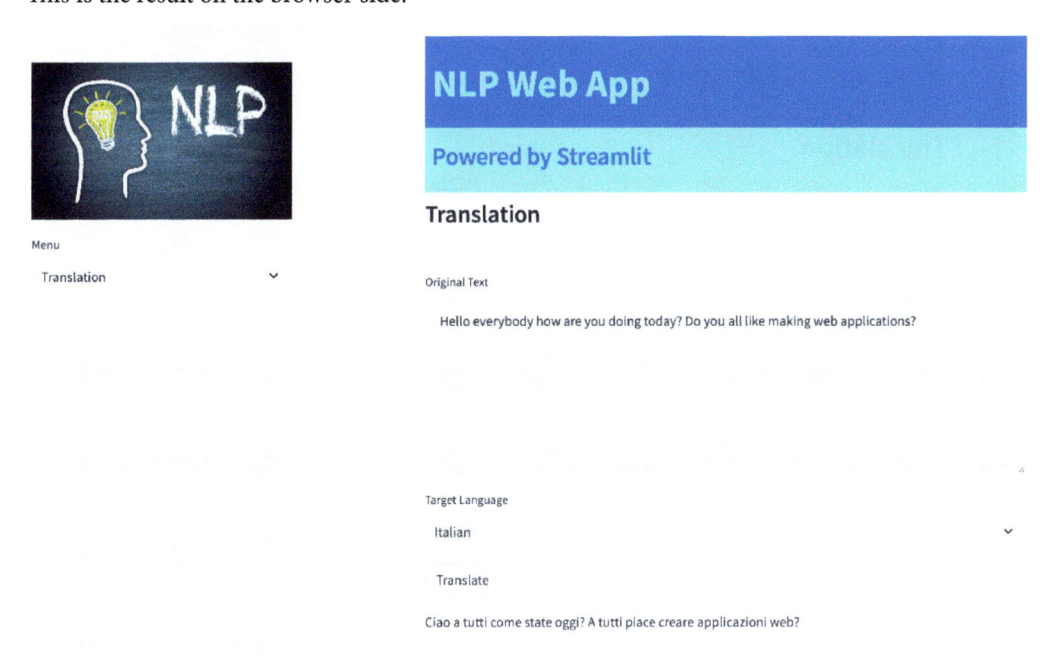

Figure 6.9: The Translation function in action

Everything is very neat and clean and works perfectly! Of course, you can personalize this feature as you like, for example, by adding more target languages or performing different kinds of checks on the input text.

Figure 6.10 shows the **Target Language** selection in action:

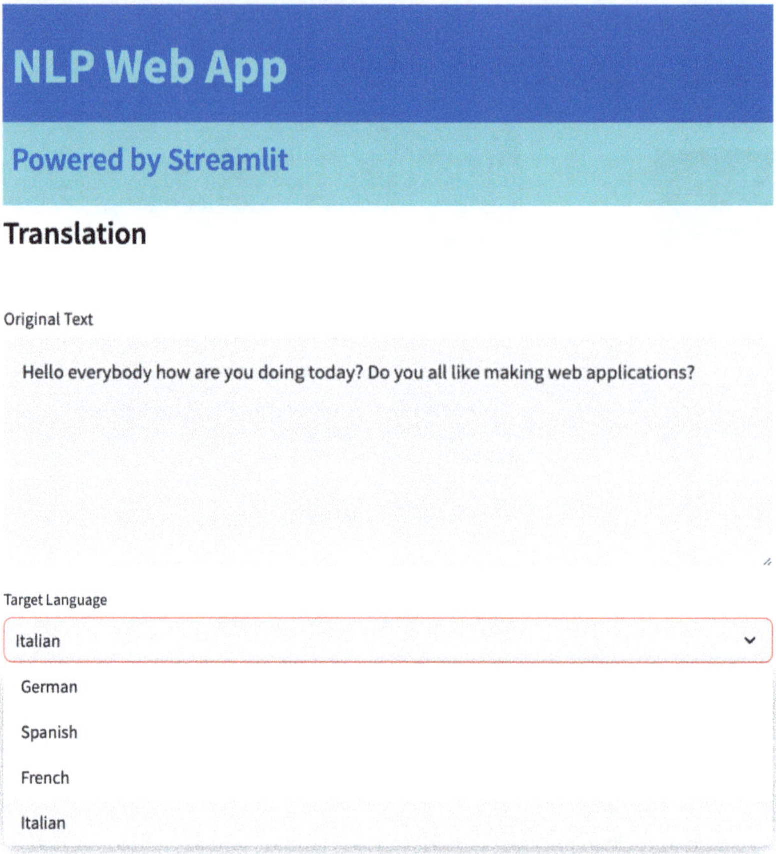

Figure 6.10: Target Language selection

Up to now, we have written less than 200 lines of code and our web application is working very well. With just a small amount of code, we were able to put together a backend and frontend, business logic running on a server, and a presentation layer living on a browser. Everything is in Python and is quite simple. This is the power of Streamlit.

Let's move on to our last NLP task: sentiment analysis. As we discovered in the introduction, it is a fascinating topic.

Diving deep into sentiment analysis

The sentiment analysis task is quite easy because we can leverage `TextBlob`, which has already been imported. So, let's start with the very poor code we have, which, at the moment, just prints a subheading on the screen:

```
168
169    if choice == "Sentiment Analysis":
170        st.subheader("Sentiment Analysis")
171        st.write("")
172
173
174
```

Figure 6.11: Sentiment Analysis section

Currently, when we select **Sentiment Analysis** from our web application menu, we just get a subheading and some white space below it.

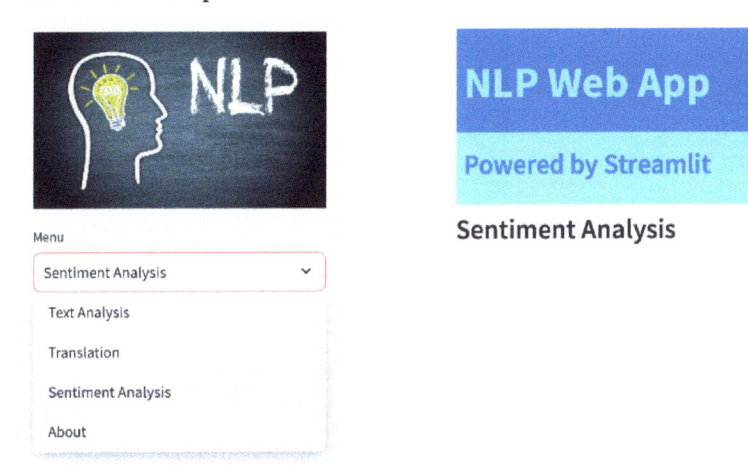

Figure 6.12: Sentiment Analysis starting point

Let us start by creating a text area, since we need somewhere to add the text we want to analyze in order to extract its sentiment. Adding a `text_area` now is really quite simple for us:

```
170    if choice == "Sentiment Analysis":
171        st.subheader("Sentiment Analysis")
172        st.write("")
173        st.write("")
174        raw_text = st.text_area("Text to analyse", "Enter a text here....", height=200)
175
```

Figure 6.13: A text_area for Sentiment Analysis

This is the result of the preceding change on the browser side:

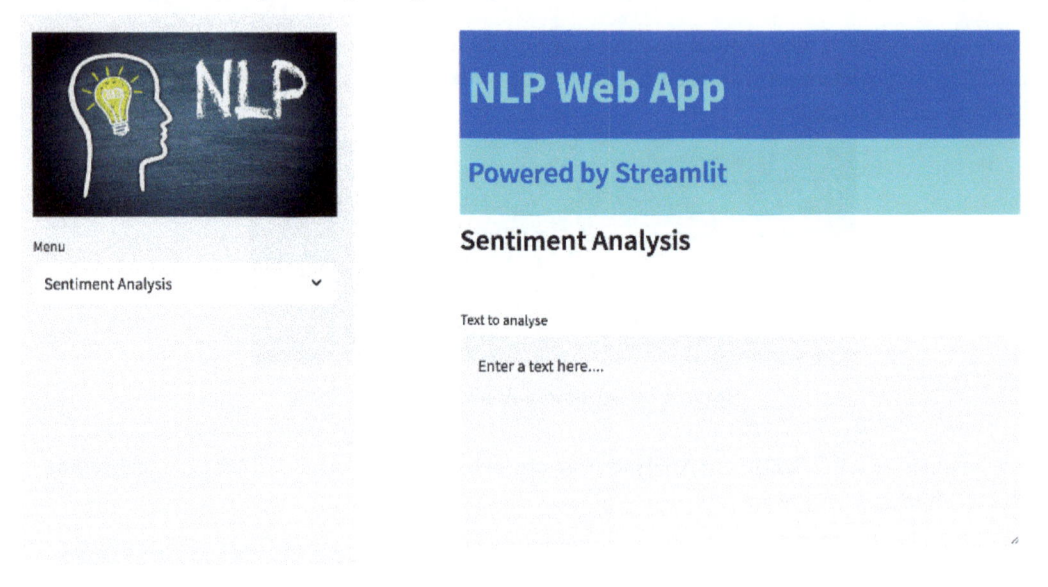

Figure 6.14: The text area in the browser

Now, we can type something in the text area and store it in a variable named, once again, `raw_data`.

As usual, a great option we have is to add a button – we can call it, for example, **Evaluate** – in order to perform our analysis. Since the text area could be empty, we also have to add a check on the `raw_text` length, and in case of missing text, we can print a warning message.

This is a simple example of the code that we can use:

```python
if choice == "Sentiment Analysis":
    st.subheader("Sentiment Analysis")
    st.write("")
    st.write("")
    raw_text = st.text_area("Text to analyse", "Enter a text here....", height=200)
    if st.button("Evaluate"):
        if len(raw_text) == 0:
            st.warning("Enter a text...")
```

Figure 6.15: Evaluate button and check of raw_text length

If `raw_text` is not empty, we can use `TextBlob` to create a `blob` object. After that, we can use the blob's `sentiment` method to get the sentiment of the text we just wrote, and at the end, we can write it on the screen. Here is the code:

```
170    if choice == "Sentiment Analysis":
171        st.subheader("Sentiment Analysis")
172        st.write("")
173        st.write("")
174        raw_text = st.text_area("Text to analyse", "Enter a text here....", height=200)
175        if st.button("Evaluate"):
176            if len(raw_text) == 0:
177                st.warning("Enter a text...")
178            else:
179                blob = TextBlob(raw_text)
180                st.info("Sentiment Analysis")
181                st.write(blob.sentiment)
182                st.write("")
```

Figure 6.16: The sentiment method provided by TextBlob

Figures 6.17 and *6.18* show the result of the latest code modification in the browser.

The first case is positive sentiment, since the polarity is very high.

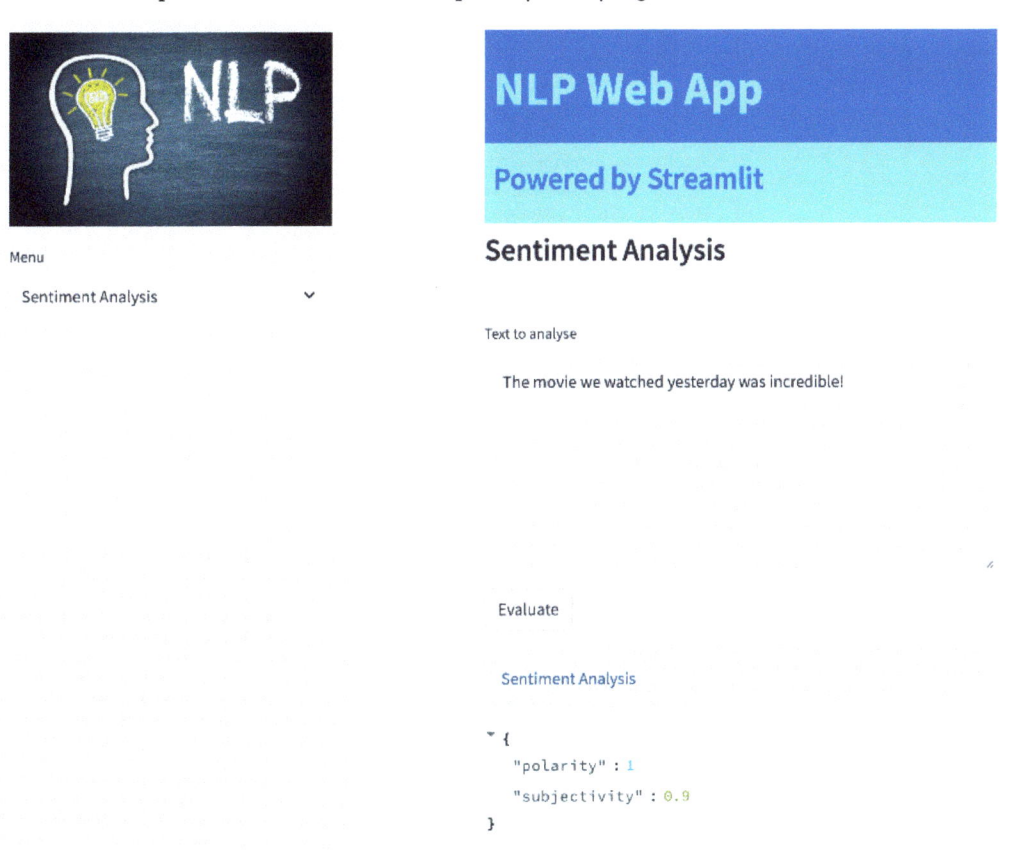

Figure 6.17: An example of positive sentiment

The second case is negative sentiment, based on the rather low polarity.

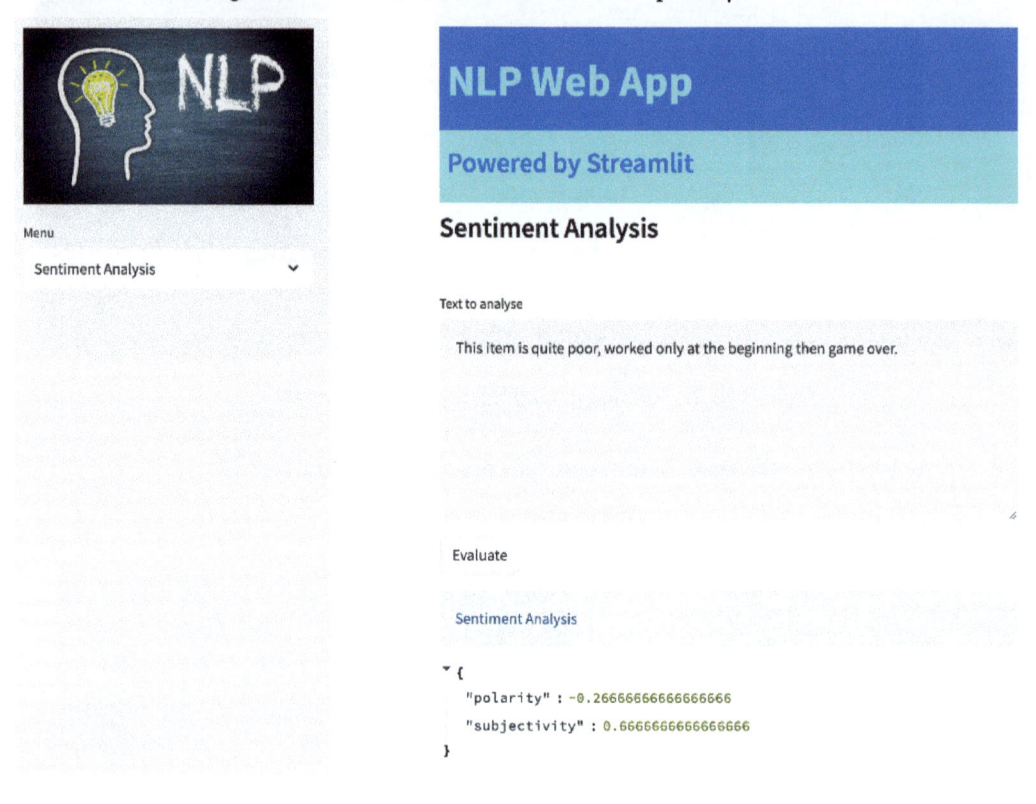

Figure 6.18: An example of negative sentiment

In *Figure 6.19*, we can see the warning that appears when the **Evaluate** button is clicked, but there is no text to be considered.

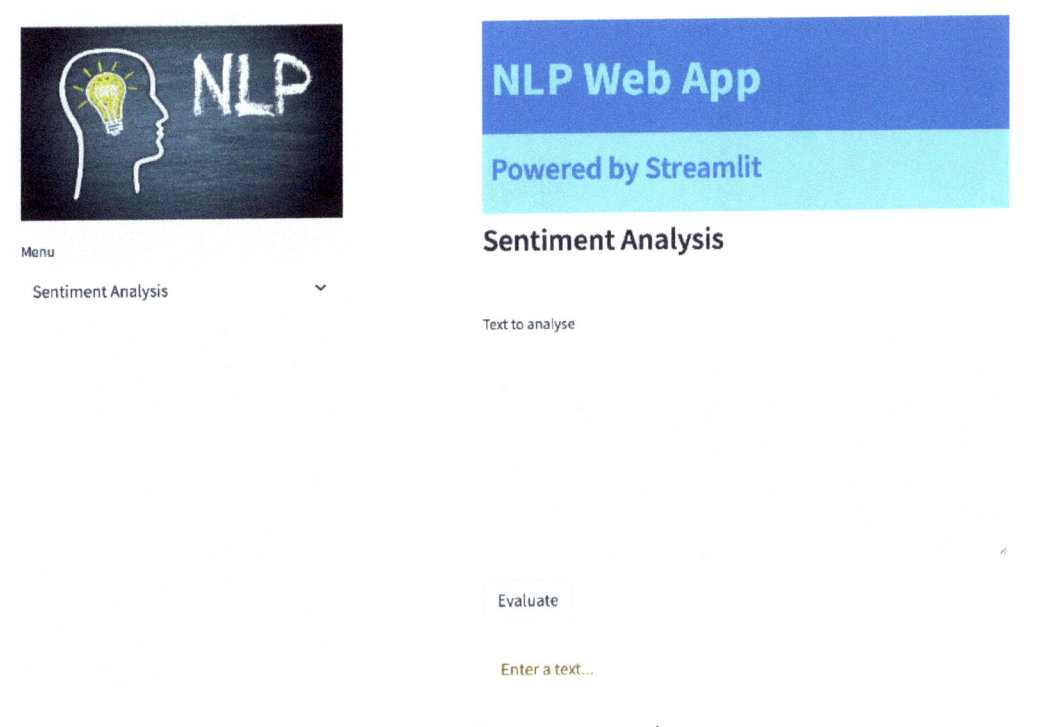

Figure 6.19: Enter a text... warning

As we can see, the TextBlob's sentiment analysis returns two values: `polarity` and `subjectivity`. Let's look in a little bit more detail at the meaning of these terms:

- **Polarity** is the real sentiment, with a value that goes from -1 up to +1. Specifically, -1 indicates very negative sentiment, +1 indicates very positive sentiment, and all values around 0 are generally considered neutral outcomes.
- **Subjectivity** can have values from 0 up to 1. Values around 0 are very objective results, while values around 1 are very subjective ones.

So, for a sentence such as *I loved that movie, it's really great!*, we get a result like the following:

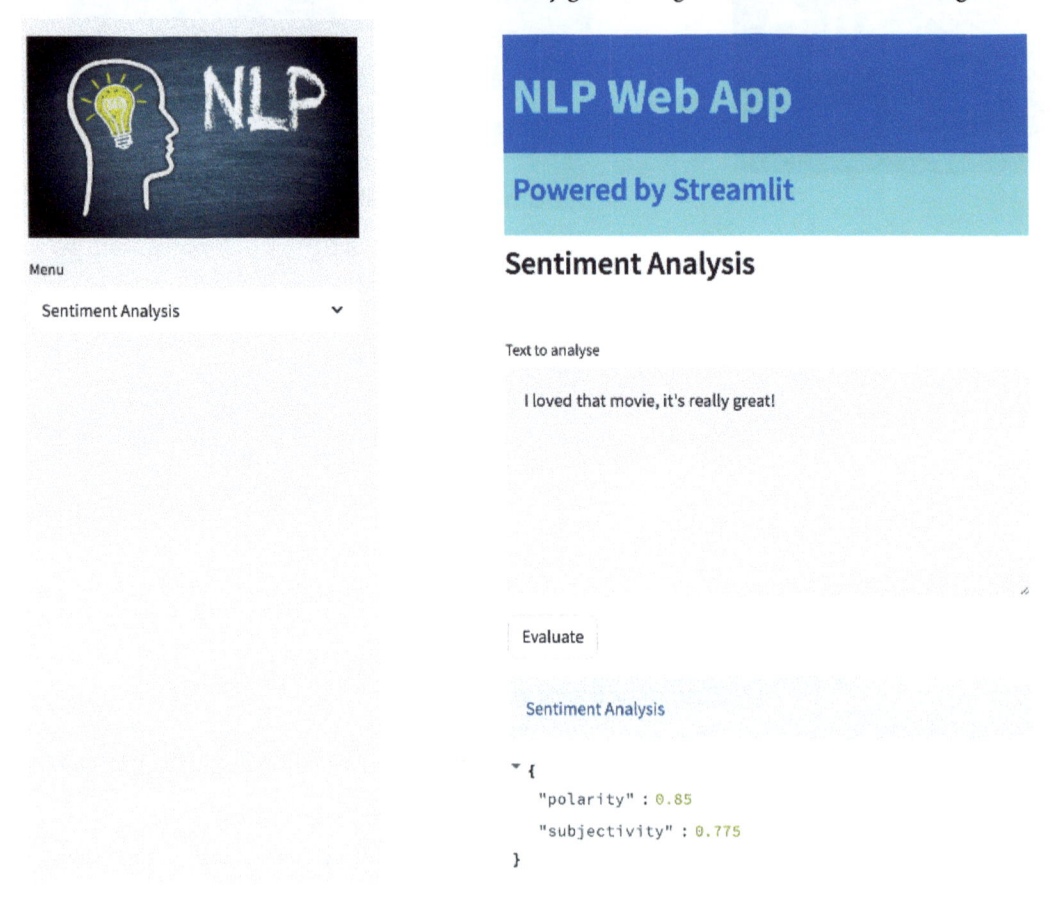

Figure 6.20: High polarity and high subjectivity

The movie received a high polarity score of 0.85 and a high subjectivity score due to the use of the first-person pronoun in *I loved*. This indicates a highly subjective opinion. Let's write something different, such as the following:

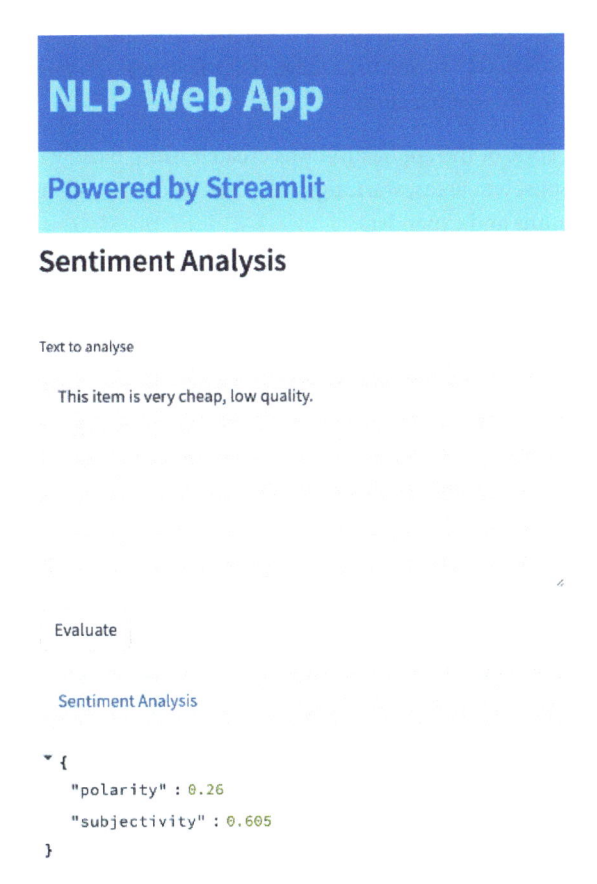

Figure 6.21: Neutral sentiment

The polarity of our statement is 0.26, indicating neutrality since we presented a factual statement. The subjectivity is almost balanced since facts hold personal and universal perspectives.

And that's all! Our first web application is really finished! We implemented all the tasks we defined at the beginning using just Python, pure Python, and some free libraries!

Let's take some time to recap what we have done so far.

Recap of our first web application

It's incredible, but we really did it! Starting from scratch, from an empty file, we created a well-working web application that performs a lot of tasks and provides us with very nice outputs.

First of all, we created a Python environment, and then we installed all the required libraries in it. After that, we started building the skeleton of our application. This point is very important because this skeleton, consisting of a menu that contains all the main features of our web application and various parts of code to manage these features, is something that we can reuse any time we want to create a new application.

The code of the application was created using basic widgets in Streamlit, that is, titles, subheaders, buttons, text areas, warnings, info, and so on, as well as some very interesting components, such as columns and expanders.

We also learned how to add some basic HTML in our web applications, as well as some basic Markdown. We used these techniques to add some beautiful customizations on the titles. We then continued by talking about customizations. We also saw a way to associate a beautiful icon and a meaningful title or name to our application's web browser window.

We delved into some fundamental concepts around NLP: tokens, lemmas, stopwords, word clouds, summarization, sentiment analysis, polarity, and objectivity. Our web app now also contains a very useful **About** section with information and working hyperlinks, which can be customized as you prefer.

Here are some screenshots of the final version of our application:

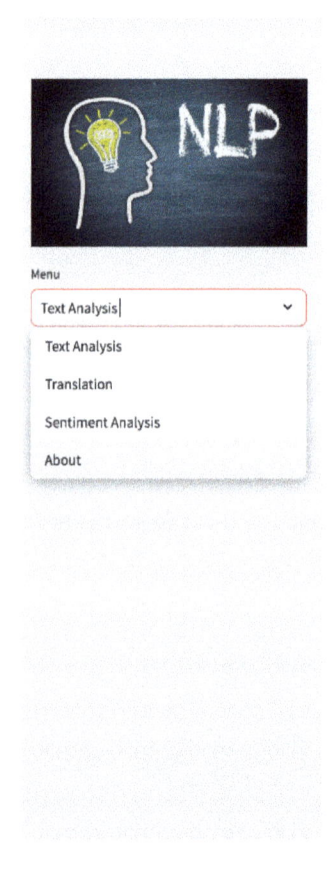

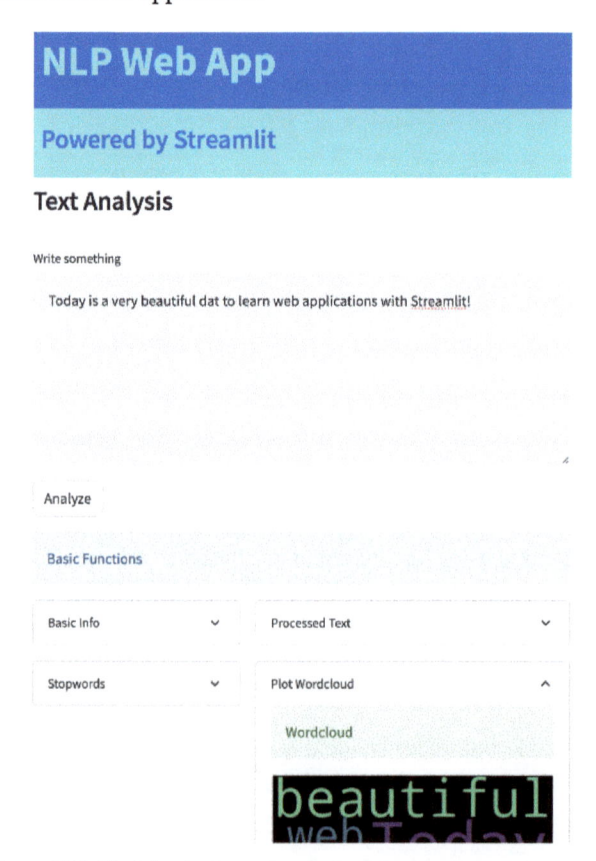

Figure 6.22: Text Analysis

In *Figure 6.22*, we can see the complete menu on the left side of the screen and the result of the **Text Analysis** function applied to the short sentence in the text area in the main part of the web app.

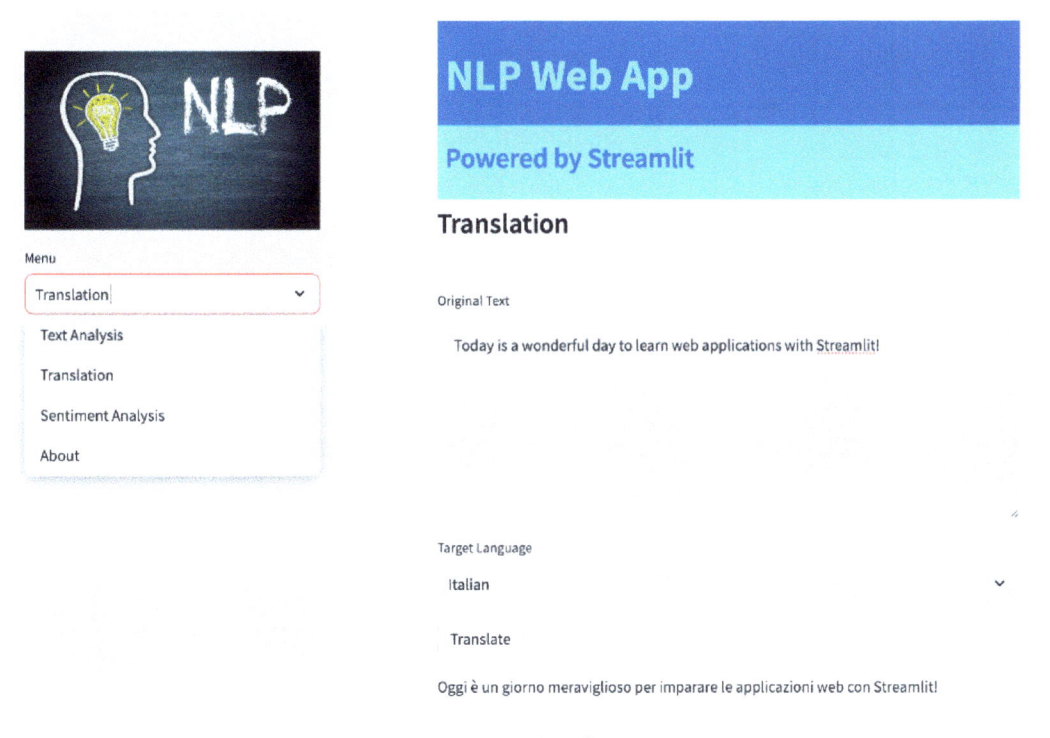

Figure 6.23: Translation

Figure 6.23 shows the behavior of the **Translation** function. This is quite self-explanatory: a sentence is typed into the text area, then a target language is selected, and finally, on pressing the **Translate** button, the translation task is performed and the result is displayed on the screen.

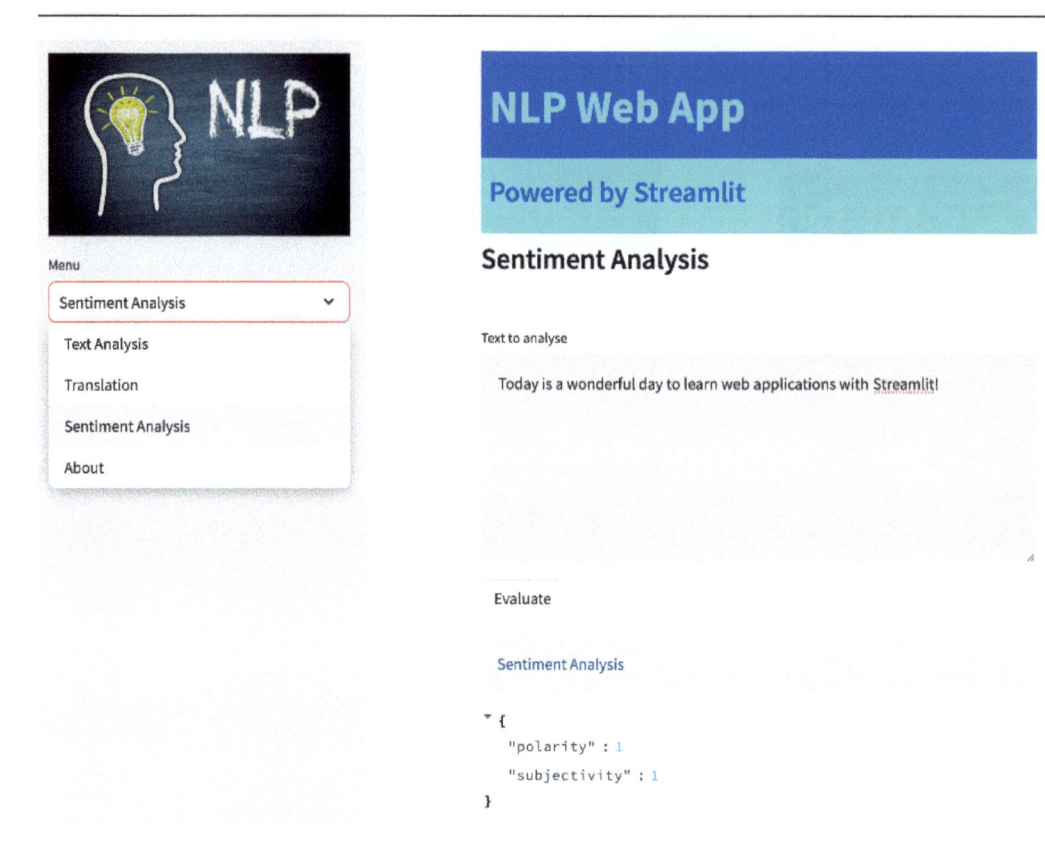

138   Implementing NLP Techniques for Text Analysis and Processing in Streamlit

Figure 6.24: Sentiment Analysis

Figure 6.24 shows an example of **Sentiment Analysis**, which in this case shows a very high polarity.

We close the sequence of screenshots from the NLP web application we made together with the **About** section, as shown in *Figure 6.25*.

Figure 6.25: The About section

The **About** section is very useful since it contains information about the author, links to external web pages, and so on.

Here is all the code we have written together up to now:

```python
# Core Pkgs
import streamlit as st
st.set_page_config(page_title="NLP Web App", page_icon="👍", layout="centered", initial_sidebar_state="auto")

# Viz Pkgs
import matplotlib.pyplot as plt
import matplotlib
matplotlib.use("Agg")
from wordcloud import WordCloud
from deep_translator import GoogleTranslator

# NLP Pkgs
from textblob import TextBlob
import neattext as nt
import spacy

from collections import Counter
import re


# Sumarization Function
def summarize_text(text, num_sentences=3):
    # Remove special characters and convert text to lowercase
    clean_text = re.sub('[^a-zA-Z]', ' ', text).lower()

    # Split the text into words
    words = clean_text.split()

    # Calculate the frequency of each word
    word_freq = Counter(words)

    # Sort the words based on their frequency in descending order
    sorted_words = sorted(word_freq, key=word_freq.get, reverse=True)

    # Extract the top `num_sentences` most frequent words
    top_words = sorted_words[:num_sentences]

    # Create the summary by joining the top words
    summary = ' '.join(top_words)

    return summary
```

Figure 6.26: NLP web application code part 1

In part 1, we imported the packages, set the page configuration, and defined the `summarize_text` function.

```python
42
43    #@st.cache_data
44    # Lemma and Tokens Function
45    def text_analyzer(text):
46        # import English library
47        nlp = spacy.load('en_core_web_sm')
48        # create an nlp object
49        doc = nlp(text)
50        #extract tokens and lemmas
51        allData = [('"Token":{},\n"Lemma":{}'.format(token.text, token.lemma_)) for token in doc]
52        return allData
53
54
55    def main():
56        """NLP web app with Streamlit"""
57
58        title_template = """
59        <div style="background-color:blue; padding:8px;">
60        <h1 style="color:cyan">NLP Web App</h1>
61        </div>
62        """
63
64        st.markdown(title_template, unsafe_allow_html=True)
65
66        subheader_template = """
67        <div style="background-color:cyan; padding:8px;">
68        <h3 style="color:blue">Powered by Streamlit</h1>
69        </div>
70        """
71
72        st.markdown(subheader_template, unsafe_allow_html=True)
73
74        st.sidebar.image("nlp.jpg", use_column_width=True)
75
76        activity = ["Text Analysis", "Translation", "Sentiment Analysis", "About"]
77        choice = st.sidebar.selectbox("Menu", activity)
78
79        if choice == "Text Analysis":
80            st.subheader("Text Analysis")
81            st.write("")
82
83            raw_text = st.text_area("Write something", "Enter a text in English...", height=200)
84
```

Figure 6.27: NLP web application code part 2

In part 2, we wrote the `text_analyzer` function, then the `main` function, which contains the main title of the application, a subheading, and the menu in the sidebar.

```python
 84
 85     if st.button("Analyze"):
 86         if len(raw_text) == 0:
 87             st.warning("Enter a text...")
 88         else:
 89             #blob = TextBlob(raw_text)
 90             st.info("Basic Functions")
 91
 92             col1, col2 = st.columns(2)
 93
 94             with col1:
 95                 with st.expander("Basic Info"):
 96                     st.info("Text Stats")
 97                     word_desc = nt.TextFrame(raw_text).word_stats()
 98                     result_desc = {"Length of Text":word_desc['Length of Text'],
 99                                    "Num of Vowels":word_desc['Num of Vowels'],
100                                    "Num of Consonants":word_desc['Num of Consonants'],
101                                    "Num of Stopwords":word_desc['Num of Stopwords']}
102                     st.write(result_desc)
103
104                 with st.expander("Stopwords"):
105                     st.success("Stop Words List")
106                     stop_w = nt.TextExtractor(raw_text).extract_stopwords()
107                     st.error(stop_w)
108
109             with col2:
110                 with st.expander("Processed Text"):
111                     st.success("Stopwords Excluded Text")
112                     processed_text = str(nt.TextFrame(raw_text).remove_stopwords())
113                     st.write(processed_text)
114
115                 with st.expander("Plot Wordcloud"):
116                     st.success("Wordcloud")
117                     wordcloud = WordCloud().generate(processed_text)
118                     fig = plt.figure(1, figsize=(20,10))
119                     plt.imshow(wordcloud, interpolation = 'bilinear')
120                     plt.axis('off')
121                     st.pyplot(fig)
122
123             st.write("")
124             st.write("")
125             st.info("Advanced Features")
126
127             col3, col4 = st.columns(2)
128
```

Figure 6.28: NLP web application code part 3

In part 3, we developed the `main` function using an `if` loop and many advanced widgets, such as columns and expanders.

```
129      with col3:
130          with st.expander("Tokens&Lemmas"):
131              st.write("T&K")
132              processed_text_mid = str(nt.TextFrame(raw_text).remove_stopwords())
133              processed_text_mid = str(nt.TextFrame(processed_text_mid).remove_puncts())
134              processed_text_fin = str(nt.TextFrame(processed_text_mid).remove_special_characters())
135              tandl = text_analyzer(processed_text_fin)
136              st.json(tandl)
137
138      with col4:
139          with st.expander("Summarize"):
140              st.success("Summarize")
141              summary = summarize_text(raw_text)
142              st.success(summary)
143
144
145  if choice == "Translation":
146      st.subheader("Translation")
147      st.write("")
148      st.write("")
149      raw_text = st.text_area("Original Text", "Write something to be translated...", height=200)
150      if len(raw_text) < 3:
151          st.warning("Please provide a text with at least 3 characters...")
152      else:
153          target_lang = st.selectbox("Target Language", ["German", "Spanish", "French", "Italian"])
154          if target_lang == "German":
155              target_lang = "de"
156          elif target_lang == "Spanish":
157              target_lang = "es"
158          elif target_lang == "French":
159              target_lang = "fr"
160          else:
161              target_lang = "it"
162
163          if st.button("Translate"):
164              translator = GoogleTranslator(source='auto', target=target_lang)  # set source and target languages
165              translated_text = translator.translate(raw_text)
166              st.write(translated_text)
167
168
```

Figure 6.29: NLP web application code part 4

In part 4, we mainly developed the **Translation** feature, making it possible to insert text and select a language.

```
167
168
169   if choice == "Sentiment Analysis":
170       st.subheader("Sentiment Analysis")
171       st.write("")
172       st.write("")
173       raw_text = st.text_area("Text to analyse", "Enter a text here....", height=200)
174       if st.button("Evaluate"):
175           if len(raw_text) == 0:
176               st.warning("Enter a text...")
177           else:
178               blob = TextBlob(raw_text)
179               st.info("Sentiment Analysis")
180               st.write(blob.sentiment)
181               st.write("")
182
183
184   if choice == "About":
185       st.subheader("About")
186       st.write("")
187
188       st.markdown("""
189       ### NLP Web App made with Streamlit
190
191       for info:
192       - [streamlit](https://streamlit.io)
193       """)
194
195
196   if __name__ == "__main__":
197       main()
```

Figure 6.30: NLP web application code part 5

In part 5, we implemented the **Sentiment Analysis** feature, leveraging the `TextBlob` library, then completed the web app by adding the **About** section.

The full listing of our web application's code makes it clear how powerful Streamlit is. Less than 200 lines of code are enough to create a fully working web application with a lot of advanced features and quite a nice look and feel. We achieved this result just using standard Python, with no need for HTML, CSS, JavaScript, and so on.

Summary

Our web application utilizing NLP is finished and running. You should be very proud of that!

We also recapped the main points and takeaways. So, what else can we do?

If we think about it, our application works very well, but only locally, or at least within the same network as the machine that we coded on.

For a web application to be defined as a real web application, it needs to be public. This means it needs to be accessible everywhere.

To be accessed everywhere, our web application needs to live on a server on the real internet with a real public URL.

To put our web application on a real server on the web, we need to deploy it, and this is exactly what we are going to do in the next chapter.

7
Sharing and Deploying Your Apps on the Cloud Using Streamlit Share

Streamlit Share is a service provided by the Streamlit framework that allows users to deploy their web applications, made with Streamlit, to the cloud with just a few clicks. Streamlit Share provides a free and easy way to share our web applications with others and make them accessible from anywhere with an internet connection.

To deploy a Streamlit app on Streamlit Share, users must connect their GitHub repository to the Streamlit Share platform. Streamlit Share takes care of the rest, automatically building and deploying the app in the cloud. Streamlit Share provides several benefits for users, including seamless deployment, automatic scaling, and easy collaboration.

Overall, deploying on Streamlit Share is a convenient and user-friendly way to deploy Streamlit web applications to the cloud and share them with others.

In the previous chapter, we finished and tested our NLP web application, so now is the perfect moment to deploy it using Streamlit Share and maybe show it to our friends and colleagues so that they can try and play with our creation using any browser.

Web applications deployed in this way are even a great "portfolio" to be shown around to prove our capabilities!

In this chapter, we're going to cover the following main topics:

- Understanding the importance of deployment
- A quick introduction to GitHub
- Getting familiar with the Streamlit Share service

Technical requirements

- In this chapter, we will use the following libraries, packages, and tools:
  - Sublime Text
  - Python 3
  - `pipenv`
  - Streamlit
  - GitHub
  - Streamlit Cloud

- The code for this chapter can be found in this book's GitHub repository: `https://github.com/PacktPublishing/Web-App-Development-Made-Simple-with-Streamlit/tree/8d935899f9f128c8cd62d93627711de7c9388b15/Chapter07`.

Understanding the importance of deployment

Web application deployment is the process of making a web application available to users. This involves copying the application's code, data, and configuration files to a web server, and configuring the server to run the application.

There are many reasons why web application deployment is important; here are a few:

- *Deployment ensures that your application is available to users*: Once your application has been deployed, it will be accessible to users on the internet. This means that they can use your application to perform tasks, such as shopping, browsing, or interacting with your business.

- *Deployment makes it easy to update your web application*: As you make changes to your web application, you can deploy them to production with a few clicks. This allows you to quickly and easily deliver new features and bug fixes to your users.

- *Deployment helps improve the security of your web application*: When you deploy your web application, you can take steps to improve its security, such as configuring firewalls and implementing security best practices. This helps protect your application from attacks and data breaches.

- *Deployment can help you improve the performance of your web application*: When you deploy your web application, you can optimize its performance by configuring the server, optimizing the code, and using caching. This can help improve the user experience and reduce the server load.

In short, web application deployment is an important part of the development process. Next, let's learn about some best practices to keep in mind related to web application deployment.

Best practices in web application deployment

By following these best practices, you can ensure that your web application is available, secure, and performant:

- *Use a staging environment*: A staging environment is a copy of your production environment that you can use to test changes to your web application before deploying them to production. This helps ensure that your changes are stable and working properly before you make them available to users.
- *Automate the deployment process*: Automation can help reduce the time and resources required to deploy your web application. There are many different tools available to help you automate the deployment process.
- *Use a version control system*: A version control system helps you track changes to your web application code. This makes it easy to roll back changes if something goes wrong during deployment.
- *Test your application thoroughly*: Before you deploy your web application, it is important to test it thoroughly. This includes testing the application's functionality, performance, and security.
- *Monitor your application after deployment*: Once your web application has been deployed, monitoring its performance and availability is important. This helps you identify and fix any problems that may occur.

By following these practices, your web applications can be deployed smoothly and successfully.

Additional benefits of web application deployment

Here are some additional benefits of web application deployment:

- *Increased scalability*: You can easily handle increased traffic by deploying your web application to a scalable infrastructure. This is important for businesses that experience spikes in traffic, such as during sales or marketing campaigns.
- *Reduced costs*: By automating the deployment process, you can reduce the time and resources required to deploy your web application. This can save you money in the long run.
- *Improved agility*: With a repeatable and automated deployment process, you can quickly and easily deploy new features and bug fixes to your web application. This gives you the agility to respond to changing customer needs.

Overall, web application deployment is a key part of the development process. So, is there a way to ease the adoption of all these best practices?

We are very lucky since Streamlit Share adopts the best practices we mentioned, by definition, so we can ensure we deploy our web application in the best possible way.

Having a service that adopts all these best practices is a big advantage for us since we can exclusively focus on the real business logic of our web apps. Our main task will be coding and making our web applications work properly, satisfying and achieving all the needs and results we want, all while being sure that the deployment and how it's shared is something perfect that we don't have to care too much about.

In the next section, we'll learn about Streamlit Share and Streamlit Cloud.

What are Streamlit Share and Streamlit Cloud?

Streamlit Share is a free service that allows you to deploy your Streamlit apps to the web with just a few clicks. Once you have created your Streamlit app, you can share it on Streamlit Share by clicking the **Share** button in the Streamlit app. This will create a unique URL for your app that you can share with anyone.

Streamlit Cloud is a service that allows you to deploy one private app and unlimited public apps, thus offering more features and flexibility than Streamlit Share. With Streamlit Cloud, you can deploy your Streamlit apps to a scalable infrastructure, add custom domains, and integrate with other services. Please check the official page to get updated information: `https://streamlit.io/cloud`.

To close this section, let's underline the importance of deployment once more. This is the easiest way to make our web apps available to anyone. Streamlit offers its own cloud service that is very easy to manage. Besides the app code, the only thing we need is a GitHub repository.

A quick introduction to GitHub

GitHub is a code hosting platform for version control and collaboration. It allows you to store your code in a central location, track changes over time, and collaborate with others on projects.

There are many reasons to use GitHub. Here are just a few:

- *Version control*: GitHub allows you to track changes to your code over time. This is essential for any project as it allows you to revert to previous code versions if necessary.
- *Collaboration*: GitHub makes it easy to collaborate with others on projects. You can create a repository and invite others to collaborate with you. This is a great way to get feedback on your code and help from others.
- *Documentation*: GitHub can be used to store documentation for your projects. This is a great way to keep track of your project's requirements, design, and implementation.
- *Hosting*: GitHub can also be used to host your projects. This means you can make your code available to others to view and download.
- *Free*: GitHub is free to use, and you can keep your repositories public or private. If you need more resources, you can opt for a paid plan and check out `https://github.com/pricing`.

- *Popular*: GitHub is the most popular code hosting platform in the world. This means that there is a large community of users and developers who can help you with your projects.
- *Feature-rich*: GitHub offers a wide range of features that make it easy for you to track changes, collaborate with others, and host your projects.
- *Secure*: GitHub uses industry-standard security measures to protect your code.

You should use GitHub for any project that you want to track changes to, collaborate on, or host. This includes personal projects, work projects, and open source projects.

Nonetheless, there are a few disadvantages to using GitHub:

- *Can be complex*: GitHub can be complex to use, especially for beginners
- *Can be slow*: GitHub can be slow at times, especially when there is a lot of traffic

These disadvantages can be overcome quite easily:

- First of all, the complexity can be mitigated by studying GitHub's syntax and functions. After doing this a few times, everything will be smoother.
- In the case of sensitive information we need to protect, we can always create private repositories – it's just a matter of understanding when this operation is truly necessary.
- Finally, in the case of big traffic, the service can be a little bit slow, but there are always intervals throughout the daytime when speed and responsiveness are not a problem.

GitHub is a key part of the Streamlit ecosystem. GitHub is related to Streamlit Share in a few ways:

- *Streamlit apps are hosted on GitHub*: When you create a Streamlit app, you can choose to host it on GitHub. This means that your app's code will be stored in a GitHub repository. This is a great way to make your app available to others to view and download.
- *Streamlit Share uses GitHub OAuth*: Streamlit Share allows you to share your app with others without having to share your GitHub username and password. When you use Streamlit Share, Streamlit will ask you to authorize it to access your GitHub account. This allows Streamlit to create a new GitHub repository for your app and deploy your app to GitHub pages.
- *Streamlit's Community Cloud is integrated with GitHub*: Streamlit's Community Cloud, as we've already explained, is a platform that makes it easy to deploy, manage, and share Streamlit apps. When you create a Streamlit app in Community Cloud, you can choose to link it to your GitHub account. This allows you to easily manage your app's code and collaborate with others on your app.

In short, if you want to create, share, and collaborate on Streamlit apps, you will need to use GitHub.

Now that we have all the theoretical information we need to start sharing our web apps in a very effective way, let's not hesitate and get started!

Getting familiar with the Streamlit Share service

Now that we've covered the theory, let's understand how to deploy our fresh NLP web application in a very easy and smooth way!

First of all, you will have to go to `https://share.streamlit.io`:

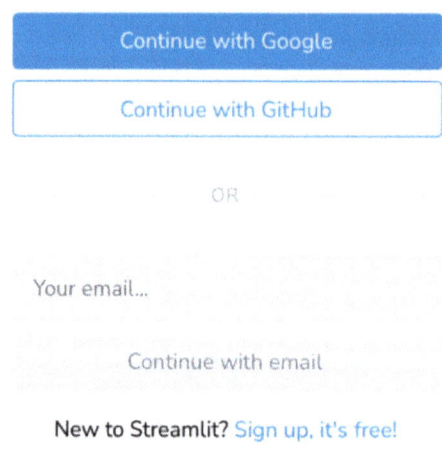

Figure 7.1: The Streamlit Share web page

When you arrive on the page, you must sign in with your GitHub account, using the email (or username) and password you use for your GitHub account. This requires you to register for a GitHub account if you do not already have one (`https://github.com`).

Now, before signing in, I strongly suggest that you carefully read Streamlit's official documentation about sharing apps since you can find very detailed information about how to share private and public apps:

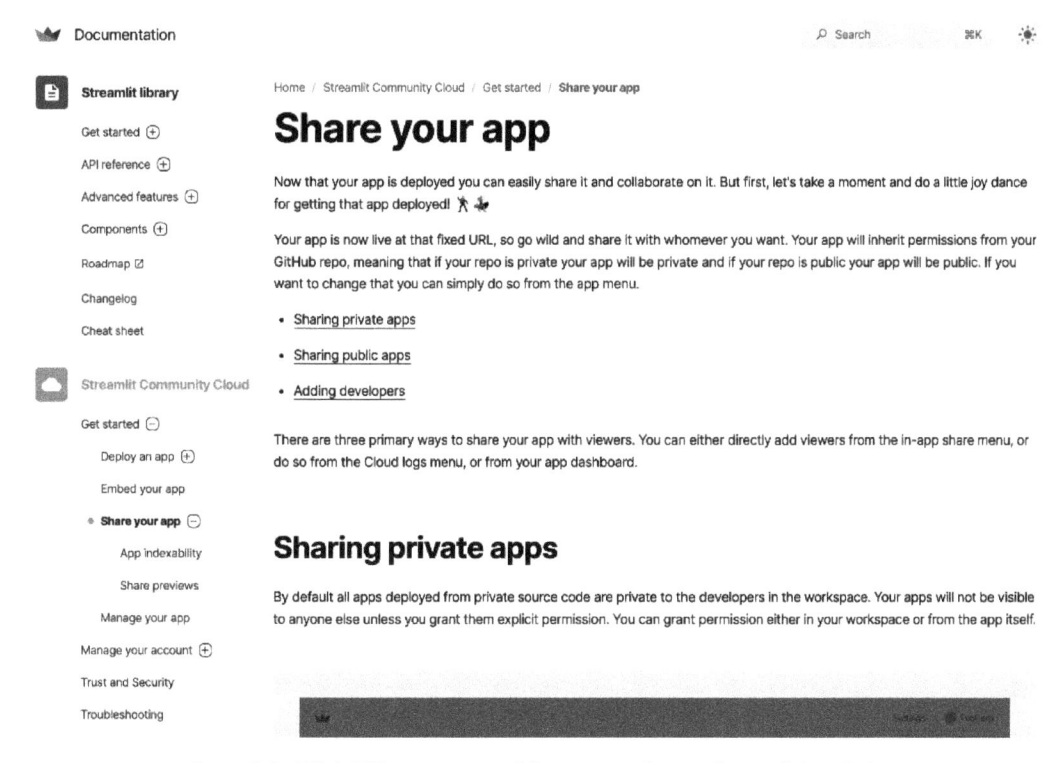

Figure 7.2: Official "Share your app" documentation on Streamlit's website

Once you've logged in with your GitHub account, you will see a page similar to the following (in mine, there are a lot of already published/deployed applications; in the beginning, yours will be empty):

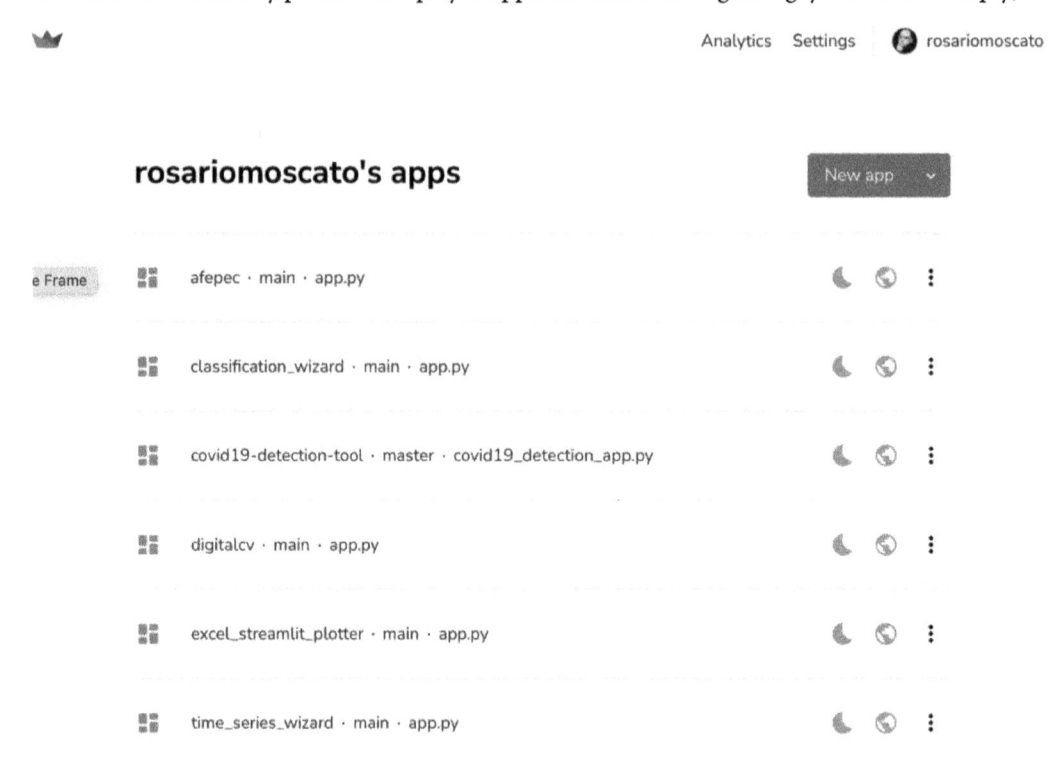

Figure 7.3: The page you get after logging in

On the top left-hand side of the page, there is the Streamlit logo, while on the right-hand side, there are the **Analytics** and **Settings** areas of the menu and your account name.

To work correctly, the web application we are going to deploy needs all the required libraries in its code. There are several ways to collect the list of all these required packages, but one of the simplest is using the `pipreqs` package. So, from the command line, let's write the following:

```
pip install pipreqs
```

This installation is very fast. Once completed, you can write, once again in the command line, a very simple instruction:

```
pipreqs my_application_folder_name
```

Here, `my_application_folder_name` is the folder where the Python file of your application lives.

This instruction will produce a file named `requirements.txt`. If you open it, you will see that it contains a list of all the packages/libraries that are required by the Python web application we will deploy:

Figure 7.4: The "requirements.txt" file

Very well – we already have everything we need! Before you start the real deployment, you must upload the Python file of the web app, so the `app.py` or `whatevername.py` file, together with the `requirements.txt` file you just made, and the `nlp.jpg` file we used as an image in the sidebar for GitHub (if you don't update the image file, you will get a runtime error). Your GitHub should contain these two files and should look like this:

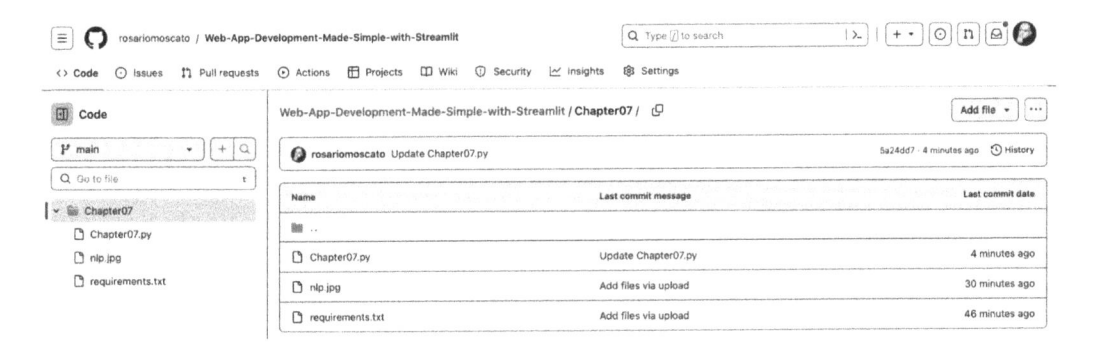

Figure 7.5: GitHub with the files needed for deployment

If you are at the stage shown in *Figure 7.5*, everything is ready for deployment. Please move back to the Streamlit Share page and click on **New app**, then **From existing repo**, as shown in *Figure 7.6*:

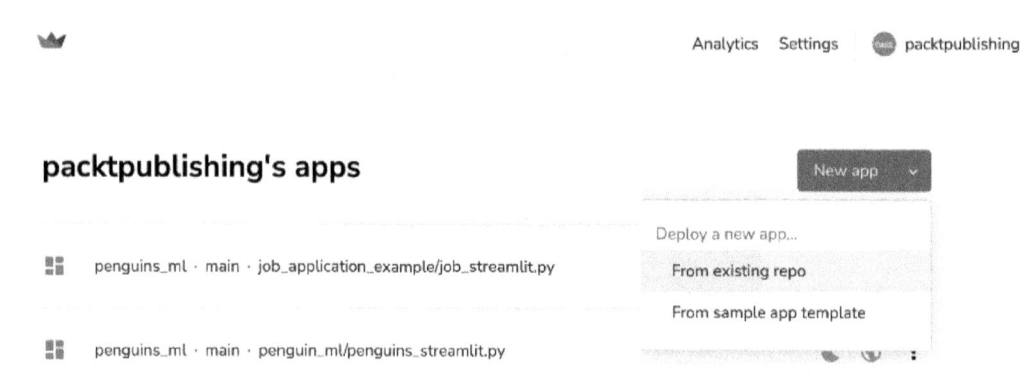

Figure 7.6: "New app" from an existing repo

Now, you will be asked to provide some information about the repository, including its name (under **Repository**), **Branch**, **Main file path**, and **App URL (Optional)**, as shown in *Figure 7.7*:

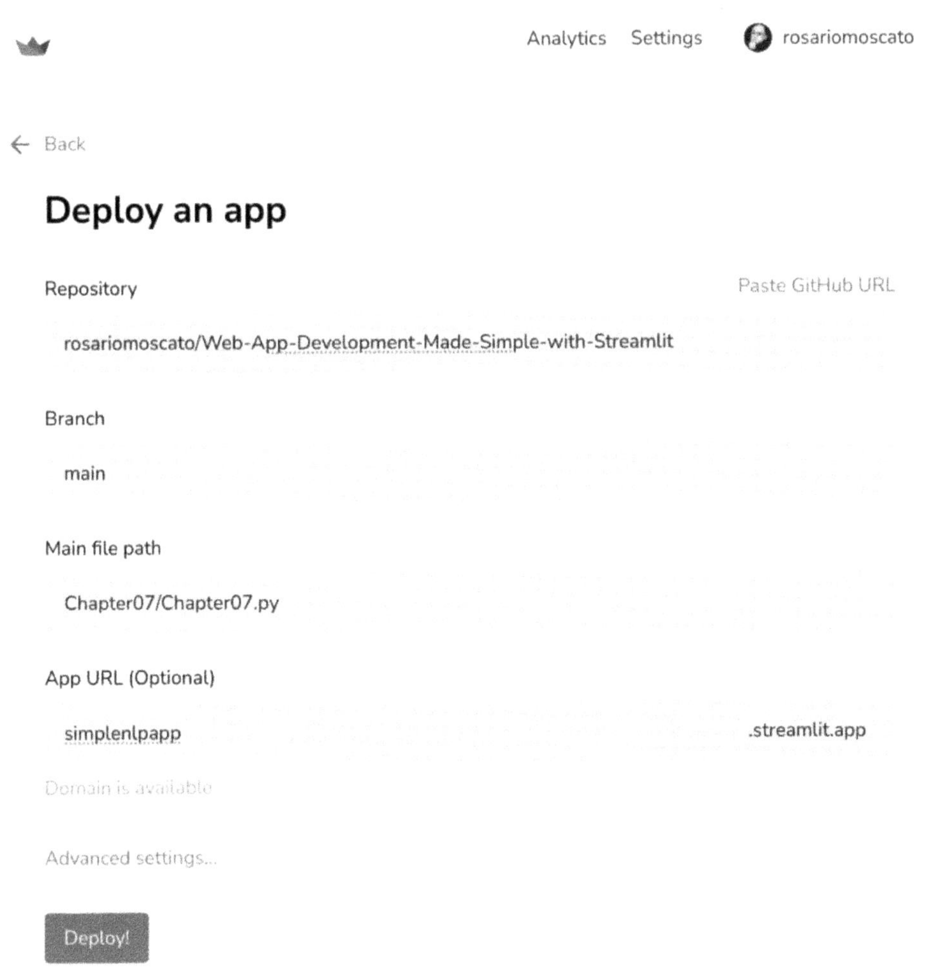
Analytics
Settings
rosariomoscato
Back
Deploy an app
Repository
Paste GitHub URL
rosariomoscato/Web-App-Development-Made-Simple-with-Streamlit
Branch
main
Main file path
Chapter07/Chapter07.py
App URL (Optional)
simplenlpapp
.streamlit.app
Domain is available
Advanced settings...
Deploy!

Figure 7.7: The information that's required to deploy the app

The information required depends on how you upload your files to GitHub. However, providing this information is simple. You must provide the name of your repository, which will be displayed as an alternative in the form. You will also need to provide the name of the branch, which is usually `main`. Additionally, you will need to provide the name of the application code file, which should be `app.py` or the name of your Python file. Finally, it is strongly suggested that you fill in the name of the public URL that everyone will use to connect to your web application. More or less, that's it! You can then click **Deploy!** and just wait for the magic to happen.

While the web application is being deployed, you should get a nice message saying **Your app is in the oven**, with an animation made up of nice images of desserts:

Figure 7.8: Your app is in the oven

After a little while, your web application will be up and running in the cloud, on the internet!

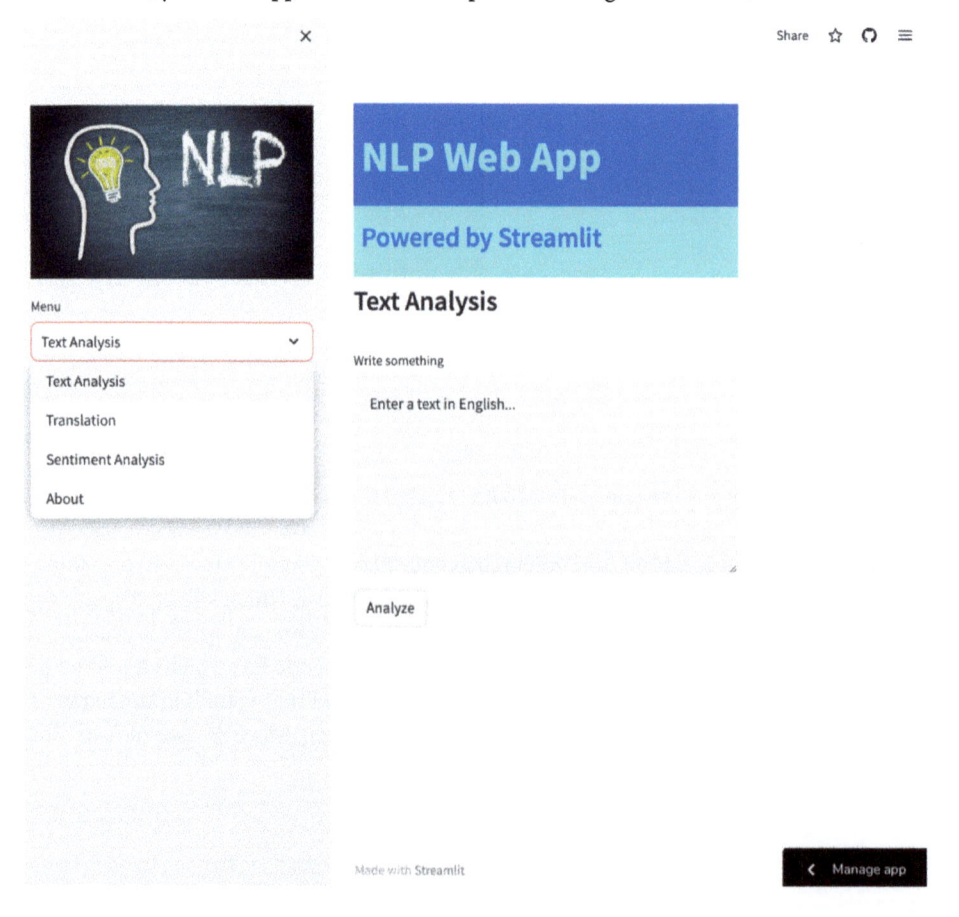

Figure 7.9: The NLP web app has been deployed

This was very easy and neat. Once our app is working on the cloud, we might want to manage it. Let's see what functions we can access by clicking on **Manage app** in the bottom-right corner of the web app:

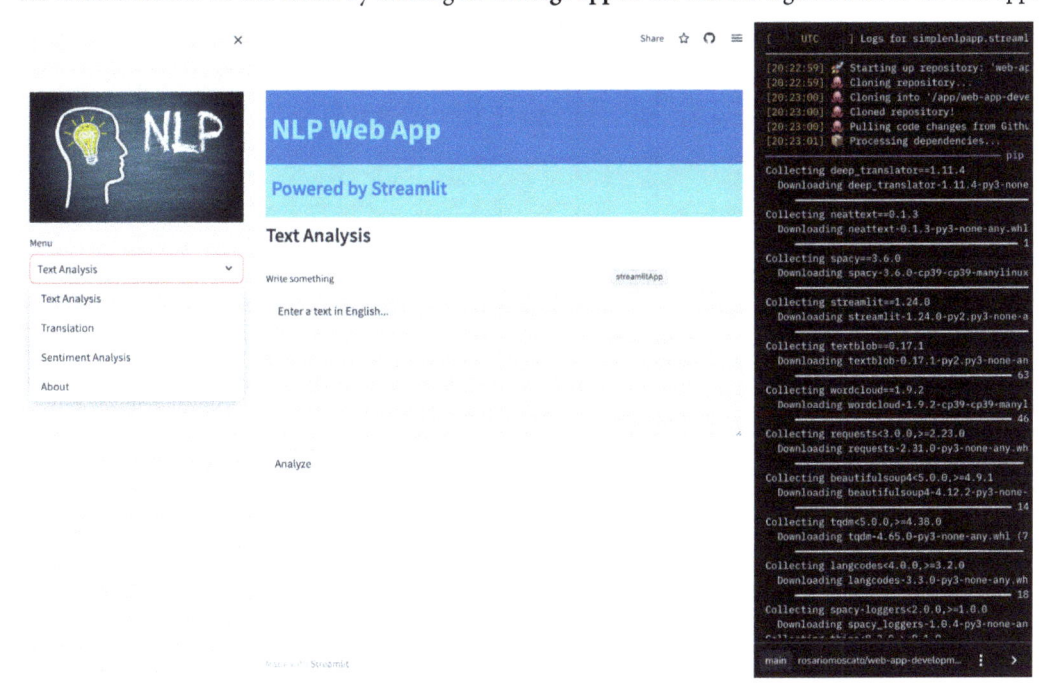

Figure 7.10: Deployment "terminal"

First of all, we will see something like an installation terminal – that is, a terminal reporting everything that is going on with our deployment. Besides this, we can click on the three dots, which will give us access to some very important functions:

Figure 7.11: Functions in Streamlit Share

First, by choosing **Download log**, we can download the deployment log, which is very useful in case of issues. After that, we can access the analytics of our app, reboot the web application, delete it, and access some settings. Moreover, we can get an overview of all the web applications we have already deployed and check the documentation or ask for support.

If we select **Settings**, we will have access to three extra voices, as shown in *Figure 7.10*:

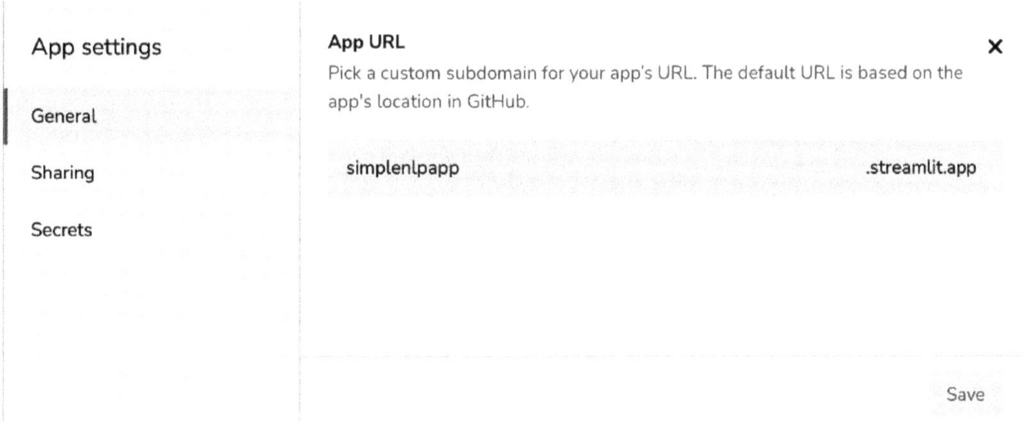

Figure 7.12: App settings

In the **General** section, we can modify the URL of our app, in the **Sharing** section, we can decide whether our web app is private or public, and in the **Secrets** section, we can specify – if we use them – the API keys for external services without sharing them with everybody.

Now, there is something else very easy but very useful we can do: we can add a badge or a button that says **Open in Streamlit** in our GitHub repository. By doing this, everyone can directly access our deployed web app very easily just by clicking this badge.

This operation is quite immediate since we just have to add a README.md file with a couple of lines of code to our repository.

So, let's add the README.md file containing the code shown in the following screenshot to our GitHub repository:

```
1   To OPEN **Simple NLP APP** click here:
2
3   [![Streamlit APP](https://static.streamlit.io/badges/streamlit_badge_black_white.svg)](https://simplenlparp.streamlit.app)
4
```

Figure 7.13: The README.md file's content

The first URL, so the first `https://`, is the link to the badge or the image, while the second one, so the second `https://`, is just the URL of the web app you just deployed, so please customize it with your app's real URL.

The following figure shows us the effect in the GitHub repository:

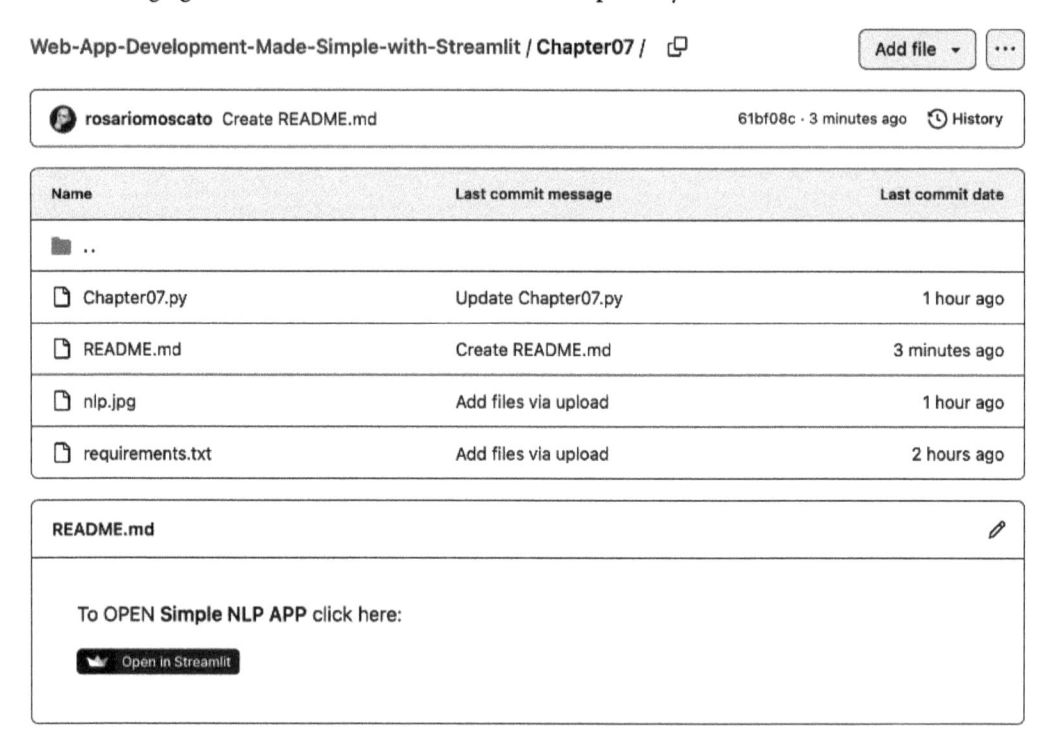

Figure 7.14: The "Open in Streamlit" badge

As we mentioned previously, upon clicking on the badge, you will be redirected to the web application we just deployed.

Before closing this chapter, please note that when we developed our NLP application after installing all the required Python packages, we downloaded the *spaCy English model* with the following command:

```
python -m spacy download en_core_web_sm
```

When we deploy an app on Streamlit Share, we just have a `requirements.txt` file. So, how do we get our spaCy English model?

If we get an error related to NOT FOUND en_core_web_sm, to fix it, we have to make a very easy change in our `requirements.txt` file – we have just to replace the line related to `spacy` with the following two lines:

```
spacy>=2.2.0,<3.0.0
https://github.com/explosion/spacy-models/releases/download/en_core_
web_sm-2.2.0/en_core_web_sm-2.2.0.tar.gz#egg=en_core_web_sm
```

In this way, the English model will be downloaded to our workspace and everything will work perfectly!

If we stop for a few seconds and think carefully, we'll understand that in this section, we achieved an incredible result. A web app that was previously living only in our little environment (our computer or our local network) is now available for anyone who has an internet connection. Anyone everywhere can interact with our web application and use it. This kind of skill is incredibly valuable. We can not only develop beautiful web apps but also make them available to anybody. Our applications can now serve an incredibly wide audience.

Summary

Congratulations! You deployed your first web application, and now, anybody can access it and enjoy it just by using the URL you specified!

If you look back now, you can consider how far we've come together. Starting from a real empty file in an empty folder, we have built up a complete web application with a lot of features.

The point is that this new web application only lives in the developer's computer or private network unless it's deployed to the cloud.

Deploying it to the cloud is what we learned to do in this chapter. App deployment is the real "big thing" since we can make our creations accessible anywhere!

Making changes and improvements to what we have already deployed is very easy since we can simply modify the code according to the new ideas, test it, and upload it to the GitHub repository. After that, in a very magical way, Streamlit Share will automatically update the deployment seamlessly.

We can upload the code on GitHub and Streamlit Share takes care of all the rest: easy!

Starting with the next chapter, we are going to implement a new web application that's even more complex than the one we've just finished. By doing this, we will learn about and master all the main advanced features of Streamlit!

Part 3: Developing Advanced Skills with a Covid-19 Detection Tool

In Part 3, the book shifts focus to more advanced Streamlit capabilities, using the development of a Covid-19 Detection Tool as a practical case study. It begins by guiding you through an advanced environment setup and package management, specifically tailored to build **artifitial intelligence (AI)**-powered web applications. This section is critical for understanding the nuances of integrating complex AI models. Then, it delves into optimizing the **user experience (UX)** of Streamlit web apps through customization and UI features, highlighting the importance of an intuitive and engaging interface. The part further explores the use of pretrained models, demonstrating how to create specialized and personalized applications, a skill crucial in the era of AI and machine learning. Finally, it covers the deployment and management of complex libraries on Streamlit Share, ensuring that you are well-equipped to handle sophisticated app requirements. This part of the book is pivotal in elevating your skills from intermediate to advanced, preparing you for professional-grade Streamlit development.

This part contains the following chapters:

- *Chapter 8, Advanced Environment Setup and Package Management for Building an AI-Powered Web App*
- *Chapter 9, Optimizing Streamlit Web App UX with Customization and UI Features*
- *Chapter 10, Utilizing Pretrained Models to Create Specialized and Personalized Web Applications*
- *Chapter 11, Deploying and Managing Complex Libraries on Streamlit Share*

8
Advanced Environment Setup and Package Management for Building an AI-Powered Web App

In *Chapters 8* through *12*, we will be building a new web app together: a tool that can detect the presence of COVID-19 from an image. To do so, we will leverage a pre-trained model (we are not delving into AI and model training but just using a pre-trained convolutional neural network) and in this way, we will learn how to integrate our AI models into our web applications by building up an entire set of services around them!

In very few words, a pre-trained model is an AI model that has been trained previously by someone else in order to make predictions – for example, classifications or regressions. To train the model, a dataset of cases related to the problem under scrutiny is typically needed. So, in the case of COVID-19 detection, a binary classification model (binary means only two possible solutions: COVID or no COVID) has been trained in the past and is now ready to be used in our web application.

This chapter covers in a deeper way what we already saw in *Chapter 4*. The chapter is designed to help you better understand how to develop a web application from scratch, adding more features that require higher skills. So, once again, we will set up a virtual environment, install and manage packages, create an app skeleton, and add a menu and decorations to the app. In this part, we will build a new web app together to acquire much more high-level skills.

In this chapter, we're going to cover the following main topics:

- Configuring our environment
- Installing and importing packages

- Building the app skeleton
- Building the menu and adding decorations

Technical requirements

- In this chapter, we will use the following libraries, packages, and tools:
  - Sublime Text
  - Python 3
  - `pipenv`
  - Streamlit
- Code in the chapter can be accessed through the following GitHub link: https://github.com/PacktPublishing/Web-App-Development-Made-Simple-with-Streamlit/tree/d5860f2916d79752d4b03c615da68f5bbdb4ed63/Chapter08

Configuring our environment

Actually, we already created a virtual environment at the beginning of the previous project, in *Chapter 4*, so we should be quite skilled at this task. Let's start by creating an empty directory, which can be simply named `covid`. So, let's write in our terminal the following instruction:

```
mkdir covid
```

Then, we can move inside the new directory just by typing the following:

```
cd covid
```

It's now time to create our virtual environment. We know that this operation is very easy since we can use `pipenv`, as we already did in *Chapter 4*. So, once again, let's write from our directory (it's very important to be inside the `covid` directory):

```
pipenv shell
```

The virtual environment will be created quite quickly, and we should be at a stage like the one in the following figure:

Installing and importing packages 167

Figure 8.1: Virtual environment creation

As shown in *Figure 8.1*, a new directory named `covid` is created. Then, we enter this directory and, by writing `pipenv shell`, we create the virtual environment, assigning to it the name of the directory. The tool we are using to make the virtual environment (`pipenv`) provides a positive output (the text in green) and automatically opens the new virtual environment. In fact, at the beginning of the last line in the screenshot, the word `covid` between the parentheses indicates that we are inside the virtual environment.

At this point, the environment is ready but still empty, since we are still missing all the libraries we are going to use in our code. Let's see what packages we need.

Installing and importing packages

Now that we are inside the `covid` directory and our virtual environment has been created, it's time to install all the packages we are going to use in our web application.

We need five different libraries:

- `Streamlit`, our wonderful framework for web applications
- `numpy`, a library for advanced numeric calculations
- `tensorflow`, the package needed to manage neural networks
- `Pillow`, a library for image management
- `opencv-python`, the computer vision package

Let's install everything by typing the following instructions one by one:

```
pipenv install streamlit numpy tensorflow Pillow opencv-python
```

This installation can take a little while. When it finishes, we should have something like this on our screen:

Figure 8.2: Package installation

We can now launch our editor, Sublime Text. You'll see that in the `covid` directory, there are now the two *famous* files, `Pipfile` and `Pipfile.lock`, containing the configuration of our virtual environment with the installed libraries and the dependencies list:

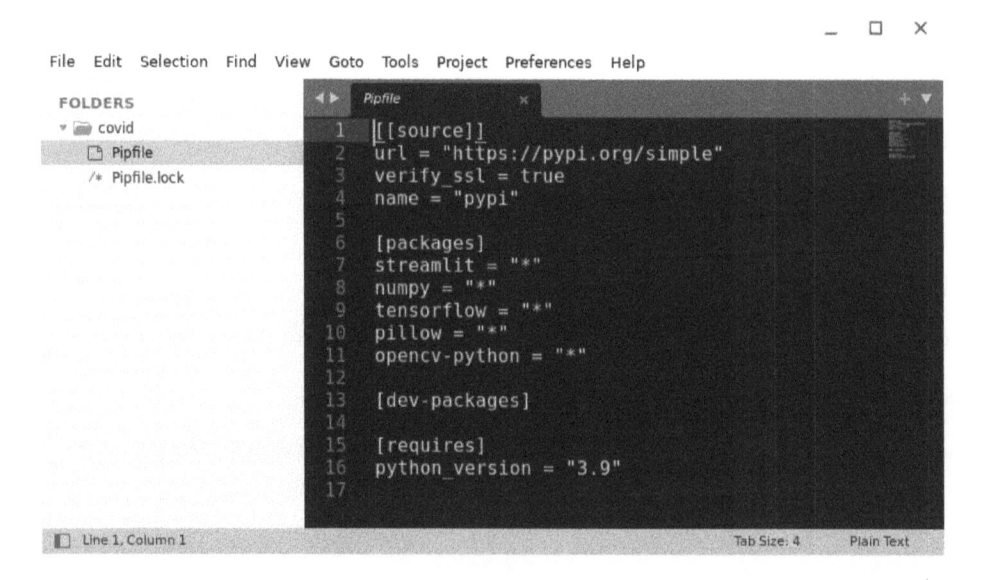

Figure 8.3: Pipfile

Now we can create a new file and call it, as usual, `app.py`, so let's write the following:

```
touch app.py
```

Everything is finally ready to start coding.

Obviously, we have to start by importing the libraries, and this is very easy, as we can see in the following figure:

```
# Core Pkgs
import streamlit as st
#st.set_page_config(page_title="Covid19 Detection Tool", page_icon="covid19.jpeg", layout='centered', initial_sidebar_state='auto')

import os
import time

# Viz Pkgs
import cv2
from PIL import Image,ImageEnhance
import numpy as np

# AI Pkgs
import tensorflow as tf
```

Figure 8.4: Importing the libraries

As for the previous web application, we need to create a main function. Let's do it by adding some `html` code just to give a title to our app, and since we already imported Streamlit, as usual, let's add as the first instruction, after the `import streamlit as st` line, the code for the page configuration (we just set the title, an icon – you can use any picture you want – and the initial sidebar state). The full code is as follows:

```
# Core Pkgs
import streamlit as st
st.set_page_config(page_title="Covid19 Detection Tool", page_icon="covid19.jpeg", layout='centered', initial_sidebar_state='auto')

import os
import time

# Viz Pkgs
import cv2
from PIL import Image,ImageEnhance
import numpy as np

# AI Pkgs
import tensorflow as tf

def main():
    """Simple Tool for Covid-19 Detection from Chest X-Ray"""
    html_templ = """
    <div style="background-color:blue;padding:10px;">
    <h1 style="color:yellow">Covid-19 Detection Tool</h1>
    </div>
    """

    st.markdown(html_templ,unsafe_allow_html=True)


if __name__ == '__main__':
    main()
```

Figure 8.5: First app draft

At the moment, we've just imported the libraries and added very few lines of code, but the web app can be launched. Let's do it by typing the following well-known instruction:

```
pipenv run streamlit run app.py
```

In the following figure, the result we get upon opening the browser on localhost port `8501` can be seen:

Covid-19 Detection Tool

Figure 8.6: First launch of the app

No errors! We can continue to build the app skeleton now.

Building the app skeleton

At this point, we should be quite expert at building the application's skeleton, since we did a very good job with the NLP web app developed previously. In fact, if you recall, we first defined and built up a simple skeleton containing just a menu with all the functions supposed to be present in the web application and only in a second moment, we implemented those functions one by one. Now we are going to adopt the same approach.

Before building up the skeleton for the *COVID* app, let us just add a couple of other decorations to our app – for example, some text just below the title and an image in the sidebar.

Building the app skeleton   171

The code with the two new lines of code is shown in the following figure:

```python
# Core Pkgs
import streamlit as st
st.set_page_config(page_title="Covid19 Detection Tool", page_icon="covid19.jpeg", layout='centered')

import os
import time

# Viz Pkgs
import cv2
from PIL import Image,ImageEnhance
import numpy as np

# AI Pkgs
import tensorflow as tf

def main():
    """Simple Tool for Covid-19 Detection from Chest X-Ray"""
    html_templ = """
    <div style="background-color:blue;padding:10px;">
    <h1 style="color:yellow">Covid-19 Detection Tool</h1>
    </div>
    """

    st.markdown(html_templ,unsafe_allow_html=True)
    st.write("A simple proposal for Covid-19 Diagnosis powered by Deep Learning and Streamlit")

    st.sidebar.image("covid19.jpeg",width=300)


if __name__ == '__main__':
    main()
```

Figure 8.7: Text below the title and sidebar creation

As we already know, the code in the third line is responsible for the web application configuration, setting the page title (`Covid-19 Detection Tool`), page icon (`covid19.jpeg image`), and page layout (`centered`).

The result produced on the web side is the following:

Figure 8.8: Image in the sidebar and text below the title

Now, let's add to the sidebar a very important widget: `file_uploader`. The instruction we will use is the following:

```
image_file = st.sidebar.file_uploader("Upload an X-Ray Image (jpg, png 
or jpeg)", type=["jpg", "png", "jpeg"])
```

As we can see on the web-side, **File Uploader** is a widget that lets us upload (or even drag and drop) an image, saving it in a variable named, in our case, `image_file`. The first argument is just a label (the text **Upload an...**), while the second argument (`type`) contains a list with the types of files users are enabled to select.

Immediately after `file_uploader`, it's a good idea to insert a check (an `if` clause) just to be sure that an image has been uploaded and, only in this case, to open it (leveraging the `Pillow` library we imported at the beginning).

Once we have the image, and only when the image we uploaded can be opened, we can perform some other actions – for example, an **Image Preview**. This new action can be executed by just nesting another `if` clause inside the previous one. So, finally, our code inside the main function will be as follows:

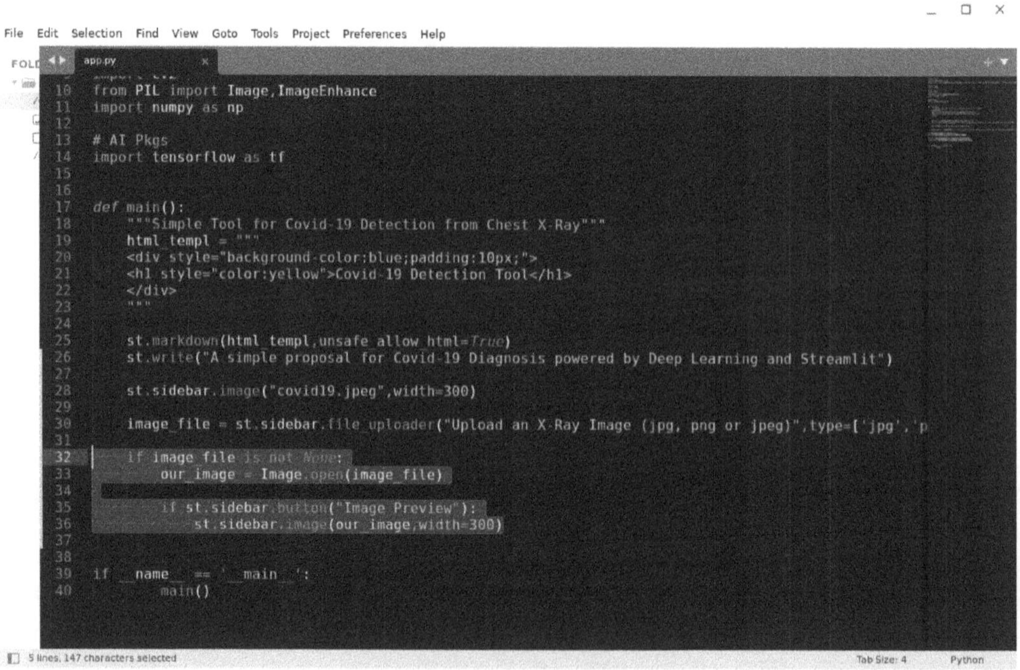

Figure 8.9: How to manage the image

Very easily, we can select an image and when we click on the **Image Preview** button, we can see it on the screen, in the sidebar, as shown in the following figure:

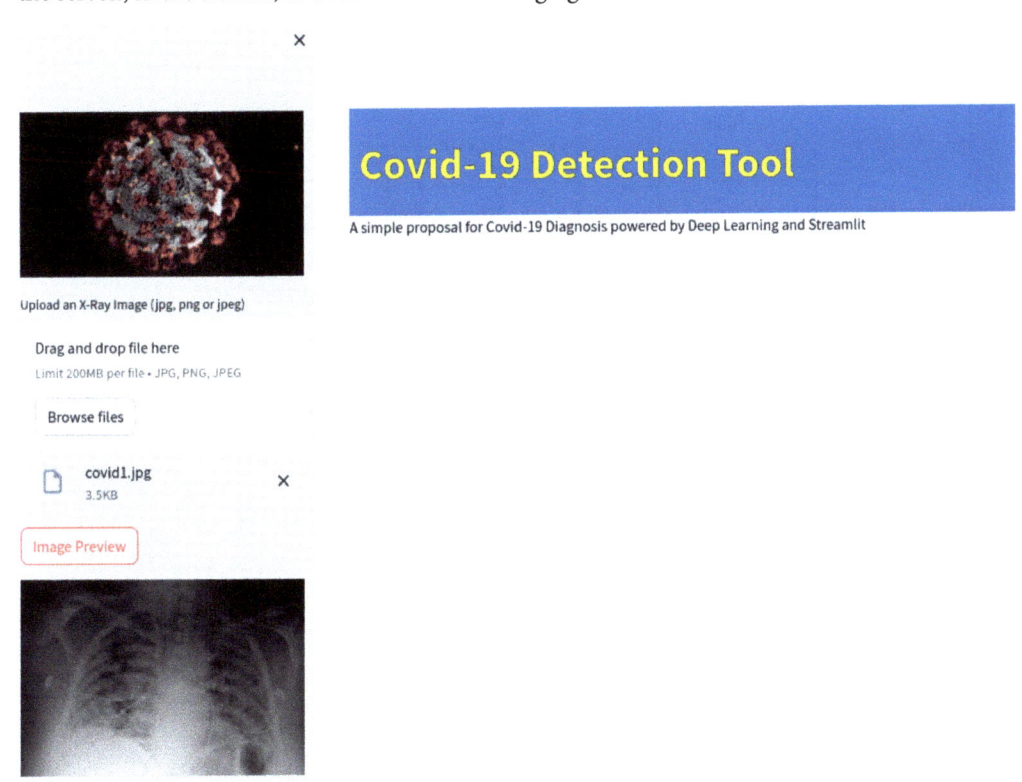

Figure 8.10: Image upload and preview in the sidebar

At this point, we have a complete app skeleton and are able to upload and show an image in the sidebar. We are now ready to build up the menu.

Building the menu and adding decorations

Now, we can add a selectbox in the sidebar, which will be the menu of the web application, and guidelines for its development. This menu will have three voices – **Image Enhance**, **Diagnosis**, and **Disclaimer and Info** – and it will be placed below the second `if` clause, the inner one, because it makes sense only if a valid image has already been uploaded. For sure, after the selectbox, we can place the three options (three `if` clauses) that will contain the code for each one of the menu voices.

We have already built up a menu in the same way in the NLP web application; the code is very easy:

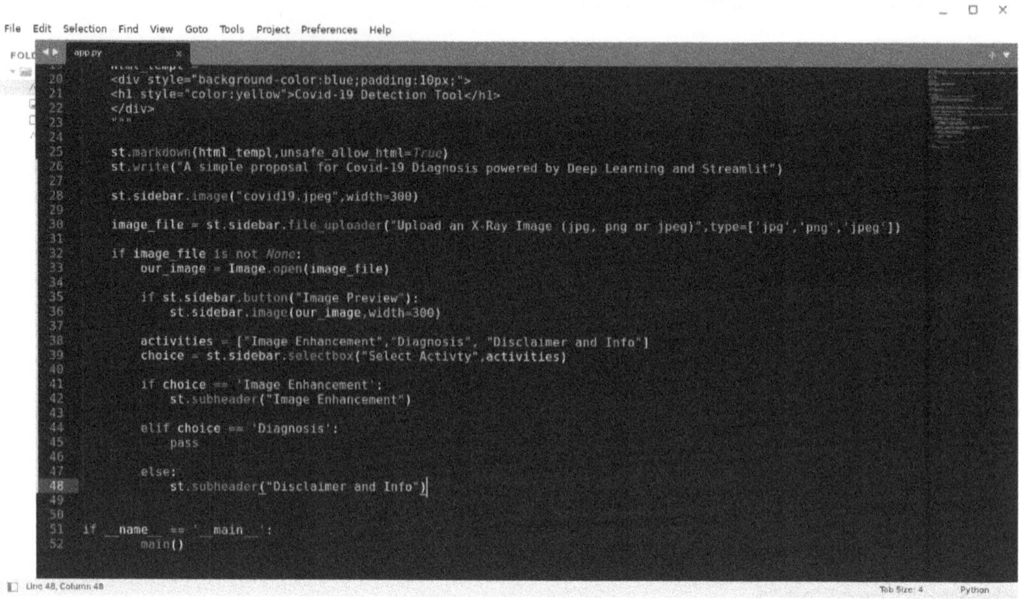
File Edit Selection Find View Goto Tools Project Preferences Help
app.py
20 <div style="background-color:blue;padding:10px;">
21 <h1 style="color:yellow">Covid-19 Detection Tool</h1>
22 </div>
23 """
25 st.markdown(html_templ,unsafe_allow_html=True)
26 st.write("A simple proposal for Covid-19 Diagnosis powered by Deep Learning and Streamlit")
28 st.sidebar.image("covid19.jpeg",width=300)
30 image_file = st.sidebar.file_uploader("Upload an X-Ray Image (jpg, png or jpeg)",type=['jpg','png','jpeg'])
32 if image_file is not None:
33 our_image = Image.open(image_file)
35 if st.sidebar.button("Image Preview"):
36 st.sidebar.image(our_image,width=300)
38 activities = ["Image Enhancement","Diagnosis", "Disclaimer and Info"]
39 choice = st.sidebar.selectbox("Select Activty",activities)
41 if choice == 'Image Enhancement':
42 st.subheader("Image Enhancement")
44 elif choice == 'Diagnosis':
45 pass
47 else:
48 st.subheader("Disclaimer and Info")
51 if __name__ == '__main__':
52 main()
Line 48, Column 48
Tab Size: 4
Python

Figure 8.11: The menu (choice) and its voice sections

Here's what we are doing:

- At *line 38*, we create a list containing all the menu voices
- Then, at *line 39*, we add a selectbox in the sidebar in order to visualize all the items contained in this list.
- After that, from *line 41* up to *line 48*, we double-check which one of menu's voices has been selected and just print the information on the screen – for example, `st.subheader` (**Image Enhancement**) or, in the case of **Diagnosis**, just `pass`.

Building the menu and adding decorations 175

The messages we print with the st.subheader or pass function (it's just a function doing nothing) are simple placeholders and, in the next chapters, we are going to develop the code related to each one of them. Here's how the app's menu looks thus far:

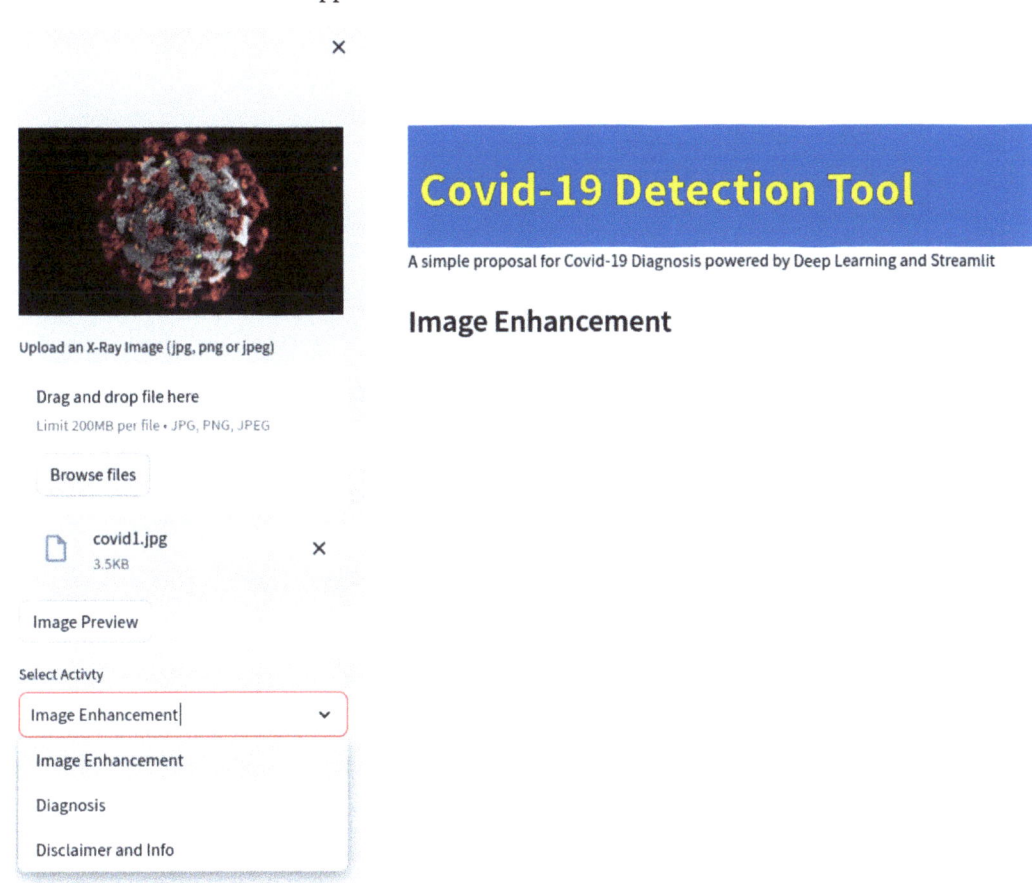

Figure 8.12: The menu in the browser

As a final decoration, before closing the chapter, we can add an **About the Author** button on the sidebar, showing in this way all the information about the author of the web application, the link to their website, their email, and so on. This is the code:

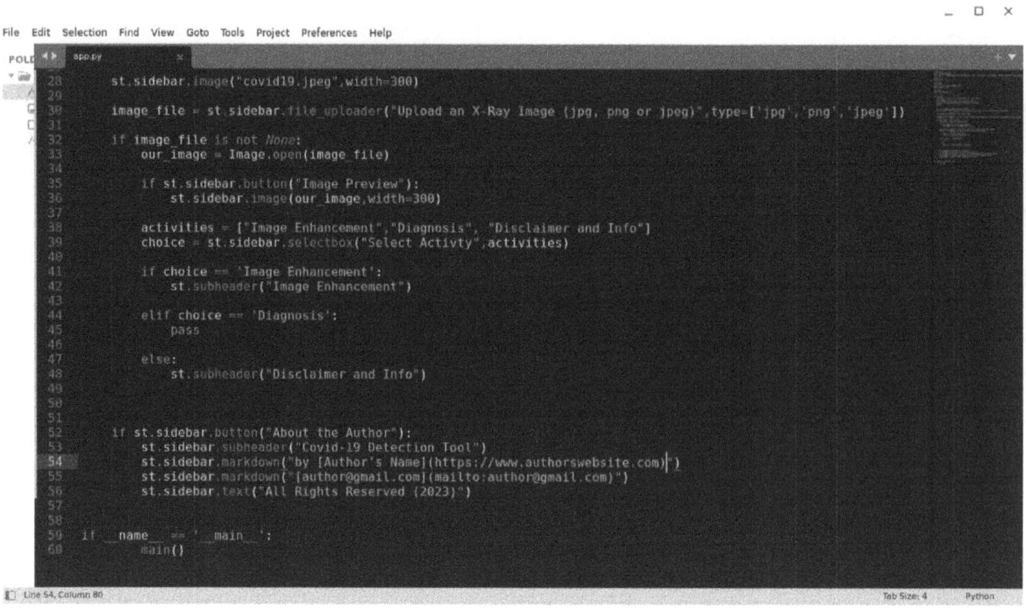

Figure 8.13: About the Author button code

This is the effect in the browser:

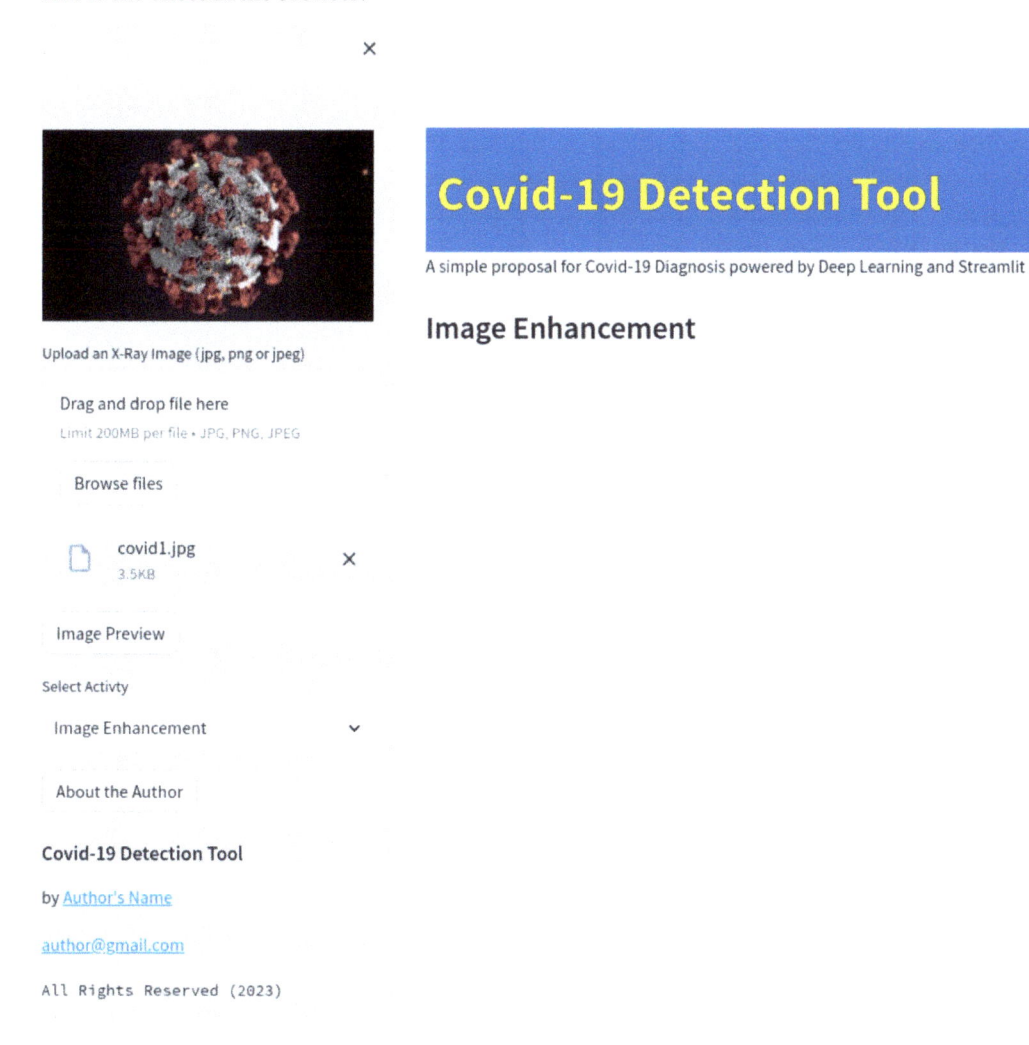

Figure 8.14: About the Author details

In this section, we created the menu for our new web application. Now, in the sidebar, there are several voices, and the user can clearly select what they want to do. This approach is very useful since it can be applied anytime we start working on a new app. On the left side, in the sidebar, we have a menu with the list of all the features available in the web application, and in the main part, we show the title and information and let the user insert data from their case.

Summary

In this chapter, we consolidated our knowledge about virtual environments and package installation. After that, as usual, we started from an empty file and developed the skeleton of our app.

First, we imported all the libraries and created a main function. We also created some nice decorations such as a title in html, a beautiful icon, and a very interesting image in the sidebar. We also discovered how to upload files by filtering their types and, once imported, we learned how to visualize those images thanks to the `Pillow` library.

Another important step was to build up the menu of our app with all its voices and, at the end, we created a button showing all the information about the author, with some linkable elements, such as their website and email address.

Starting from the next chapter, we will focus on developing the three voices of the menu, which,, at the moment, are just empty containers: **Image Enhance**, **Diagnosis**, and **Disclaimer and Info**.

9

Optimizing Streamlit Web App UX with Customization and UI Features

In *Chapter 8*, we started the development of a new web application, *Covid-19 Detection Tool*. We have already created the virtual environment and the application skeleton, together with some basic decorations. It's time now to focus on the three main sections of our new tool: **Image Enhancement**, **Diagnosis**, and **Disclaimer and Info**.

Contrast and **Brightness** are UI elements that allow users to adjust the contrast and brightness of images. These features can help improve the visibility and clarity of the displayed image. Sliders and radio buttons are widgets that allow users to interact with and manipulate data within the web app. Sliders allow users to set a value within a range by dragging a slider button, while radio buttons allow users to select a single option from a group of options. Overall, contrast, brightness, sliders, and radio buttons are powerful UI features that enable us to create very engaging and interactive web applications for COVID-19 detection. In the case of applications that make predictions or forecasts, such as the one we are building together, it's always very important to add a *Disclaimer* in order to not provide any kind of wrong message to the users.

By developing these new features, we have the chance to learn how to use the more advanced techniques and skills of Streamlit.

In this chapter, we're going to cover the following main topics:

- Dealing with more advanced web app features
- Adding the **Image Enhancement** section using the Pillow library
- Adding the **Disclaimer and Info** section

Technical requirements

- In this chapter, we'll use the following libraries, packages, and tools:
  - Sublime Text
  - Python 3
  - `pipenv`
  - Streamlit
  - Pillow
  - `numpy`

- The code in the chapter can be accessed through the following GitHub link: `https://github.com/PacktPublishing/Web-App-Development-Made-Simple-with-Streamlit/tree/f1bd9c354072092c268f27621680c858ce93c823/Chapter09`

Dealing with more advanced web app features

In *Chapter 8*, we stopped our development at the point shown in the following figure:

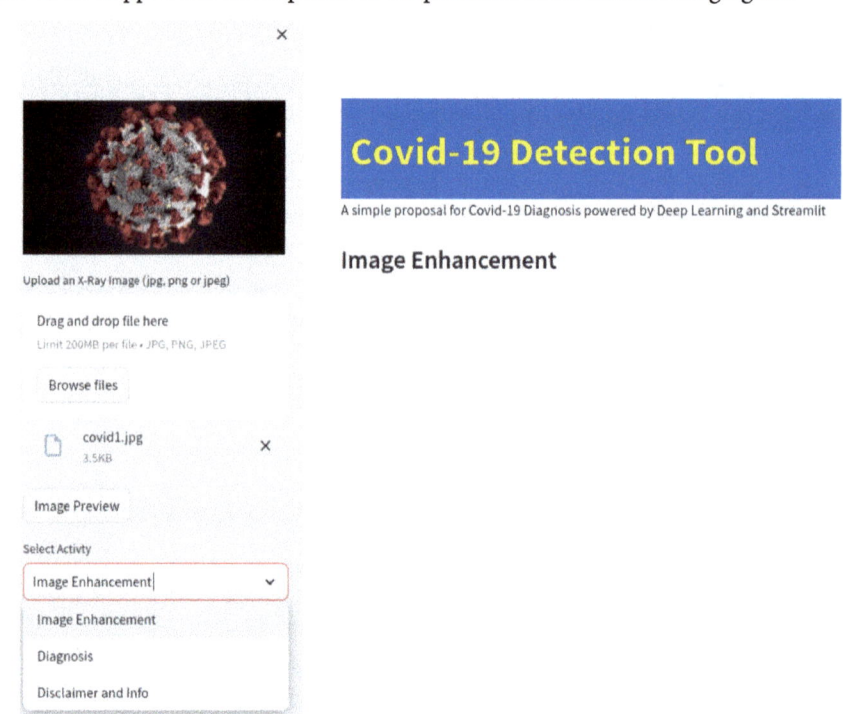

Figure 9.1: Chapter09 starting point

So, let's start working on the menu's three voices: **Image Enhancement**, **Diagnosis**, and **Disclaimer and Info**. Before that, since we are entering some advanced features of Streamlit and considering that new versions are released quite often, it's very important to remember how Streamlit's official documentation (https://docs.streamlit.io/) is always the best place to get detailed info about all the available components and APIs; for example, in case you have any doubts about, let's say, the **Image** widget, you can just search for it in the **API reference** menu on the left side of the official documentation page or directly in the search bar in the top-right corner and check out all the results.

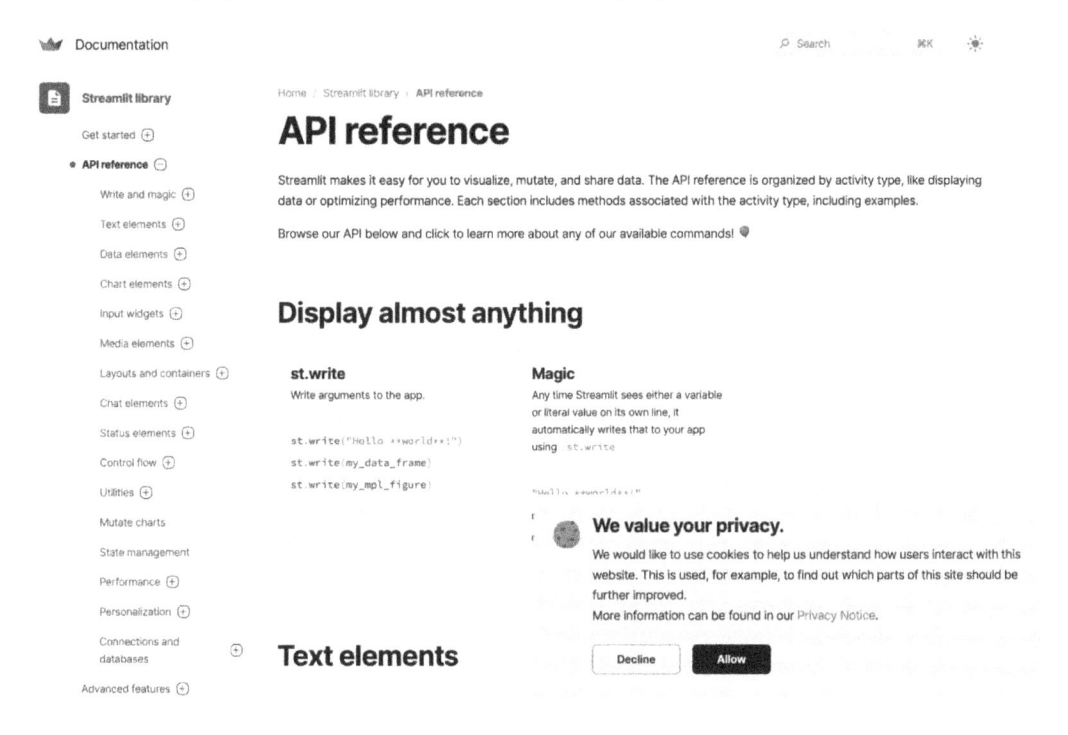

Figure 9.2: Streamlit's official documentation

Let's open our code in Sublime Text and let's continue with our development since, at the moment, we have only an empty menu.

We have already defined a list of voices for our menu, which is called `activities`, and an `if` clause that checks which of these voices has been selected and put in a variable named `choice`; our job now is to write the business logic for each one of these three possibilities:

```python
activities = ["Image Enhancement","Diagnosis", "Disclaimer and Info"]
choice = st.sidebar.selectbox("Select Activty",activities)

if choice == 'Image Enhancement':
    st.subheader("Image Enhancement")

elif choice == 'Diagnosis':
    pass

else:
    st.subheader("Disclaimer and Info")
```

Figure 9.3: The points where the business logic has to be inserted

We know very well that `pass` is just a placeholder, so we can start our coding from the first one of the menu voices: **Image Enhancement**.

Images can be enhanced in many ways – for example, by changing their brightness or contrast. So we can use some radio buttons in the sidebar to give the user the faculty to choose what kind of enhancement they want to perform.

The radio buttons, as we should know, have a couple of mandatory arguments: a label (a title) and a list of all the items that can be selected:

```python
if choice == 'Image Enhancement':
    st.subheader("Image Enhancement")

    enhance_type = st.sidebar.radio("Enhance Type", ["Original", "Contrast", "Brightness"])

elif choice == 'Diagnosis':
```

Figure 9.4: Radio button for Image Enhancement

As usual, the list of items in the radio button contains all the features we want to show on the screen:

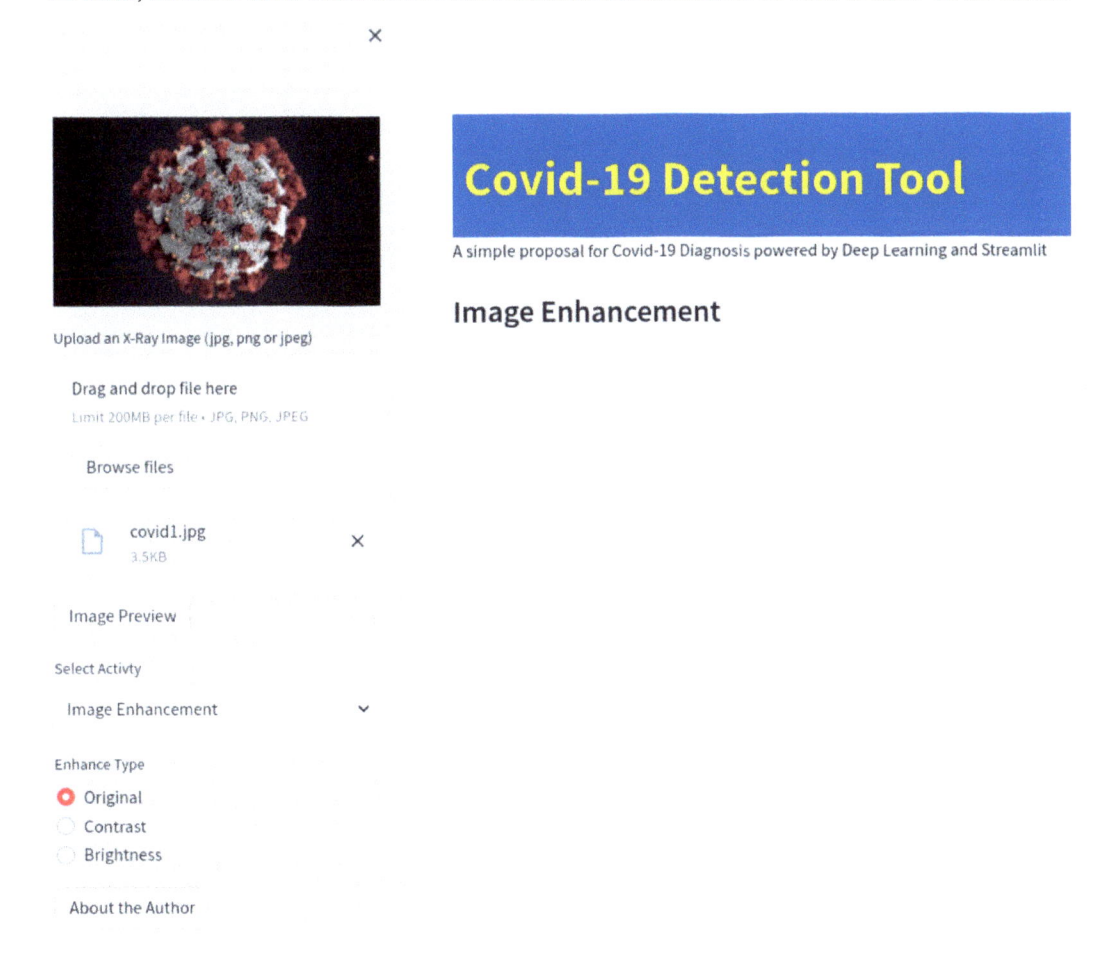

Figure 9.5: Radio button in the browser

It's quite clear that now we need some `if` clauses. This is because if the `enhance_type` variable is `Original`, we need to do something; if it's `Contrast`, we need to do something different, and if it's `Brightness`, we need to do something else:

```
if choice == 'Image Enhancement':
    st.subheader("Image Enhancement")

    enhance_type = st.sidebar.radio("Enhance Type", ["Original", "Contrast", "Brightness"])

    if enhance_type == "Contrast":
        pass

    elif enhance_type == "Brightness":
        pass

    else:
        pass

elif choice == 'Diagnosis':
    pass
```

Figure 9.6: If clauses for "Image Enhancement"

As already said, `pass` is just a placeholder, so let's take care of these `if` clauses one by one. The first one is `Contrast`.

Adding the Image Enhancement section using the Pillow library

Among the libraries we imported at the beginning, there is **Pillow**. It contains a module named `ImageEnhance` that can actually take care of all the features related to any kind of image enhancement for us. This means that we can use the `Contrast` and `Brightness` methods already included in Pillow's `ImageEnhance` module because all the functions we need, and many others, have been already implemented for us.

Pillow, or **Python Imaging Library**, is a very powerful library and it can do more than the things we are showing in this book. For this reason, we suggest taking a look at its official page on PyPI (`https://pypi.org/project/Pillow/`) and reading all the documentation contained there.

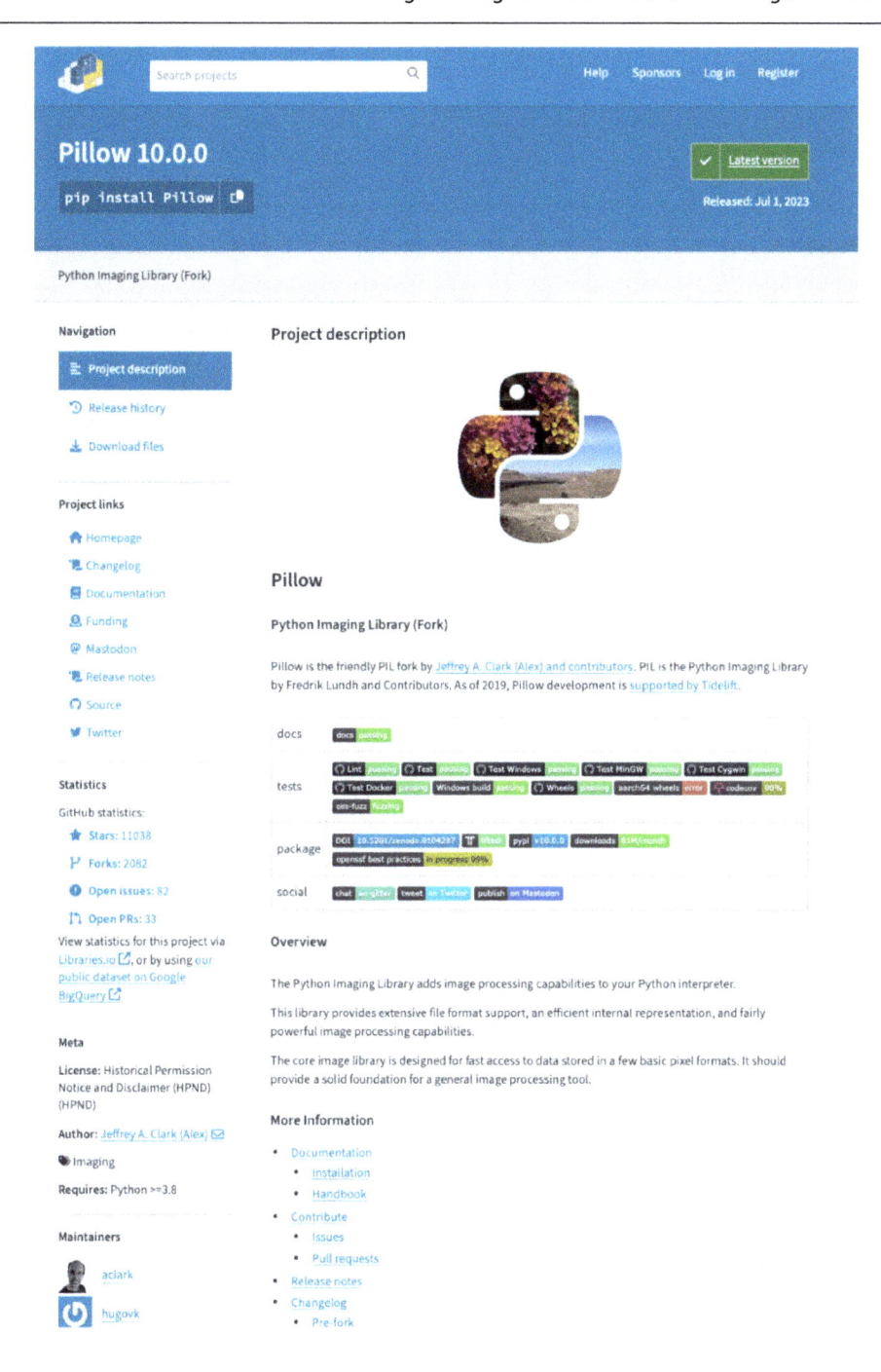

Figure 9.7: The Pillow page on PyPI

Let's start with `Contrast`.

Contrast

As shown in *Figure 9.8*, managing `Contrast` with Pillow's methods is really very simple:

```python
if choice == 'Image Enhancement':
    st.subheader("Image Enhancement")
    
    enhance_type = st.sidebar.radio("Enhance Type", ["Original", "Contrast", "Brightness"])
    
    if enhance_type == "Contrast":
        c_rate = st.slider("Contrast", 0.5, 5.0)
        enhancer = ImageEnhance.Contrast(our_image)
        img_output = enhancer.enhance(c_rate)
        st.image(img_output, width=600, use_column_width=True)
    
    elif enhance_type == "Brightness":
        pass
```

Figure 9.8: The Contrast feature

In the `if` case immediately after the subheader, we start by adding a *slider*. The values on this slider go from `0.5` to `5.0`; you can play with this range to check the different behaviors.

After adding the slider, we need to instantiate an `ImageEnhance.Contrast` object using the image we opened previously (`our_image`) with `file_uploader`. Then, we apply the `enhance` method to this image with the value selected by using the slider.

Finally, the result is printed on the screen thanks to `st.image`, one of Streamlit's classic widgets.

This is the result from the browser's perspective:

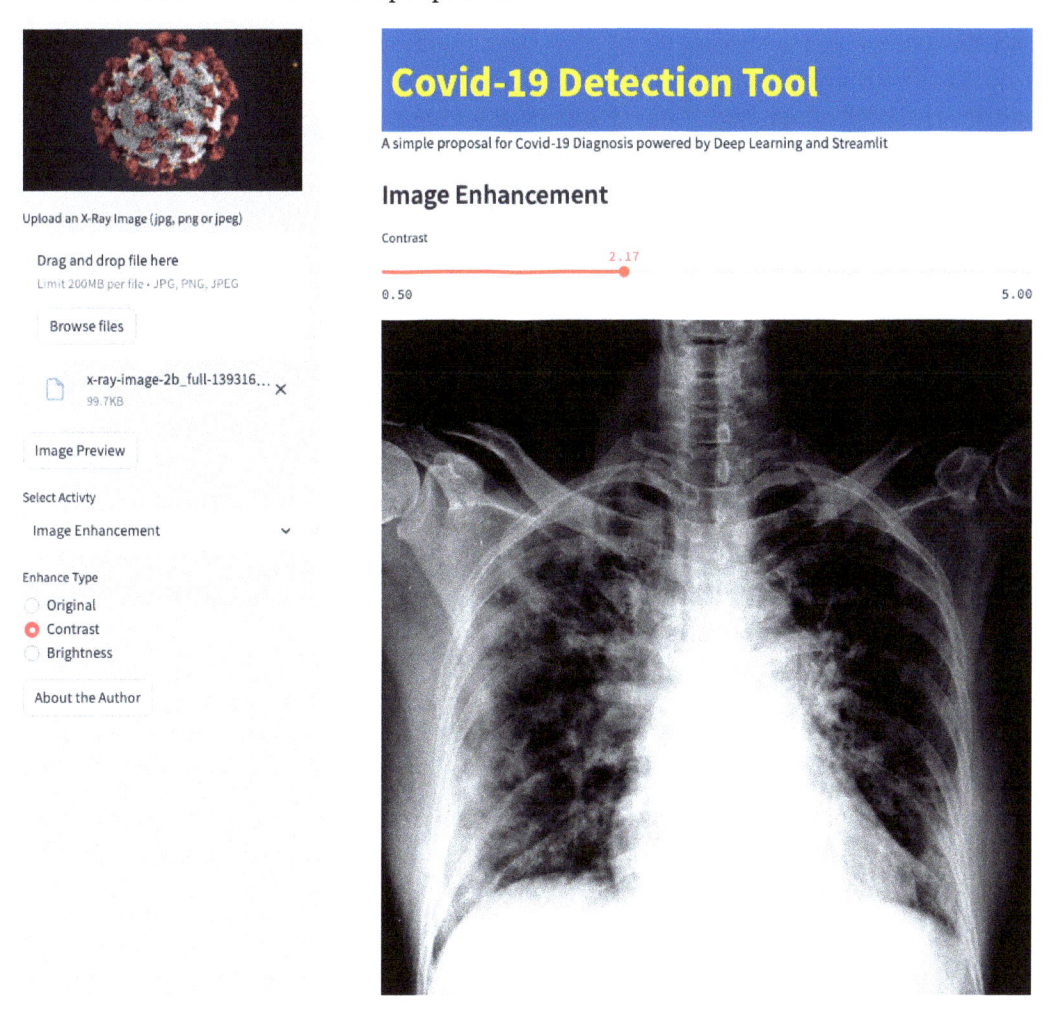

Figure 9.9: The Contrast feature in action

It gives a very nice result, and managing this kind of image enhancement with Pillow is really very easy.

As we just saw, Pillow contains the `Contrast` function out of the box. So, it's quite obvious to imagine that it contains a `Brightness` function as well.

Brightness

In fact, the code we need to write for the `Brightness` feature is more or less the same as that for the `Contrast` feature. We can type the following:

```python
if choice == 'Image Enhancement':
    st.subheader("Image Enhancement")
    
    enhance_type = st.sidebar.radio("Enhance Type", ["Original", "Contrast", "Brightness"])
    
    if enhance_type == "Contrast":
        c_rate = st.slider("Contrast", 0.5, 5.0)
        enhancer = ImageEnhance.Contrast(our_image)
        img_output = enhancer.enhance(c_rate)
        st.image(img_output, width=600, use_column_width=True)
    
    elif enhance_type == "Brightness":
        c_rate = st.slider("Brightness", 0.5, 5.0)
        enhancer = ImageEnhance.Brightness(our_image)
        img_output = enhancer.enhance(c_rate)
        st.image(img_output, width=600, use_column_width=True)
    
    else:
        pass

elif choice == 'Diagnosis':
    pass
```

Figure 9.10: The Brightness feature

The preceding code is exactly the same as the code we wrote for `Contrast`, but this time, we are using the `ImageEnhance.Brightness` method instead of the `ImageEnhance.Contrast` method.

So, once again, we set a value for the brightness using a slider, create an `enhancer` object from the image opened thanks to `file_uploader`, apply the brightness to this image, and print the result on the screen.

This is the result in our web application:

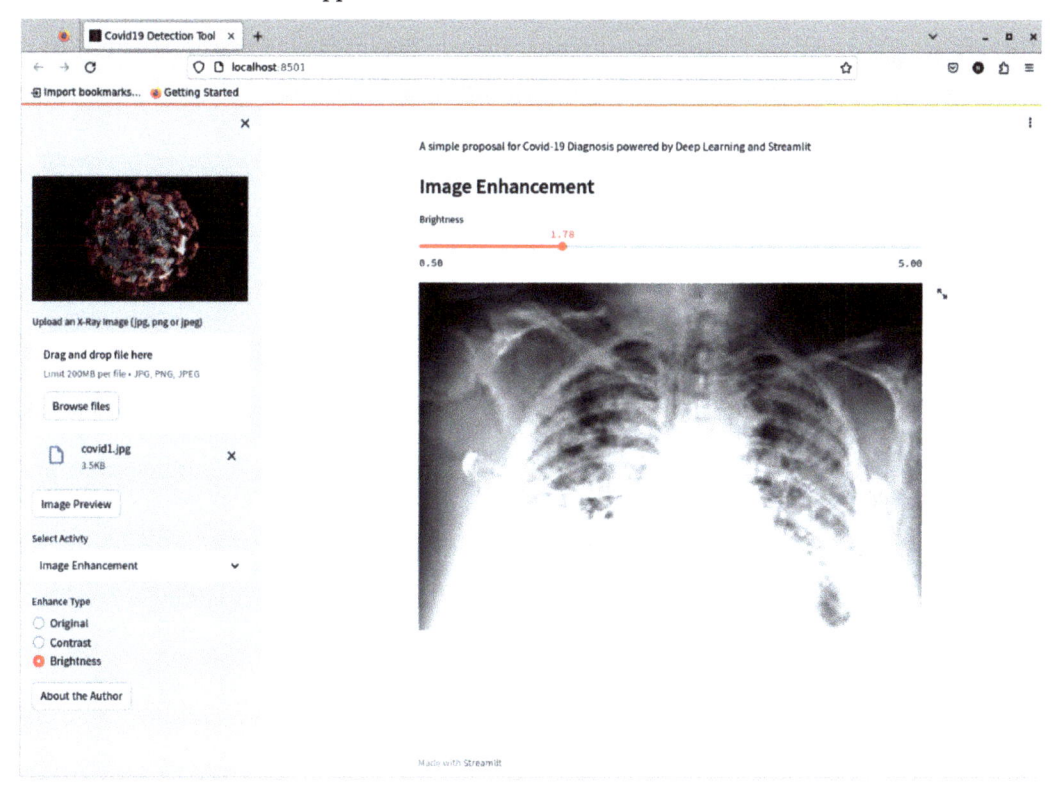

Figure 9.11: The Brightness feature in action

In both cases, `Brightness` and `Contrast`, you can change the strength of the effect by selecting different values using the slider, and if you don't like the outcome, you can always change the range that we set as 0.5 to 5.0.

The final option we can select using the radio button is `Original`.

Original

In the case of the **Original** voice, things are very easy since we don't need sliders and values as in the case of **Brightness** and **Contrast**, and we don't need to modify anything. We just need to get the image we opened with `file_uploader` and show it on the screen. The code is as follows:

```python
if choice == 'Image Enhancement':
    st.subheader("Image Enhancement")

    enhance_type = st.sidebar.radio("Enhance Type", ["Original", "Contrast", "Brightness"])

    if enhance_type == "Contrast":
        c_rate = st.slider("Contrast", 0.5, 5.0)
        enhancer = ImageEnhance.Contrast(our_image)
        img_output = enhancer.enhance(c_rate)
        st.image(img_output, width=600, use_column_width=True)

    elif enhance_type == "Brightness":
        c_rate = st.slider("Brightness", 0.5, 5.0)
        enhancer = ImageEnhance.Brightness(our_image)
        img_output = enhancer.enhance(c_rate)
        st.image(img_output, width=600, use_column_width=True)

    else:
        st.text("Original Image")
        st.image(our_image, width=600, use_column_width=True)

elif choice == 'Diagnosis':
    pass
```

Figure 9.12: The Original Image feature

If you want, you can try to set the `use_column_width` argument in `st.image` to `False` and check the result, or, if you prefer, you can specify a width size different from `600`.

This is the effect in the browser:

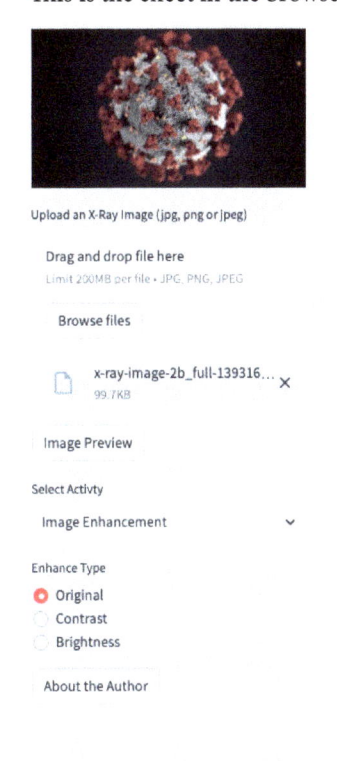

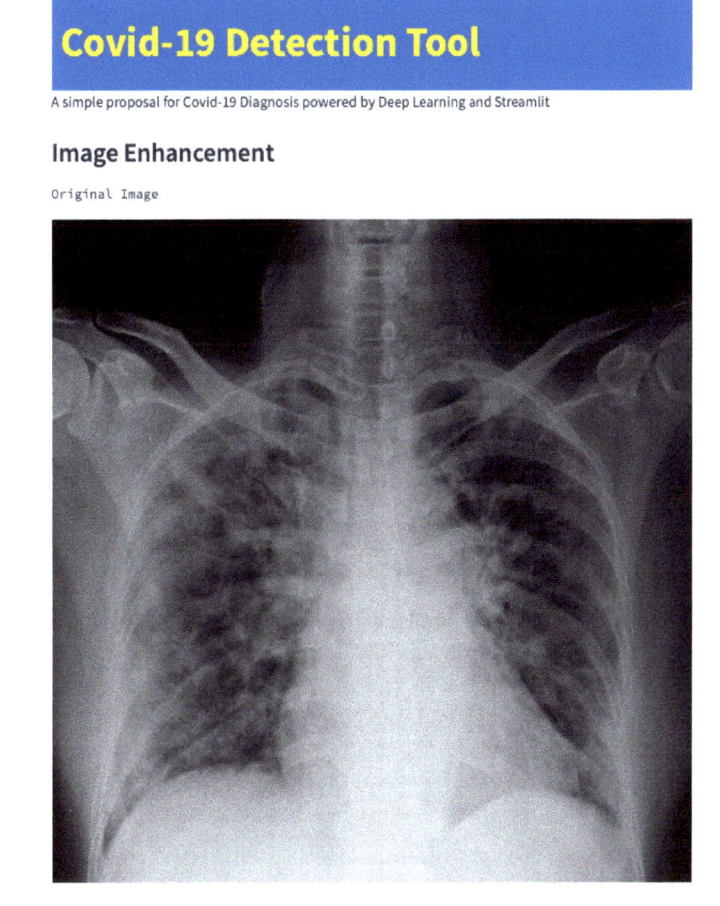

Figure 9.13: The Original Image feature in action

With the **Original** image feature, we can consider the **Image Enhancement** voice of the menu completed. Thanks to the Pillow library, we could implement all features of this voice in a very smooth way. This is one of the best aspects of Python, and you can always find a nice package that already has all the features you need!

Let's move on to the **Disclaimer and Info** section. The **Diagnosis** section is a little bit more complex, so we will leave that for the next chapter.

Adding the Disclaimer and Info section

Dealing with applications that provide predictions, especially health predictions, can be a little bit dangerous, so a good practice is to write down a disclaimer to avoid any kind of misunderstanding.

The disclaimer of this web application, named **Disclaimer and Info**, also serves the function of providing some information about the model used to predict COVID-19 from images and about the dataset that was used to train that model.

In short, the main purpose of the disclaimer is to clarify that the application is just a demo of Streamlit's capabilities and doesn't have any value from a medical point of view. Additionally, the disclaimer also contains some information about the AI model used to make the predictions.

In *Chapter 10*, we will see that every time we need to make predictions, a good strategy is to use a machine learning model.

In particular, the model used in our web application is a so-called **convolutional neural network (CNN)** developed using the library named `tensorflow` and using a dataset comprising 206 images of affected people and 206 images of healthy individuals.

> **Additional information**
>
> CNNs are particular neural network architectures that perform very well with problems related to images, such as image classification. What we want to do with this application is precisely the classification of images, specifically X-ray images of the chest, to discover whether or not they show cases of COVID-19. Discovering whether or not a given image represents a COVID-19 case is a classic problem of binary classification, which means understanding whether something is true or false. CNNs are very good classifiers for this type of task. However, for better performance, they need a large number of images, so a big dataset is required to train these models.
>
> The CNN we used performs quite well, even if it was trained with a limited number of images. The model performs well when classifying images representing COVID-19 cases and healthy individuals, but its predictive performance is poor for images representing SARS cases (SARS is rather close to Covid-19).

The disclaimer has to be inserted in the `else` part of the `if` clause related to the menu, as shown in the following figure:

```
elif choice == 'Diagnosis':
    pass

else:
    st.subheader("Disclaimer and Info")
```

Figure 9.14: The insertion point of the disclaimer

We can decide to write this disclaimer in many ways, but a very easy one is just to use some `st.write` objects. In this way, we can have very clear, well-presented, formatted text, and we can add links to some websites that can be used as references. We are using the **Markdown** syntax, so it's possible to use bold, italics, bullet points, lists, and so on.

> **Note**
> The websites linked in the text are real websites that inspired the author to create this tool during the first COVID-19 lockdown. If you want to check them out, they are quite interesting!

Here is the code we can use to add the disclaimer:

```
else:
    st.subheader("Disclaimer and Info")
    st.subheader("Disclaimer")
    st.write("**This Tool is just a DEMO about Artificial Neural Networks so there is no clinical value in its diagno
    st.write("**Please don't take the diagnosis outcome seriously and NEVER consider it valid!!!**")
    st.subheader("Info")
    st.write("This Tool gets inspiration from the following works:")
    st.write("- [Detecting COVID-19 in X-ray images with Keras, TensorFlow, and Deep Learning](https://www.pyimagesea
    st.write("- [Fighting Corona Virus with Artificial Intelligence & Deep Learning](https://www.youtube.com/watch?v=
    st.write("- [Deep Learning per la Diagnosi del COVID-19](https://www.youtube.com/watch?v=dpa8TFg1H_U&t=114s)")
    st.write("We used 206 Posterior-Anterior (PA) X-Ray [images](https://github.com/ieee8023/covid-chestxray-dataset/
    st.write("Since dataset was quite small, some data augmentation techniques have been applied (rotation and bright
    st.write("Unfortunately in our test we got 5 cases of 'False Negative', patients classified as healthy that actua
    st.write("The model is suffering of some limitations:")
    st.write("- small dataset (a bigger dataset for sure will help in improving performance)")
    st.write("- images coming only from the PA position")
    st.write("- a fine tuning activity is strongly suggested")
    st.write("")
    st.write("Anybody has interest in this project can drop me an email and I'll be very happy to reply and help.")
```

Figure 9.15: The code used for the Disclaimer section

Actually, this code is just a proposal. You don't need to copy it in your version of the *COVID-19 Detection Tool* web application. You can modify it as you like, and if you decide to use another model to make the predictions (nowadays, it's quite easy to find several pretrained models online, for example, `https://ieeexplore.ieee.org/document/9340145` or `https://www.nature.com/articles/s41598-023-33685-z`), you can insert the information about your own version and your new model, together with an explanation about its performances and accuracy.

Here's the **Disclaimer** section for my version of the app:

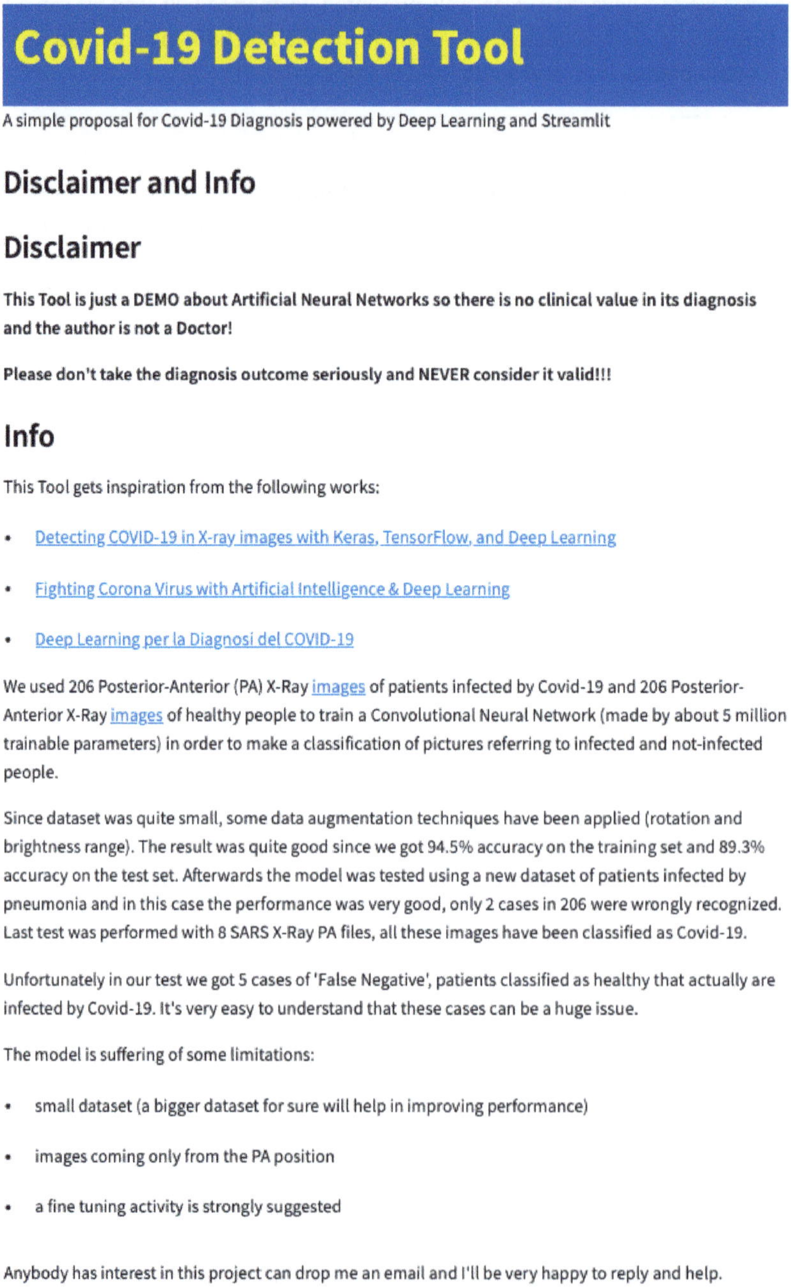

Covid-19 Detection Tool

A simple proposal for Covid-19 Diagnosis powered by Deep Learning and Streamlit

Disclaimer and Info

Disclaimer

This Tool is just a DEMO about Artificial Neural Networks so there is no clinical value in its diagnosis and the author is not a Doctor!

Please don't take the diagnosis outcome seriously and NEVER consider it valid!!!

Info

This Tool gets inspiration from the following works:

- Detecting COVID-19 in X-ray images with Keras, TensorFlow, and Deep Learning

- Fighting Corona Virus with Artificial Intelligence & Deep Learning

- Deep Learning per la Diagnosi del COVID-19

We used 206 Posterior-Anterior (PA) X-Ray images of patients infected by Covid-19 and 206 Posterior-Anterior X-Ray images of healthy people to train a Convolutional Neural Network (made by about 5 million trainable parameters) in order to make a classification of pictures referring to infected and not-infected people.

Since dataset was quite small, some data augmentation techniques have been applied (rotation and brightness range). The result was quite good since we got 94.5% accuracy on the training set and 89.3% accuracy on the test set. Afterwards the model was tested using a new dataset of patients infected by pneumonia and in this case the performance was very good, only 2 cases in 206 were wrongly recognized. Last test was performed with 8 SARS X-Ray PA files, all these images have been classified as Covid-19.

Unfortunately in our test we got 5 cases of 'False Negative', patients classified as healthy that actually are infected by Covid-19. It's very easy to understand that these cases can be a huge issue.

The model is suffering of some limitations:

- small dataset (a bigger dataset for sure will help in improving performance)

- images coming only from the PA position

- a fine tuning activity is strongly suggested

Anybody has interest in this project can drop me an email and I'll be very happy to reply and help.

Figure 9.16: The disclaimer in the browser

Adding the Disclaimer and Info section   195

The result is very clean and neat because we used headers, bold, lists with bullet points, and hyperlinks to external websites.

As usual, let's print the code we have implemented up to now in order to be sure that everything for our web application is written correctly without mistakes:

```
# Core Pkgs
import streamlit as st
st.set_page_config(page_title="Covid19 Detection Tool", page_icon="covid19.jpeg", layout='centered', initial_sidebar_state='auto')

import os
import time

# Viz Pkgs
import cv2
from PIL import Image,ImageEnhance
import numpy as np

# AI Pkgs
import tensorflow as tf


def main():
    """Simple Tool for Covid-19 Detection from Chest X-Ray"""
    html_templ = """
    <div style="background-color:blue;padding:10px;">
    <h1 style="color:yellow">Covid-19 Detection Tool</h1>
    </div>
    """

    st.markdown(html_templ,unsafe_allow_html=True)
    st.write("A simple proposal for Covid-19 Diagnosis powered by Deep Learning and Streamlit")

    st.sidebar.image("covid19.jpeg",width=300)

    image_file = st.sidebar.file_uploader("Upload an X-Ray Image (jpg, png or jpeg)",type=['jpg','png','jpeg'])

    if image_file is not None:
        our_image = Image.open(image_file)

        if st.sidebar.button("Image Preview"):
            st.sidebar.image(our_image,width=300)

        activities = ["Image Enhancement","Diagnosis", "Disclaimer and Info"]
        choice = st.sidebar.selectbox("Select Activty",activities)

        if choice == 'Image Enhancement':
            st.subheader("Image Enhancement")

            enhance_type = st.sidebar.radio("Enhance Type",["Original","Contrast","Brightness"])

            if enhance_type == "Contrast":
                c_rate = st.slider("Contrast",0.5,5.0)
                enhancer = ImageEnhance.Contrast(our_image)
                img_output = enhancer.enhance(c_rate)
                st.image(img_output,width=600,use_column_width=True)
```

Figure 9.17: The first part of the code

To recap, in *Figure 9.17*, we have the first part of the code, where we import all the relevant libraries, set up the page title and icon, define the `main` function, and inside it, we put an image in the sidebar together with the menu of the app.

This menu contains three voices: **Image Enhancement**, **Diagnosis**, and **Disclaimer and Info**. Inside **Image Enhancement**, we can select between three options: **Original**, **Contrast**, and **Brightness**.

```
        elif enhance_type == "Brightness":
            c_rate = st.slider("Brightness", 0.5, 5.0)
            enhancer = ImageEnhance.Brightness(our_image)
            img_output = enhancer.enhance(c_rate)
            st.image(img_output, width=600, use_column_width=True)

        else:
            st.text("Original Image")
            st.image(our_image, width=600, use_column_width=True)


    elif choice == 'Diagnosis':
        pass

    else:
        st.subheader("Disclaimer and Info")
        st.subheader("Disclaimer")
        st.write("**This Tool is just a DEMO about Artificial Neural Networks so there is no clinical value in its diagnosis and the author is not
        st.write("**Please don't take the diagnosis outcome seriously and NEVER consider it valid!!!**")
        st.subheader("Info")
        st.write("This Tool gets inspiration from the following works:")
        st.write("- [Detecting COVID-19 in X-ray images with Keras, TensorFlow, and Deep Learning](https://www.pyimagesearch.com/2020/03/16/detecti
        st.write("- [Fighting Corona Virus with Artificial Intelligence & Deep Learning](https://www.youtube.com/watch?v=_bDHOwASVS4)")
        st.write("- [Deep Learning per la Diagnosi del COVID-19](https://www.youtube.com/watch?v=dpa8TFg1H_U&t=114s)")
        st.write("We used 206 Posterior-Anterior (PA) X-Ray [images](https://github.com/ieee8023/covid-chestxray-dataset/blob/master/metadata.csv)
        st.write("Since dataset was quite small, some data augmentation techniques have been applied (rotation and brightness range). The result wa
        st.write("Unfortunately in our test we got 5 cases of 'False Negative', patients classified as healthy that actually are infected by Covid-
        st.write("The model is suffering of some limitations:")
        st.write("- small dataset (a bigger dataset for sure will help in improving performance)")
        st.write("- images coming only from the PA position")
        st.write("- a fine tuning activity is strongly suggested")
        st.write("")
        st.write("Anybody has interest in this project can drop me an email and I'll be very happy to reply and help.")



    if st.sidebar.button("About the Author"):
        st.sidebar.subheader("Covid-19 Detection Tool")
        st.sidebar.markdown("by [Author's Name](https://www.authorswebsite.com)")
        st.sidebar.markdown("[author@gmail.com](mailto:author@gmail.com)")
        st.sidebar.text("All Rights Reserved (2023)")


if __name__ == '__main__':
    main()
```

Figure 9.18: The second part of the code

In the second part of the code, shown in *Figure 9.18*, we complete the **Disclaimer and Info** and **About the Author** sections, while we leave the **Diagnosis** part blank for now.

Summary

In this chapter, we have completed two of the three voices composing the menu of our *COVID-19 Detection Tool* web application.

To deal with the **Image Enhancement** voice, we leveraged the Pillow library, which is a very powerful library that makes it possible to manage some quite powerful functions, such as image contrast and brightness, with very few lines of code.

We also created multiple selections for the user, adopting radio buttons and `if` clauses. Radio buttons are a very clean and powerful way to propose selections, and there is no way to put any kind of ambiguity in the process.

Using sliders in combination with image visualization is a powerful tool to adjust various parameters, such as contrast and brightness. Sliders provide the user with the ability to precisely and continuously select the desired value for any given parameter.

Another important trick to underline is that every time we modified images (for example, to perform brightness adjustments), we worked on their copies and not on the original image. In this way, it was quite simple to move back to the original situation just showing the image that was loaded thanks to `file_uploader`.

We also learned how well-formatted text that leverages the Markdown syntax can be full of information to the user – for example, to show the technologies used and the sources and documents of inspiration. For sure, this clean and nicely formatted text is the perfect way to create disclaimers to avoid any future problems.

In the next chapter, we will learn how to integrate artificial intelligence and machine learning models into our web applications.

10
Utilizing Pretrained Models to Create Specialized and Personalized Web Applications

So far, we have used Streamlit's components and libraries, made in Python, to create and build up our web application. However, with Streamlit, we can do even more.

This incredible framework is extremely powerful when used with **artificial intelligence** (**AI**) models to make predictions. Developing **machine learning** (**ML**) models or neural networks is something very complex and outside the scope of this book, but considering that there are a lot of pretrained models available that perform well to provide solutions for many different use cases, knowing how to use them in our web application to increase their effectiveness and usefulness is something very important.

Simply put, importing and using pretrained ML models in Streamlit is an advanced technique for creating very powerful web applications. Users can import any kind of pretrained model and use it to make predictions on new data within their Streamlit web apps. This opens a world of new, more customized, and specialized applications tailored to any kind of specific needs.

In this chapter, we'll cover the following main topics:

- Understanding the benefits of pretrained ML models
- Creating customized web apps to improve user experience
- Utilizing predictions from ML

Technical requirements

- In this chapter, we will be using the following libraries, packages, and tools:
  - Sublime Text
  - Python 3
  - `pipenv`
  - Streamlit
  - OpenCV
  - Pillow
  - `numpy`
  - `tensorflow`

- The code for this chapter can be found in this book's GitHub repository: https://github.com/PacktPublishing/Web-App-Development-Made-Simple-with-Streamlit/tree/7c29f4eca8b189b4f711cc8f724c6dee9dba60ab/Chapter10.

Understanding the benefits of pretrained ML models

In this short section, I will try to clarify why using pretrained ML models inside our web applications can be a very good and valuable idea.

ML has rapidly evolved in recent years, offering unprecedented opportunities to enhance web applications with intelligent and predictive features. Streamlit, a popular Python library for creating interactive web applications, has gained immense popularity due to its simplicity and flexibility. When combined with pretrained ML models, Streamlit can empower developers to build web applications that leverage the vast potential of AI.

Pretrained ML models are models that have been trained on large datasets for various tasks, such as image recognition, natural language processing, and more. These models have learned rich data representations and can be fine-tuned for specific applications. Incorporating pretrained models into Streamlit web applications can significantly enhance their capabilities and provide a seamless user experience.

Here are some of the key benefits associated with using pretrained AI models:

- **Efficient development**: One of the primary benefits of using pretrained models is the reduction in development time. Instead of starting from scratch and training a model from the ground up, developers can leverage existing pretrained models, saving both time and resources. Streamlit's straightforward interface complements this efficiency by enabling developers to quickly integrate these models into their applications.

- **Improved user experience**: Pretrained models bring state-of-the-art capabilities to web applications, enabling features such as image recognition, sentiment analysis, and language translation. Users can interact with the application more naturally, making it more engaging and user-friendly. For example, a product recommendation system powered by a pretrained model can enhance the shopping experience on an e-commerce website built with Streamlit.
- **Scalability and performance**: Pretrained models are often designed to handle complex tasks, making them suitable for a wide range of applications. Streamlit's ability to efficiently serve web applications makes it a perfect companion for pretrained models. Whether it's processing large datasets or performing real-time predictions, the combination of Streamlit and pretrained models ensures high scalability and performance.
- **Customization and fine-tuning**: While pretrained models provide a solid foundation, developers can fine-tune these models to adapt them to specific requirements. Streamlit's flexibility allows for the easy integration of customized models and tailored user interfaces. This combination empowers developers to create unique and highly specialized applications.

The potential applications of pretrained ML models within Streamlit-based web applications are vast and diverse. Here are some examples:

- **Healthcare**: Streamlit applications can utilize pretrained models for medical image analysis, disease diagnosis, and patient risk prediction, providing valuable tools for healthcare professionals
- **E-commerce**: Recommender systems powered by pretrained models can enhance product discovery, boosting sales and user satisfaction
- **Natural language processing**: Sentiment analysis, chatbots, and language translation can improve user interactions in various applications, from customer support to social media platforms
- **Finance**: Fraud detection, credit scoring, and stock market prediction can benefit from the predictive power of pretrained models, helping businesses make informed decisions

To summarize, the fusion of pretrained ML models and Streamlit-based web applications represents a promising frontier in the world of AI-driven development. This synergy allows developers to create intelligent and interactive web applications quickly and efficiently. As technology advances, this combination's potential applications are limited only by our imagination. By harnessing the power of pretrained models within Streamlit, we can deliver cutting-edge solutions that transform the way we interact with web applications, making them smarter, more engaging, and more useful to users across various domains.

Creating customized web apps to improve user experience

Now, it's time to complete our *Covid-19 Detection Tool* web application. So far, we have implemented several features, such as **Image Enhancement** and **Disclaimer and Info**, but we are still missing the **Diagnosis** section. *Figure 10.1* shows what we have completed so far:

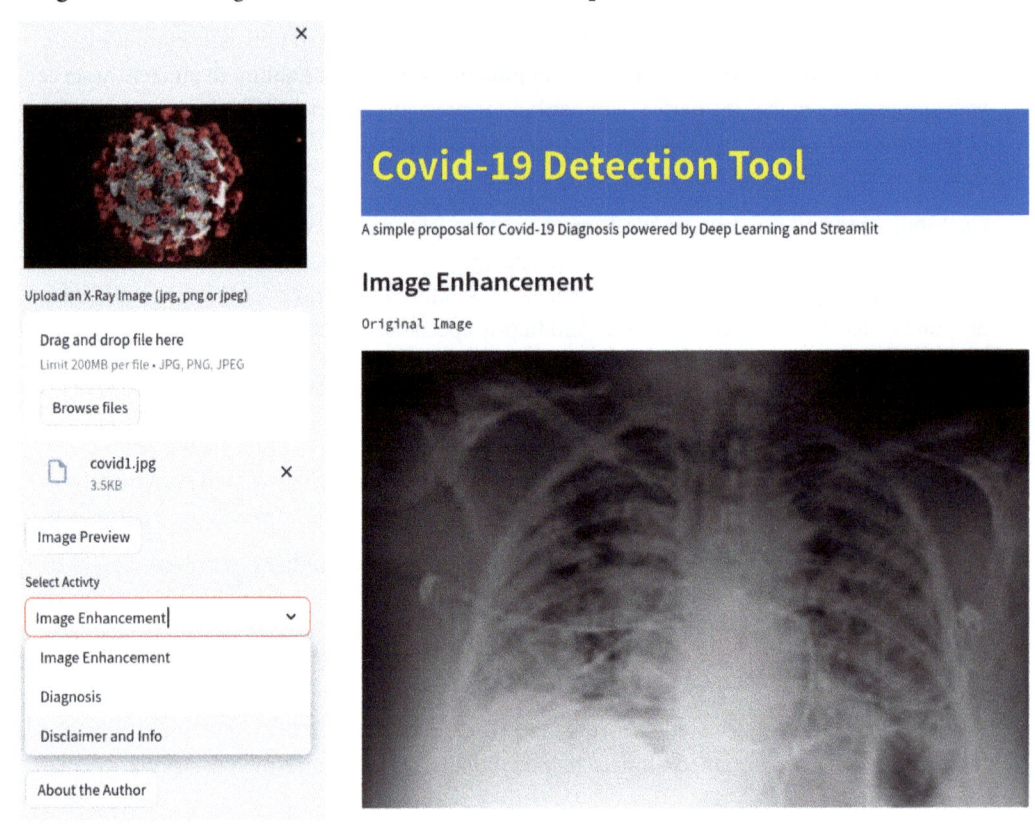

Figure 10.1: The Covid-19 Detection Tool web app we've developed so far

As I mentioned in *Chapter 9*, the task of **Diagnosis** is to understand from a picture, specifically from an X-ray of the chest, whether or not a patient has Covid-19.

This kind of prediction can be performed using a pretrained AI model, which in our case is a **convolutional neural network** (**CNN**). A CNN is a neural network with a peculiar structure or shape that performs very well regarding tasks related to computer vision. **Computer vision**, in a few words, means to make computers understand what's going on with a picture, its content, the objects represented inside it, and so on.

So, let's see how it is possible to use a pretrained AI model inside Streamlit to perform, in this case, a computer vision task, but more generally, a prediction.

We need to start from the point where we stopped in *Chapter 9*: the `if` clause related to the **Diagnosis** voice of the menu, as shown in the following figure:

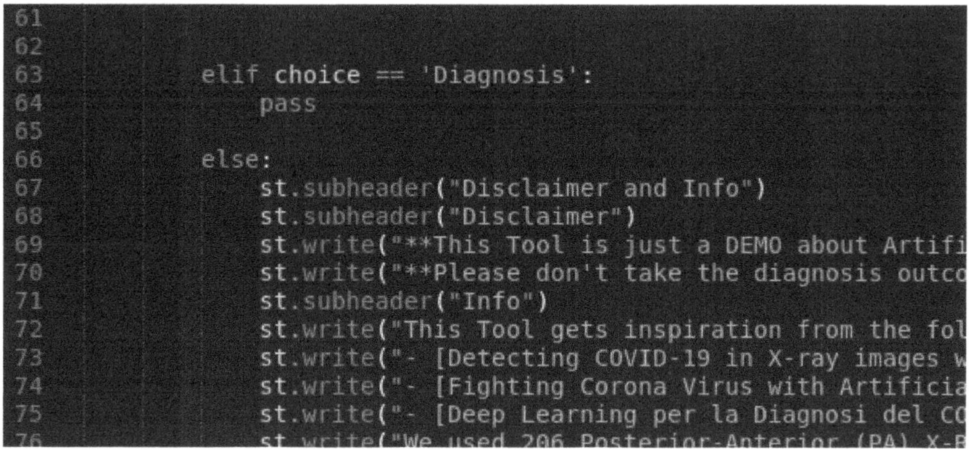

```
elif choice == 'Diagnosis':
    pass

else:
    st.subheader("Disclaimer and Info")
    st.subheader("Disclaimer")
    st.write("**This Tool is just a DEMO about Artifi
    st.write("**Please don't take the diagnosis outco
    st.subheader("Info")
    st.write("This Tool gets inspiration from the fol
    st.write("- [Detecting COVID-19 in X-ray images w
    st.write("- [Fighting Corona Virus with Artificia
    st.write("- [Deep Learning per la Diagnosi del CO
    st.write("We used 206 Posterior-Anterior (PA) X-R
```

Figure 10.2: The "Diagnosis" voice of the menu

The first step is to add a button in the sidebar. In this way, when the user clicks on this button (its label will be **Diagnosis**), the tool will perform a binary classification while leveraging the pretrained model to predict whether or not the X-ray image represents a case of Covid-19.

Adding the button, as we know, is very easy – it's just a matter of typing the following immediately after `choice=='Diagnosis'`:

```
if st.sidebar.button('Diagnosis'):
```

The CNN we are going to use was trained with black and white images. So, first of all, when the user clicks on the **Diagnosis** button, the X-ray image must be converted into a black and white image. However, the image – the original X-ray image before the black and white transformation – must be converted into an array (because this is the format we need to manipulate images). We are lucky since this operation is very simple when using `numpy`, a library that we've already imported. The three lines of code we need are as follows:

```
new_img = np.array(our_image.convert('RGB'))
new_img = cv2.cvtColor(new_img, 1) #0 is original, 1 is grayscale
Gray = cv2.cvtColor(new_img, cv2.COLOR_BGR2GRAY)
```

The code in the first line changes the image into an array, the second line converts the image into a grayscale domain, and the final one converts it into a pure black and white image. Please note that we are leveraging `cv2`, the Python library for computer vision that was imported at the beginning of the file.

This black and white image is saved in a variable named `gray`.

> **Note**
>
> Studying the several Python packages we are importing and using is outside the scope of this book; however, having a look at the `cv2` (OpenCV) official website https://opencv.org/) can be a very interesting activity.

After converting the uploaded image, we are ready to write some text on the screen (`"Chest X-Ray"`) to give our operation some context and print the black and white image:

```
st.text("Chest X-Ray")
st.image(gray, width=400, use_column_width= True)
```

Here's the code we've added so far:

```
        elif choice == 'Diagnosis':
            if st.sidebar.button("Diagnosis"):
                new_img = np.array(our_image.convert('RGB')) #our image is converted into an array
                new_img = cv2.cvtColor(new_img,1) #0 is original, 1 is grayscale
                gray = cv2.cvtColor(new_img, cv2.COLOR_BGR2GRAY)
                st.text("Chest X-Ray")
                st.image(gray, width=400, use_column_width=True)

        else:
            st.subheader("Disclaimer and Info")
```

Figure 10.3: The code we've added to the Diagnosis menu

From the browser's point of view, you should get something like this:

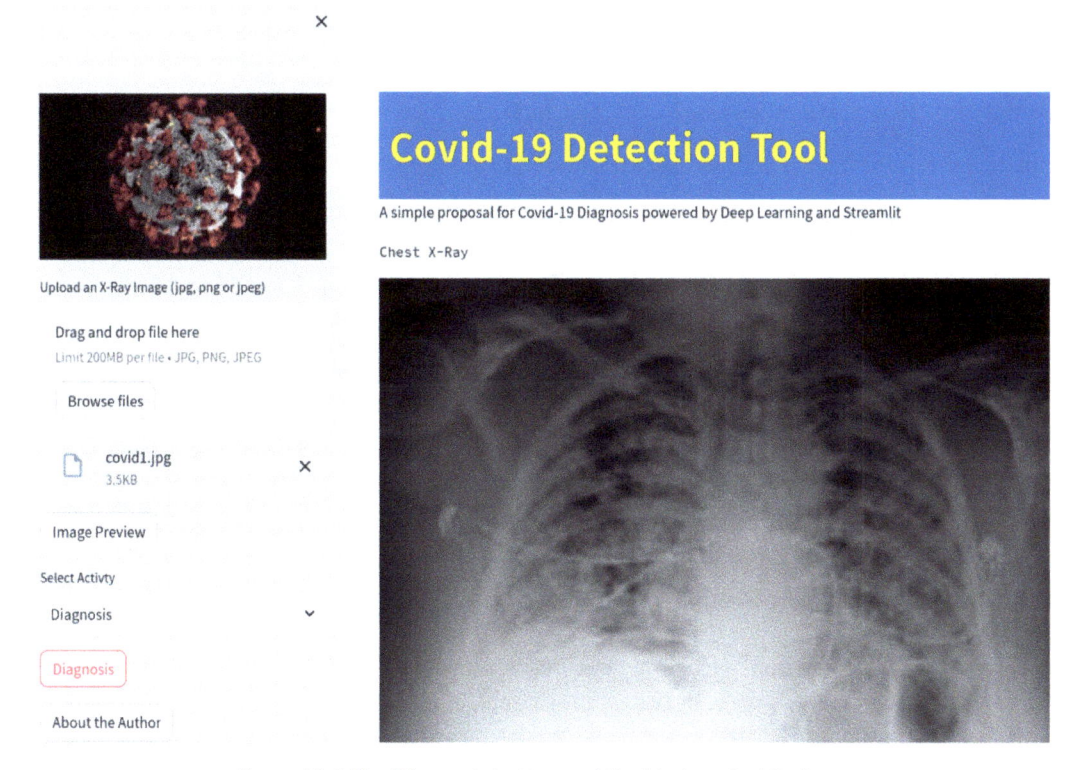

Figure 10.4: The Diagnosis button and the black and white image

Since the CNN was trained with black and white images in a specific format in terms of size and values, before performing the prediction, we must pre-process the image we are interested in to get the same format that the neural network is expecting.

The neural network was trained with images that had a size of 200 pixels by 200 pixels and their values went from 0 up to 1, where 0 was black and 1 was white.

The code we need to write to make sure the image we uploaded will be in the format needed by the neural network is as follows:

```
IMG_SIZE = (200, 200)
img = cv2.equalizeHist(gray)
img = cv2.resize(img, IMG_SIZE)
img = img/255 #normalization
```

The first line is just an image size definition that is saved in a constant. The second line performs image equalization, an operation that potentially increases the clarity of our image. The third line resizes the image according to the `IMG_SIZE` dimension saved in the constant, and the final instruction normalizes the image (usually, the values of gray tones go from 0 (black) to 255 (white); dividing everything by 255, we have values from 0 to 1, which are black and white, respectively).

Figure 10.5 shows the lines of code we just explained:

```
elif choice == 'Diagnosis':
    if st.sidebar.button("Diagnosis"):
        new_img = np.array(our_image.convert('RGB')) #our image is converted into an array
        new_img = cv2.cvtColor(new_img,1) #0 is original, 1 is grayscale
        gray = cv2.cvtColor(new_img, cv2.COLOR_BGR2GRAY)
        st.text("Chest X-Ray")
        st.image(gray, width=400, use_column_width=True)

        #X-Ray Imge Pre-processing
        IMG_SIZE = (200, 200)
        img = cv2.equalizeHist(gray)
        img = cv2.resize(img, IMG_SIZE)
        img = img/255 #normalization

else:
    st.subheader("Disclaimer and Info")
```

Figure 10.5: Pre-processing the X-ray image

The library we are using to manage neural networks is named `tensorflow` and it requires the images in a precise format (n,m,p,q), where n, m, p, and q are integers. Unfortunately, the shape of our image is only (200,200). So, before we use it for prediction, we must resize it; this is the instruction we should use:

```
X_Ray = img.reshape(1, 200, 200, 1)
```

By processing the image in this way, we have a very good input for ML classifiers. We'll learn how to deal with this task in the next section.

Utilizing predictions from ML

At this point, everything is ready. Now, to be able to perform predictions about Covid-19 from an X-ray image, we need to load our pretrained model (available in this chapter's GitHub repository; the link can be found in the *Technical requirements* section) and use it with the uploaded picture (pre-processed according to the code we wrote in the *Creating customized web apps to improve user experience* section). As explained in the *Understanding the benefits of pretrained ML models* section, using a pretrained model is an easy and fast way to solve a problem without spending time developing an AI model by ourselves. In our specific case, we can predict the presence of Covid-19 from an image just by loading and using a model developed and made available by others.

Let's start writing:

```
model = tf.keras.models.load_model("./models/Covid19_CNN_Classifier.h5")
```

In the preceding code, `tf` is the alias of `tensorflow`, and `keras` is a module inside it. So, we just pass to the `load_model` method the path to our pretrained model (please note that the file type of `tensorflow` models is `h5`) and save it into a variable named `model`. Please note that the pretrained CNN was put in a directory named `models`, so if you changed its position, please update the path in the code accordingly.

This is the code we've implemented so far:

```
elif choice == 'Diagnosis':
    if st.sidebar.button("Diagnosis"):
        new_img = np.array(our_image.convert('RGB')) #our image is converted into an array
        new_img = cv2.cvtColor(new_img,1) #0 is original, 1 is grayscale
        gray = cv2.cvtColor(new_img, cv2.COLOR_BGR2GRAY)
        st.text("Chest X-Ray")
        st.image(gray, width=400, use_column_width=True)

        #X-Ray Imge Pre-processing
        IMG_SIZE = (200, 200)
        img = cv2.equalizeHist(gray)
        img = cv2.resize(img, IMG_SIZE)
        img = img/255 #normalization

        # Image reshaping according to tensorflow format
        X_Ray = img.reshape(1, 200, 200, 1)

        #Pre-trained CNN Model loading
        model = tf.keras.models.load_model("./models/Covid19_CNN_Classifier.h5")

    else:
```

Figure 10.6: Image reshaping and model loading

Our model variable has a method named `predict` that returns the probability of the prediction in a list containing two elements: the probability of no Covid and the probability of Covid. Since we are performing a binary classification (true or false, so no Covid or Covid) we want to know whether or not the picture represents a case of Covid; we can do this using the `argmax` method of `np` (`numpy`). `argmax` checks the values of a list and provides the index of the maximum value, which in our case is 0 or 1 (0 in the case of no Covid and 1 in the case of Covid). So, if the prediction result is a list such as [0.70, 0.30], `argmax` will return 0; the first index starts from 0 (because 0.70 is greater than 0.30), which means that the diagnosis is no Covid since the probability of no Covid is 70%, while the probability of Covid is 30%.

To complete the **Diagnosis** voice of the menu, we can add the following code:

```
diagnosis_proba = model.predict(X_Ray)
diagnosis = np.argmax(diagnosis_proba, axis=1)
```

Here is the code we implemented:

```
elif choice == 'Diagnosis':
    if st.sidebar.button("Diagnosis"):
        new_img = np.array(our_image.convert('RGB')) #our image is converted into an array
        new_img = cv2.cvtColor(new_img,1) #0 is original, 1 is grayscale
        gray = cv2.cvtColor(new_img, cv2.COLOR_BGR2GRAY)
        st.text("Chest X-Ray")
        st.image(gray, width=400, use_column_width=True)

        #X-Ray Imge Pre-processing
        IMG_SIZE = (200, 200)
        img = cv2.equalizeHist(gray)
        img = cv2.resize(img, IMG_SIZE)
        img = img/255 #normalization

        # Image reshaping according to tensorflow format
        X_Ray = img.reshape(1, 200, 200, 1)

        #Pre-trained CNN Model loading
        model = tf.keras.models.load_model("./models/Covid19_CNN_Classifier.h5")

        #Diagnosis (Prediction== Binary Classification)
        diagnosis_proba = model.predict(X_Ray)
        diagnosis = np.argmax(diagnosis_proba,axis=1)
```

Figure 10.7: How we get the prediction

At this point, we have everything we need to display the result on the screen.

Now, as the first frontend element, we must create a progress bar in the sidebar that indicates the status of the diagnosis prediction. For this, we can write the following:

```
my_bar = st.sidebar.progress(0)
```

A progress bar always works with a timer, so we should *import time* at the very beginning of our Python file. This is the reason we did this when we started this project (see *Figure 8.4* in *Chapter 8*). Let's continue by adding the following code:

```
for percent_complete in range(100):
    time.sleep(0.05)
    my_bar.progress(percent_complete + 1)
```

In this way, we create a `for` loop that sleeps for `0.05` seconds and then activates the progress bar, extending it by `1` unit (the progress bar was instantiated with a value of 0), repeating this operation `100` times since our progress bar's range goes from 0 up to `100` units.

This progress bar indicates that the prediction is ongoing until it reaches its maximum value and stops extending.

When the progress bar is completely extended, we can print the diagnosis on the screen, explaining what kind of prediction we are dealing with. For this, we can type the following:

```
if diagnosis == 0:
st.sidebar.success("DIAGNOSIS: NO COVID-19")
else:
st.sidebar.error ("DIAGNOSIS: COVID-19")
```

This is the code we added for the frontend part – that is, the part that is visualized in the browser:

```
elif choice == 'Diagnosis':
    if st.sidebar.button("Diagnosis"):
        new_img = np.array(our_image.convert('RGB')) #our image is converted into an array
        new_img = cv2.cvtColor(new_img,1) #0 is original, 1 is grayscale
        gray = cv2.cvtColor(new_img, cv2.COLOR_BGR2GRAY)
        st.text("Chest X-Ray")
        st.image(gray, width=400, use_column_width=True)

        #X-Ray Imge Pre-processing
        IMG_SIZE = (200, 200)
        img = cv2.equalizeHist(gray)
        img = cv2.resize(img, IMG_SIZE)
        img = img/255 #normalization

        # Image reshaping according to tensorflow format
        X_Ray = img.reshape(1, 200, 200, 1)

        #Pre-trained CNN Model loading
        model = tf.keras.models.load_model("./models/Covid19_CNN_Classifier.h5")

        #Diagnosis (Prediction== Binary Classification)
        diagnosis_proba = model.predict(X_Ray)
        diagnosis = np.argmax(diagnosis_proba,axis=1)

        my_bar = st.sidebar.progress(0)

        for percent_complete in range(100):
            time.sleep(0.05)
            my_bar.progress(percent_complete + 1)

        #Diagnosis Cases: No-Covid=0, Covid=1
        if diagnosis == 0:
            st.sidebar.success("DIAGNOSIS: NO COVID-19")
        else:
            st.sidebar.error("DIAGNOSIS: COVID-19")
```

Figure 10.8: How we get the prediction and visualize it on the screen

210   Utilizing Pretrained Models to Create Specialized and Personalized Web Applications

This is the result in the browser in the case of a no Covid prediction:

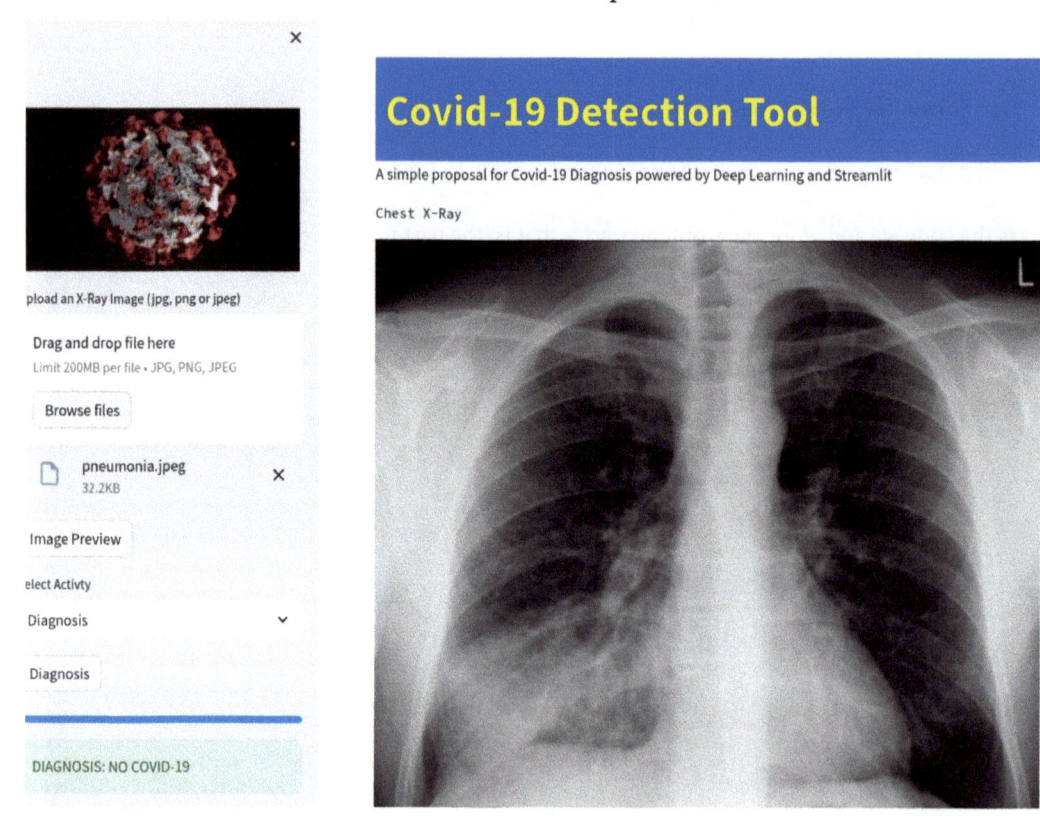

Figure 10.9: No Covid diagnosis

Since the model we are using to perform the prediction is just a *toy model* and there is no clinical value in the diagnosis that's made using it, it's better to add a final disclaimer to our application.

Let's add something like this:

```
st.warning("This Web App is just a DEMO about Streamlit and Artificial
Intelligence and there is no clinical value in its diagnosis!")
```

Our final code for the **Diagnosis** voice of the menu is as follows:

Figure 10.10: Complete code for the "Diagnosis" voice of the menu

And this is the disclaimer on the browser:

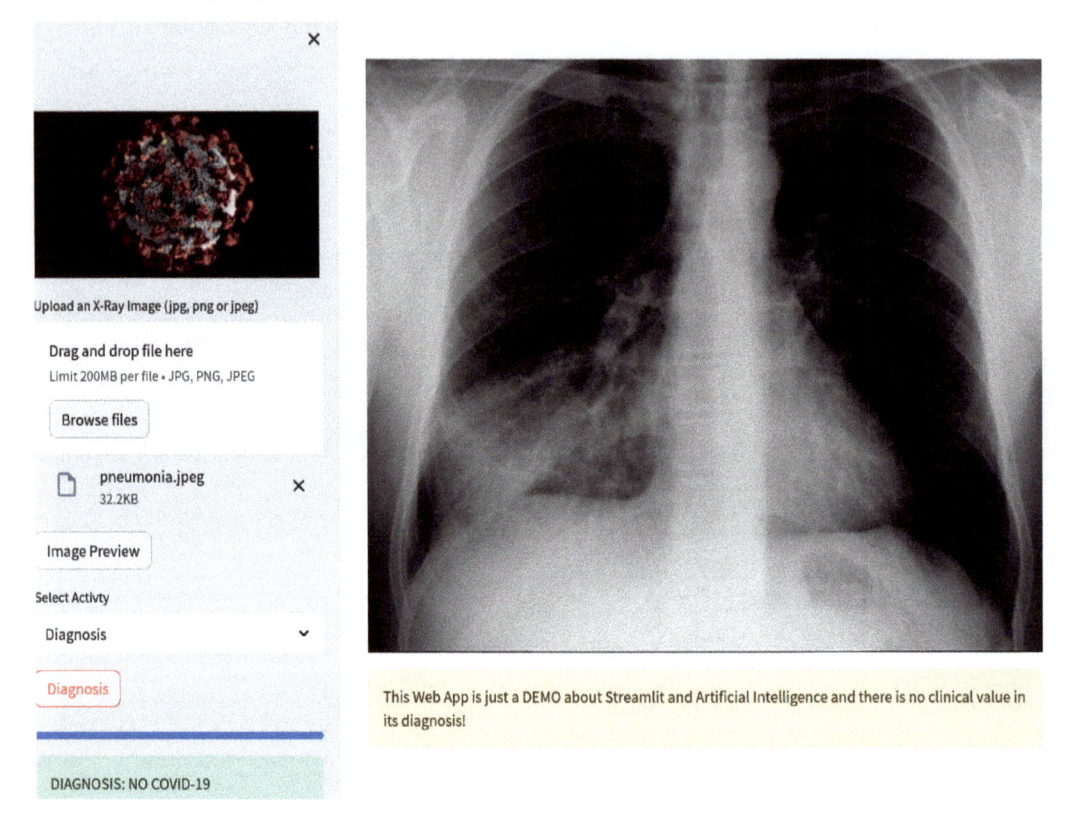

Figure 10.11: Prediction with the disclaimer

Please remember that the point here is not to get a very well-performing model to predict cases of Covid-19 but to understand how to integrate AI models inside Streamlit.

Let's dive deeper into what we achieved in this chapter.

First of all, in addition to `tensorflow`, as in the case of our web application, AI models can be trained with other packages such as `scikit-learn`. Due to this, it's very important that before loading the model into your Streamlit web application, you carefully read the documentation of the specific package that was used to train the model. Different packages usually adopt different syntaxes to load their models. This means that according to the model you decide to adopt, you must use a different syntax in your code.

The second and most important point is that the web application we just implemented is quite powerful since it performs several complex tasks, such as image enhancements, diagnosis, and more. Even though it's complex, when we count the lines of code we wrote down, we will see that from the very beginning to the end, we wrote just about 130 lines of Python, comments included. This is the real power of Python and Streamlit together. In a few lines of code, we implemented a web application that performs several complex tasks, even leveraging AI. On top of that, we have all the typical widgets that are typically included in very professional applications, such as different kinds of text, buttons, progress bars, and more.

As usual, and considering that this time the code is even more complex, here are some screenshots of the complete transcript of the web application we just completed:

```
# Core Pkgs
import streamlit as st
st.set_page_config(page_title="Covid19 Detection Tool", page_icon="covid19.jpeg", layout='centered', initial_sidebar_state='auto')

import os
import time

# Viz Pkgs
import cv2
from PIL import Image,ImageEnhance
import numpy as np

# AI Pkgs
import tensorflow as tf


def main():
    """Simple Tool for Covid-19 Detection from Chest X-Ray"""
    html_templ = """
    <div style="background-color:blue;padding:10px;">
    <h1 style="color:yellow">Covid-19 Detection Tool</h1>
    </div>
    """

    st.markdown(html_templ,unsafe_allow_html=True)
    st.write("A simple proposal for Covid-19 Diagnosis powered by Deep Learning and Streamlit")

    st.sidebar.image("covid19.jpeg",width=300)

    image_file = st.sidebar.file_uploader("Upload an X-Ray Image (jpg, png or jpeg)",type=['jpg','png','jpeg'])

    if image_file is not None:
        our_image = Image.open(image_file)

        if st.sidebar.button("Image Preview"):
            st.sidebar.image(our_image,width=300)

        activities = ["Image Enhancement","Diagnosis", "Disclaimer and Info"]
        choice = st.sidebar.selectbox("Select Activty",activities)

        if choice == 'Image Enhancement':
            st.subheader("Image Enhancement")

            enhance_type = st.sidebar.radio("Enhance Type",["Original","Contrast","Brightness"])

            if enhance_type == "Contrast":
                c_rate = st.slider("Contrast",0.5,5.0)
                enhancer = ImageEnhance.Contrast(our_image)
                img_output = enhancer.enhance(c_rate)
                st.image(img_output,width=600,use_column_width=True)
```

Figure 10.12: Part 1 of the Covid-19 Detection Tool web app

First, we imported the libraries and defined the main function. The main function starts by creating a beautiful title and then continues with the presence of a `file_uploader` widget. After that, there is a menu containing three voices – **Image Enhancement**, **Diagnosis**, and **Disclaimer and Info**:

```
       st.image(img_output, width=600, use_column_width=True)

    elif enhance_type == "Brightness":
        c_rate = st.slider("Brightness", 0.5, 5.0)
        enhancer = ImageEnhance.Brightness(our_image)
        img_output = enhancer.enhance(c_rate)
        st.image(img_output, width=600, use_column_width=True)

    else:
        st.text("Original Image")
        st.image(our_image, width=600, use_column_width=True)

elif choice == 'Diagnosis':
    if st.sidebar.button("Diagnosis"):
        new_img = np.array(our_image.convert('RGB')) #our image is converted into an array
        new_img = cv2.cvtColor(new_img,1) #0 is original, 1 is grayscale
        gray = cv2.cvtColor(new_img, cv2.COLOR_BGR2GRAY)
        st.text("Chest X-Ray")
        st.image(gray, width=400, use_column_width=True)

        #X-Ray Imge Pre-processing
        IMG_SIZE = (200, 200)
        img = cv2.equalizeHist(gray)
        img = cv2.resize(img, IMG_SIZE)
        img = img/255 #normalization

        # Image reshaping according to tensorflow format
        X_Ray = img.reshape(1, 200, 200, 1)

        #Pre-trained CNN Model loading
        model = tf.keras.models.load_model("./models/Covid19_CNN_Classifier.h5")

        #Diagnosis (Prediction== Binary Classification)
        diagnosis_proba = model.predict(X_Ray)
        diagnosis = np.argmax(diagnosis_proba,axis=1)

        my_bar = st.sidebar.progress(0)

        for percent_complete in range(100):
            time.sleep(0.05)
            my_bar.progress(percent_complete + 1)

        #Diagnosis Cases: No-Covid=0, Covid=1
        if diagnosis == 0:
            st.sidebar.success("DIAGNOSIS: NO COVID-19")
        else:
            st.sidebar.error("DIAGNOSIS: COVID-19")

        st.warning("This Web App is just a DEMO about Streamlit and Artificial Intelligence and there is no clinical valu
```

Figure 10.13: Part 2 of the Covid-19 Detection Tool web app

Then, we mainly dealt with the **Image Enhancement** feature and completed the **Diagnosis** part. In this part, we pre-processed the image, prepared it for the ML model, loaded the classification model and a pretrained CNN, executed the prediction, and introduced some nice widgets, such as the progress bar:

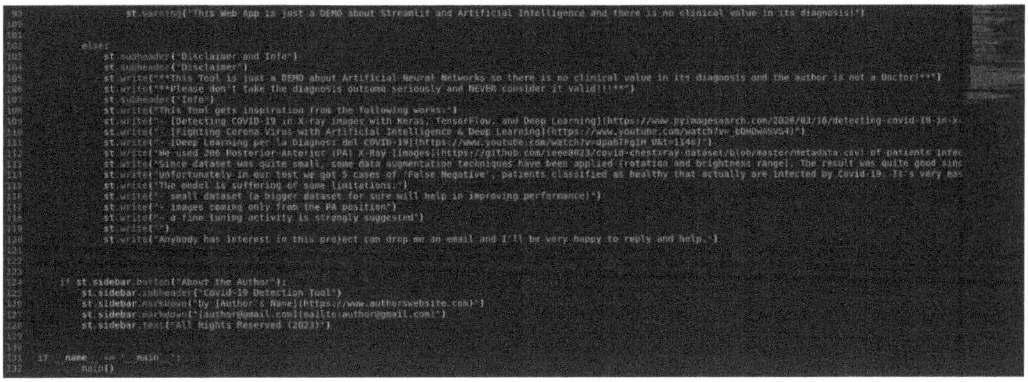

Figure 10.14: Part 3 of the Covid-19 Detection Tool web app

Finally, we just suggested simple text for the **Disclaimer and Info** section and created the **About the Author** information page.

Summary

This chapter was very important since we learned how to integrate AI into our web applications.

AI is a highly disruptive technology that can completely change the game when managed and leveraged properly in our applications. In this chapter, we learned that it is possible to include AI models developed and trained separately in Streamlit. Several packages and tools can create AI models, and almost all these models can be included in Streamlit; it's only a matter of checking the proper documentation and following the rules.

Loading AI models into our web applications is only one part of the process since each model needs to be fed information in a specific format. For this reason, all the data we provide as input to the model that we decide to use must be pre-processed so that it's compliant with that specific format. This is the reason why we spent a good amount of our time manipulating and transforming the image of the X-ray we uploaded in a format that's compatible with the CNN model we used. The uploaded image was converted into black and white, then resized and reshaped.

Having the input in the proper format is extremely important; otherwise, the model will not understand what to do and will generate a runtime error. After pre-processing the image, we focused on the prediction; we learned how to perform predictions and interpret them. Finally, we covered the frontend part and took care of visualizing the predictions in the web browser using beautiful effects such as the progress bar. We observed that when dealing with sensitive topics such as health, it's good practice to include a disclaimer to avoid potential issues.

Having a working application is a very good starting point but it is not the real conclusion of our job. As we already did with the natural language processing web application, we still have to deploy our new tool to the cloud because only with deployment is it possible to build a well-done and well-performing application available to a very wide customer base. This is exactly what we are going to do in the next chapter.

11
Deploying and Managing Complex Libraries on Streamlit Share

Let's continue our exploration of deployment on Streamlit Share, a service provided by the Streamlit framework that allows users to deploy their web applications, implemented with Streamlit, to the cloud with just a few clicks. This time, we have to pack up the *Covid-19 Detection Tool* app and try to deploy it. Many heavy libraries will be involved here, so this time, the task is a little bit more complex.

When we deal with heavy files, the deployment task becomes more difficult because GitHub has some limitations regarding file size; in fact, it is not possible to directly upload files with a size over 25 MB. In the case of our *Covid-19 Detection Tool* app, unfortunately, the file of the AI model is over 25 MB. Files to be uploaded on GitHub can't be any bigger than this, at least at the time of writing this book.

There are some techniques we can use to bypass this limit; I'll show you a rather smart way to do this in this chapter.

In this chapter, we'll cover the following main topics:

- Consolidating cloud deployment skills
- Avoiding bad behavior
- Managing difficult libraries
- Deploying the app on Streamlit Cloud

Technical requirements

- In this chapter, we will use the following libraries, packages, and tools:
  - Sublime Text
  - Python 3

- pipenv
- Streamlit
- GitHub
- Streamlit Cloud

• The code for this chapter can be found in this book's GitHub repository: `https://github.com/PacktPublishing/Web-App-Development-Made-Simple-with-Streamlit/tree/8e8d3b20f3de84b5ce02bc2352f86ad1c8018a4a/Chapter11`

Consolidating cloud deployment skills

Considering that we are at *Chapter 11* of this book, we should be aware of the fact that implementing a web application is only one part of the process and that the process ends only when the web app is deployed and shared.

We already understand the importance of web application deployment as we covered this when we created the NLP web application in the first part of this book, as well as because it's one of the first things we see when we land on Streamlit's website:

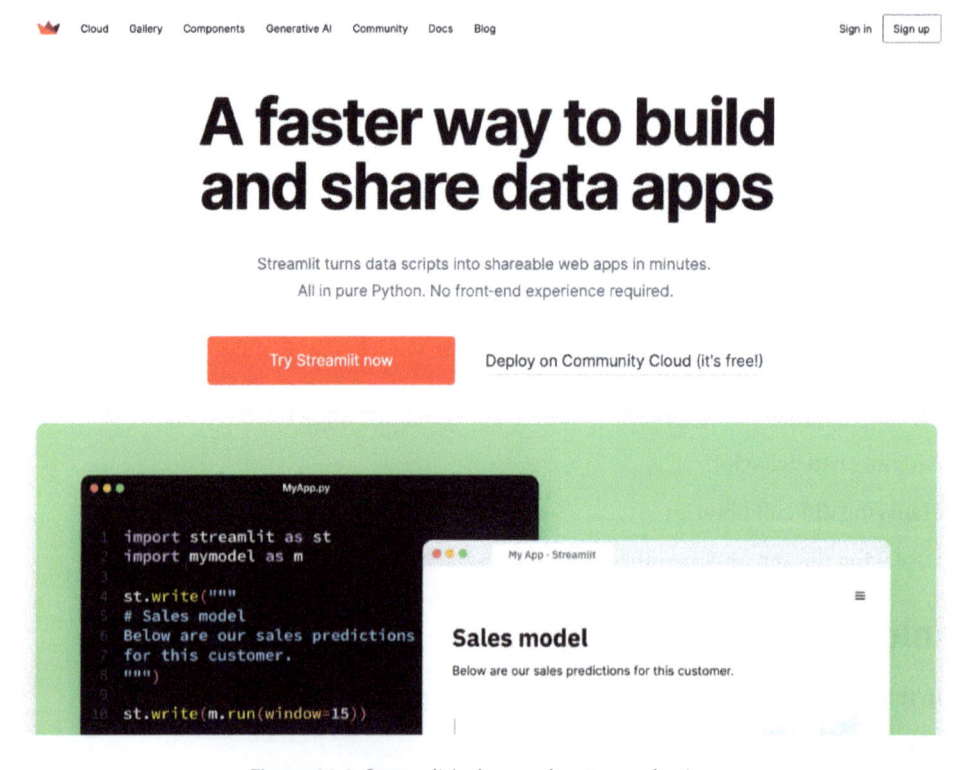

Figure 11.1: Streamlit's slogan about app sharing

When we click on the **Cloud** voice of the main menu, we are redirected to a page containing a quick video about the deployment and an important declaration: **Deploy, manage, and share your apps with the world, directly from Streamlit — all for free**:

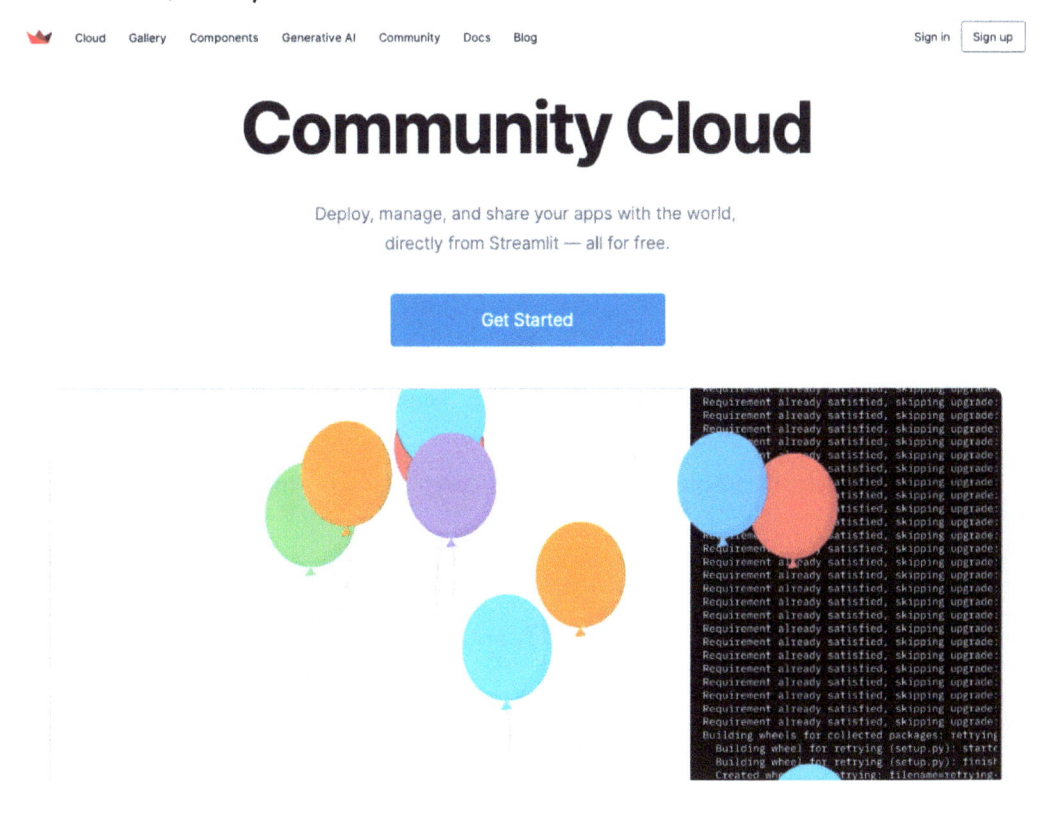

Figure 11.2: Streamlit Cloud

The most important message here is *share your apps with the world*. A web application is something that lives on the web – that's its real essence.

When we deployed the NLP application, we adopted quite a smooth process:

1. We created a requirements file.
2. We hosted the web application on GitHub.
3. We signed into Streamlit Cloud.
4. We shared the web application through a Streamlit Cloud/GitHub connection.

The procedure will be the same for our *Covid-19 Detection Tool* app, with one important difference: we must manage an external and large file – that is, the CNN pretrained model needed to detect Covid-19 cases. Let's learn how to deal with this kind of large artifact.

Avoiding bad behavior

Bad behavior is any kind of missing, wrong, or incomplete action that produces a runtime problem during the deployment, where the result is the deployment task failing. For this reason, in this section, we will learn about the steps that are required to complete any deployment.

Creating a list of all the packages that were installed and used to develop the Python code

The first thing we need to run our web application is the list of all the packages that were installed and used to develop the Python code. As we know, there are several ways to get this list, but the easiest one is to use `pipreqs`. Let's take a look:

1. First of all, let's install `pipreqs` by typing the following command in the Terminal:

   ```
   pipenv install pipreqs (simply "pip install pipreqs" if you are not using pipenv)
   ```

2. Then, we can create the `requirements.txt` file with the following simple instruction:

   ```
   pipreqs ./covid
   ```

   Here, `covid` is the name of the directory containing all the code for our web application.

3. Finally, let's check that the required file contains everything by simply writing the following instruction:

   ```
   cat ./covid/requirements.txt
   ```

Figure 11.3 shows the contents of the `requirements.txt` file:

```
(covid) rosario@penguin:~/covid$ cat requirements.txt
numpy==1.24.3
opencv_python==4.8.0.74
Pillow==9.5.0
streamlit==1.25.0
tensorflow==2.13.0
(covid) rosario@penguin:~/covid$
```

Figure 11.3: The requirements.txt file

Now that we have all the code and the requirements file, we are ready to create a dedicated repository on GitHub.

Creating a GitHub repository

Let's log into GitHub with the same account we will be using later on to connect to Streamlit Cloud.

Once on GitHub, we can create a new repository by following these steps:

1. Click on the **New** tab on the **Repositories** page. We should see the following screen:

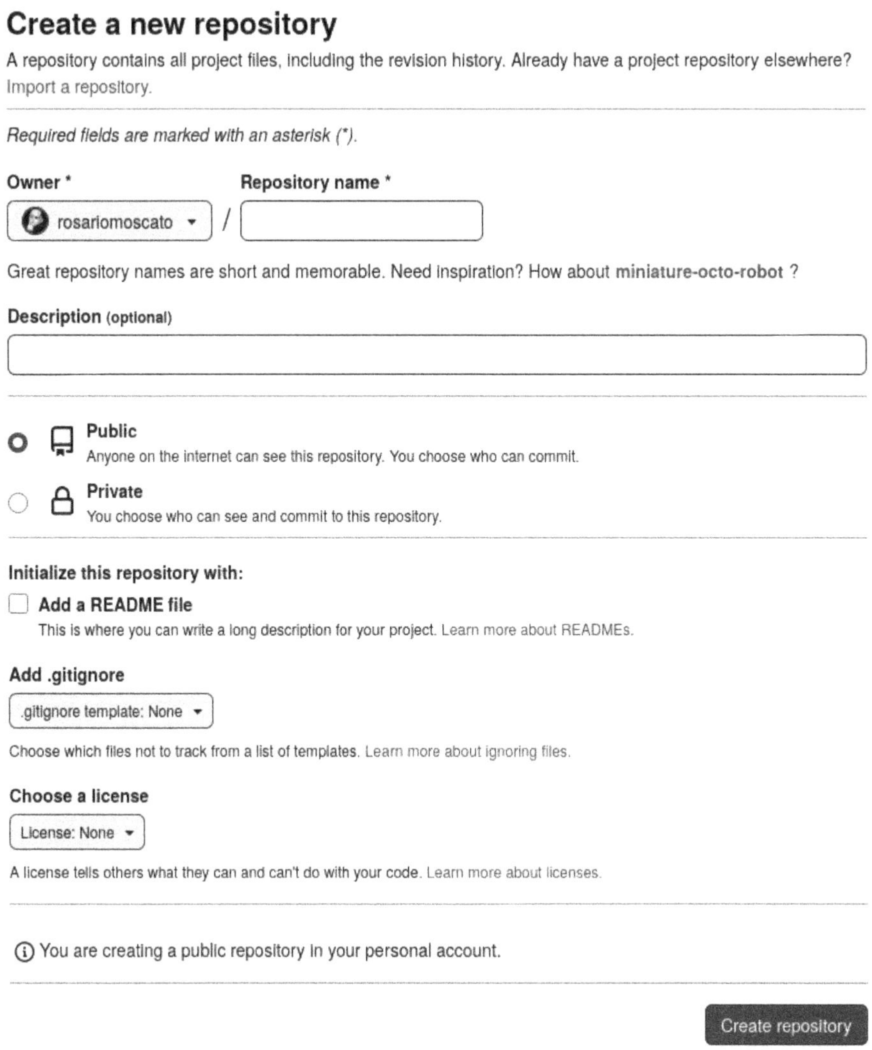

Figure 11.4: Creating a new repository on GitHub

2. Insert a repository name, such as `covid19-book`, and add a description (this is not necessary).

3. Keep the repository public and check **Add a README file**.
4. Finally, click **Create repository**.

After a little while, we'll get the following page:

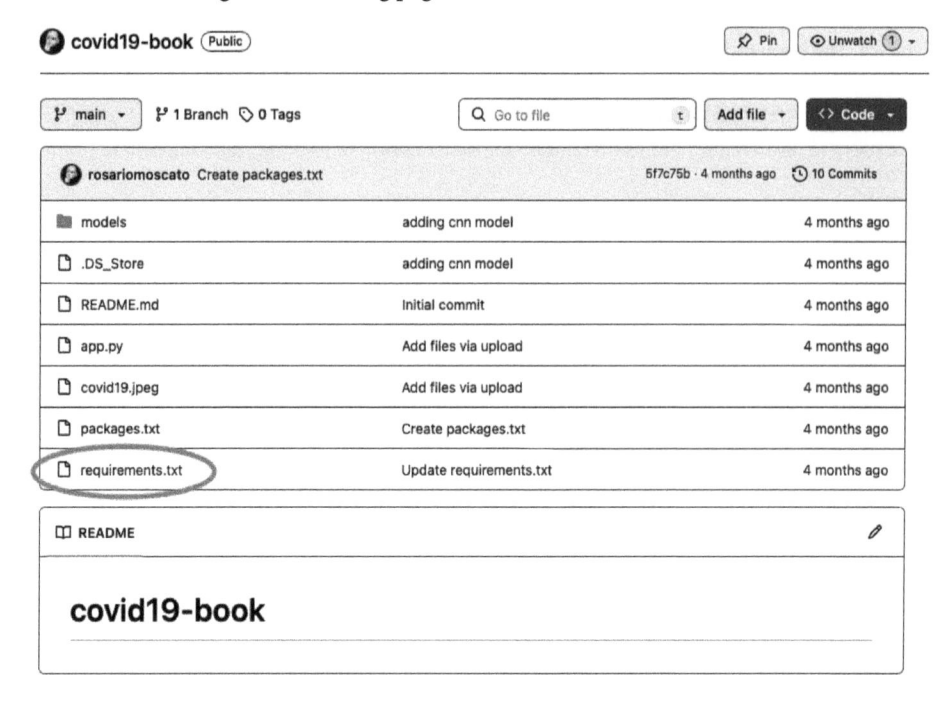

Figure 11.5: The new repository is empty

As we can see, the new repository is empty. We must add the Python file and the `requirements.txt` file to it. This operation is very easy – we just need to click **Add file** and upload the files of our interest.

In principle, we are ready to go to Streamlit Cloud to deploy the application and share it with the world.

However, every time we are at this stage of the deployment process, we must pay great attention to our actions. If we try to deploy the files contained in the newly created repository to Streamlit Cloud, we'll get a runtime error and the application won't run. Let's learn how to fix that.

Avoiding runtime errors

To avoid runtime errors during deployment, we have to think about what our web application needs to run properly.

The first item we need is the Covid-19 image that we display in the left sidebar of our *Covid-19 Detection Tool* app. This operation is very easy since we just have to add the `covid19.jpeg` file to our repository.

The second point of attention is that the Streamlit version available at the time of writing this book has some problems with the `opencv` library: there are issues when it attempts to import this library. To avoid this issue, we must create a new file in the repository by clicking **Add file**, and then selecting **Create new file**. We must call this file `packages.txt`. This new file must contain the following instruction:

`libgl1`

In this way, all the right dependencies will be installed by Streamlit Cloud at deployment time.

The third item we must pay extra attention to when using the *Covid-19 Detection Tool* app is as follows. When we upload the X-ray image and click on **Diagnosis** to determine whether or not it represents a case of Covid-19, the pretrained CNN model is run. If the web application is unable to locate the model, we may encounter issues.

The point of attention here is that uploading the AI model file is not enough because if we double-check the code we wrote on *line 81*, we'll see that this model must be put inside a directory named `models`, living at the same level as the `app.py` file. In short, we must recreate the same files and directory order indicated in our Python code in our GitHub repository; otherwise, the files we need – specifically the CNN model – will never be found:

```
62
63        elif choice == 'Diagnosis':
64            if st.sidebar.button("Diagnosis"):
65                new_img = np.array(our_image.convert('RGB')) #our image is converted into an array
66                new_img = cv2.cvtColor(new_img,1) #0 is original, 1 is grayscale
67                gray = cv2.cvtColor(new_img, cv2.COLOR_BGR2GRAY)
68                st.text("Chest X-Ray")
69                st.image(gray, width=400, use_column_width=True)
70
71                #X-Ray Imge Pre-processing
72                IMG_SIZE = (200, 200)
73                img = cv2.equalizeHist(gray)
74                img = cv2.resize(img, IMG_SIZE)
75                img = img/255 #normalization
76
77                # Image reshaping according to tensorflow format
78                X_Ray = img.reshape(1, 200, 200, 1)
79
80                #Pre-trained CNN Model loading
81                model = tf.keras.models.load_model("./models/Covid19_CNN_Classifier.h5")
82
83                #Diagnosis (Prediction== Binary Classification)
84                diagnosis_proba = model.predict(X_Ray)
85                diagnosis = np.argmax(diagnosis_proba,axis=1)
86
```

Figure 11.6: Line 81 indicates where we need to put the CNN model file

Finally, a rather big issue arises. When we try to upload `Covid19_CNN_Classifier.h5`, we discover that this operation is not possible since the file is larger than 25 MB and GitHub on the web only accepts files that are smaller than this size.

In the next section, we'll learn how to manage this problem.

Managing difficult libraries

To fix the problem of file size, we must install the GitHub Desktop application, which at the time of writing is only available for Windows or macOS. So, follow these steps:

1. Download the GitHub Desktop application from `desktop.github.com` and install it.
2. Then, log into your GitHub account and authorize. You should see the following window:

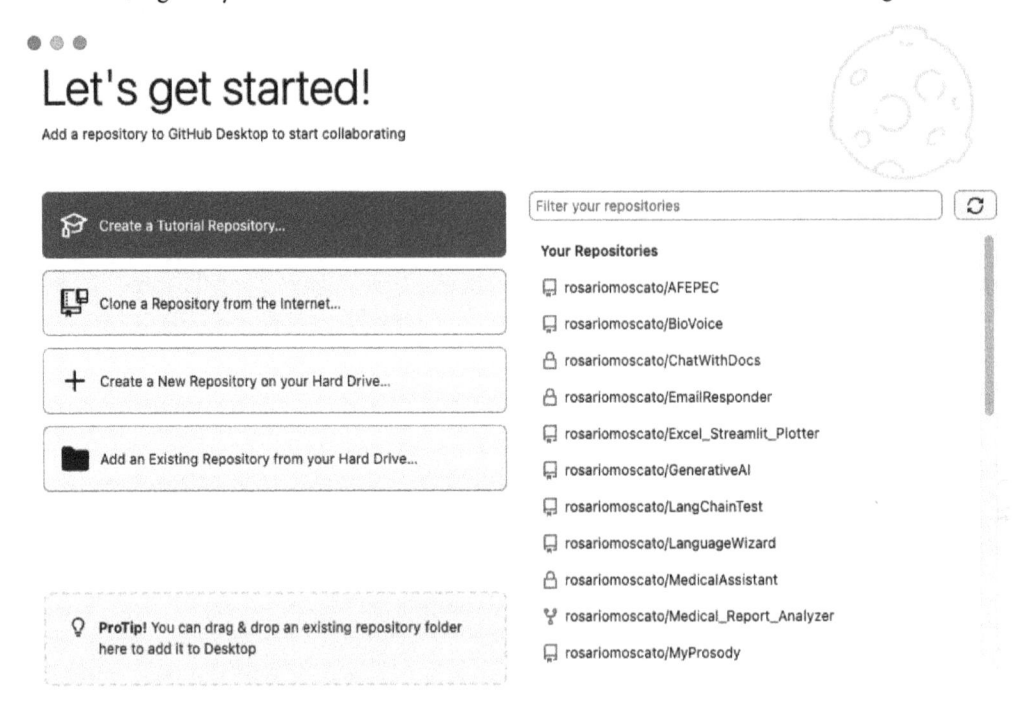

Figure 11.7: GitHub Desktop application

3. Now, select the `covid19-book` repository (if you used another name, you must look for it) and click **Clone...**.

A clone of the repository will be created on your machine, as shown in *Figure 11.8*:

Figure 11.8: Cloning the GitHub repository locally

4. Once the cloning operation is finished, open the local folder of the repository on your Mac Finder or via Windows File Explorer, as shown in *Figure 11.9*:

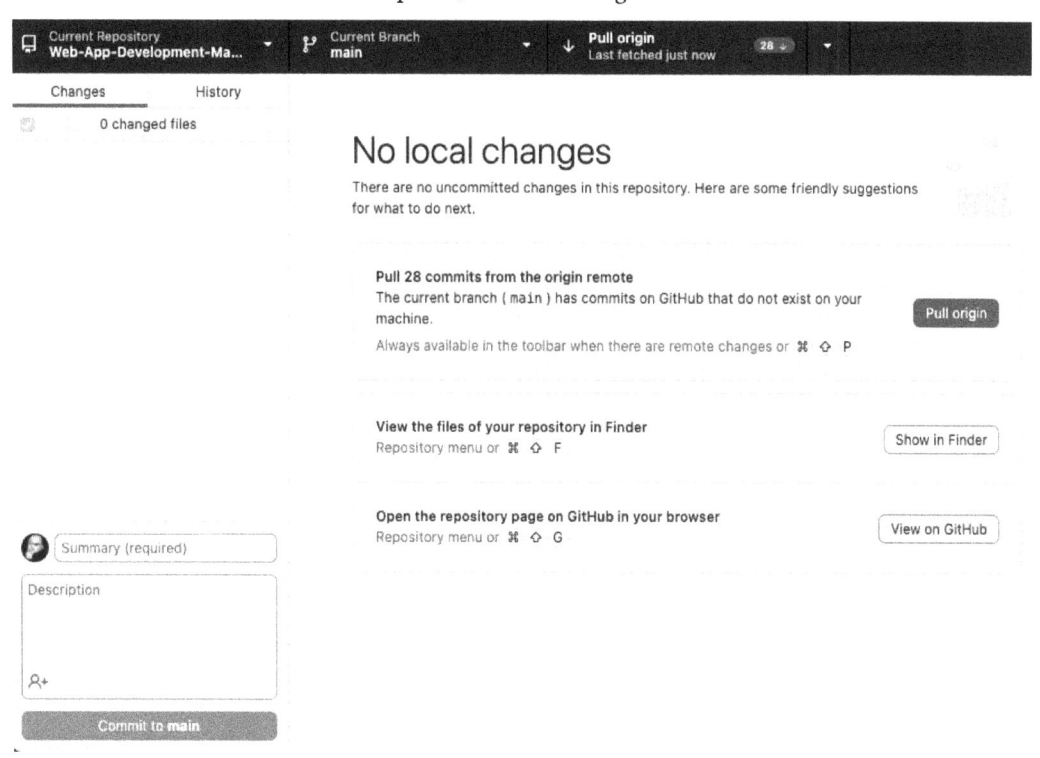

Figure 11.9: Local folder of the repository

5. Now, create the `models` directory and copy the `Covid19_CNN_Classifier.h5` file inside it:

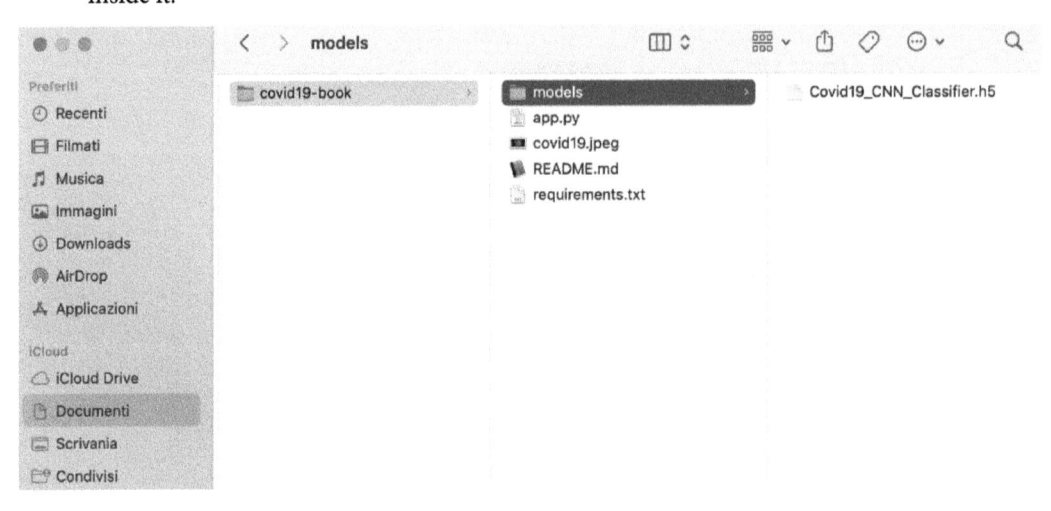

Figure 11.10: Big file copied into the proper directory

6. Move back to the GitHub Desktop application. Here, you will see the big file we just added. Write something in the **Summary (required)** text box, such as `adding cnn model`, and click **Commit to main**:

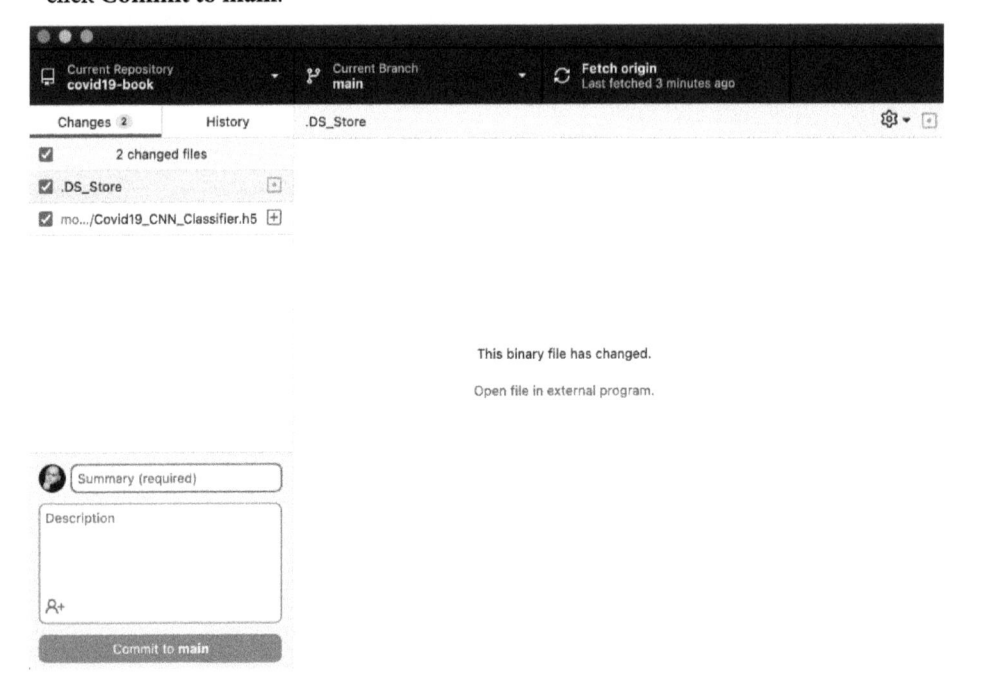

Figure 11.11: Big file copied into the proper directory

7. Now, select **Push origin**, as suggested in *Figure 11.12*:

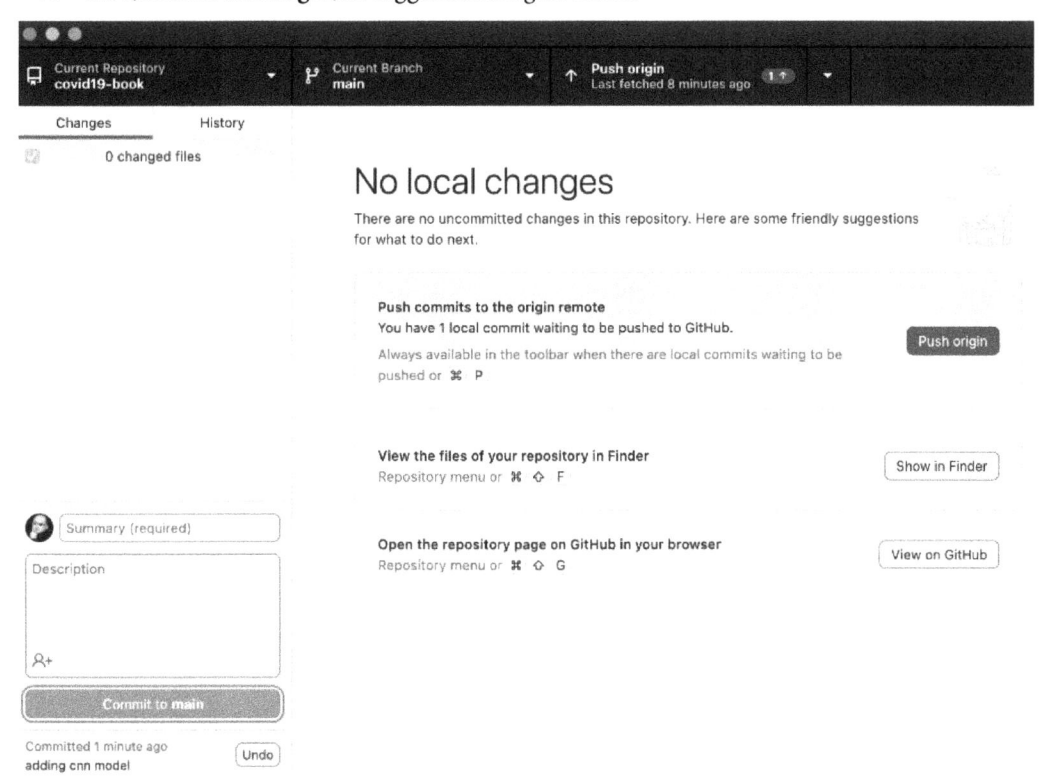

Figure 11.12: Push origin

Now, you can check in your browser whether the big file is included in your GitHub repository:

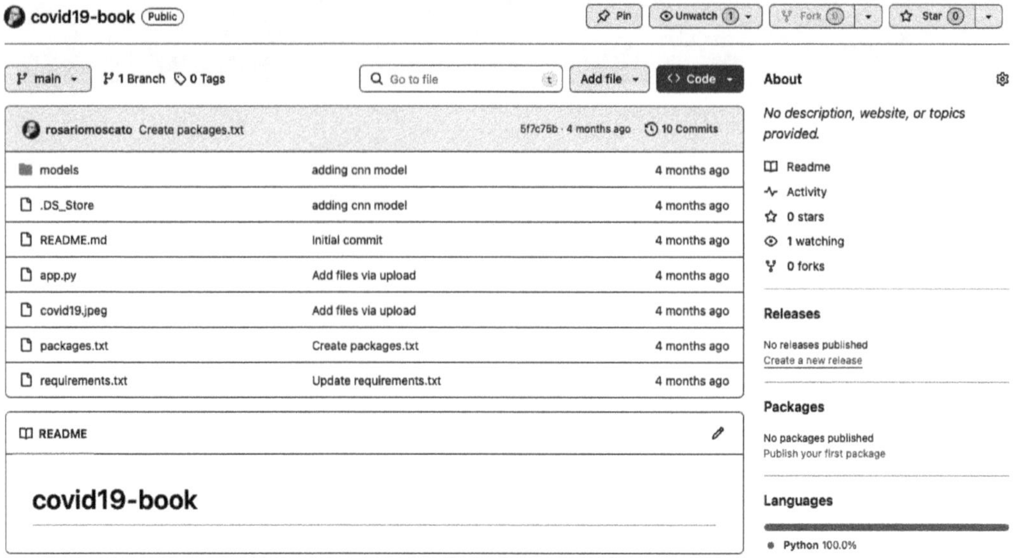

Figure 11.13: The GitHub repository containing all the necessary files

What we have learned here is very important since it is common to deal with difficult libraries or heavy files is quite frequent, and knowing how to manage this issue properly makes a big difference. Managing this kind of issue makes it possible to deploy any kind of web application we could develop.

Deploying the app on Streamlit Cloud

The hardest part is over. From here on, we can follow the same procedure we adopted for the NLP web application. Here are the steps:

1. Sign into Streamlit Cloud by selecting **Continue with Github**, authorizing and using the same account you used for GitHub.

2. Once you're in, select **New app**.

You should only have the application we created in *Chapter 7* among the deployed applications. The window should look like what's shown in *Figure 11.14*:

rosariomoscato's apps

afepec · main · app.py

classification_wizard · main · app.py

covid19-book · main · app.py

covid19-detection-tool · master · covid19_detection_app.py

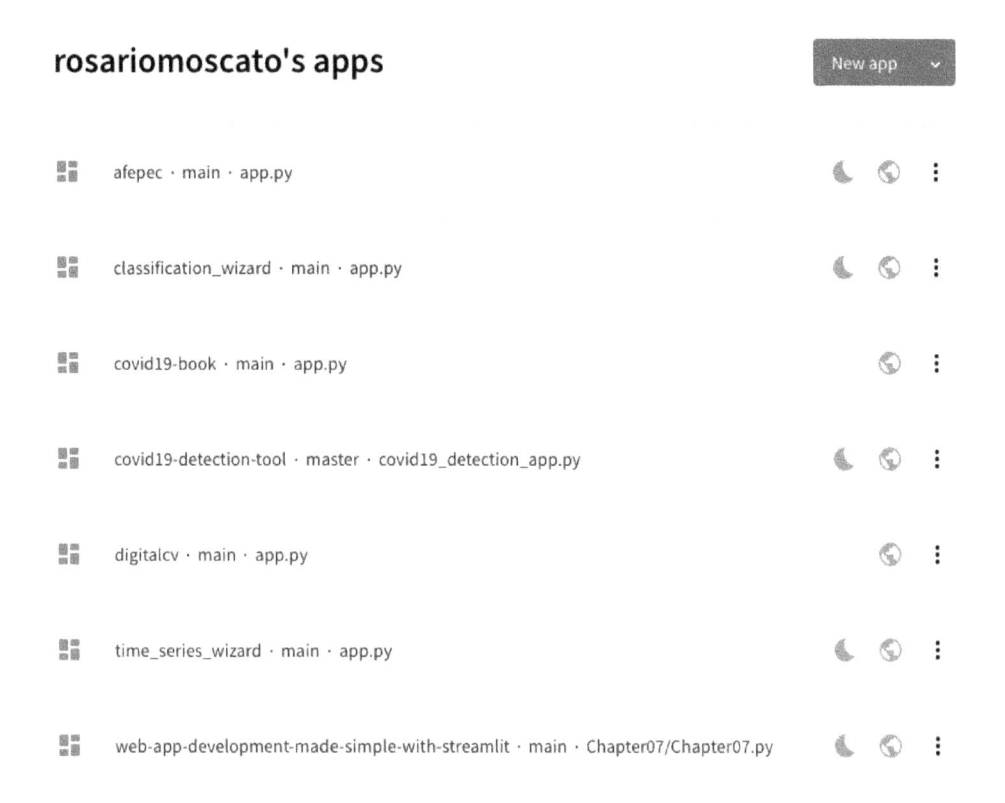

digitalcv · main · app.py

time_series_wizard · main · app.py

web-app-development-made-simple-with-streamlit · main · Chapter07/Chapter07.py

Figure 11.14: Creating a new app on Streamlit Cloud

1. After selecting **New app**, in the new form, choose the right repository, the main branch, and the name of the Python file (it should be app.py), and specify a meaningful name to the app URL, as shown in *Figure 11.15*:

Deploy an app

Repository — Paste GitHub URL

rosariomoscato/covid19-book

Branch

main

Main file path

app.py

App URL (Optional)

covid19-book-chapter11 .streamlit.app

Domain is available

Advanced settings...

[Deploy!]

Figure 11.15: Deploying the web app on Streamlit Cloud

2. When everything is ready, click **Deploy!** and wait since **Your app is in the oven**:

Your app is in the oven

Figure 11.16: Deploying animation

At the end of this process, your *Covid-19 Detection Tool* app will be deployed and ready to be shared with everyone.

Here's how our new web application looks once the deployment process is completed:

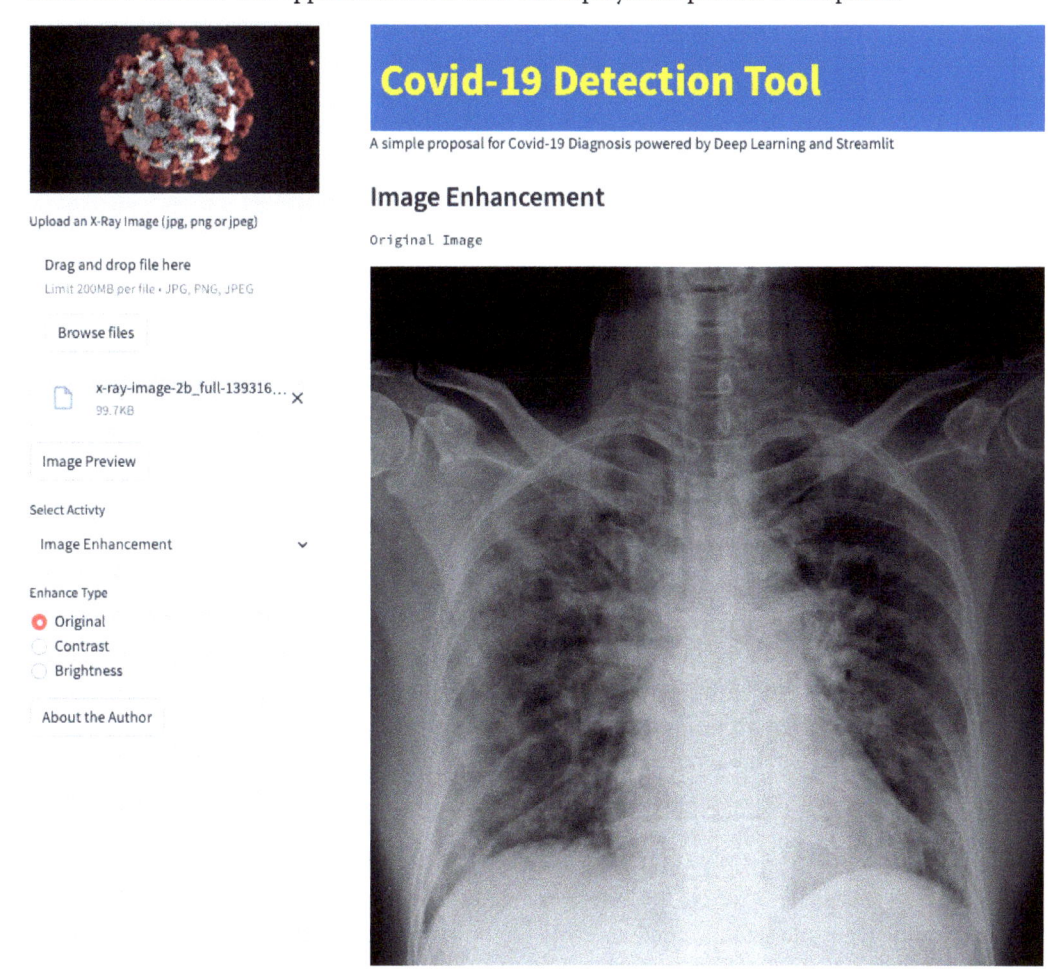

Figure 11.17: The Covid-19 Detection Tool app deployed on Streamlit Cloud

As shown in *Figure 11.17*, the application now lives on the web, and its URL is self-explanatory since it contains `covid19-book-chapter11` in it.

Once again, it's very important to highlight how crucial proper deployment capabilities are in the web application development process. We can only consider this process completed once the web application lives on the cloud and anybody can use it. The contents of this chapter have enabled us to deploy any kind of web app, even those including difficult libraries and big files.

> **Important note**
> Depending on the versions of the packages you installed, it might be necessary to install the `opencv-python` library as well. If you get this suggestion during deployment, just install the library as usual (using `pipenv install...`), add it to the `requirements.txt` file, and let the standard deployment process from GitHub be completed.

Summary

Great job! Deploying the *Covid-19 Detection Tool* app was complex. As we saw, there are many potential problems to avoid.

First of all, we needed to recreate the same structure of files and directories that were used in the Python code, and not forget to also include the picture files in the GitHub repository.

The second problem was allowing Streamlit Cloud to manage all the dependencies related to `opencv`. To do this, it was necessary to add a `packages.txt` file to the repository containing the instructions to get these dependencies.

Finally, we found out that GitHub – at least its online version – only manages files that are smaller than 25 MB, but sometimes, such as with the CNN AI model, we need to upload bigger files. This operation requires us to install the GitHub Desktop application and the local (on our computers) cloning of the repository. Once we have the repository on our computers, we can add this big file and push it back toward the origin (the Git *server*). In this way, even our AI model file, which is over 50 MB, will be hosted in the GitHub repository of interest.

Once we've tackled all these issues, we are ready to deploy the web application to Streamlit Cloud and share it with everybody.

Starting from the next chapter, we are going to cover some very advanced topics, such as smart file uploading, adding login and signup functionality to our web apps, managing databases, and more.

Part 4: Advanced Techniques for Secure and Customizable Web Applications

Part 4 of the book is dedicated to mastering advanced techniques that are essential for creating secure and highly customizable web applications. It starts with an exploration of smart file uploading methods, tailored for professional-grade web applications, ensuring efficient and user-friendly file management. The section then addresses the critical aspect of security, providing in-depth guidance on creating secure login and signup processes, a cornerstone for any web application dealing with user data. Next, it dives into the customization of pages, personalization of themes, and implementation of multi-page layouts, allowing for a more tailored and engaging user experience. The part also covers enhancing web applications with forms, session state management, and the use of customizable subdomains, adding a layer of sophistication and functionality to web apps. The book concludes with key takeaways and a thoughtful conclusion, encapsulating what you have learned and preparing you for the future of web app development. This final part is essential for those looking to elevate their web apps from functional to exceptional, focusing on customization, security, and advanced user engagement.

This part has the following chapters:

- *Chapter 12, Smart File Uploading – Advanced Techniques for Professional Web Applications*
- *Chapter 13, Creating a Secure Login and Signup Process for Web Applications*
- *Chapter 14, Customizing Pages, Personalizing Themes, and Implementing Multi-Pages*
- *Chapter 15, Enhancing Web Apps with Forms, Session State, and Customizable Subdomains*
- *Chapter 16, Takeaways and Conclusion*

12
Smart File Uploading – Advanced Techniques for Professional Web Applications

At this point of our journey, we have almost acquired all the skills we need to implement and deploy well-working and nice-looking web applications. Anyway, our web apps still have a quite "naive" aspect and are a little bit far from professional ones. Starting with this chapter, we will deal with some advanced techniques that will help make our products look more complete and professional.

Let's start with the file uploader, a widget that we already used in the *Covid-19 Detection Tool* app when we were asked to upload an X-ray image of the chest.

What we want to do now is move the file uploader to another level, deeply customizing it to automatically detect the type of file we are going to open and adopt the appropriate actions. This kind of behavior gives our web applications a very professional standing and makes them easy to use.

In this chapter, we're going to cover the following main topics:

- Understanding the customized features of the file uploader
- Creating a suitable file uploader for web apps
- Simplifying web apps with smart components

Technical requirements

- In this chapter, we'll use the following libraries, packages, and tools:
    - Sublime Text
    - Python 3

- pipenv
- Streamlit
- docx2txt
- pdfplumber

• The code for this chapter can be found in this book's GitHub repository: https://github.com/PacktPublishing/Web-App-Development-Made-Simple-with-Streamlit/tree/57674ee5b5c58769120051cfb466f4b4d658c20c/Chapter12

Understanding the customized features of the file uploader

Uploading a file is a simple task. There are several ways to do it, and these different approaches have different effects on the so-called *user experience*: the way users perceive the application itself. Moreover, a better-implemented uploading feature can speed up the entire application, making things easier for the users. Let's imagine that we want to upload a file containing text. It could be a .txt file, so a plain text file, but also a .docx file, a Microsoft Word file, or even a .pdf file. One approach is to ask the customer, *what kind of file do you need to upload (.txtx, .docx, .pdf)?* If the user replies .txt, the application will launch the file_uploader widget customized for this file format; if the answer is .docx, the file_uploader widget customized for Microsoft Word will be executed, and so on. This kind of approach works perfectly, but it's a little bit too complex.

What if the user updated a file and the web application recognized its type automatically without human intervention?

Let's learn how to implement this feature according to both approaches, one requiring information from the user and another that's completely automated.

Creating a new virtual environment

First, we'll create a new virtual environment dedicated to this chapter. So, follow these steps:

1. Create a new folder and call it FileUploader.
2. Next, move to the newly created folder and, once inside it, as usual, write pipenv shell to create the virtual environment.

The instructions are shown in *Figure 12.1*:

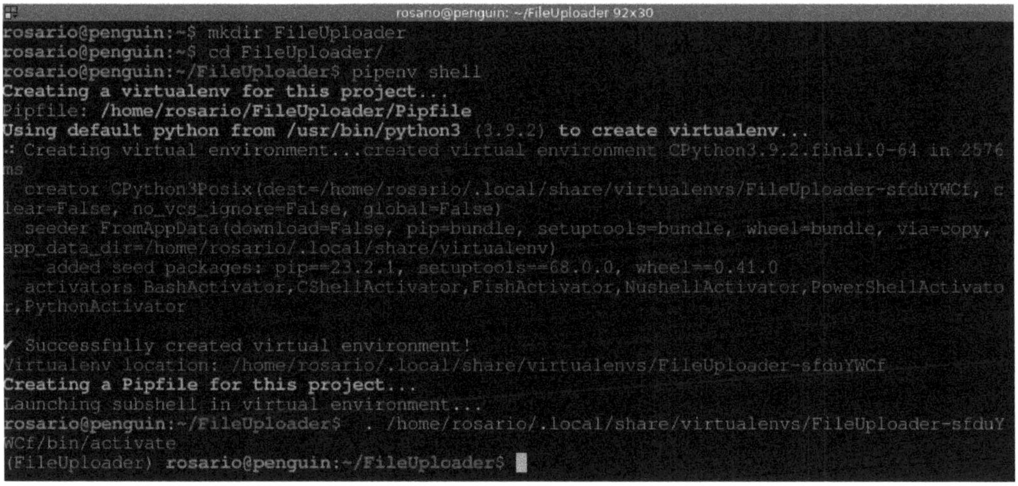

Figure 12.1: Creating a new virtual environment dedicated to this chapter

3. After that, the only library we need is Streamlit, so let's type the following:

    `pipenv install streamlit`

    After a few seconds, our environment will be equipped with the latest Streamlit version that's available.

4. As usual, before we start coding, we have to create an empty Python file, which is a very easy operation. We can do this by writing the following instruction:

    `touch app.py`

Here, app.py is the name of our file.

We can open the app.py file with our favorite IDE, such as Sublime Text.

Building the app skeleton

When we have an empty file, the best starting option is to always use the *skeleton* we adopted in the two web applications we implemented previously. So, we can import the libraries – in this case, just streamlit – and then define a main function containing the menu. The menu for this chapter's app is quite light in that it just contains two voices: **Dropfiles** and **About**.

In the following figure, we can see how short the skeleton we are using for this specific case is:

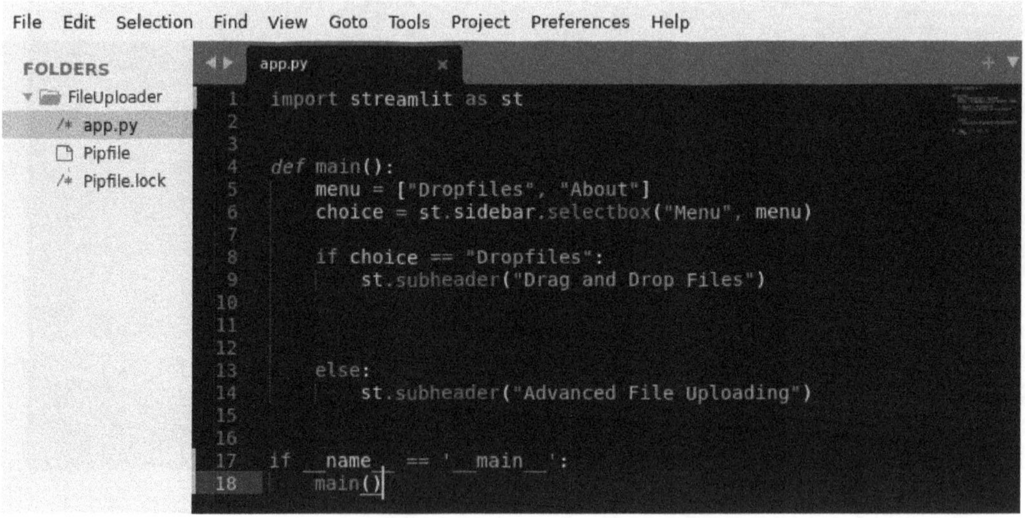
File Edit Selection Find View Goto Tools Project Preferences Help
FOLDERS
FileUploader
app.py
Pipfile
Pipfile.lock
app.py
import streamlit as st
def main():
menu = ["Dropfiles", "About"]
choice = st.sidebar.selectbox("Menu", menu)
if choice == "Dropfiles":
st.subheader("Drag and Drop Files")
else:
st.subheader("Advanced File Uploading")
if __name__ == '__main__':
main()

Figure 12.2: The skeleton of our app

Here's a breakdown of the code shown in *Figure 12.2*:

- On *line 1*, we import the library (here, `streamlit`), while on *line 4*, we define the `main` function – that is, the function containing the business logic of our app.
- On *line 5*, we have a list named `menu` containing the values of the web application menu (the functions this web application can offer).
- On *line 6*, we create a select box starting from the menu list in the sidebar.
- On *lines 8* and *13*, we add an `if` clause that enters the proper code to execute according to the selection that was performed in the selectbox on *line 6*.

With that, we have the skeleton of our app. Now, we can write the following instruction in the terminal:

```
pipenv run streamlit run app.py
```

At this point, we can start the web application and see it in our browser:

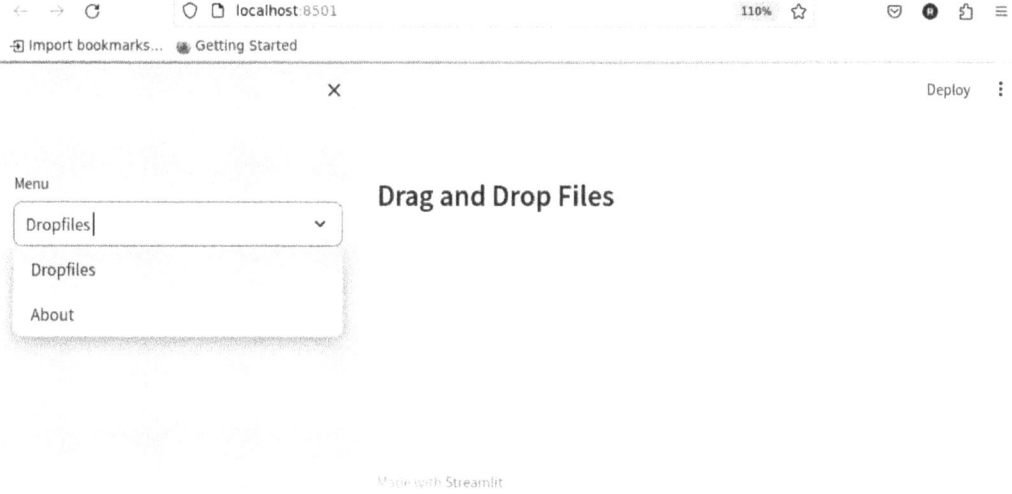

Figure 12.3: First execution of our new web app

As we can see, in the sidebar, there is a selectbox offering the two options in the menu.

Let's focus on the **Dropfile** voice of the menu.

Creating a radio button for the app menu

We can use a radio button to let the user indicate what kind of file they would like to upload. Let's add the following code:

```
file_selection = st.radio("Select the file type", ['TXT', 'DOCX', 'PDF'])
```

In this way, the file selection is stored in a variable named `file_selection`. So far, our app looks as follows:

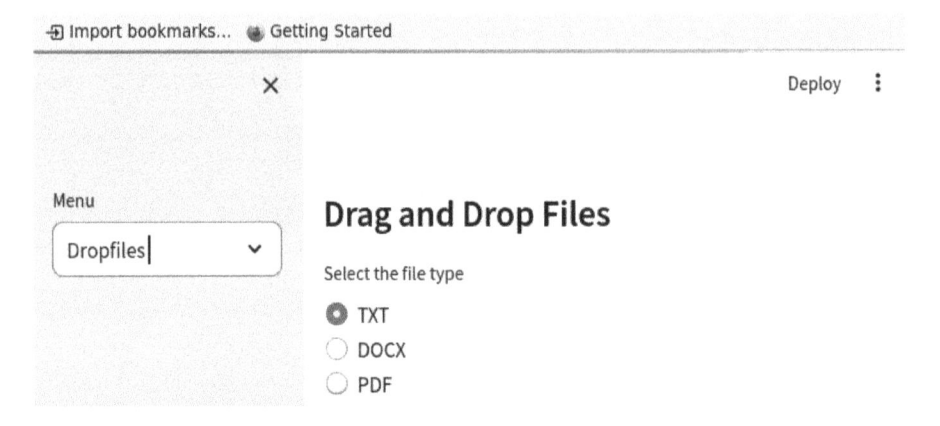

Figure 12.4: Selecting the file type with radio buttons

Once the user selects an option, we are ready to open `file_uploader` using the file type as the selected option. The following code can be adopted in this case:

```
raw_text_file = st.file_uploader("Upload File", type=['txt'])
if raw_text_file is not None:
try:
raw_text = str(raw_text_file.read(),"utf-8")
st.info("Text from TXT file")
st.write(raw_text)
except:
st.warning("TXT File Fetching Problem...")
```

Quite easily, after uploading the file (with the `txt` type), we can check that the file is not null, read it using `utf-8` encoding, and visualize it on the screen. If the uploaded file is null, we just print a warning on the screen stating **TXT File Fetching Problem...**.

Figure 12.5 shows the code in the IDE:

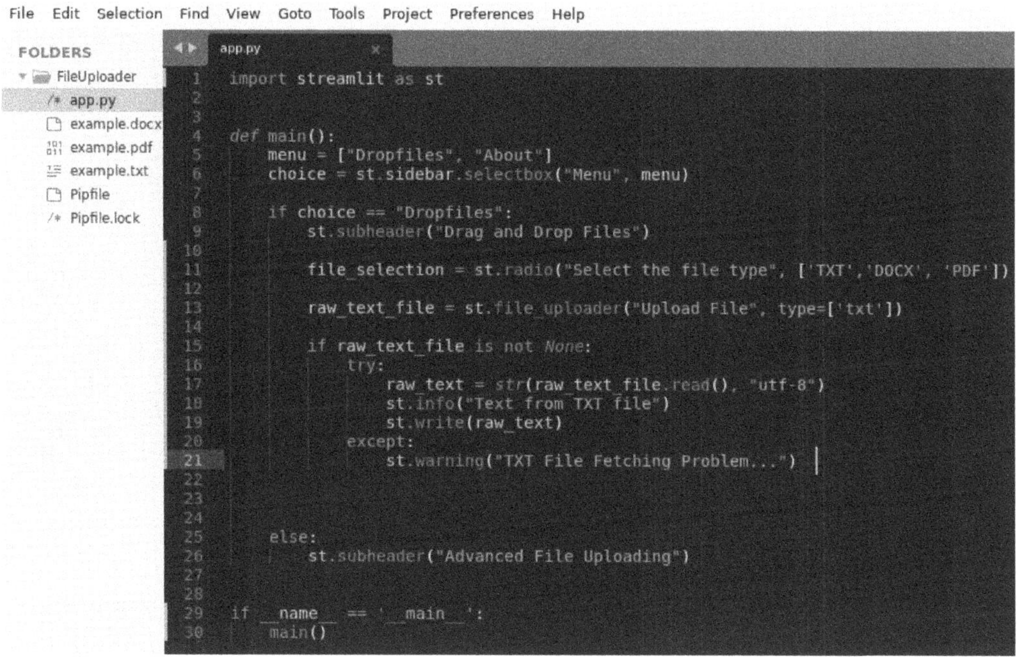
File Edit Selection Find View Goto Tools Project Preferences Help
FOLDERS
FileUploader
app.py
example.docx
example.pdf
example.txt
Pipfile
Pipfile.lock
app.py
import streamlit as st
def main():
menu = ["Dropfiles", "About"]
choice = st.sidebar.selectbox("Menu", menu)
if choice == "Dropfiles":
st.subheader("Drag and Drop Files")
file_selection = st.radio("Select the file type", ['TXT','DOCX', 'PDF'])
raw_text_file = st.file_uploader("Upload File", type=['txt'])
if raw_text_file is not None:
try:
raw_text = str(raw_text_file.read(), "utf-8")
st.info("Text from TXT file")
st.write(raw_text)
except:
st.warning("TXT File Fetching Problem...")
else:
st.subheader("Advanced File Uploading")
if __name__ == '__main__':
main()

Figure 12.5: Uploading a .txt file

When we move to the browser, something interesting happens. Even if we have three different files containing text in our directory – that is, `'txt'`, `'docx'`, and `'pdf'` – since we specify `txt` as the type, the file uploader just sees and can open the `.txt` file:

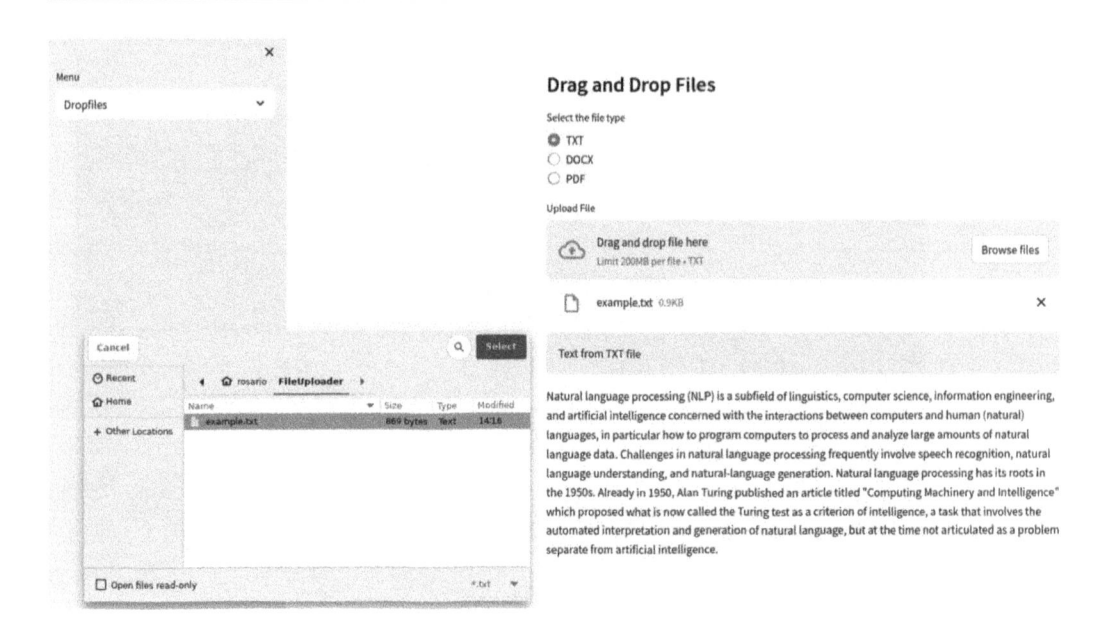

Smart File Uploading – Advanced Techniques for Professional Web Applications

Figure 12.6: In the directory on the left, there are three different files, but we can only open the .txt file

At this point, to manage other file types, we should write more or less the same code we used for the `txt` type but also specify the different types. So, the code can evolve into something like this:

Figure 12.7: Asking the user for the type of file

The code in *Figure 12.7* contains a couple of `pass` calls for `.docx` and `.pdf` files. If you want to complete the related functions, you must import the proper library and read the content of the files.

The real point here is that when approaching file uploading in this way, even if the code works very well technically, we are forced to do a couple of operations we don't like that much:

- Asking the user about the type of file at the beginning
- Repeating (we just copy and paste) a lot of code that is redundant

Now that we've explored this solution, let's try to implement something much more elegant and cleaner that can automatically read the type of file, without asking the user.

Creating a suitable file uploader for web apps

As you can imagine, this time, we are not using the radio button. Instead, we are directly uploading the files. So, referring to *Figure 12.7*, let's comment all the code between *lines 11* and *31*.

Immediately in the subheading, on *line 10*, we can add `file_uploader`, this time including all three types:

```
raw_text_file = st.file_uploader('Upload File', type=['txt', 'docx', 'pdf'])
```

When we try to upload the file from the browser, this time in our directory, we will see all three types of files and be able to select one of them.

As we did on *line 15* in the code presented in *Figure 12.5*, we can check that the file is not null by writing the following:

```
if raw_text_file is not None:
```

After this `if` clause, we must get the details of the file. We need these details to understand which type of file we selected and how to manage it. By using the `raw_file_text` variable, which contains the file we uploaded, we can use three methods named `name`, `type`, and `size` to collect the details we need.

These details will be put into a dictionary; we are calling it `file_details`. Let's see it in the code:

Figure 12.8: The code for file upload and file detail detection

This is the result in the browser:

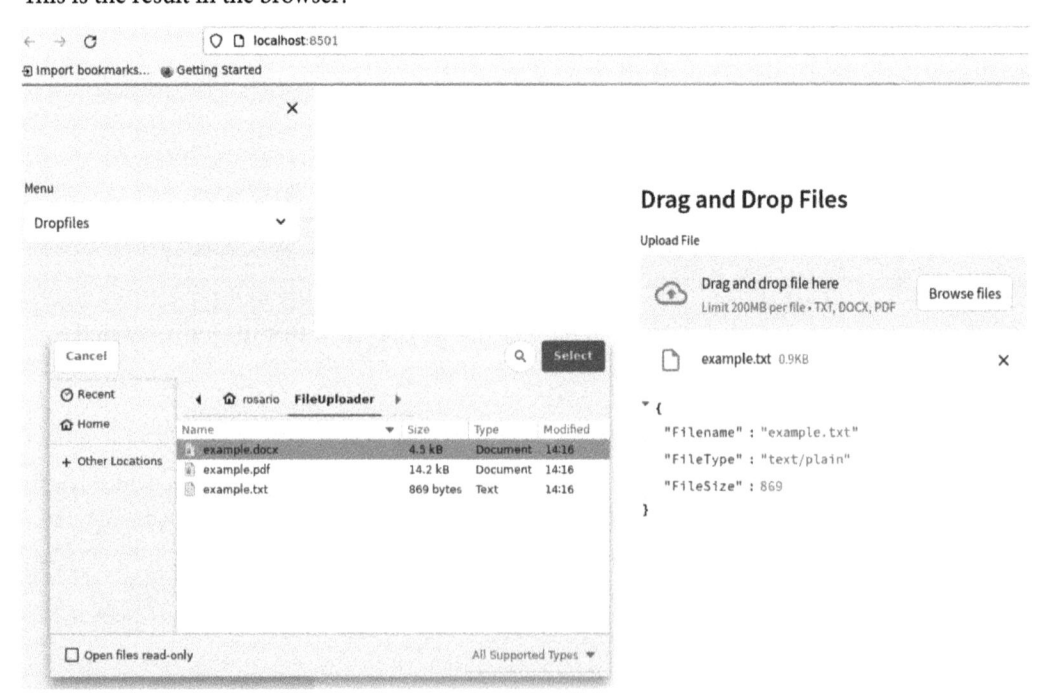

Figure 12.9: File upload and file detail detection in the browser

As we can see, in the directory, we have all three types of files and can select any one of them since the information about the file details has been intercepted correctly. In the case of the `.txt` file, we got the correct filename, the `text/plain` type, and its size.

Let's see what type we get for the `.docx` and `.pdf` files. The `.docx` file, as shown here, has a very long type file:

Drag and Drop Files

Upload File

Drag and drop file here
Limit 200MB per file • TXT, DOCX, PDF

Browse files

example.docx 4.5KB

```
{
  "Filename" : "example.docx"
  "FileType" :
  "application/vnd.openxmlformats-officedocument.wordprocessingml.document"
  "FileSize" : 4517
}
```

Figure 12.10: The .docx file

Meanwhile, the `.pdf` file has a shorter name:

Drag and Drop Files

Upload File

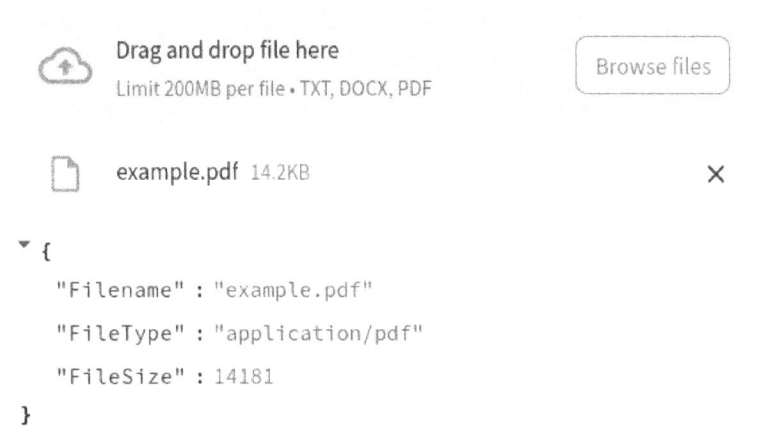

Drag and drop file here
Limit 200MB per file • TXT, DOCX, PDF

Browse files

example.pdf 14.2KB

```
{
  "Filename" : "example.pdf"
  "FileType" : "application/pdf"
  "FileSize" : 14181
}
```

Figure 12.11: The .pdf file

These three different types of files are all we need to manage file uploading automatically. To open the .pdf and .docx files, we need to install the proper libraries (pdfplumber and docx2txt). So, please write the following command in your terminal:

```
pipenv install pdfplumber docx2txt
```

The first package takes care of .pdf files, while the second takes care of .docx files.

Once the installation is finished, we must import these libraries into our app.py file by typing the following:

```
import docx2txt
import pdfplumber
```

With that, we have everything we need. So, referring to *Figure 12.8*, continuing from *line 15* of our code, we can write the following:

```
if raw_text_file.type == "text/plain":
try:
        raw_text = str(raw_text_file.read(), "utf-8")
st.info("Text from TXT file")
except:
st.write("TXT File Fetching Problem...")
```

The preceding code checks that the type of file we uploaded is text/plain. In this case, it reads it, stores its content in a variable named raw_text, and prints a label on the screen saying just **Text from TXT file**. This check happens in a try cycle; so, in case of an error, a simple exception will be printed on the screen.

The same code we used for the .txt file has to be used for the other kind of files; the only differences are the type of the files and the libraries needed to read the content of the files (the two libraries we just imported – that is, pdfplumber and docx2txt).

Let's look at the code shown in *Figure 12.12*:

```python
import streamlit as st
import pdfplumber
import docx2txt


def main():
    menu = ["Dropfiles", "About"]
    choice = st.sidebar.selectbox("Menu", menu)

    if choice == "Dropfiles":
        st.subheader("Drag and Drop Files")

        raw_text_file = st.file_uploader("Upload File", type=['txt', 'docx', 'pdf'])
        if raw_text_file is not None:
            file_details = {"Filename":raw_text_file.name, "FileType": raw_text_file.type, "FileSize": raw_text_file.size}
            st.write(file_details)

            # Check file type
            if raw_text_file.type == "text/plain":
                try:
                    raw_text = str(raw_text_file.read(), "utf-8")
                    st.info("Text from TXT file")
                except:
                    st.warning("TXT File Fetching Problem...")
            elif raw_text_file.type == "application/pdf":
                try:
                    pdf_file = pdfplumber.open(raw_text_file)
                    p0 = pdf_file.pages[0]
                    raw_text = p0.extract_text()
                    st.info("Text from PDF file")
                except:
                    st.warning("PDF File Fetching Problem...")
            else:
                try:
                    raw_text = docx2txt.process(raw_text_file)
                    st.info("Text from DOCX file")
                except:
                    st.warning("DOCX File Fetching Problem...")

            # Print the file content
            st.write(raw_text)
```

Figure 12.12: The code that automatically uploads the files

On *line 27*, we used `pdfplumber` because the file type is `"application/pdf"`, while on *line 35*, we used `docx2txt` because the file to open is a `.docx` file.

Finally, on *line 42*, we automatically print the contents of the opened file on the screen.

This is the result in the case of a `.docx` file; please note the very long name of the file type:

Drag and Drop Files

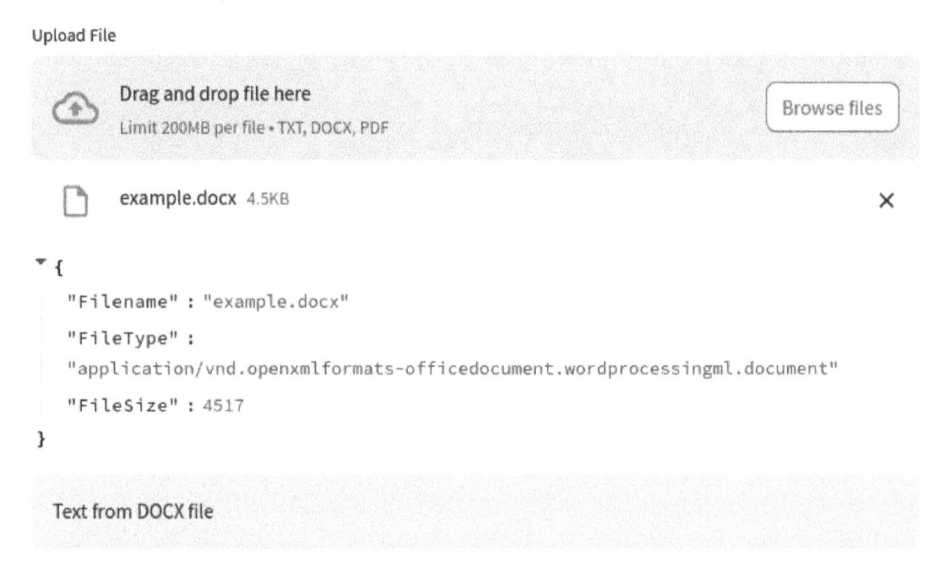

Upload File

⛅ **Drag and drop file here**
Limit 200MB per file • TXT, DOCX, PDF   [Browse files]

📄 **example.docx** 4.5KB   ✕

```
▼ {
    "Filename" : "example.docx"
    "FileType" :
    "application/vnd.openxmlformats-officedocument.wordprocessingml.document"
    "FileSize" : 4517
}
```

Text from DOCX file

Natural language processing (NLP) is a subfield of linguistics, computer science, information engineering, and artificial intelligence concerned with the interactions between computers and human (natural) languages, in particular how to program computers to process and analyze large amounts of natural language data.

Challenges in natural language processing frequently involve speech recognition, natural language understanding, and natural-language generation.

Natural language processing has its roots in the 1950s. Already in 1950, Alan Turing published an article titled "Computing Machinery and Intelligence" which proposed what is now called the Turing test as a criterion of intelligence, a task that involves the automated interpretation and generation of natural language, but at the time not articulated as a problem separate from artificial intelligence.

Figure 12.13: A .docx file is automatically recognized and opened

The application behavior with a `.pdf` file is the same:

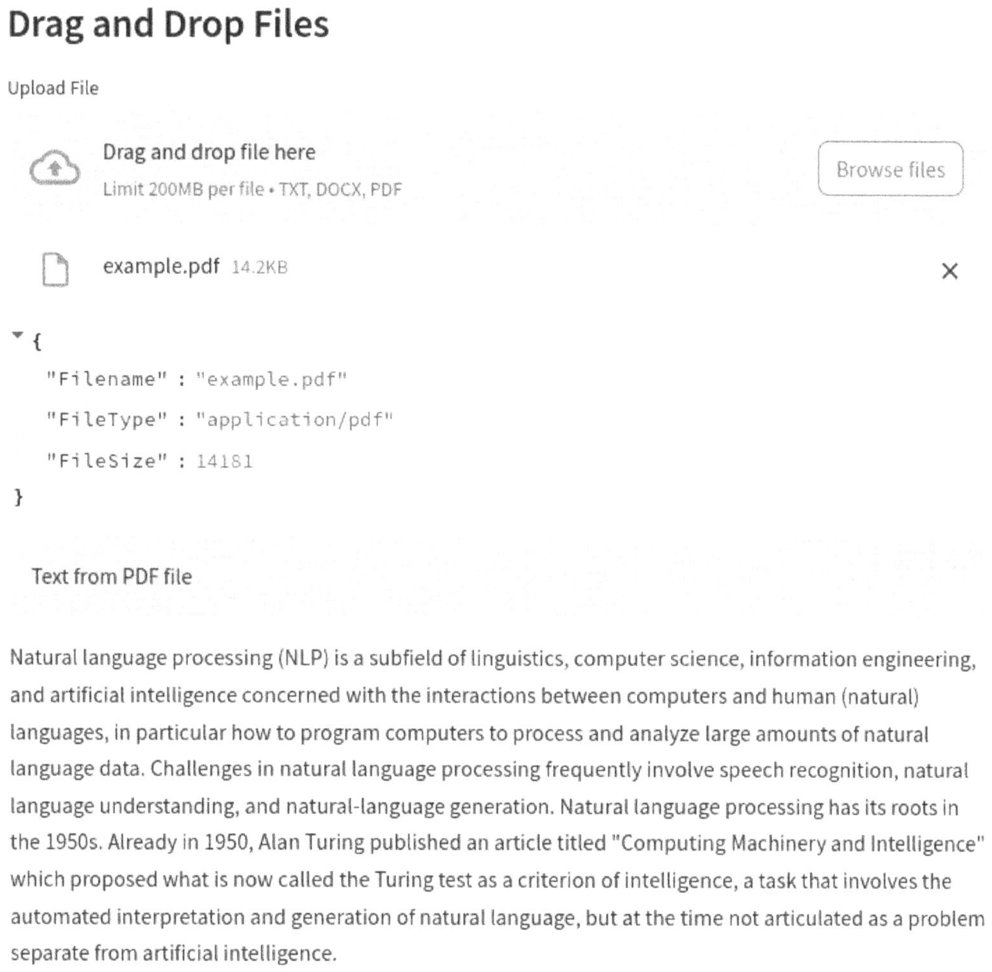

Drag and Drop Files

Upload File

```
Drag and drop file here                                    Browse files
Limit 200MB per file • TXT, DOCX, PDF
```

example.pdf 14.2KB   ✕

▼ {
     "Filename" : "example.pdf"
     "FileType" : "application/pdf"
     "FileSize" : 14181
  }

Text from PDF file

Natural language processing (NLP) is a subfield of linguistics, computer science, information engineering, and artificial intelligence concerned with the interactions between computers and human (natural) languages, in particular how to program computers to process and analyze large amounts of natural language data. Challenges in natural language processing frequently involve speech recognition, natural language understanding, and natural-language generation. Natural language processing has its roots in the 1950s. Already in 1950, Alan Turing published an article titled "Computing Machinery and Intelligence" which proposed what is now called the Turing test as a criterion of intelligence, a task that involves the automated interpretation and generation of natural language, but at the time not articulated as a problem separate from artificial intelligence.

Figure 12.14: A .pdf file is automatically recognized and opened

So far, we have learned two ways of uploading files: asking the user about the file type and making the file uploading process automated. Both approaches are valid, and which one you should choose depends on the use case. Simplifying our web apps with smart components should always be the preferred solution.

Simplifying web apps with smart components

So far in this chapter, we have learned about the principles of effective web application design. Now, we can move toward the user experience, which should always be simple, intuitive, and aesthetically pleasing.

The approach with the radio button, from a functional point of view, works very well but makes things a little bit too complex because it requires the user's intervention at the beginning and draws an ugly radio button on the screen.

The other approach is very neat and extremely clean because just a file uploader widget is present on the screen and the user can select the file by just clicking on it (or using drag and drop) without any other kind of intervention.

This is possible because the web app intercepts the file type property and uses it to open the file and read its content by selecting the proper library.

This kind of approach is quite smart and delineates the difference between an application made by a rookie and an application that looks very professional.

Summary

In this chapter, we learned how to manage file uploading in different ways and according to different approaches: first, by specifying the file type at any time to trigger the proper function, and second by making the file type detection automatic and seamless.

While the first approach involves the user, the second one makes our application usage very smooth.

In the next chapter, we will continue exploring advanced features and solutions to make our web applications more professional.

13
Creating a Secure Login and Signup Process for Web Applications

Let's continue our exploration of advanced techniques to make our web applications look professional and work well.

In this chapter, we are going to learn how to implement a login and signup page made with **Secure Hash Algorithm 256** (**SHA-256**) encryption and connected to a database in a secure and user-friendly way. By adopting this approach, we will be able to authenticate our web app users and store their credentials permanently. The login and signup page typically consists of a form where users can enter their username and password to access the web application. When a user logs in, their credentials are hashed using SHA-256 and compared to the stored hash in the database (in this context, we are using **SQLite3**). If the hashes match, the user is authenticated and granted access to the application. The signup page allows new users to create an account by entering their desired username and password.

In this chapter, we're going to cover the following main topics:

- Understanding the logic behind the login and signup page
- What is SHA-256 and why should we use it?
- Connecting to a relational database and interacting with it
- Retrieving or saving credentials from and to the database

Technical requirements

- In this chapter, we'll use the following libraries, packages, and tools:
    - Sublime Text
    - Python 3
    - `pipenv`
    - Streamlit
    - Pillow
    - `Sqlite3`
    - `hashlib`

- The code for this chapter can be found in this book's GitHub repository: https://github.com/PacktPublishing/Web-App-Development-Made-Simple-with-Streamlit/tree/main/Chapter13.

Understanding the logic behind the login and signup page

When a user creates an account on a website or application, they are typically asked to provide a username and password. The username is a unique identifier for the user, while the password is a secret that only the user should know.

The website or application then stores the username and password in a database. However, the password is not stored in plain text. Instead, it's converted into a **hash**. A hash is a one-way function, meaning that it is easy to calculate the hash of a password, but it is very difficult to reverse the process and calculate the password from the hash.

This is done for security reasons. If a hacker were to gain access to the database, they would not be able to read the passwords in plain text. They would only be able to read the hashes. Even if the hacker knew the hashing algorithm used, it would still be very difficult for them to crack the password.

When a user logs in, they are asked to enter their username and password. The website or application then calculates the hash of the password that the user entered and compares it to the hash that is stored in the database. If the two hashes match, then the user is successfully logged in.

Here is a step-by-step explanation of the logic behind the login and signup page:

1. The user enters their username and password on the signup page.
2. The website or application converts the password into a hash.
3. The website or application saves the username and password hash in the database.

4. The user is redirected to the login page.
5. The user enters their username and password on the login page.
6. The website or application calculates the hash of the password that the user entered and compares it to the hash that is stored in the database.
7. If the two hashes match, then the user is successfully logged in.
8. If the two hashes do not match, then the user is not successfully logged in.

There are a few reasons it is important to store the username and password hashes permanently in a database:

- To allow users to log into their accounts
- To allow users to recover their passwords if they forget them
- To prevent unauthorized access to user accounts

If the username and password hashes were not stored permanently in a database, then users would not be able to log into their accounts or recover their passwords if they forgot them. Additionally, unauthorized users would be able to gain access to user accounts simply by guessing the correct username and password.

It is important to note that even though passwords are stored as hashes in the database, it is still possible for hackers to crack them. However, it is much more difficult to crack a hash than it is to crack a plain text password.

Here are some tips for creating strong passwords:

- Use a mix of uppercase and lowercase letters, numbers, and symbols
- Make your password at least 12 characters long
- Avoid using common words or phrases in your password such as `qwerty`, `12345678`, `user`, `admin`, and so on
- Do not use your name, birthday, or other personal information in your password
- Use a different password for each website or application that you use

At this point, the importance of a signup/login page should be clear, as well as the importance of avoiding weak passwords. It's time to understand what a secure hash algorithm is.

What is SHA-256 and why should we use it?

SHA-256 is a cryptographic hash function that produces a 256-bit hash value from a data input. It is part of the *SHA-2 family of hash functions* (for more details, please check out https://justcryptography.com/sha-2/) that were designed by the **National Security Agency** (**NSA**) and published by the **National Institute of Standards and Technology** (**NIST**) in 2001.

SHA-256 is a widely used hash function for a variety of applications, including the following:

- **Password storage**: SHA-256 is used to store passwords securely. When a user creates an account on a website or application, their password is converted into an SHA-256 hash and stored in the database. When the user logs in, their password is converted into an SHA-256 hash and compared to the hash stored in the database. If the two hashes match, then the user is successfully logged in.

- **Digital signatures**: SHA-256 can be used to create digital signatures. A **digital signature** is a cryptographic technique that allows the sender of a message to verify their identity and the integrity of the message. To create a digital signature, the sender calculates the SHA-256 hash of the message and then encrypts the hash with their private key. The sender then sends the message and the encrypted hash to the recipient. The recipient calculates the SHA-256 hash of the message and then decrypts the encrypted hash with the sender's public key. If the two hashes match, then the recipient can be sure that the message is authentic and has not been tampered with.

- **File integrity verification**: SHA-256 can be used to verify the integrity of files. To do this, the SHA-256 hash of the file is calculated and then stored. When the file is needed, the SHA-256 hash of the file is calculated again and compared to the stored hash. If the two hashes match, then the file is known to be intact.

SHA-256 is considered to be a very secure hash function. It is resistant to collision attacks, meaning that it is very difficult to find two different inputs that produce the same hash value. It is also resistant to preimage attacks, meaning that it is very difficult to find the input that produces a given hash value.

Here are some reasons why you should use SHA-256:

- It is a very secure hash function
- It is widely used and supported
- It is relatively easy to implement
- It is free to use

If you need a secure way to store passwords, create digital signatures, or verify the integrity of files, then SHA-256 is a good choice.

Now that we have all the information we need, let's start coding. As usual, we have to follow some typical steps to set up a new virtual environment:

1. Create a new directory named `Login_Skeleton`.
2. Enter this directory and write `pipenv shell` to create a new virtual environment.
3. Install the `streamlit` and `pillow` packages.

4. Create a new empty Python file named app.py.
5. Launch your IDE (Sublime Text).

Figure 13.1 shows all these steps, from creating the new directory to installing the required libraries:

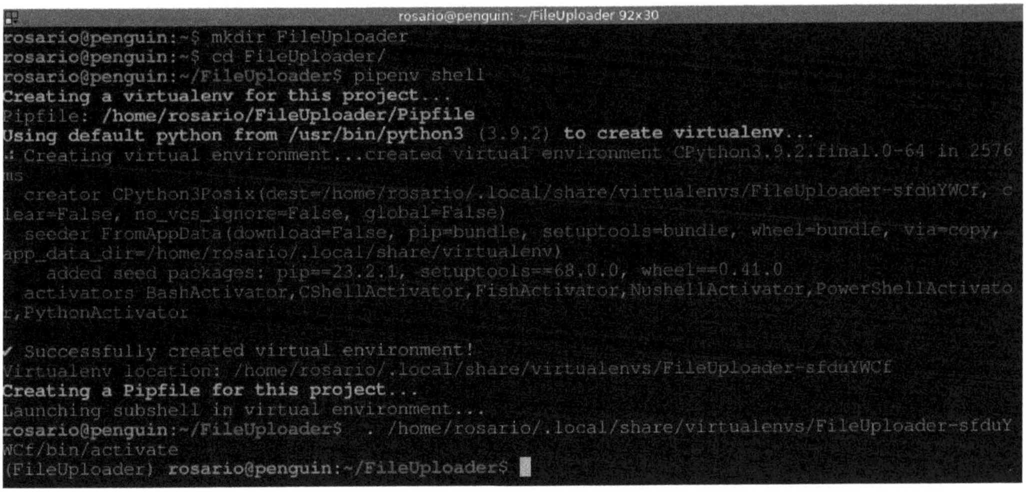

Figure 13.1: Virtual environment and app.py file preparation

Now, we are ready to edit the Python code in the app.py file.

Inside Sublime Text, we can start writing the code for our new login/signup web app, as shown in *Figure 13.2*:

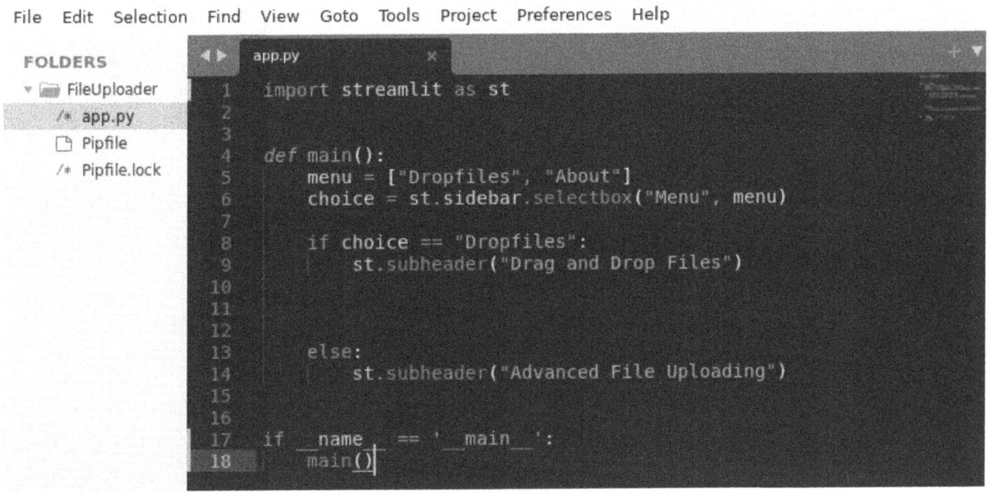

Figure 13.2: Starting code

The preceding code should be quite familiar. Here's a breakdown of what we did:

- At the very beginning, on *lines 1* and *2*, we import the necessary libraries – in this case, `streamlit` and `Pillow`.
- After that, on *line 5*, we create a `main()` function:
    - In the `main()` function, we write some HTML code in the `html_temp` variable (*line 8*) to set a big title in the web app that specifies the background color, the padding, and the text color
    - Then, we visualize the HTML code using the `st.markdown` instruction (*line 14*)
- Next, we create a list on *line 16* that contains the voices of the menu we want to visualize and add a selectbox in the sidebar on the left-hand side of the screen.
- Then, we check the selection (*line 19*) and if it is `Home`, we do something: at the moment, we just write some text in the `subheader` format. Meanwhile, if the selection is `Login` *(line 25)*, we pass (we will develop the code for this in the *Creating the Login menu* subsection); the same goes for `Signup` (*line 28*).
- Finally, we add an `About` section (*line 32*), where we are free to write anything we want.

Please note that in the **Home** section, just after the header, we can visualize an image thanks to the `st.image` instruction. This image, named `login.png`, must be present in the same directory as the `app.py` file, as shown in the **Folder** section of the editor in *Figure 13.2*.

As usual, when we execute the following command, the web application will be executed:

```
pipenv run streamlit run app.py
```

The result in the browser is quite simple and clean:

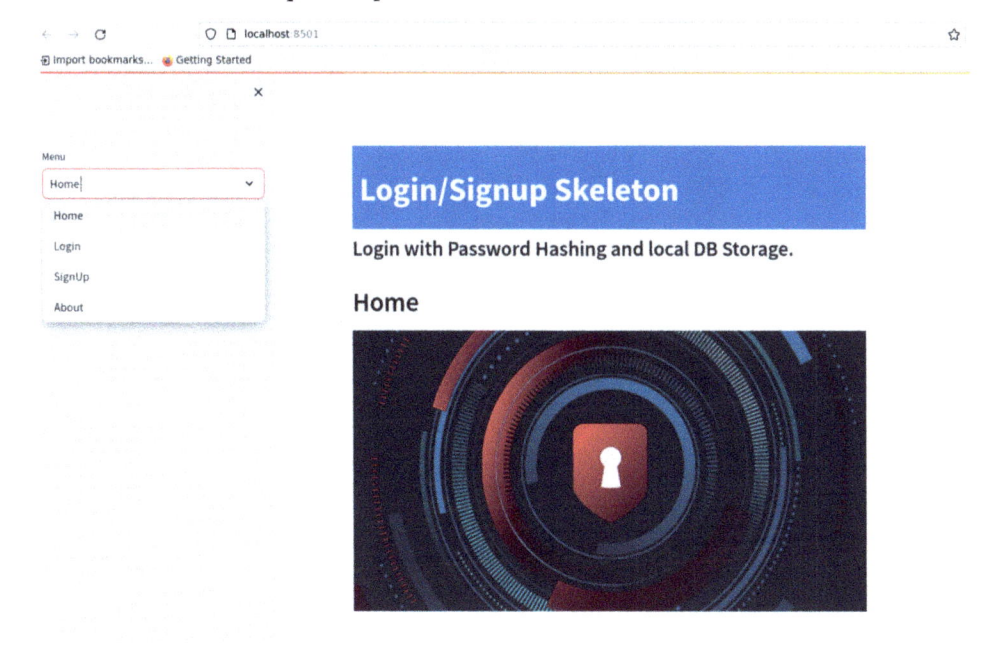

Figure 13.3: The login/signup web app in the browser

On the left, we have the sidebar with the menu, while in the middle, there is the **Home** section with a beautiful picture.

The skeleton is ready. Now, it's time to connect our web app to a database so that we can save all username/password data and use it at the proper time.

Connecting to a relational database and interacting with it

As explained in the *Understanding the logic behind the login and signup page* section, we want to save the accounts in a database. So, we have to import the database libraries. As mentioned previously, we are using a **SQLite3** database. So, first of all, let's install its Python library by typing the following:

```
pipenv install sqlite3
```

Then, simply import the library by writing `import sqlite3` in our `app.py` file.

Making a SQLite3 database work for us is a quite simple task. For this, we need to open a *connection* to the database by specifying its name (in our case, `userdata.db`) as an argument and creating a *cursor* to execute operations in it.

On *lines 6* and *7* in *Figure 13.4*, the connection and cursor are created:

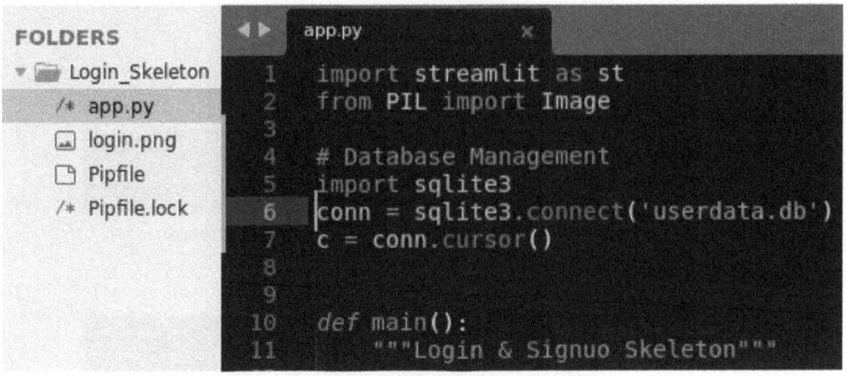
FOLDERS
Login_Skeleton
app.py
login.png
Pipfile
Pipfile.lock
app.py
1 import streamlit as st
2 from PIL import Image
3
4 # Database Management
5 import sqlite3
6 conn = sqlite3.connect('userdata.db')
7 c = conn.cursor()
8
9
10 def main():
11 """Login & Signuo Skeleton"""

Figure 13.4: The connection to the database and its cursor

To recap, the *connection* (`conn`) opens a connection to the database while the *cursor* (`c`) makes it possible to operate inside the database. Essentially, we need three different operations:

- Table creation
- Data insertion
- Data retrieval

The best way to implement these operations is to create a specific function dedicated to each of these operations, as shown in the following figure:

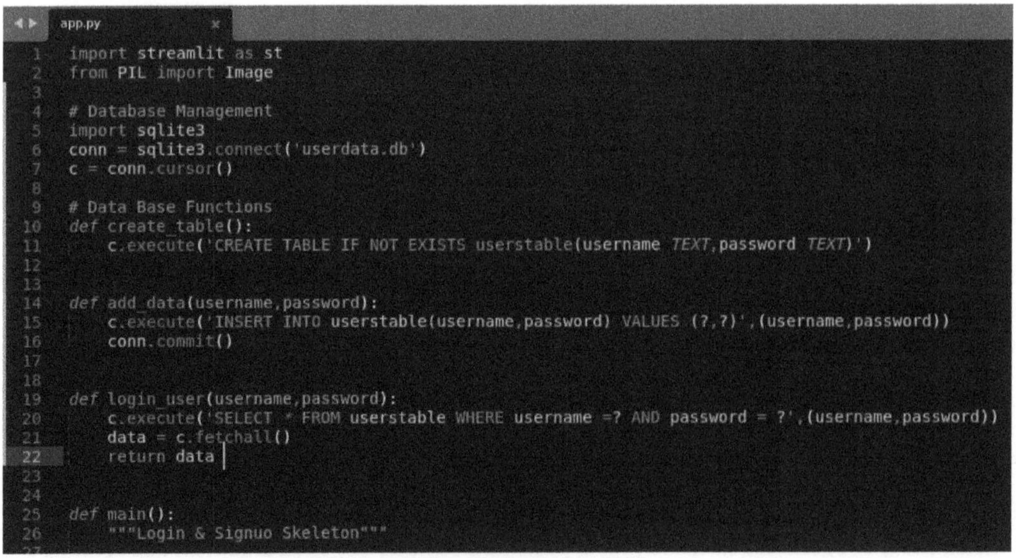
app.py
1 import streamlit as st
2 from PIL import Image
3
4 # Database Management
5 import sqlite3
6 conn = sqlite3.connect('userdata.db')
7 c = conn.cursor()
8
9 # Data Base Functions
10 def create_table():
11 c.execute('CREATE TABLE IF NOT EXISTS userstable(username TEXT,password TEXT)')
12
13
14 def add_data(username,password):
15 c.execute('INSERT INTO userstable(username,password) VALUES (?,?)',(username,password))
16 conn.commit()
17
18
19 def login_user(username,password):
20 c.execute('SELECT * FROM userstable WHERE username =? AND password = ?',(username,password))
21 data = c.fetchall()
22 return data
23
24
25 def main():
26 """Login & Signuo Skeleton"""

Figure 13.5: The database functions

Let's take a closer look at these three functions:

- The first one is named `create_table`. Simply put, this function creates a table named `userstable`, but only if this table is not already present in the database. The `userstable` table has two columns named `username` and `password`, each of which contains text. It's important to understand that the `CREATE TABLE` instruction is given to the database using the cursor we created in *Figure 13.4*. So, the cursor, leveraging the opened connection, makes it possible to *deliver* operations (or functions) to the database.

- The second function is named `add_data` because it oversees data insertion or values inside the `userstable` table we created with the `create_table` function. So, we pass two values to the `add_data` function – a username and a password – as an argument and it inserts these two values in the `userstable` table in the following order: the username value in the `username` column and the password value in the `password` column. Once again, the cursor oversees carrying out the instruction. `conn.commit()` is extremely important because, without this *commit*, the new username and values won't be stored in the database.

- The third function is named `login_user` and, similar to the `add_data` function, has two arguments: `username` and `password`. It takes these two values and looks for them inside the `userstable` table, then retrieves (`fetchall`) all the results and puts them in a variable named `data`. This `data` variable is returned as the final output of the function. In this way, it is possible to check when a username and a password are present in the database. Once again, the cursor oversees carrying out the commands.

With these three functions ready, we can move on to the **Login** voice of the menu in the `app.py` file.

Creating the Login menu

First, we need a couple of text inputs, one for the username and one for the password, after which we can put them in the sidebar. So, let's add two new lines, as shown on *lines 46* and *47* in the following figure:

```
36      menu = ["Home", "Login", "SignUp", "About"]
37      choice = st.sidebar.selectbox("Menu", menu)
38
39      if choice == "Home":
40          st.subheader("Login with Password Hashing and local DB Storage.")
41          st.header("Home")
42
43          st.image("login.png", use_column_width = True)
44
45      elif choice == "Login":
46          username = st.sidebar.text_input("Username")
47          password = st.sidebar.text_input("Password",type='password')
48
49      elif choice == "SignUp":
50          pass
```

Figure 13.6: Text input for username and password

Upon specifying `type='password'` on *line 47*, the password we type will be hidden; by clicking on the *eye* icon, we can see the password clearly in the browser, as shown in the following figure:

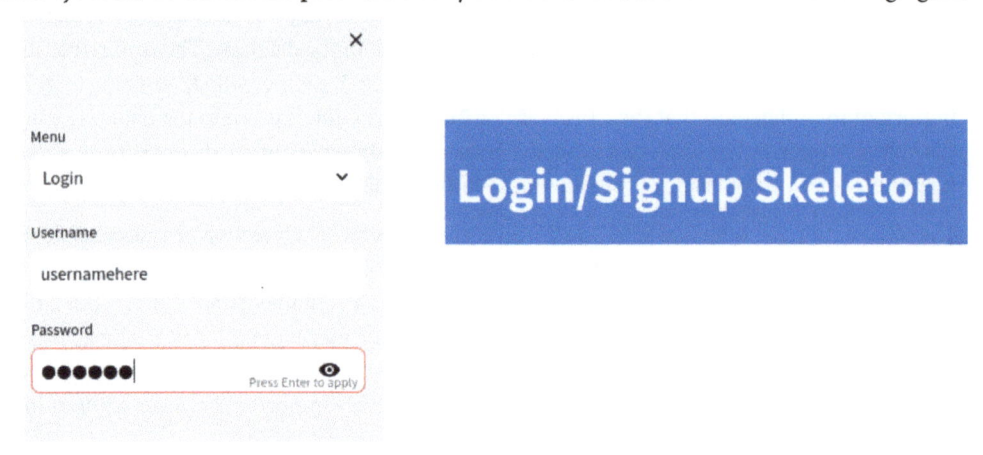

Figure 13.7: The password is hidden

At this point, the logic behind the login should be quite clear: we insert a username and a password and look for them in the database to understand whether a specific user is allowed to log into our app or not.

As usual, let's have a look at the code that performs this function:

```
36        menu = ["Home", "Login", "SignUp", "About"]
37        choice = st.sidebar.selectbox("Menu", menu)
38
39        if choice == "Home":
40            st.subheader("Login with Password Hashing and local DB Storage.")
41            st.header("Home")
42
43            st.image("login.png", use_column_width = True)
44
45        elif choice == "Login":
46            username = st.sidebar.text_input("Username")
47            password = st.sidebar.text_input("Password",type='password')
48
49            if st.sidebar.checkbox("Login"):
50                st.subheader("NAME of YOUR APP Here!")
51                create_table()
52
53                result = login_user(username,password)
54
55                if result:
56                    st.success("Logged In as: {}".format(username))
57                    task = st.selectbox("Task",["Task A","Task B"])
58
59
60                else:
61                    st.warning("Incorrect Username/Password")
```

Figure 13.8: The "Login" section's code

Here's a breakdown of what the code in *Figure 13.8* does:

- On *line 49*, we added a checkbox; when it is selected, a new subheading is printed in the `main` section of the web app.
- After that, on *line 51*, the `create_table` function, which we described previously, is executed. In this way, a new table named `userstable` will be created in the database, but only if it doesn't exist already.
- On *line 53*, the `login_user` function is executed, with the username and password that were inputted using the two `text_inputs` widgets on *lines 46* and *47* as arguments.
- If the result of the data fetching is positive, we print the **Logged in…** message with *success* and show a selectbox with a couple of tasks (just some placeholders); otherwise, we print a *warning* stating the **Incorrect Username/Password** message.

If you try to log in now, you'll get the **Incorrect Username/Password** message since no data is present in the database.

To populate the database, we must implement the `SignUp` function. Let's see how.

Creating the Sign Up menu

The logic is the same as that for the `Login` function but we must make a couple of changes, as shown in the following code:

```python
    elif choice == "Login":
        username = st.sidebar.text_input("Username")
        password = st.sidebar.text_input("Password",type='password')

        if st.sidebar.checkbox("Login"):
            st.subheader("NAME of YOUR APP Here!")
            create_table()

            result = login_user(username,password)

            if result:
                st.success("Logged In as: {}".format(username))
                task = st.selectbox("Task",["Task A","Task B"])



            else:
                st.warning("Incorrect Username/Password")


    elif choice == "SignUp":
        st.subheader("Create An Account")
        new_username = st.text_input("Username")
        new_password = st.text_input("Password",type='password')
        if st.button("Sign Up"):
            create_table()

            add_data(new_username,new_password)

            st.success("You have successfully created an Account")

    else:
        st.subheader("About Section")
```

Figure 13.9: The "SignUp" section code

Here's a breakdown of what we did:

- On *lines 66* and *67*, we have two `text_input` widgets to collect the username and the password, but this time, we are putting them in the `main` section of the web app and not in the sidebar.
- After that, on *line 68*, we add a button with a label of `Sign Up`. When this button is pushed, we execute the `create_table` function (we must ensure that the `userstable` table exists; otherwise, we will get a runtime error).
- On *line 71*, we execute the `add_data` function. We've already explained this function (see *Figure 13.5*), so we know that by passing the username and password that have been inputted by the `text_input` widgets to it, we create a new record in the database. This new record will contain the new username and password.
- Finally, on *line 73*, we print a beautiful *success* message to confirm the creation of the account.

Let's see the web application in action.

Running the app

In the menu, select **Sign Up** and insert a new username, such as `user1`, and a password, such as `12345` (please remember that during real usage, you should use a stronger password):

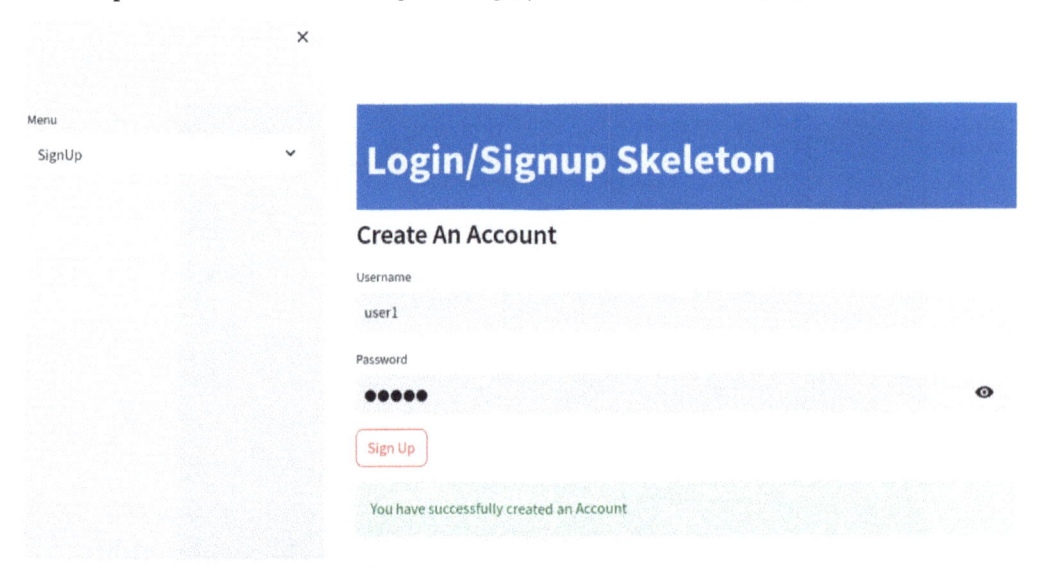

Figure 13.10: Using Sign Up to create a new account

Then, click on the **Sign Up** button; you'll get a **You have successfully created an Account** message.

With that, we have inserted our first account into our database. This means we can try to log in.

Select **Login** from the menu, type the username (**user1**) and password (**12345**), and enter the web application. We'll get a **Logged in as: user1** message and the list of tasks (I repeat, these are just placeholders):

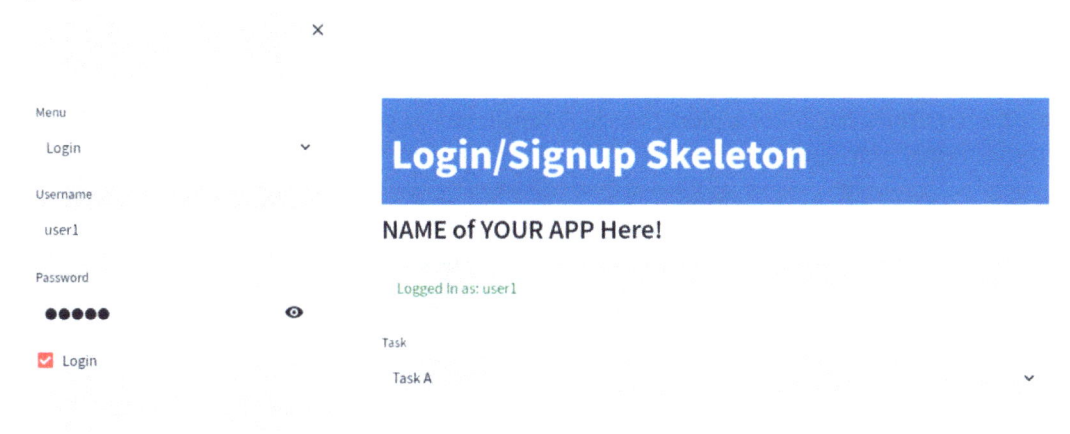

Figure 13.11: Using "Login" to enter the web application

When we try to log in with an incorrect username or password, we get the following output:

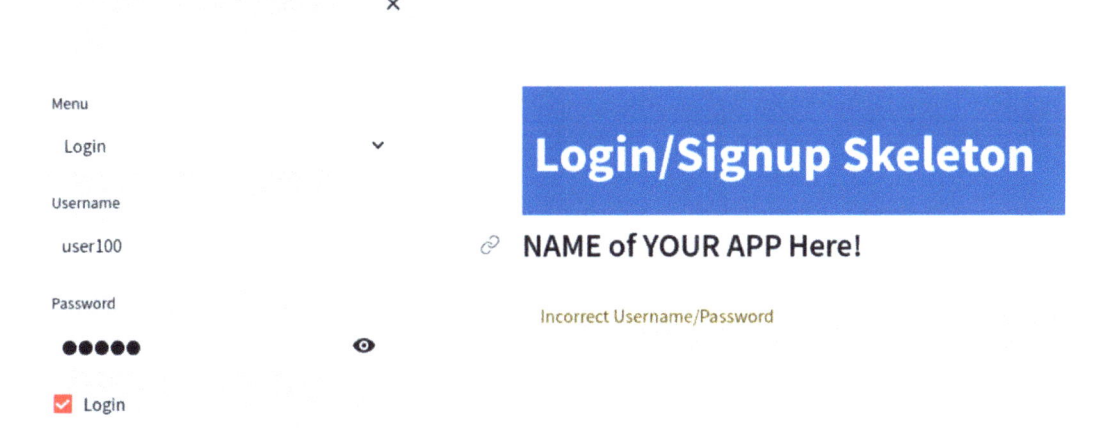

Figure 13.12: Logging in with the wrong username/password

We typed `user100`, but this username is not present in the database, so it is not possible to log in. We cannot enter the web application and for this reason, we cannot see the list of tasks.

The web application is working very well. Next, we'll add a nice graphical user interface to our app.

Adding a graphical user interface

From the command line, please install **DB Browser for SQLite**, a very nice graphical interface for managing SQLite databases. Type the following instruction:

```
sudo apt install sqlitebrowser
```

Once the installation has finished, please launch the application; a graphical user interface, as shown in the following figure, should appear:

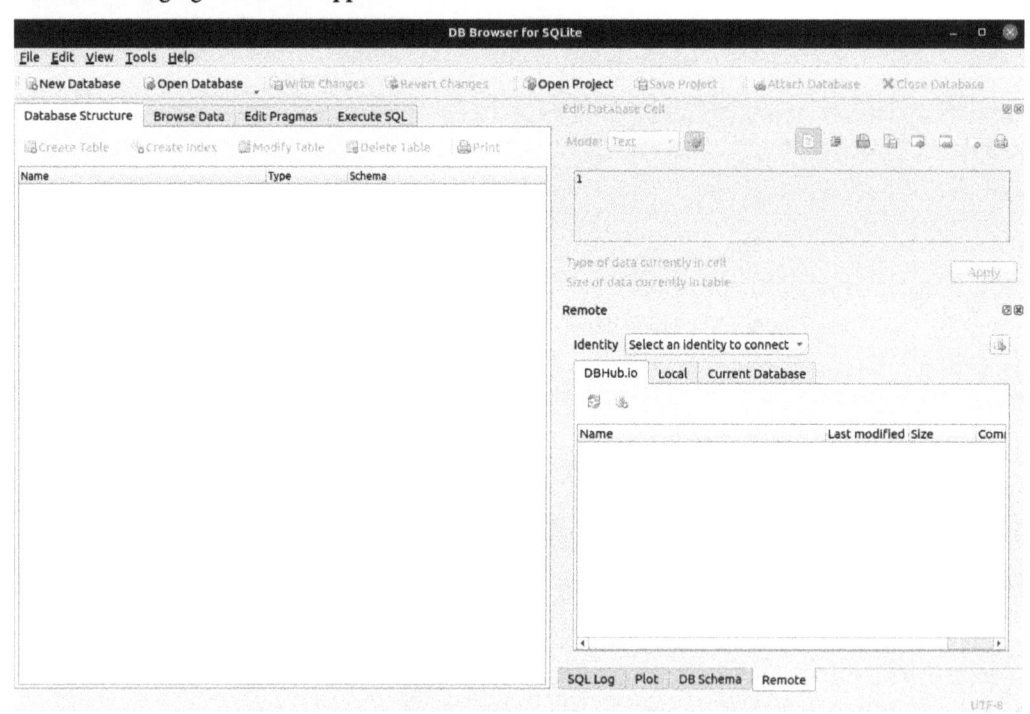

Figure 13.13: DB Browser for SQLite

With that, we are ready to open the database we created in our web app:

1. Click on **File | Open Database**.
2. As shown in the `Login_Skeleton` directory, there is a file named `userdata.db`. Select it and open it:

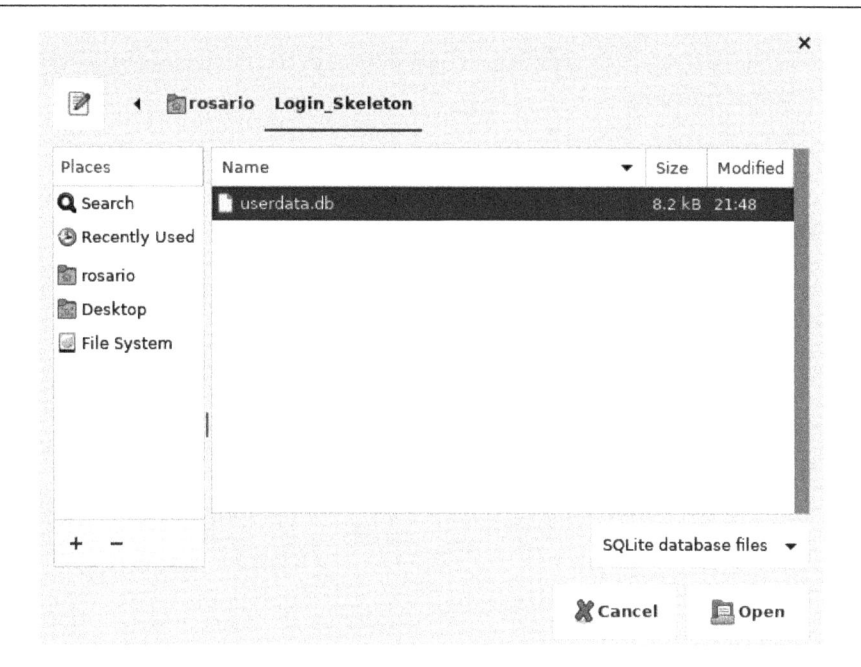

Figure 13.14: Opening the userdata.db database

You should see your database's structure, as shown in the following figure:

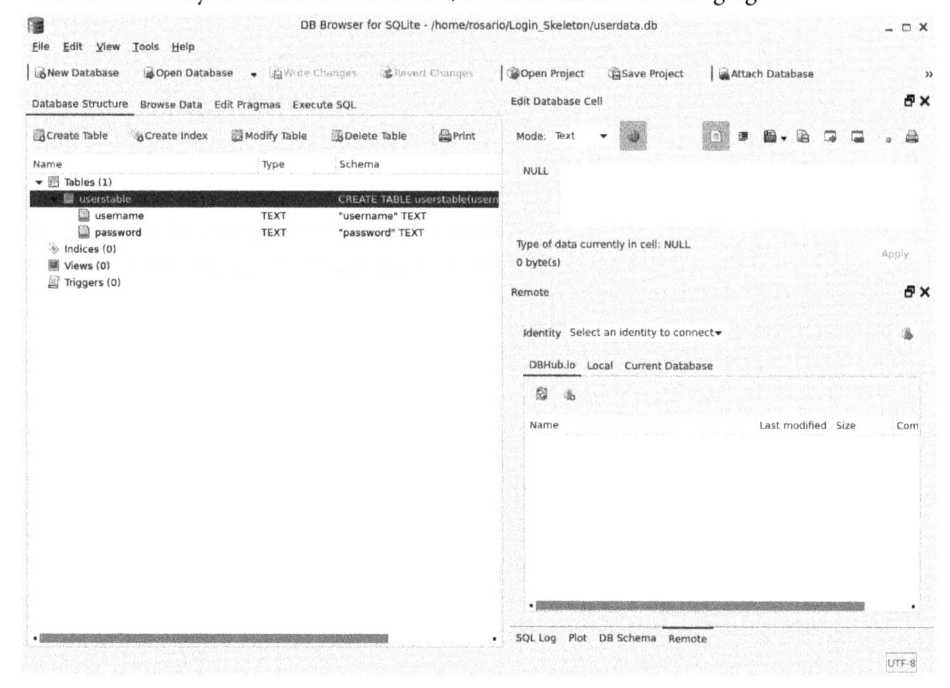

Figure 13.15: The database's structure

As we know, the database has a table named `userstable`, and this table has two text columns: `username` and `password`.

3. Select the `Browse Data` tag.

   As shown in the following figure, the `userstable` table contains the account we created previously – the one where the username is equal to **user1** and the password is equal to **12345**:

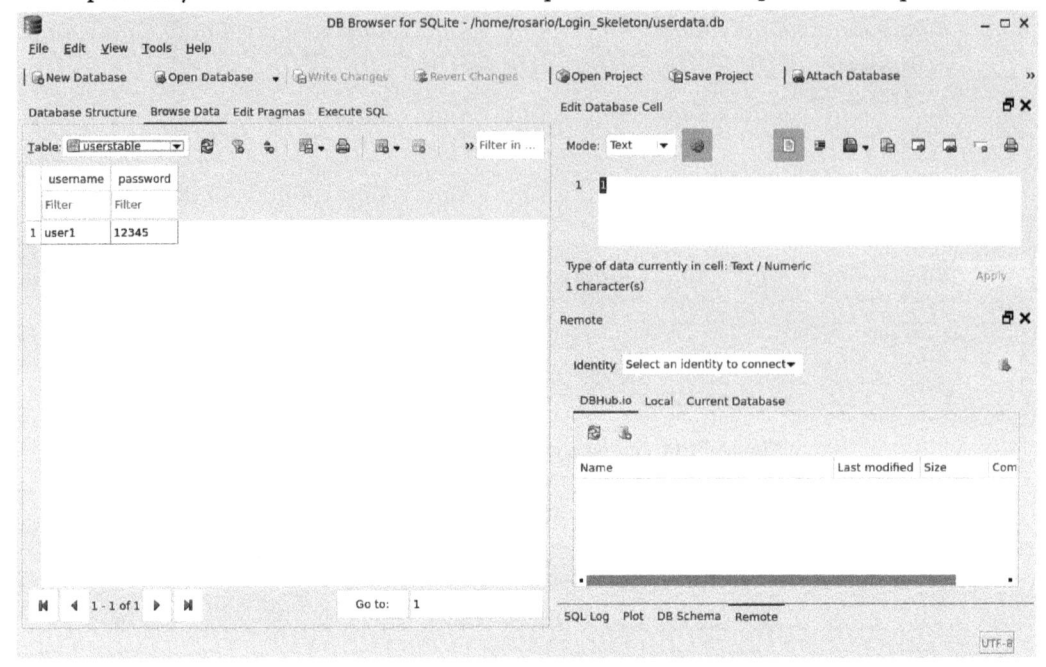

Figure 13.16: The account saved in our table

There is one big problem related to security here: the password is in *plain text*. Anybody that can access the `userdata.db` file in our database can read it. This is the reason why we must introduce hashing encryption in our code – to make it almost impossible for anybody to discover our passwords in such an easy way. We'll see how in the next section.

Retrieving or saving credentials from and to the database

From a theoretical point of view, we have already discussed what a hash is and why we should use one. From a practical point of view, there are many Python packages available (for example, `sha256` and `pycrypto`), but one of the easiest to use that's also very effective is `hashlib`. This library is installed in Python by default, so we don't have to install it in our virtual environment; all we have to do is import it into our `app.py` file.

While leveraging `hashlib`, all we need to do is use its `sha256` method to create the hash encryption of the password. Once again, let me highlight that *SHA-256* is a very strong form of encryption from a security perspective.

These are the new lines of code we need for the hashing process:

```
1   import streamlit as st
2   from PIL import Image
3
4   # Database Management
5   import sqlite3
6   conn = sqlite3.connect('userdata.db')
7   c = conn.cursor()
8
9   #Hashing Function (passlib,hashlib,bcrypt,scrypt)
10  import hashlib
11
12  def make_hashes(password):
13      return hashlib.sha256(str.encode(password)).hexdigest()
14
15
16  # Data Base Functions
17  def create_table():
18      c.execute('CREATE TABLE IF NOT EXISTS userstable(username TEXT,password TEXT)')
19
```

Figure 13.17: The make_hashes function

Here's a breakdown of what we did:

- On *line 5*, we imported `hashlib`.
- On *lines 12* and *13*, we created a new function named `make_hashes`. This function has just one input argument: the password. This password is passed to the `sha256` method, which creates a hashing from it. This hashing is converted into hexadecimal and returned.

As we know, there is no way to decode a hashing. This means that once we convert the password into a hash, we cannot convert it back again. So, to complete the authentication/login of a user, we must type the password into `text_input`, convert it into its hashing, and compare the result with the hashing stored in the database. If the two hash codes are the same, this means that the inputted password is correct; otherwise, it is different from the saved one.

Implementing this procedure requires us to make a few modifications to our code:

1. First, we must convert the inputted password into a hashing. This can be done using the `make_hashes` function we just discussed.
2. Then, we need to compare this hashing with the one saved in the database.

The first code change affects the **Login** section, as shown in the following figure:

```
52      elif choice == "Login":
53          username = st.sidebar.text_input("Username")
54          password = st.sidebar.text_input("Password",type='password')
55
56          if st.sidebar.checkbox("Login"):
57              st.subheader("NAME of YOUR APP Here!")
58              create_table()
59
60              hashed_pswd_init = make_hashes(password)
61              result = login_user(username,check_hashes(password,hashed_pswd_init))
62
63              if result:
64                  st.success("Logged In as: {}".format(username))
65                  task = st.selectbox("Task",["Task A","Task B"])
66
67
68              else:
69                  st.warning("Incorrect Username/Password")
70
```

Figure 13.18: The hashing of the inputted password

Here's what we are doing in the preceding code:

- On *line 60*, we make a hash of the inputted password.
- On *line 61*, leveraging the `check_hashes` function, we compare the hashed password with the one (with the hashing) saved in the database. If they are the same, then the login process is successful.

Let's write the `check_hashes` function; the code is very short, as shown in the following figure:

```
1   import streamlit as st
2   from PIL import Image
3
4   # Database Management
5   import sqlite3
6   conn = sqlite3.connect('userdata.db')
7   c = conn.cursor()
8
9   #Hashing Function (passlib,hashlib,bcrypt,scrypt)
10  import hashlib
11
12  def make_hashes(password):
13      return hashlib.sha256(str.encode(password)).hexdigest()
14
15  def check_hashes(password,hashed_text):
16      if make_hashes(password) == hashed_text:
17          return hashed_text
18      return False
```

Figure 13.19: The "check_hashes" function

Here's what we are doing in the preceding code:

- On *line 15*, we define the new function, which has only two arguments: a password (clear text) and the hashed text (the hashing of the password saved in the database).
- On *line 16*, we can see that if the hashing of the password (which we get using the `make_hashes` function) is the same as the one stored in the database, we return the hashed text (the hashed version of the password); otherwise, we return `False`.

So, moving back to *line 61* of the code shown in *Figure 13.18*, when `check_hashes` returns the hashed password, the `result` variable is `True` and the code enters the `success` part of the `if` cycle. Otherwise, when `check_hashes` returns `False`, the `result` variable is `False` as well, and the code enters in the `else` part of the `if` cycle, denying the login.

Now, if we try to log into the web application using the account we saved previously (**user1**, **12345**), we'll fail and get a warning. The reason is that in our database, we saved the password without introducing the hashing, so the password is stored in clear text.

To complete all the login/signup web application coding, we must change the **SignUp** section a little bit, making sure that the passwords of the accounts are saved in their own hashing version:

```
76
77      elif choice == "SignUp":
78          st.subheader("Create An Account")
79          new_username = st.text_input("Username")
80          new_password = st.text_input("Password",type='password')
81          if st.button("Sign Up"):
82              create_table()
83
84              hashed_pswd = make_hashes(new_password)
85              add_data(new_username,hashed_pswd)
86
87              st.success("You have successfully created an Account")
88
89      else:
90          st.subheader("About Section")
```

Figure 13.20: The final "SignUp" section

Here's what we are doing in the preceding code:

- On *line 84*, we create the hashing of the inputted password
- On *line 85*, we save it in the database, together with its related username

270　　Creating a Secure Login and Signup Process for Web Applications

At this point, we've finished coding. We can try out the entire set of features of the web application, starting with creating a new account with a username of `user2` and a password of `09876`:

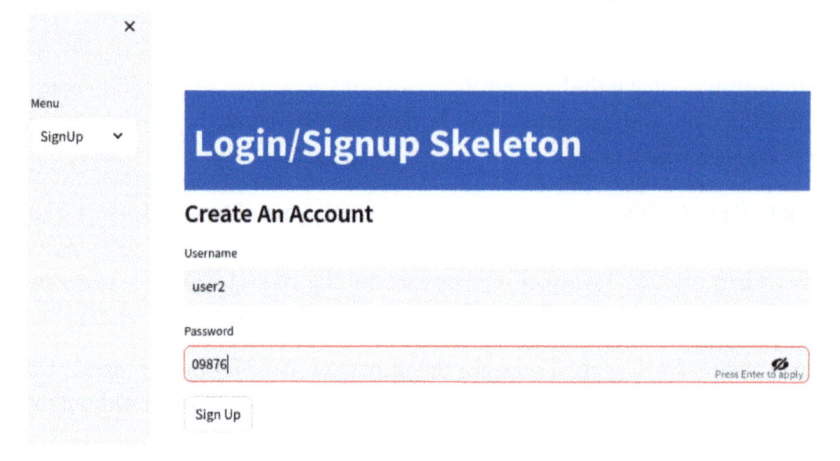

Figure 13.21: Creating a new account

As we can see, in the database browser, the new password has been saved as a hashing code:

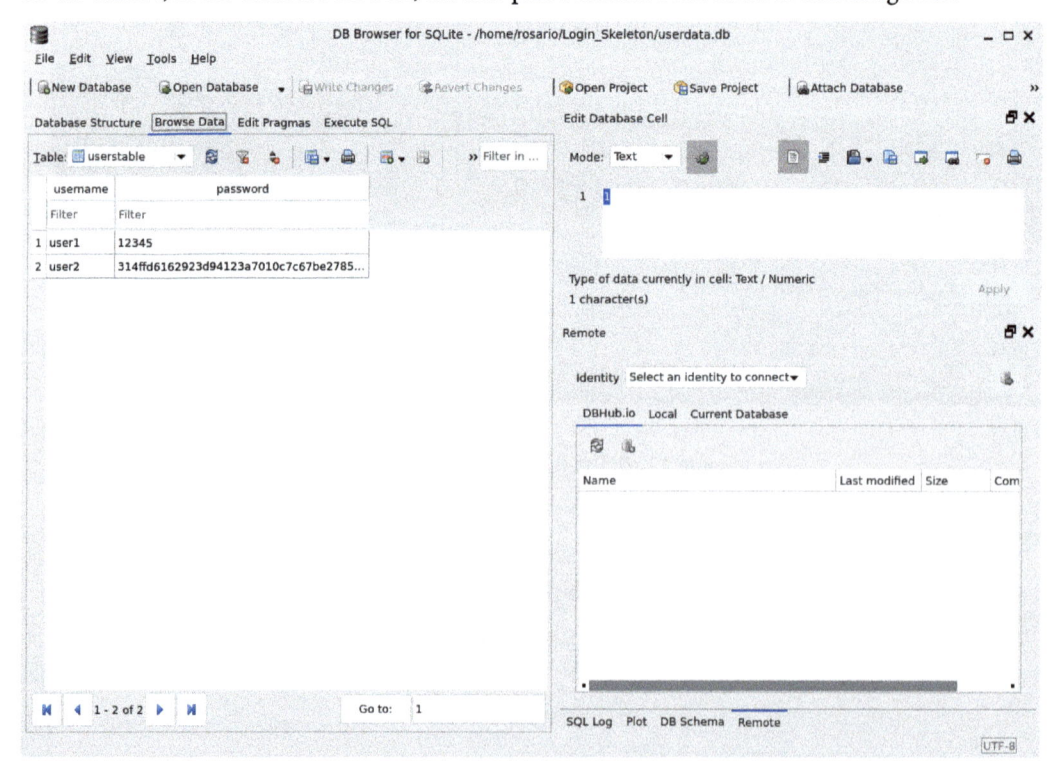

Figure 13.22: The new password in its hashing version

Anybody who gets the database file can read its content but cannot understand what the password is since getting the plain text from the hashing is quite impossible.

Let's try to log in:

Figure 13.23: Logging in with the new account

The inputted password is converted into its hash and compared with the one stored in the database; since the two hashes match, we get the following result:

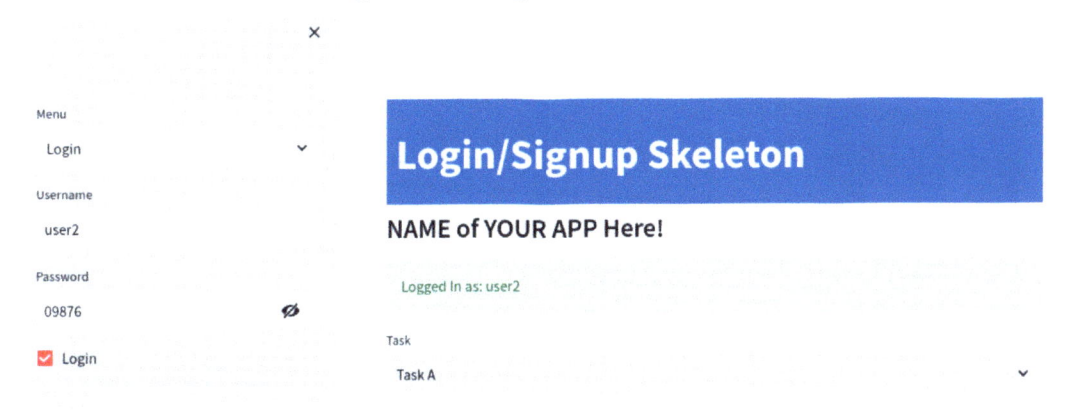

Figure 13.24: The login was successful

The login process has been completed with success, and the user can access the application's tasks.

It's very interesting to understand that even if the given text differs in a very small element from another, its hashing will be completely different. Add another account to the database, this time with a password such as `09875`, and check how different its hashing is from the one coming from the `09876` password.

This chapter was full of complex information, but the result we got is very valuable: a complete app skeleton that can be used in all our web applications that need to manage signing up, logging in, hashing, and saving data permanently in a database.

As usual, here is all the code we developed:

```python
import streamlit as st
from PIL import Image

# Database Management
import sqlite3
conn = sqlite3.connect('userdata.db')
c = conn.cursor()

#Hashing Function (passlib,hashlib,bcrypt,scrypt)
import hashlib

def make_hashes(password):
    return hashlib.sha256(str.encode(password)).hexdigest()

def check_hashes(password,hashed_text):
    if make_hashes(password) == hashed_text:
        return hashed_text
    return False


# Data Base Functions
def create_table():
    c.execute('CREATE TABLE IF NOT EXISTS userstable(username TEXT,password TEXT)')


def add_data(username,password):
    c.execute('INSERT INTO userstable(username,password) VALUES (?,?)',(username,password))
    conn.commit()


def login_user(username,password):
    c.execute('SELECT * FROM userstable WHERE username =? AND password = ?',(username,password))
    data = c.fetchall()
    return data


def main():
    """Login & Signuo Skeleton"""

    html_temp = """
    <div style=background-color:{};padding:10px;border-radius:10px">
    <h1 style="color:{};text-align:center;">Login/Signup Skeleton</h1>
    </div>
    """

    st.markdown(html_temp.format('royalblue','white'),unsafe_allow_html=True)

    menu = ["Home", "Login", "SignUp", "About"]
    choice = st.sidebar.selectbox("Menu", menu)
```

Figure 13.25: Signup/login skeleton – part 1

In the first part of the code, we started importing the libraries (*lines 1-5*) and then created the connection and the cursor to the database (*lines 6-7*). After that, we imported the hashlib library (*line 10*) and created the make_hashes and check_hashes functions (*lines 12 and 15*). On *lines 22 and 26*, we defined two functions to create new tables and add data to the database, and on *line 31*, we defined the function that manages user login.

On *line 37*, we defined the `main` function, introduced some HTML code just to make the app more beautiful, and implemented the application menu:

```python
51      if choice == "Home":
52          st.subheader("Login with Password Hashing and local DB Storage.")
53          st.header("Home")
54
55          st.image("login.png", use_column_width = True)
56
57      elif choice == "Login":
58          username = st.sidebar.text_input("Username")
59          password = st.sidebar.text_input("Password",type='password')
60
61          if st.sidebar.checkbox("Login"):
62              st.subheader("NAME of YOUR APP Here!")
63              create_table()
64
65              hashed_pswd_init = make_hashes(password)
66              result = login_user(username,check_hashes(password,hashed_pswd_init))
67
68              if result:
69                  st.success("Logged In as: {}".format(username))
70                  task = st.selectbox("Task",["Task A","Task B"])
71
72
73              else:
74                  st.warning("Incorrect Username/Password")
75
76
77      elif choice == "SignUp":
78          st.subheader("Create An Account")
79          new_username = st.text_input("Username")
80          new_password = st.text_input("Password",type='password')
81          if st.button("Sign Up"):
82              create_table()
83
84              hashed_pswd = make_hashes(new_password)
85              add_data(new_username,hashed_pswd)
86
87              st.success("You have successfully created an Account")
88
89      else:
90          st.subheader("About Section")
91
92
93  if __name__ == '__main__':
94      main()
```

Figure 13.26: Signup/login skeleton – part 2

In the second part of the code, we managed the menu. So, if the user selects **Login**, we implement the proper code (*lines 57-74*). When the user selects **Sign Up**, we implement the code dedicated to this function (*lines 77-87*). Finally, on *line 90*, we have the **About** section.

This chapter is very important because an application almost always needs to manage accounts and therefore usernames and passwords. To accomplish this task properly, encrypting the password very securely is the key.

Summary

In this chapter, we understood the logic behind login and signup pages and learned a very solid way of implementing and managing accounts according to the best practices summarized here.

When users sign up on our web apps, they provide a username and a password. The username serves as their unique identifier, while the password is a secret known only to them. For security, these credentials are stored in a database, but the passwords are not kept as plain text. Instead, they are converted into a hash, a one-way function that is easy to compute from a password but hard to reverse. This ensures that even if a hacker accesses the database, they can't easily decipher the passwords.

During login, the user's entered password is hashed and compared with the stored hash; if they match, the user is granted access. Storing these hashes is crucial for allowing users to log in and recover passwords. Although hacking these hashes is possible, it is much more difficult than cracking plain text passwords.

Implementing robust business code is the main target of any web application since by doing this, it is possible to address any kind of problem that the code is supposed to solve. Giving customers more beautiful interfaces, well-designed applications, and very customized tools is another key skill that a real web application designer should have. This is exactly what we are going to discuss in the next chapter.

14
Customizing Pages, Personalizing Themes, and Implementing Multi-Pages

Streamlit recently added many advanced features to make customizing our apps easier and more accurate. Now, it's possible to configure our pages so that we can hide the *burger menu* or the footer, for example. It's possible to change many standard links and deeply personalize themes, colors, and styles. Finally, it's possible to deal with multi-pages natively, naming and configuring folders in a very specific way.

All these new features are a very powerful way to deeply customize our web applications, making their look and behavior exactly the way we imagined during the design stage of the project.

In this chapter, we're going to cover the following main topics:

- Understanding new features related to deep customization
- Creating deeply customized pages
- Understanding theming and `.toml` files
- Exploring the multi-pages feature

Technical requirements

- In this chapter, we will be using the following libraries, packages, and tools:
    - Sublime Text
    - Python 3

- pipenv
- Streamlit

- The code for this chapter can be found in this book's GitHub repository: https://github.com/PacktPublishing/Web-App-Development-Made-Simple-with-Streamlit/tree/e54d7b3d8840a3971ab8241acf6a1a6212e51f77/Chapter14

Understanding new features related to deep customization

For this chapter, no new packages are needed – all we need is Streamlit. Let's start by creating a new empty Python file; as usual, you can call it `app.py`. Then, open the IDE. We can start coding by just importing `streamlit` and adding a title both in the sidebar and in the main part of the web application, as shown in *Figure 14.1*:

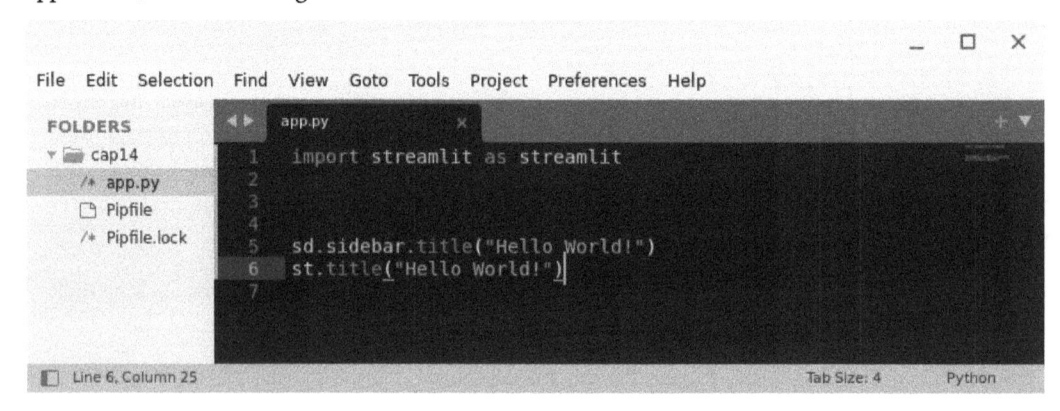

Figure 14.1: The starting code

Launching the application opens the browser on localhost at port `8501` and, as usual, we get something like this:

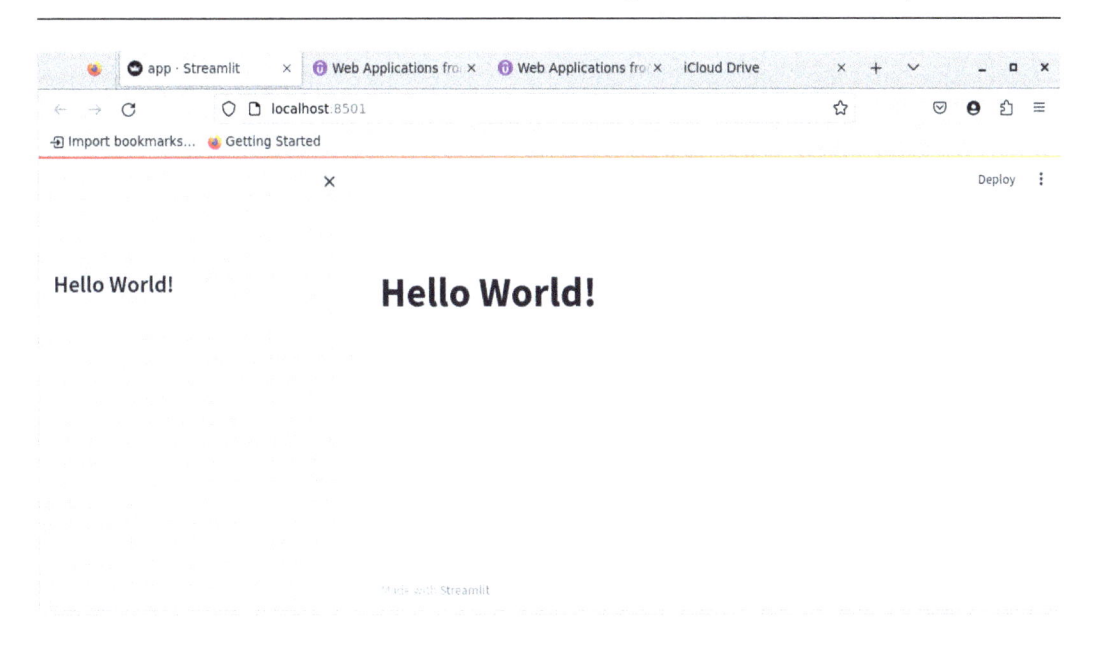

Figure 14.2: The starting web app

This is very simple: we get the same title in the sidebar and the main part of the web app. Taking a closer look, we can find some very interesting elements that can be customized:

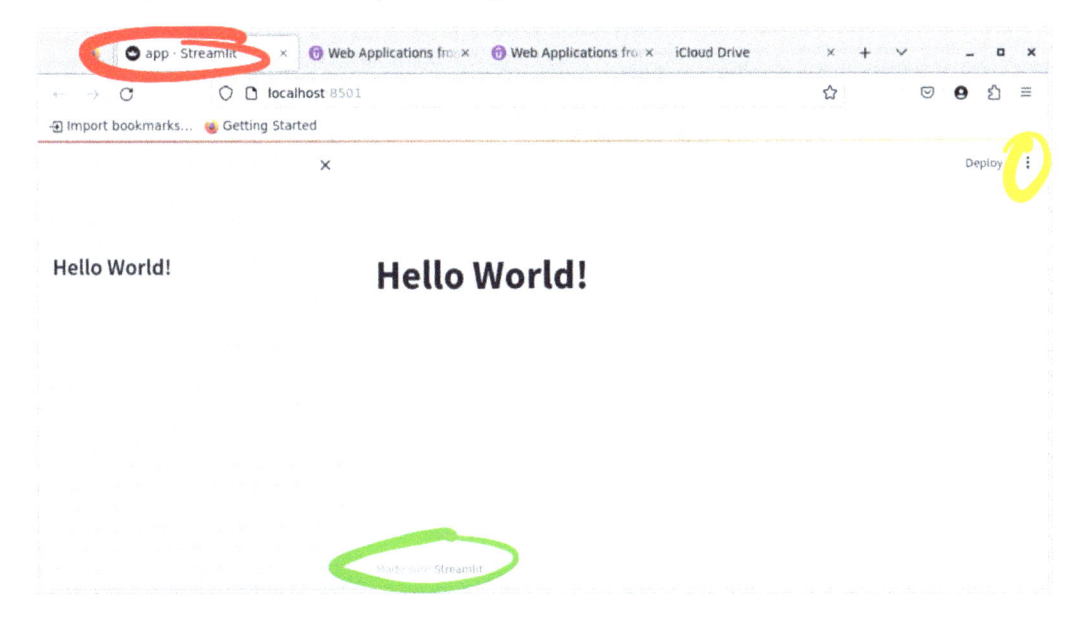

Figure 14.3: App title and icon, footer, and menu

In *Figure 14.3*, we have the following:

- In red, we can see the *title* and *icon* of our web application. At the moment, these are the default ones: Streamlit's icon and our Python filename.
- In green, we can see the so-called *footer*.
- In yellow, we can see the *three points menu*. In previous versions of Streamlit, this was the so-called *hamburger menu*.

Let's start from the *three points menu* and click on it. We'll get the following pop-up menu:

Rerun R

Settings

Print

Record a screencast

About

Developer options

Clear cache C

Figure 14.4: The "three points" menu

In this pop-up menu, there are several voices:

- **Rerun**, to rerun the web app after a change in the code
- **Print**, to print the screen
- **Record a screencast**, to record our web app
- **Clear cache**, to clear the cache with just one click

The other two voices, **About** and **Settings**, are very interesting because they can be customized, helping us in personalizing the look and feel of our application.

Let's open **Settings**. We'll get the following new window:

Settings

Development

☑ Run on save
Automatically updates the app when the underlying code is updated.

Appearance

☐ Wide mode
Turn on to make this app occupy the entire width of the screen

Choose app theme, colors and fonts

Use system setting ⌄

Edit active theme

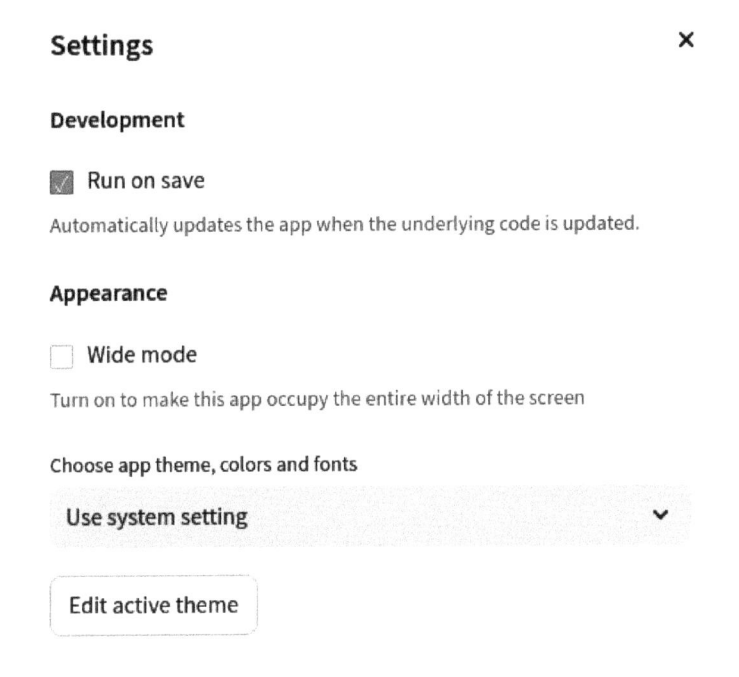

Figure 14.5: Settings

From this menu, we can automatically update the app when the underlying code is updated. We can also choose to run it in wide or normal mode and set the theme; this can be **Light**, **Dark**, or the same as our system's settings (**Use system setting**).

The customization level is even deeper. In fact, by clicking on **Edit active theme**, we'll see the following window:

Edit active theme

(screenshot of the Streamlit Edit active theme panel)

- Primary color: #FF4B4B
- Background color: #FFFFFF
- Text color: #31333F
- Secondary background color: #F0F2F6
- Font family: Sans serif

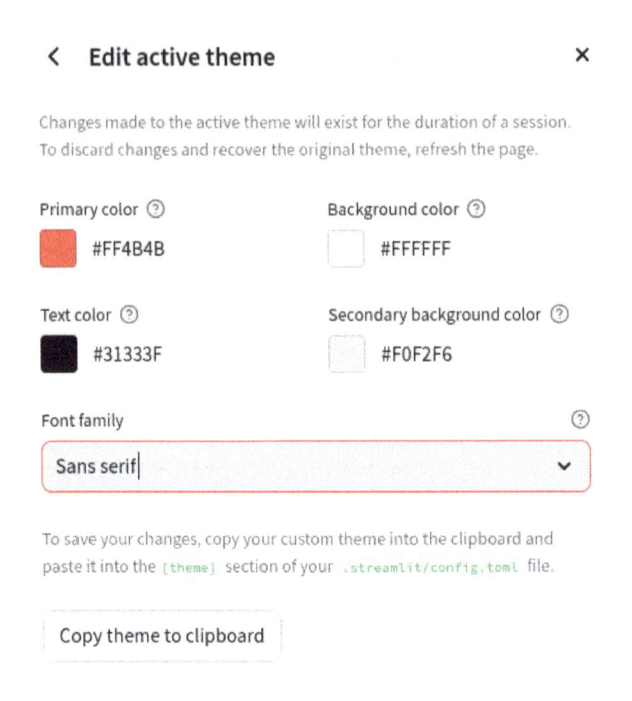

Figure 14.6: The Edit active theme window

From this window, we can customize the **Primary color**, **Text color**, **Background color**, and **Secondary background color** value. Moreover, we can select the font from a list, and we can copy the configuration to the clipboard.

As indicated in the note below the font selection, if we want to make these choices permanent, we must edit a file named `config.toml` in the `.streamlit` directory; it's a hidden folder. We'll take care of this file later, in the *Understanding theming and .toml files* section.

Now, it's time to see how we can customize our pages.

Creating deeply customized pages

Now, let's move back to the code, taking care of the title and icon marked in red in *Figure 14.3*:

Figure 14.7: The set_page_config method

On *line 3*, immediately after `import streamlit as st`, we set the page configuration using the `st.set_page_config` method. In this way, we can customize the page title and icon (an emoji or even a PNG or an ICO file is supported), set the layout of the content in the main section (it can be wide or centered), and decide whether the sidebar is expanded or collapsed at start time.

The result, with the configuration reported in *Figure 14.7*, is as follows:

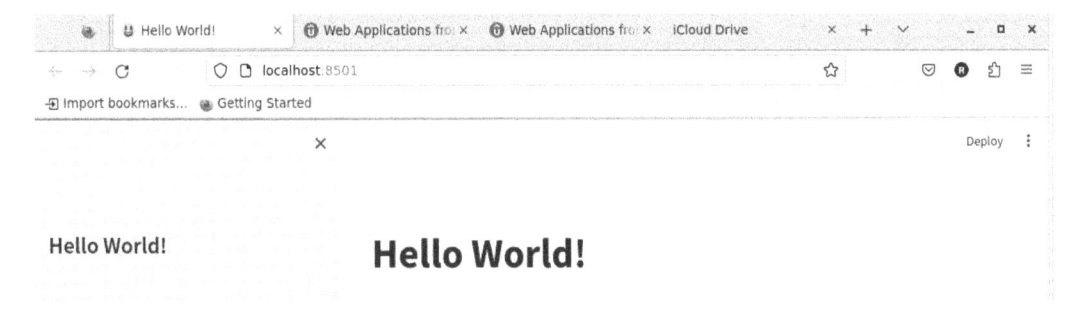

Figure 14.8: A customized page

It is up to you to try different settings while using all the available parameters.

Customizing Pages, Personalizing Themes, and Implementing Multi-Pages

With the `set_page_config` method, we can do even more. In fact, by adding the few lines of code shown in *Figure 14.9*, we can modify the *three points menu* and the **About** section:

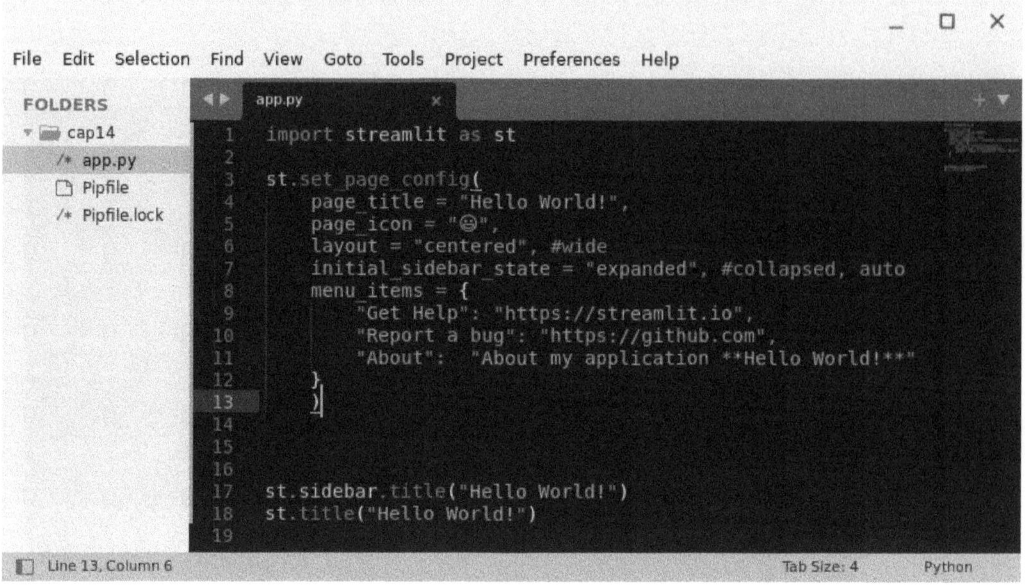

```python
import streamlit as st

st.set_page_config(
    page_title = "Hello World!",
    page_icon = "😊",
    layout = "centered", #wide
    initial_sidebar_state = "expanded", #collapsed, auto
    menu_items = {
        "Get Help": "https://streamlit.io",
        "Report a bug": "https://github.com",
        "About":  "About my application **Hello World!**"
    }
)


st.sidebar.title("Hello World!")
st.title("Hello World!")
```

Figure 14.9: Full customization with set_page_config

Here's a breakdown of what we did in the preceding code:

- On *lines 9* and *10*, we added two voices to the *three points menu* called **Get Help** and **Report a bug**. They direct the users to the Streamlit website and GitHub, respectively. You can insert any kind of URL you wish here.

- On *line 11*, we added a note that will be shown in the **About** option of the menu; this note supports the standard Markdown syntax.

Figure 14.10 shows the new *three points menu* and the customized **About** section side by side:

Figure 14.10: The customized three points menu and About section

Next, referring to the *footer* shown in *Figure 14.3*, let's learn how to remove it with a very short instruction:

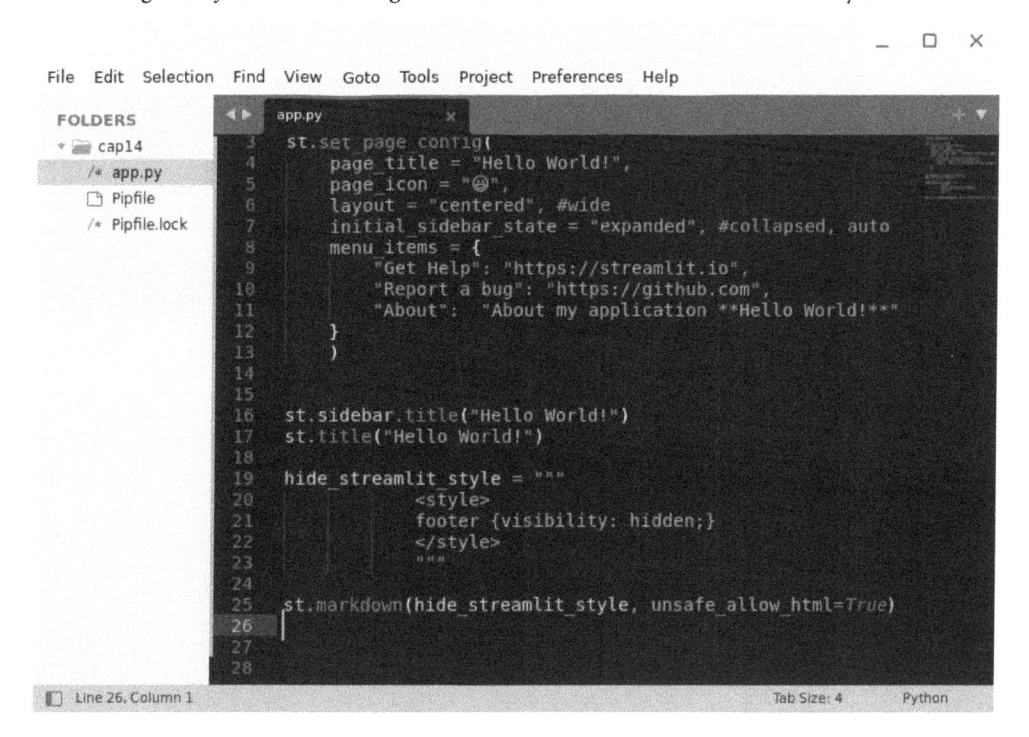

Figure 14.11: Instruction to remove the footer

Here's what we are doing in the preceding code:

- On *line 19*, we added very simple html code to set the footer's visibility to *hidden*
- On *line 25*, as usual, using `st.markdown` with `unsafe_allow_html`, we used that `html` code

It is quite interesting that just by adding another line of code before the `footer` row, we can easily remove the *three point menu* as well. The final code is as follows:

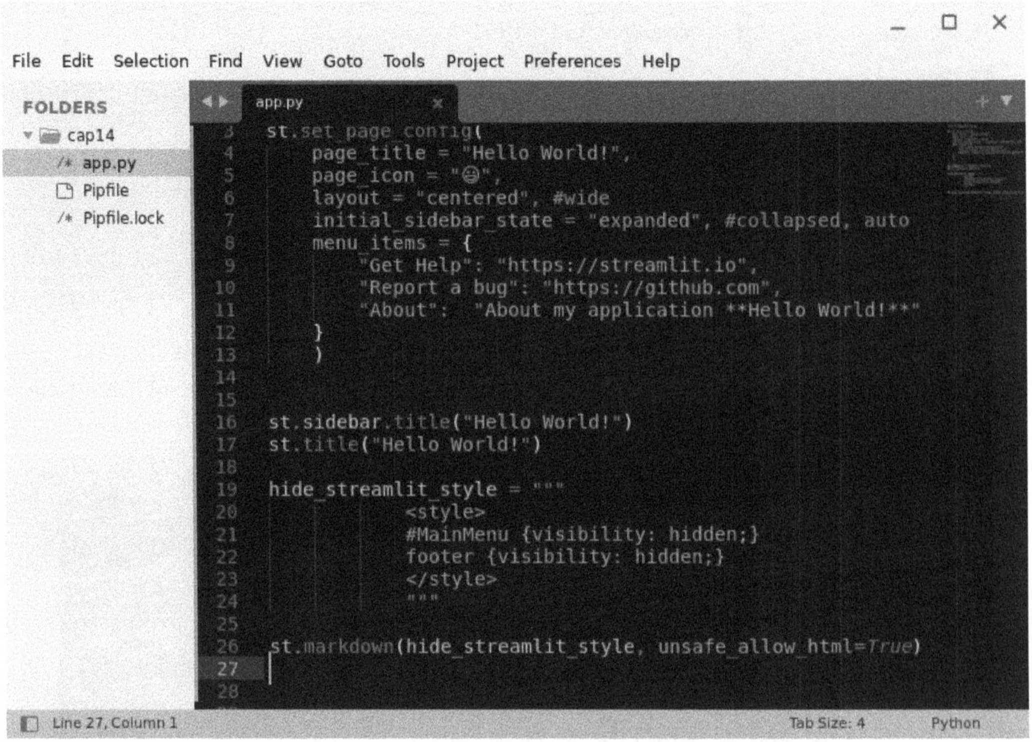
File Edit Selection Find View Goto Tools Project Preferences Help
FOLDERS
cap14
app.py
Pipfile
Pipfile.lock
app.py
st.set_page_config(
page_title = "Hello World!",
page_icon = "😀",
layout = "centered", #wide
initial_sidebar_state = "expanded", #collapsed, auto
menu_items = {
"Get Help": "https://streamlit.io",
"Report a bug": "https://github.com",
"About": "About my application **Hello World!**"
}
)
st.sidebar.title("Hello World!")
st.title("Hello World!")
hide_streamlit_style = """
<style>
#MainMenu {visibility: hidden;}
footer {visibility: hidden;}
</style>
"""
st.markdown(hide_streamlit_style, unsafe_allow_html=True)
Line 27, Column 1
Tab Size: 4
Python

Figure 14.12: The instruction to remove the footer and main menu

The web application looks as follows:

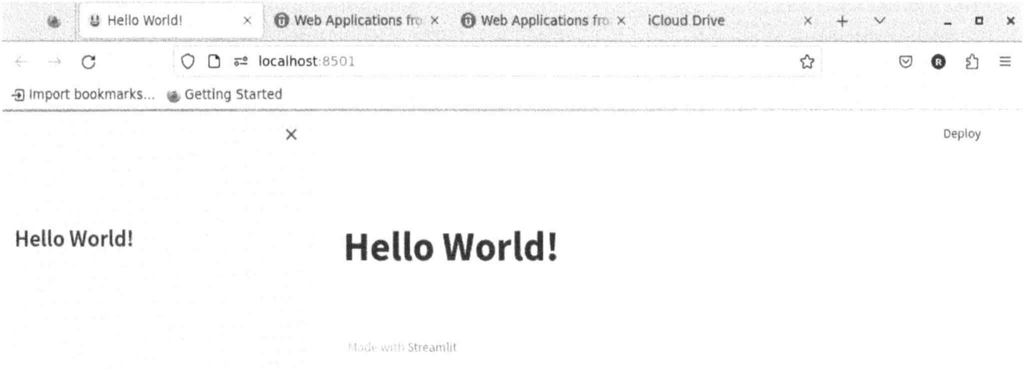

Figure 14.13: The web app without a footer and main menu

In this section, we learned how to customize our pages by leveraging the `set_page_config` instruction. Moreover, we learned how to remove the `footer` row and the *three points menu* from our Streamlit pages. In the next section, we'll learn how to work on *themes*.

Understanding theming and .toml files

At the beginning of this chapter, in the *Understanding new features related to deep customization* section, we learned how to change the theme of our web apps directly from the browser. Streamlit has supported natively custom theming since version 0.79.0, which means that we can customize our theme directly from the backend without working in the browser.

We've already seen that there is a hidden directory named `.streamlit` and that inside this directory, there is a file named `config.toml`.

If we want to customize the theme, first of all, we must open this `config.toml` file, then add the following instructions to it:

```toml
[theme]
primaryColor="#F63366"
backgroundColor="#FFFFFF"
secondaryBackgroundColor="#F0F2F6"
textColor="#262730"
font="sans serif"
```

Figure 14.14: Theme configuration with the config.toml file

The configuration in *Figure 14.14* is the classical light theme. If you want to have a completely different effect, you can use your preferred color codes and choose a font between Sans-serif, Serif, or Monospace. To get a quick indication of color codes, try to look for *HTML Color Codes* on the internet or check a website such as `https://html-color.codes/`.

For example, let's say we adopt the following HTML color codes:

```
[theme]
primaryColor="#F63366"
backgroundColor="#ff5733"
secondaryBackgroundColor="#ffd133"
textColor="#335bff"
font="monospace"
```

Figure 14.15: A completely different theme configuration

We will get a rather strong result, as shown in the following figure:

Figure 14.16: A rather strong theme with a Monospace font

Very simple! Customizing the theme is just a matter of using HTML color codes and a TOML file. Now, let's learn what *multi-pages* are.

Exploring the multi-pages feature

Multi-pages in Streamlit are a way to organize your app into multiple pages, each with its own content. This can be useful for large apps with a lot of functionalities, or for apps that need to be divided into different sections for different users.

To create a multi-page app in Streamlit, you simply need to create a new folder called `pages` in the same folder as your main app file. Then, create new Python files inside the `pages` folder, each of which will represent a different page in your app.

Once you have created your pages, you can start adding content to them. You can use any Streamlit widgets and functions that you want, just like you would in a regular Streamlit app.

When you run your app, Streamlit will automatically detect the pages in the `pages` folder and add them to a navigation bar in the sidebar. Users can then click on the different pages to navigate between them.

According to the preceding explanation, everything sounds easy; as we are going to see, it really is.

Creating multi-pages

Let's build a simple multi-pages web application. As usual, we'll start by building the skeleton of the app:

1. First, we'll create a new file. We will call it `app.py`.
2. Then, open the `app.py` file in Sublime Text and import `streamlit`.
3. Now, create a `main` function that displays just the title, as shown in *Figure 14.17*:

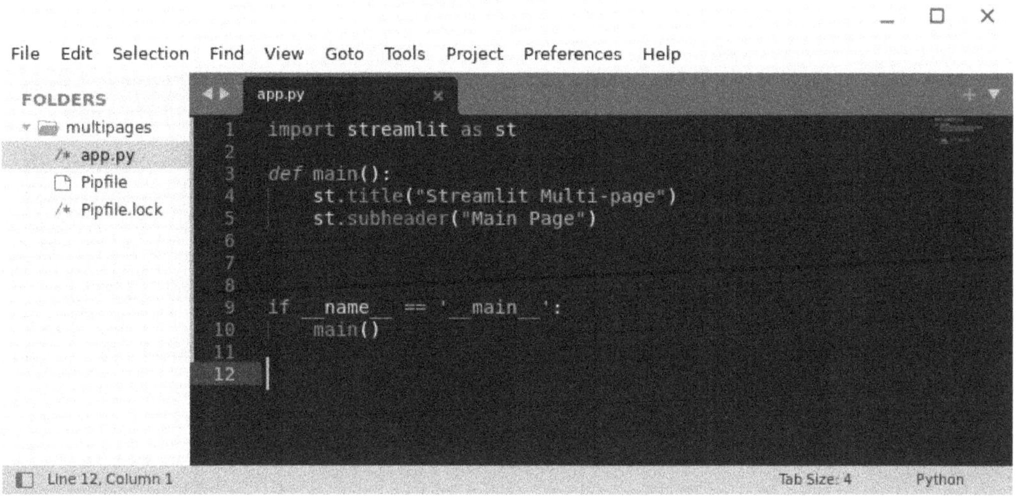

Figure 14.17: The basic skeleton for our "multi-page" web app

As you can imagine, the preceding code produces a rather simple web app in the browser. This is the result:

Figure 14.18: The starting point

Please note that the theme is still the one we configured in the *Understanding theming and .toml files* section.

Now, let's create a directory named `pages`. This directory must be at the same level as our main file – that is, it must be in the same folder as the `app.py` file. We can write the following instruction in the terminal:

```
mkdir pages
```

Now, we can move inside this `pages` directory and then create a new file named `page1.py`. To do so, we must write the following instruction in the terminal:

```
cd pages
touch page1.py
```

The structure of our folders is shown in *Figure 14.19*:

Figure 14.19: The structure of our folders and files

Exploring the multi-pages feature | 289

There is a `root` directory containing the `app.py` file and a directory named `pages`. There is also a file named `page1.py` inside the `pages` directory.

If we check our browser, we'll see that Streamlit automatically recognized the presence of two pages – one named `app` and another named `page1`:

Figure 14.20: Two pages in the sidebar

The names of the two pages in the sidebar are the same as the names of the Python files in our directories, just without `.py`.

Upon clicking on `page1`, we get an empty page because the `page1.py` file is still empty. Let's move back to Sublime Text and add some code to it:

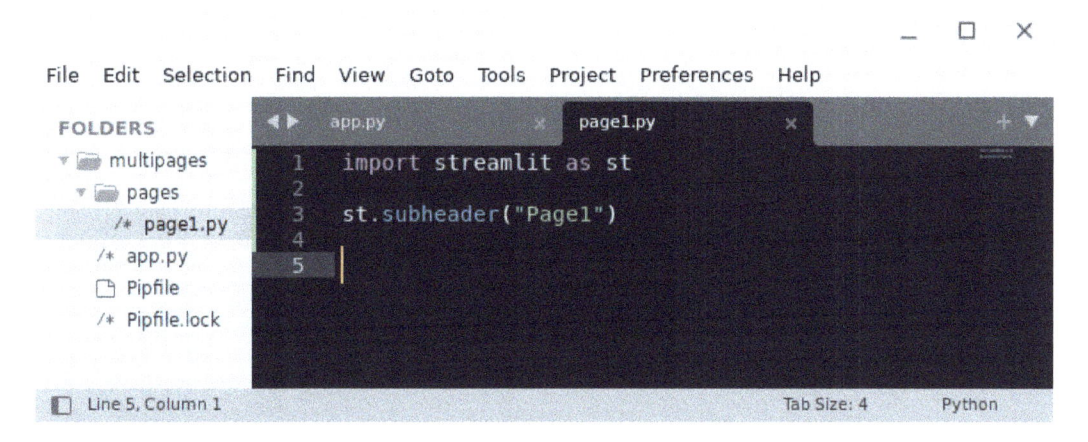

Figure 14.21: Some simple code to add to the page1.py file

The new code is very simple – it just prints **Page1** on the screen. This is the result:

Figure 14.22: The result after clicking on page1

We can continue in the same way by creating a new file named `page2.py` inside the `pages` directory. In the terminal, we can simply write the following:

```
cd pages
touch page2.py
```

Then, moving to Sublime Text, we can edit the `page2.py` file in the same way we did with `page1.py`, as shown in the following figure:

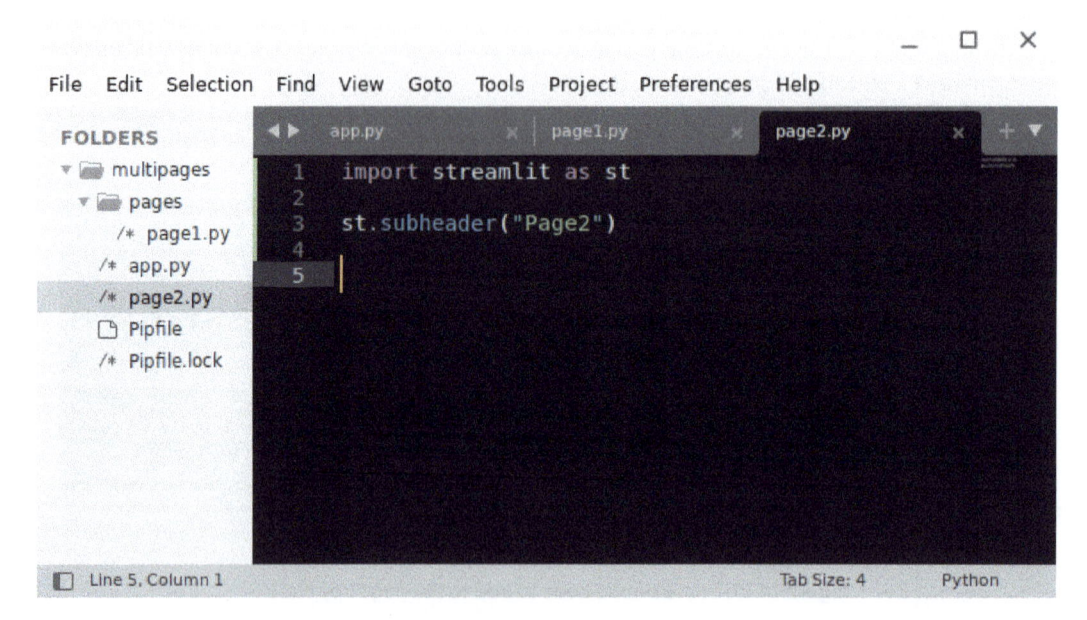

Figure 14.23: Some simple code to add to the page2.py file

This is the result in the web application:

Figure 14.24: A new page in our multi-page web application

As we can see, we have a new page in the list in the sidebar. After clicking **page2**, a new page can be visualized in the main part of the web application.

Let's create another file inside the `pages` directory, this time naming it `new_feature.py`. We'll add the same code we used for `page1.py` and `page2.py` to it. This is the result in the browser:

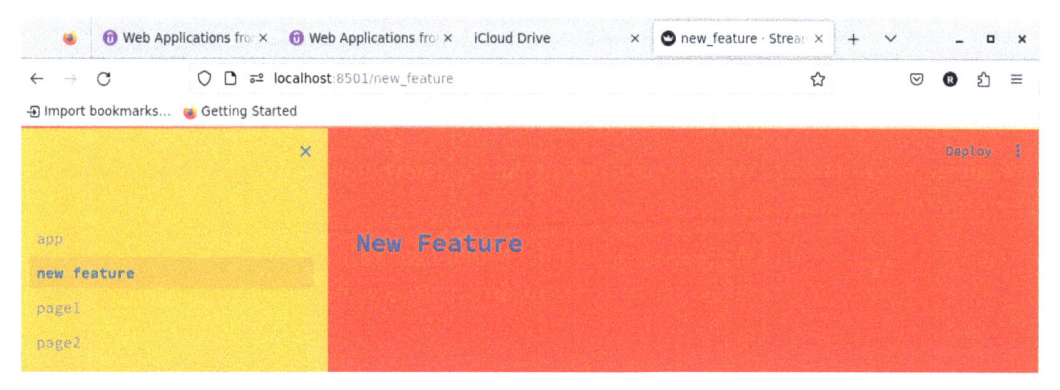

Figure 14.25: The pages in the sidebar are in alphabetical order

We can see that the pages in the sidebar are ordered alphabetically. If we want to change the order of the pages, we must change their names in a specific way.

In the terminal, write the following:

```
mv page1.py 01_page1.py
```

In this way, we renamed the old `page1.py` to `01_page1.py`.

Similarly, we can rename the old `page2.py` to `02_page2.py` and the old `new_feature.py` to `03_new_feature.py`:

```
mv page2.py 02_page2.py
mv new_feature.py 03_new_feature.py
```

If we check our browser now, we'll see that the page order is different:

Figure 14.26: The pages in the sidebar now follow a customized order

The order of the pages in the sidebar now follows the changes we applied to the files since we placed 01, 02, and 03 at the beginning of their names.

As we can see, Streamlit is very smart since it doesn't put the numeration at the beginning of the page names, only their real names.

If we check the address bar of the browser shown in *Figure 14.26*, we'll see that the *new feature* page URL is `localhost:8501/new_feature`. So, Streamlit uses the page names to change the URL accordingly.

Passing a variable from one page to another

Multi-pages is something very powerful since it is possible to pass variables from one page to another. Let's learn how to leverage this feature.

Let's make a little change to our `app.py` file – that is, to the main page – as shown in the following screenshot:

Figure 14.27: A new variable in the "app.py" file

On *line 3*, we created a text variable named `my_variable` that is printed on the screen on *line 8*. This is the result in the web application:

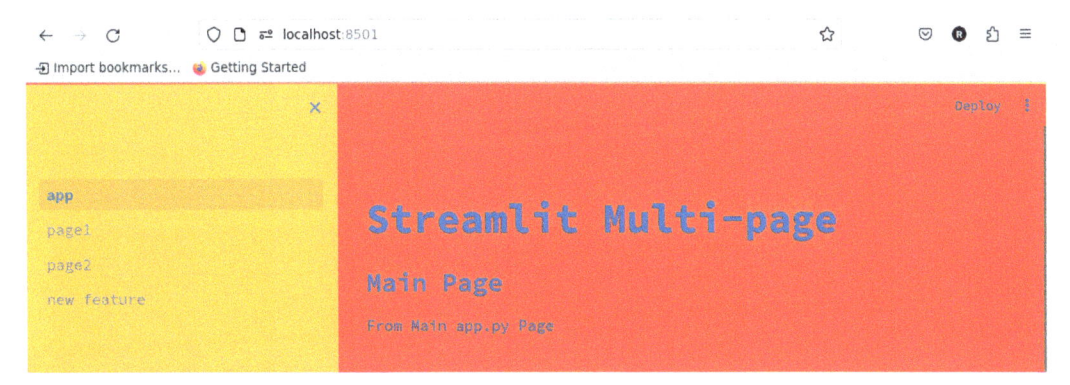

Figure 14.28: The new variable shown on the app page

On the main page – that is, the **app** page – we can visualize the content of `my_variable` that was created in the `app.py` file.

Now, in Sublime Text, we will change the `01_page1.py` code, as shown in the following screenshot:

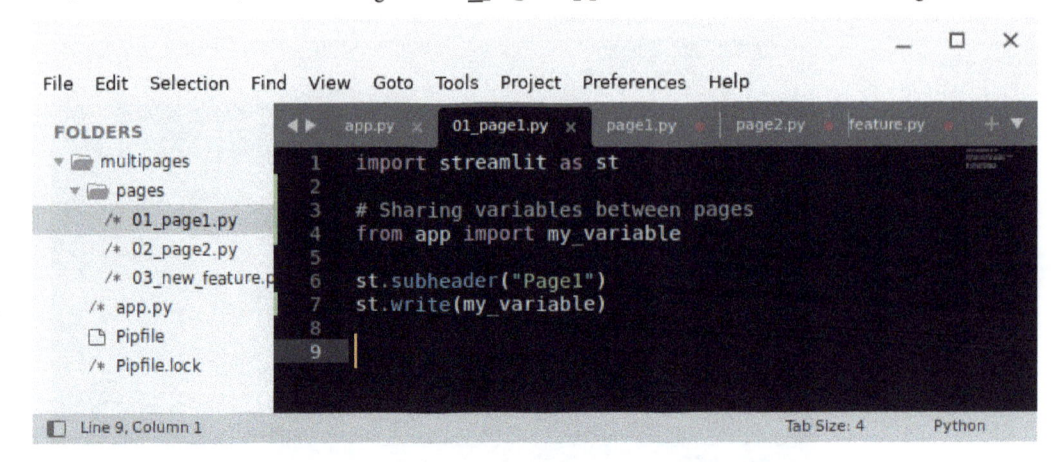

Figure 14.29: Code changes in the "01_page1.py" file

Here's what we are doing:

- On *line 4*, we imported `my_variable` from the `app` file.

    Please note that according to the specific syntax, we do not need to write `from app.py` but simply `from app` – that is, excluding the `.py` from the filename.

- Then, on *line 7*, we printed the imported variable on the screen.

This is the result in the web application:

Figure 14.30: The new variable shown on the page1 page

The result is very interesting: here, we are showing the content of a variable that has been created on another page on **page1**!

Let's also modify the `02_page2.py` file in the following way:

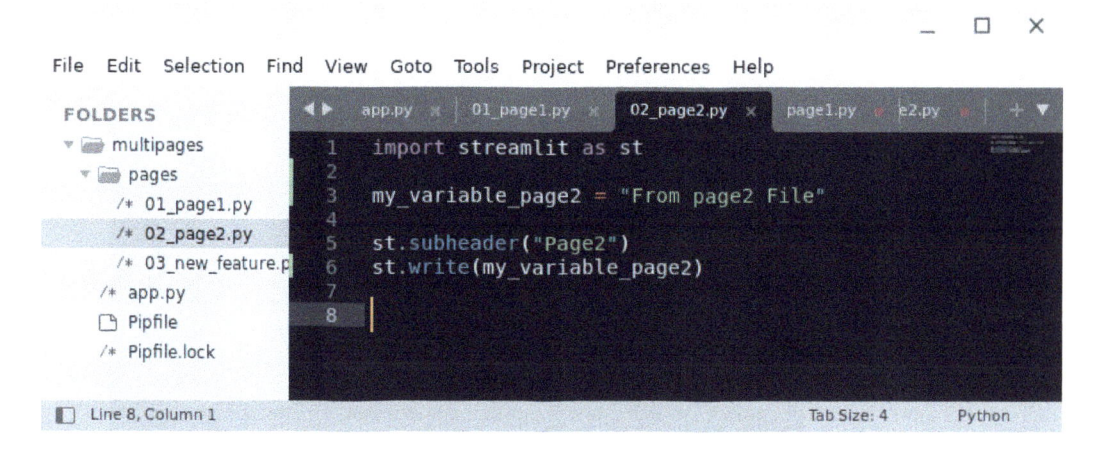

Figure 14.31: A new variable in the 02_page2.py file

On *line 3*, we introduce a new variable that is printed on *line 6*. This is the result in the web application:

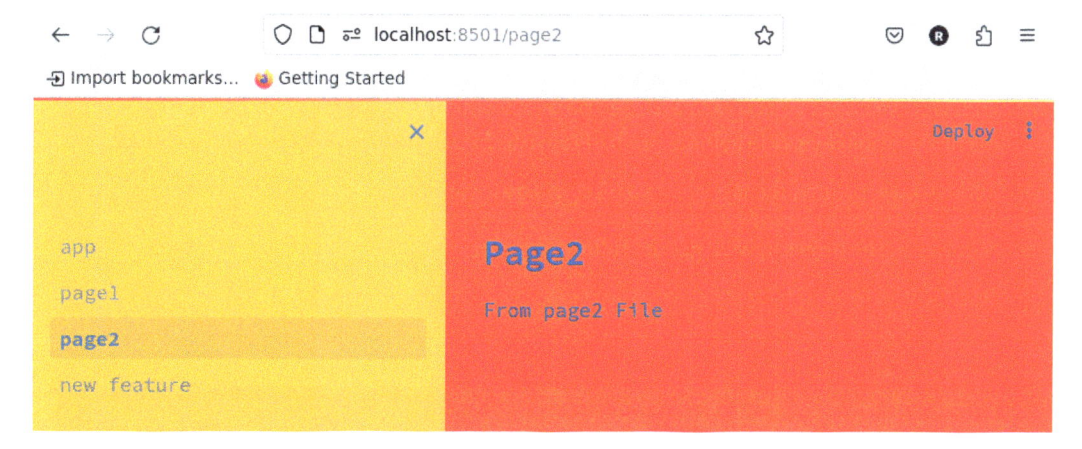

Figure 14.32: The new variable shown on the page2 page

Now, let's try to print the variable we created on page2 on page1. To achieve this result, this time, for the 01_page1.py file, we must use slightly different code, as shown in the following figure:

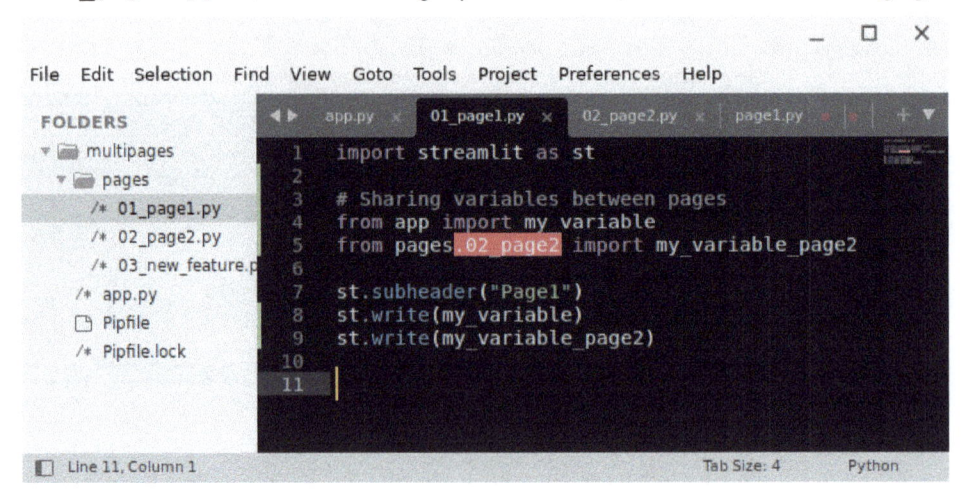

Figure 14.33: The new code for the "01_page1.py" file

Here's what we did:

- On *line 5*, we imported my_variable_page2 from the 02_page2.py file. However, since this file is inside the pages folder, we had to write from pages.02_page2 import....

- On *line 9*, we printed the my_variable_page2 variable.

When we move to the browser, we'll get the following error:

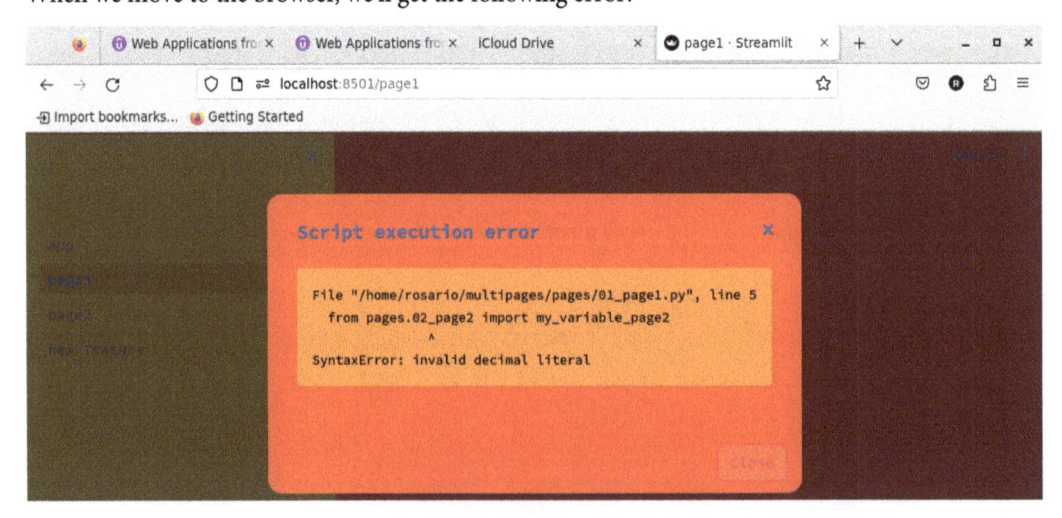

Figure 14.34: A script execution error

As the error explains, we are facing an *invalid decimal literal*. This means that when we tried to import from pages.02_page2..., as shown in *Figure 14.33*, Streamlit couldn't manage 02 at the beginning of the filename.

To fix this issue, we must rename the file in the following way:

```
mv 02_page2.py page2.py
```

Accordingly, we must change the code in the 01_page1.py file, as follows:

Figure 14.35: The final code changes to the 01_page1.py file

Now, we are correctly importing from pages.page2. Checking our browser, we'll see that everything works fine:

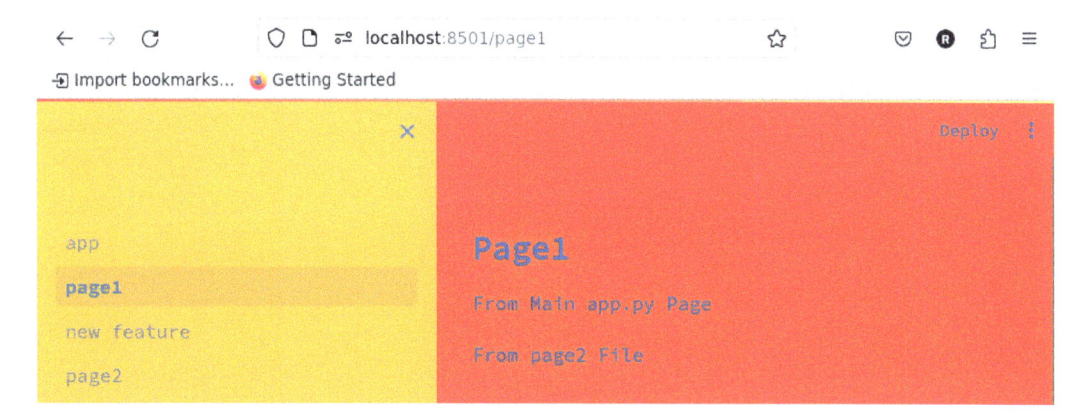

Figure 14.36: page1 showing variables from other pages

page1 shows a variable from the main page (`app.py`) and a variable from `page2.app`, which means that variables are correctly exchanged among different pages.

This is proof that to exchange variables among files, we don't have to put numbers in the filenames.

Our main task is to implement web applications that completely satisfy specific needs, such as disease detection, as we did with the *Covid-19 Detection Tool* app; however, making these applications very beautiful and easy to use is also very important. Deep customization is how we can make our application very attractive and simple to use.

Summary

In this chapter, we focused on advanced customization techniques in Streamlit. We delved into the new features that enable deep customization, allowing for more personalized and complex web pages. This chapter guided you through the process of creating highly customized pages, emphasizing the ability to tailor the user interface and functionality to specific requirements.

A significant portion of this chapter was dedicated to understanding theming and the use of TOML files. This involves exploring how themes can be manipulated to change the look and feel of a Streamlit app, making it more appealing and brand-aligned. The use of TOML files was explained in detail, demonstrating how they can be used to define and manage these themes efficiently.

Finally, this chapter explored Streamlit's multi-pages feature. We learned how to structure a Streamlit application into multiple pages, thereby enhancing its organization and user navigation. We offered practical examples and best practices for implementing multi-page applications, ensuring you can effectively organize complex Streamlit projects into more manageable and user-friendly formats. This comprehensive chapter has empowered you to elevate your Streamlit applications to new levels of customization and sophistication.

In the next chapter, we'll learn how to enhance our web applications with Streamlit's forms, Session State, and customizable subdomain features.

15
Enhancing Web Apps with Forms, Session State, and Customizable Subdomains

In Streamlit, *forms*, *Session State*, and *customizable subdomains* are all features that allow for more advanced customization and functionality in web applications.

Forms allow users to create interactive forms within their Streamlit web app that can be used to collect user input and perform actions based on a specific group of inputs. Forms can contain a variety of input elements, such as text fields, drop-down menus, and checkboxes.

Session State is a feature that allows users to store and persist data across different sessions of their web app. This can be useful for storing user preferences or app settings.

Finally, *customizable subdomains* allow users to create a custom subdomain for their Streamlit app that can be useful for branding or creating a more memorable URL (instead of using the standard anonymous URL proposed automatically).

In this chapter, we're going to cover the following main topics:

- What are forms and when and why do we use them?
- What is Session State and when do we use it?
- What are customizable subdomains and what possibilities do they offer?

Technical requirements

- In this chapter, we'll be using the following libraries, packages, and tools:
    - Sublime Text
    - Python 3
    - `pipenv`
    - Streamlit

- The code in this chapter can be accessed through the following GitHub link: `https://github.com/PacktPublishing/Web-App-Development-Made-Simple-with-Streamlit/tree/217479d2112ded99cfdd820a85709296ba5356b2/Chapter15`

What are forms and when and why do we use them?

Streamlit forms is a feature that allows you to create interactive web forms in your Streamlit apps. These forms enable you to collect user input through different widgets such as textboxes, selects, checkboxes, and more. When a user submits a form, Streamlit automatically captures the input values and makes them available to your Python code.

Using Streamlit forms is simple. You can define the form boundaries with `st.form()` and add widgets within it. Streamlit provides a variety of input components that make it easy for users to enter information such as text input, number input, and so on. This integration with Python eliminates the need for manual form handling.

Streamlit forms offer customization options to improve the user experience. You can add labels, default values, and tooltips to guide users. Additionally, you can control a form's layout and style to match your app's design.

Form submission is always triggered by a submit button, allowing you to capture user input and perform actions based on it.

To summarize, forms are groups of widgets, and we can run different groups of forms independently of one another. Let's write some simple code to show this feature:

What are forms and when and why do we use them? 301

Figure 15.1: Starting point for forms

The preceding code is extremely simple: after importing `streamlit`, we just print a title on the screen. Here is the result:

Figure 15.2: Starting point from the browser perspective

To introduce forms in our code, we essentially have two approaches. Let's take a look at them one by one.

The context manager approach

The first way to introduce forms in our code is the *context manager approach*, an elegant approach that uses the `with` instruction. The `with` instruction makes it possible to *declare* the form just at the beginning of the code block (on *line 8* in *Figure 15.3*) and then just use instructions in the usual way, typing `st.` with the name of the widget. So, write this code:

```python
import streamlit as st

def main():
    st.title("Streamlit Forms Tutorial")


    # Method 1: with (Context Manager Approach)
    with st.form(key='form1'):
        firstname = st.text_input("Firstname")
        lastname = st.text_input("Lastname")
        complete_name = firstname + " " + lastname

        submit_button = st.form_submit_button(label="Register")

        if submit_button:
            st.success("Hello {} you have been regstered!".format(complete_name))



if __name__ == '__main__':
    main()
```

Figure 15.3: The context manager approach

Here's a breakdown of the code shown in *Figure 15.3*:

- On *line 8*, we created a form leveraging the `with` instruction. Please note that the only argument of the form is its key, and it can be any kind of text.

- After that, on *lines 9* and *10*, we inserted a couple of widgets in our new form, specifically a couple of `text_input` instances used to save the first name and last name of a hypothetical user.

- On *line 11*, we just merged the first and last names.

- *Line 13* is very important because each form needs to be activated by a submit button, which must be created using the `form_submit_button` method. In this case, as an argument, we use the label to be visualized in the form.

- Finally, on *line 15*, we used an `if` clause to double-check whether the button has been pushed; if it has, we print a success message.

This is the result in the browser:

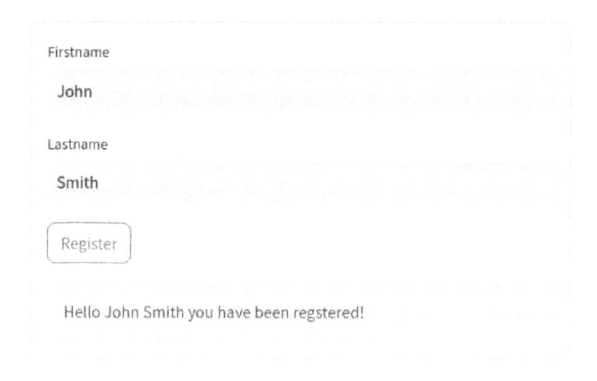

Figure 15.4: Result using the context manager approach in the browser

When we click on the **Register** button, a greeting message appears on the screen. Please note that this message is inside the form box: the gray box containing the two text_input instances and the button.

To keep the message out of the form, we can slightly change the code, as shown in the following figure:

```python
import streamlit as st

def main():
    st.title("Streamlit Forms Tutorial")


    # Method 1: with (Context Manager Approach)
    with st.form(key='form1'):
        firstname = st.text_input("Firstname")
        lastname = st.text_input("Lastname")
        complete_name = firstname + " " + lastname

        submit_button = st.form_submit_button(label="Register")

    if submit_button:
        st.success("Hello {} you have been regstered!".format(complete_name))




if __name__ == '__main__':
    main()
```

Figure 15.5: Keeping the success message outside the form

Now, the `if` clause indentation has been changed to be exactly below the `with` instruction, which means below the form – that is, outside its code block. This is the result:

Streamlit Forms Tutorial

Firstname

Mary

Lastname

Smith

Register

Hello Mary Smith you have been regstered!

Figure 15.6: A different position for the greeting message

Let's now see the second approach, a classic one, used to introduce forms.

The classic approach

The classic approach is quite straightforward, since it doesn't require the `with` instruction:

```python
import streamlit as st

def main():
    st.title("Streamlit Forms Tutorial")


    # Method 1: with (Context Manager Approach)
    with st.form(key='form1'):
        firstname = st.text_input("Firstname")
        lastname = st.text_input("Lastname")
        complete_name = firstname + " " + lastname

        submit_button = st.form_submit_button(label="Register")

        if submit_button:
            st.success("Hello {} you have been regstered!".format(complete_name))

    # Method 2: no 'with' and submitting message outside
    form2 = st.form(key='form2')
    username = form2.text_input("Username")
    jobtype = form2.selectbox("Job", ["Streamlit Master", "NBA Player", "Sailorman"])
    submit_button2 = form2.form_submit_button("Login")

    if submit_button2:
            st.success("Hello {} you logged in!".format(username))



if __name__ == '__main__':
    main()
```

Figure 15.7: The classic approach to introduce forms in our code

Here's what we are doing this time:

- On *line 19*, we directly introduce the form.

- After that, on *lines 20* and *21*, we create two new widgets, `text_input` and `selectbox`, respectively.

- On *line 22*, we create a submit button. As usual, an `if` clause oversees whether or not the submit button has been pushed. It's important to understand that, in this case, the indentation of the `if` clause will always be at the same level as that of the form, so the success message will always be outside the form box.

Here's how the two forms created using the two approaches look in the browser:

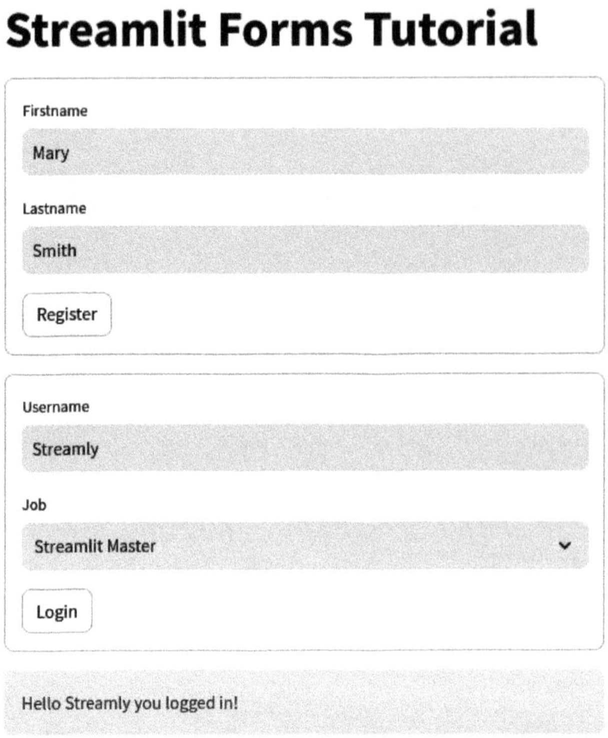

Figure 15.8: Two forms created with the context manager and classic approaches

Please note that we can insert data (this means using widgets) independently into the two forms. In fact, the two submit buttons are completely unrelated.

Forms are a very powerful way of keeping widgets and components segregated in a specific area of our web app. Let's now see how to deal with so-called *sessions*.

What is Session State and when do we use it?

Streamlit was launched in 2019, and *statefulness* was a little problem for quite a long time since states weren't managed natively. However, starting from version 0.8.4, things changed, and the official claim (https://blog.streamlit.io/session-state-for-streamlit/) was as follows:

You can now store information across app interactions and rerun!

To be honest, that claim is really perfect because it conveys everything about sessions. Streamlit's **Session State** feature offers an efficient and sophisticated approach to session management. This feature enables the storage of variables across multiple reruns, facilitates the creation of interactive events on input widgets, and allows the use of callback functions to manage these events effectively.

The robust capabilities of Session State enhance the development of various applications. These capabilities include the following:

- Integrating widgets that are interdependent
- Developing engaging stateful games, such as Battleship and Tic-Tac-Toe
- Conducting data and image annotation tasks
- Extending functionalities for diverse and complex uses, such as persistence of user data across multiple requests and efficient management of resources and data

Typically, using Streamlit without Session State means that interacting with a widget initiates a rerun, causing the variables defined in the script to reset with each execution. In contrast, employing Session State enables the preservation of variable values across reruns, which is particularly beneficial when there is a need to maintain variable states without reinitialization.

Let's use the following code to see a little example in action and understand more. Start by writing the following code:

```python
import streamlit as st

def main():
    st.title("Streamlit Session State Tutorial")

    st.subheader("Counter Example")

    # Streamlit runs from top to bottom on every iteration so
    # we check if 'count' has already been initialized in st.session_state
    # if no, the initialize count to 0
    # if count is already initialized, don't do anything

    if 'count' not in st.session_state:
        st.session_state.count = 0


    # Create a button which will increment the counter
    increment = st.button('Increment')
    if increment:
        st.session_state.count += 1

    # A button to decrement the counter
    decrement = st.button('Decrement')
    if decrement:
        st.session_state.count -= 1

    st.write("Count =", st.session_state.count )



if __name__ == '__main__':
    main()
```

Figure 15.9: Session State in code

The idea behind Session State is simple and genial: Streamlit always runs from top to bottom on every iteration, so we check whether a variable of our interest (`count` in the example) has already been initialized in `st.session_state`. If it is not initialized yet, we initialize it to a specific value (0 in our case); otherwise, we don't do anything.

So, `st.session_state` is just a kind of *collection* that saves variables we don't want to initialize every time.

The preceding code is very easy. Here's a breakdown:

- On *line 13*, we check whether the `count` variable is not in `session_state`; in this case, we initialize it to 0
- On *line 19*, we create a button to increment the count variable and we perform this operation using `st.session_state.count`; in this way, we remember the `count` variable's value
- On *line 24*, we do the same, but decrementing the `count` variable
- Finally, on *line 28*, we visualize a little message on the screen showing the `count` variable value

This is the result in the browser:

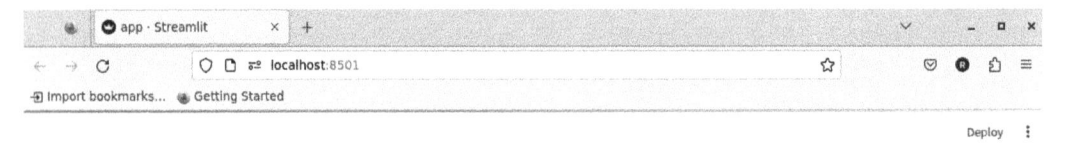

Figure 15.10: Session State in action

Please verify that every time you click on the **Increment** or **Decrement** button, the value of **Count** is automatically updated.

The code in *Figure 15.9* demonstrates the persistence of values across reruns. However, let's explore a more intricate scenario. In Streamlit, it is feasible to assign *callbacks* to various widgets, such as `st.button` or `st.slider`. This is achieved by utilizing the `on_change` argument, allowing for more advanced interactivity and functionality.

A callback, often referred to as a *call-after* function, is a segment of executable code that is provided as an argument to another piece of code. This arrangement anticipates that the receiving code will execute the callback at a specified moment. Typical scenarios for such execution include user interactions such as clicking a button or adjusting a slider – essentially, whenever a change is detected.

Utilizing Session State enables the management of events linked to modifications in a widget or button clicks through callback functions. This implies that when a callback function is associated with a widget, any alteration in the widget initiates a specific sequence: the callback function is executed first, followed by a top-to-bottom execution of the application.

Let's see callbacks in action:

```python
import streamlit as st

def main():
    st.title("Streamlit Session State Tutorial")

    st.subheader("Counter Example")

    # Streamlit runs from top to bottom on every iteration so
    # we check if 'count' has already been initialized in st.session_state
    # if no, the initialize count to 0
    # if count is already initialized, don't do anything

    if 'count' not in st.session_state:
        st.session_state.count = 0

    # Create a button which will increment the counter
    increment = st.button('Increment')
    if increment:
        st.session_state.count += 1

    # A button to decrement the counter
    decrement = st.button('Decrement')
    if decrement:
        st.session_state.count -= 1

    st.write("Count =", st.session_state.count )

    st.subheader("Callback Example - Mirrored Widgets")

    def update_first():
        st.session_state.second = st.session_state.first

    def update_second():
        st.session_state.first = st.session_state.second

    st.text_input(label="Textbox 1", key="first", on_change=update_first)
    st.text_input(label="Textbox 2", key="second", on_change=update_second)

if __name__ == '__main__':
    main()
```

Figure 15.11: Callbacks in code

Here's a breakdown of the code in *Figure 15.11*:

- On *line 32*, we define a callback function named `update_first`. This function updates the value of the *second* variable contained in the `session_state` widget to the value of the *first* variable always stored in the `session_state` widget.
- On *line 35*, we define a second callback function that is exactly the same as the first one, but updates the value of the *first* variable according to the value of the *second* one.
- On *lines 39 and 40*, we introduce two `text_input` widgets. Among their arguments, as usual, we can find a label and a key, but this time there is something new: `on_change`.

    Here, the callbacks enter action when a change happens in the widgets (so, when some text is inserted) when the `update_first` function is executed at *line 39* and the `update_second` function is executed on *line 40*.

In this way, we create two widgets with mirrored values. This is the result in the browser:

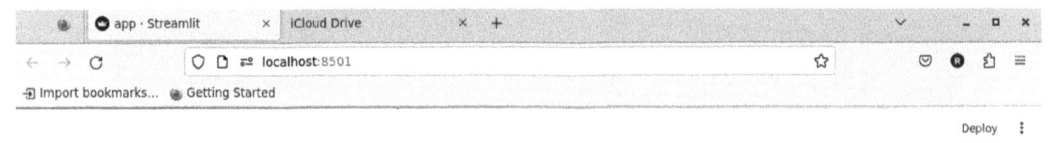

Figure 15.12: Result of the callback action

As we can see, every time we insert text into the first input box, the second one is updated, and vice versa.

Session State is perhaps one of the most powerful features of Streamlit. Please learn carefully how to leverage it.

Let's now see the advantages offered by *customizable subdomains*.

What are customizable subdomains and what possibilities do they offer?

We have already deployed two applications on Streamlit Cloud: the *NLP App* and the *COVID-19 Detection Tool*. So, we are quite familiar with the process, and even how to solve problems arising due to big files or a need for unconventional libraries.

Upon deploying our application on Community Cloud, it is assigned an automatically generated subdomain, which is structured based on our GitHub repository. This subdomain, unique to our application, serves as a means to share the app with others. Nevertheless, the default subdomain can often be cumbersome and not particularly user-friendly. For instance, a subdomain such as the following may not be easily memorable:

```
https://streamlit-demo-self-driving-streamlit-app-8jya0g.streamlit.app
```

To enhance shareability and recognition, we have the option to establish a custom subdomain. This customization allows the subdomain to better represent the content of our app, our personal brand, or any other preferred aspect. The custom URL would then be formatted as follows:

```
<your-custom-subdomain>.streamlit.app
```

Enhancing Web Apps with Forms, Session State, and Customizable Subdomains

To tailor the subdomain of your application within Streamlit's Cloud workspace, follow these straightforward steps:

1. Navigate to the right of your app, click on the ⋮ overflow menu, and then select **Settings**:

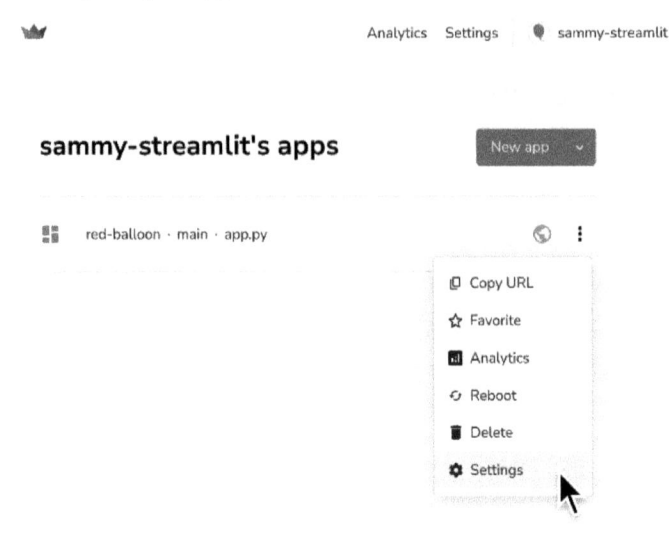

Figure 15.13: Deployed app settings on Streamlit Cloud

2. In the app settings modal, access the **General** tab. Here, you'll find your app's current unique subdomain.
3. Choose a custom subdomain that is between 6 and 63 characters long for your app's URL.
4. Click **Save** to confirm:

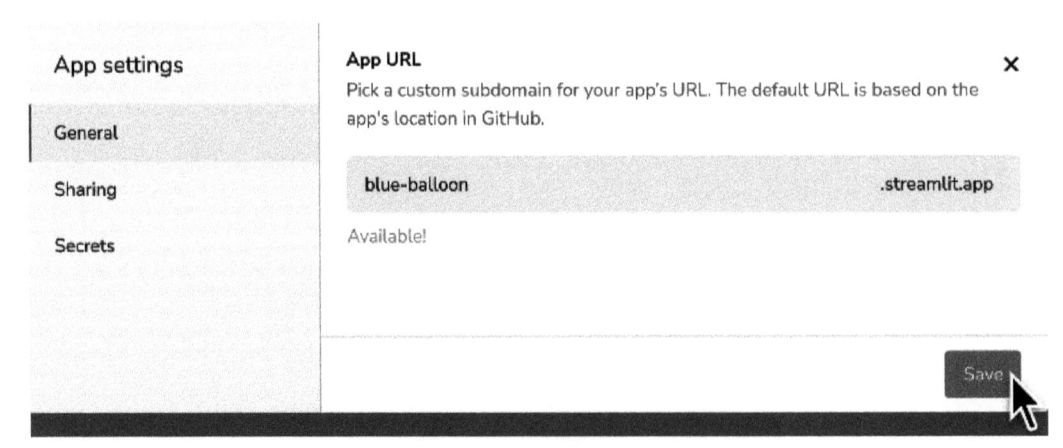

Figure 15.14: A new subdomain for our app

This process is quick and efficient. Once completed, your app will be accessible via the newly set custom subdomain URL. In cases where the chosen custom subdomain is unavailable (for instance, if it is already in use), an error message will be displayed, prompting you to select a different subdomain, as shown in the following screenshot:

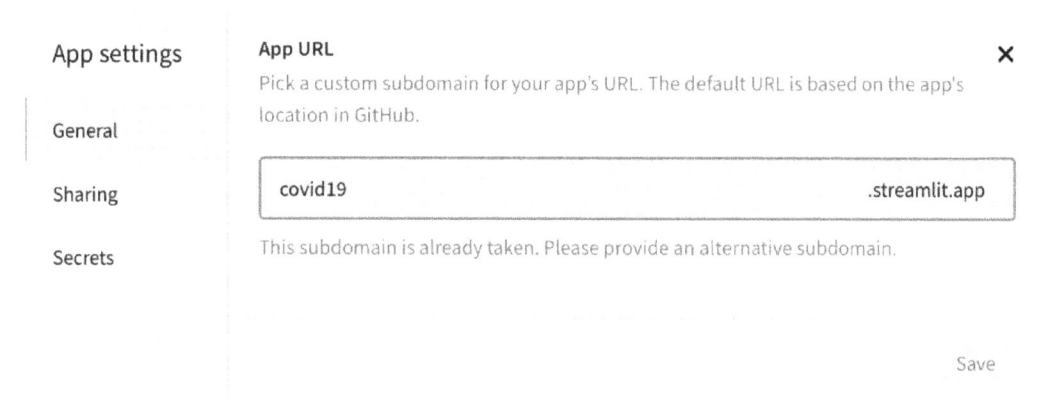

Figure 15.15: "This subdomain is already taken" error message

Being able to select a subdomain name that perfectly suits the aim of our web application is a very powerful customization.

Summary

In this chapter, we covered some topics that can really increase the level of our web applications.

First of all, we saw what forms are and how to use them, discovering that having independent groups of widgets inside our web apps can make a big difference. All we need to do is define these forms and include some widgets inside them, using a button to trigger the widgets. Even the button is customizable since it can be included in the form or placed outside it.

Further, we learned that Session State is an incredibly powerful weapon in our hands. At last, we can persist the values of our variables, and this opens up an incredible scenario of use cases to us. Moreover, thanks to callbacks, we can decide what to do when a user interacts with our widgets, calling back fully customized functions that completely match our needs.

Finally, by customizing the subdomains of our deployed web applications, we achieved two targets: we made them much easier to remember and we gave them a very professional touch!

In the next and final chapter, we are going to sum up the long journey we've made together, highlighting considerations about the Streamlit framework, discussing what the very important takeaways are, and giving some suggestions for the next steps.

16
Takeaways and Conclusion

Together, we've traveled quite a long road. Starting from learning how to create a working environment, we went through the basics of Streamlit usage. After that, we became more advanced users, and we learned a very professional way of creating web applications.

Moreover, we saw how to deploy and publish our creations on the cloud. From a wide perspective, we also acquired some very useful skills related to automatic file detection and upload, database connection, login and sign-up page creation and account management, theming, Session State, forms, and subdomains—a very long journey!

There are also a lot of takeaways, and these can make web application creation easier in the future:

- Skills for creating a very cheap (free) and effective development environment
- A web app skeleton working template with menus and decorations
- Skills for deploying and uploading web apps on the cloud
- A useful know-how (with working skeleton template) about web apps with images
- A very powerful technique for creating, populating, and using databases in our web application
- A very important skill for implementing session states and multi-page applications (with a working code example)
- Deep knowledge of the main and advanced Streamlit widgets
- The capacity to easily understand future versions and improvements of the framework

In this chapter, we're going to cover the following main topics:

- How and when to use our web app working template
- How and when to use databases and advanced skills
- How to deploy web applications on the cloud

How and when to use our web app working template

There are some operations that we must always do, such as preparing the virtual environment and installing all the proper libraries. These operations are the real foundation of our activity of web application creation.

Once our environment is ready, we can start writing our code. This activity requires a deep comprehension of the problems we are asked to solve and a clear implementation strategy. At this point, the template or skeleton that we developed together and used to build up the NLP application and the Covid-19 detection tool becomes our strongest friend. It is perfect for breaking down the problem into several sub-problems and assigning each one of these sub-problems to a specific function. The list of all the required functions will be displayed in the menu in the sidebar, letting the user select a specific function and proceed with the execution. We also saw that, in the template, there are already some nice decorators included, such as titles, icons and images.

If we want to be more specific, we can say that knowing how and when to use a web application template, such as the one we made together, is crucial for efficient and effective web application development.

Here's a breakdown of how to use such a template:

- **Installation and setup**: After opening the template, you'll find installation and setup instructions for the libraries. Follow these steps to create a project directory, install dependencies, and configure your development environment if needed.

- **Customize content**: Modify the template to fit your specific requirements. This may involve changing the user interface, adding or removing features, or altering the default content. Templates are typically designed to be customizable, so you can adapt them to your project's needs.

- **Add application logic**: Implement the application's business logic, which is the core functionality that differentiates your project from others. This may include data processing, calculations, data visualization, or any other tasks relevant to your application.

- **Styling and theming**: Customize the visual aspects of your application, such as colors, fonts, and layouts, to match your brand or design preferences. Many templates provide options for styling and theming.

- **Testing**: Thoroughly test your application to ensure that it works as intended and is free of bugs or issues. This includes testing user interactions, data handling, and responsiveness.

- **Continuous improvement**: As your application evolves, you can revisit the template to make updates or improvements. Templates are designed to be flexible and adaptable to accommodate changes in your project.

After knowing how to use a web application template, let's see when to use one:

- **Prototyping**: Templates are excellent for quickly prototyping ideas. You can use a template as a starting point to visualize your concept and gather feedback.
- **Learning and education**: If you're new to web development or a particular framework, such as Streamlit, templates can be educational. You can dissect a template's code to learn how different components and features work.
- **Rapid development**: When time is limited, using the template can help you accelerate development. You can leverage pre-built components and functionalities to get your application off the ground faster.
- **Consistency across projects**: If you work on multiple projects or within a team, using templates can ensure consistency in design and structure. This is particularly valuable when maintaining a portfolio of applications.
- **Focus on unique features**: Templates handle common tasks and functionalities, allowing you to focus on implementing unique features or solving specific problems relevant to your project.

To summarize, the web application template/skeleton is a valuable tool for development, offering a structured and efficient approach to building web applications. Use it when you want to save time, ensure consistency, prototype ideas, or accelerate development. Also, customize it to meet your specific project requirements. The template is particularly beneficial when it aligns with your project goals and reduces the need to reinvent common components and functionalities.

The template is a fundamental way of staying organized and speeding up our work. Another extremely important feature is saving information in a database.

How and when to use databases and advanced skills

In *Chapter 13*, when we talked about login and signup, we explained how to deal with databases in Streamlit, while in *Chapters 14* and *15*, we covered topics such as customized pages, multi-pages, themes, forms, subdomains, and Session State.

Now, it may sound trivial, but you should consider using databases in Streamlit when you need to store and manage data for your web application. Databases are useful when you want to do the following:

- **Persist data**: Save information (such as user profiles, user-generated content, or application settings) so that it's available even after closing the web app.
- **Access large amounts of data**: Handle and retrieve a lot of data efficiently, such as records in a sales database or user comments on a website.
- **Collaborate**: Share and update data across multiple users or devices. Databases help you keep information consistent and up to date.

When working with databases in Streamlit, or any web application, it's important to follow the best security practices, which include the following:

- **Use prepared statements**: When writing SQL queries, use prepared statements or parameterized queries to prevent SQL injection attacks. Streamlit has a library called `sqlite3` that allows you to work with databases.

- **Secure database credentials**: Store your database credentials (such as usernames and passwords) in a secure environment, such as environment variables or a configuration file. Never hardcode them in your code.

- **Implement authentication**: If your application allows users to access or modify data, implement user authentication and authorization to control who can do what in your app.

- **Regularly update and patch**: Keep your database software and libraries up to date to fix security vulnerabilities. This is important for both your application and the database system itself.

- **Data encryption**: If sensitive data is stored in the database, ensure it's encrypted both at rest (when stored on the server) and in transit (when data is transmitted between your app and the database).

In simple terms, databases are like organized storage spaces for your app's data. They're useful for saving, accessing, and managing information securely. To use them safely in Streamlit, follow the best practices to protect your data and ensure your app runs smoothly. Avoid common mistakes such as not handling errors, exposing sensitive data, or overloading the database.

Here's a brief recap of some advanced Streamlit features:

- **Customized pages**: Streamlit allows you to create customized pages within your web application. Each page can have unique content, layout, and functionality. This feature is beneficial when you want to organize your application into different sections, such as a homepage, a dashboard, and a settings page. You can use Streamlit's layout components to design and structure each page as you like.

- **Multiple pages**: Streamlit offers the ability to create web applications with multiple interconnected pages. This allows you to build complex applications with different views, navigation, and interactions. You can use Streamlit's built-in navigation elements, such as buttons or links, to move between pages within your app. Multi-page applications are useful for creating applications with a hierarchical structure or when you need to guide users through different steps.

- **Themes**: Streamlit provides the ability to customize the visual appearance of your application with themes. Themes are collections of predefined styles and colors that you can apply to your app. This feature lets you create a consistent and visually appealing design that matches your branding or personal preferences.

- **Forms**: Streamlit allows you to create interactive forms within your web application. Forms are a way to gather user input through widgets such as text inputs, sliders, and checkboxes. You can use forms to collect data, settings, or preferences from users and process that information in your application.

- **Subdomains**: Subdomains in Streamlit enable you to serve different applications or sections of your app from distinct subdomains of your website. This is especially useful when you want to host multiple Streamlit apps under different URLs, each with its own functionality or content. Subdomains help in creating a modular and organized structure for your web application, allowing for efficient navigation and scalability.

- **Session State**: Session State in Streamlit lets you store and manage data across different interactions and pages during a user's session. It's a way of maintaining variables or user-specific data that persists as the user interacts with your app. This feature is useful if you want the application to remember user settings, selections, or other information gained during users' visits. This can provide a more personalized and dynamic user experience.

To recap, Streamlit offers a variety of features to enhance the functionality and appearance of your web applications. You can create customized pages for different sections, design multi-page applications with navigation, style your app with themes, collect user input using forms, use subdomains for modularity, and maintain session-specific data with Session State. These features provide you with the flexibility and tools needed to build interactive and user-friendly web applications using Streamlit.

After developing our web application, which uses a database to save information, it's time to deploy it.

How to deploy web applications on the cloud

A web application lives on the web, and after the implementation of both the NLP app and the COVID-19 detection tool, we completed the deployment of both web apps on Streamlit Cloud.

Let's recall why deploying web applications on the cloud is so important.

Deploying web applications on the cloud offers several significant advantages:

- **Global accessibility**: Cloud-hosted applications are accessible from anywhere with an internet connection, enabling a broad user reach. Users can access your app without needing to install it locally.

- **Scalability**: Cloud platforms can easily scale your application to handle increased traffic or demand. This means your app remains responsive even during traffic spikes.

- **Reliability and redundancy**: Cloud providers offer high availability and redundancy, reducing the risk of downtime. Data is often backed up and replicated across multiple data centers.

- **Security**: Cloud providers invest heavily in security measures, including data encryption, firewalls, and identity management. Your application can benefit from these robust security features.

- **Simplified maintenance**: Cloud providers handle infrastructure management, such as server maintenance and updates. This allows developers to focus on app development rather than server administration.

Streamlit Cloud is a cloud-based platform specifically designed for deploying and sharing Streamlit applications. Streamlit Cloud is tailored to streamline the deployment process for these applications.

Besides the common advantages of deploying on a generic cloud, Streamlit's cloud service offers some more specific features:

- **Seamless deployment**: Streamlit Cloud simplifies the deployment process, removing the need for complex server configurations. Developers can deploy their Streamlit applications with minimal effort.
- **Real-time updates**: Streamlit Cloud automatically updates your app when you push changes to your code repository. Users always see the latest version without manual intervention.
- **Collaboration**: Developers can easily share their applications with specific collaborators or keep them private. This is valuable for both public-facing and internal projects.
- **Analytics and monitoring**: Streamlit Cloud provides tools to track usage, performance, and errors in your application. This data is valuable for optimizing and improving your app over time.

In conclusion, deploying web applications on the cloud, particularly with Streamlit Cloud, offers a streamlined and user-friendly approach to sharing Streamlit applications with a global audience. The advantages of global accessibility, scalability, cost efficiency, and simplified maintenance make cloud hosting a popular choice for web app deployment. Streamlit Cloud, tailored to Streamlit applications, simplifies the deployment process and enhances the accessibility and usability of your data-driven web applications.

Farewell!

In closing, as we reach the end of the final chapter of this book, I want to express my sincere appreciation to you for embarking on this journey of exploring Streamlit. We've come a long way together, delving into the world of web application development with this incredible Python library. Your dedication to mastering Streamlit and its many functionalities is truly commendable.

Remember that technology is ever-evolving and new features and improvements are continually being introduced. To stay at the forefront of web application development, I encourage you to periodically visit Streamlit's official website. There, you'll find the latest updates and features and resources that will help you stay informed and empowered in your web application projects.

As we bid farewell, I want to extend my best wishes to you, dear readers. I thank you for your time, your passion for learning, and your determination to explore the world of Streamlit. May your future endeavors in web application development be filled with creativity and success. Good luck on your coding journey, and thank you for being a part of this exciting exploration of Streamlit. Farewell!

Index

Symbols

.toml files 285

A

advanced customization techniques 276-280
advanced web app features
　dealing with 180-184
AI-Powered web app
　decorations, adding 175-178
　environment, configuring 166, 167
　menu, building 176-178
　packages, importing 170
　packages, installing 167-172
　skeleton, building 172-175
app skeleton
　building 73-78
artificial intelligence (AI) 199

B

bad behavior
　avoiding 220
　GitHub repository, creating 221, 222
　package list, creating 220
　runtime errors, avoiding 222, 223

C

call-after function 309
callback 309
classic approach 305, 306
cloud-based web application
　versus local-based web application 7
cloud deployment skills 218, 219
computer vision 202
computing methods
　scenario 4, 5
context manager approach 301-304
convolutional neural network (CNN) 192, 202
customizable subdomains 299, 311-313
　providing, advantages 311-313
customized pages
　creating 281-285
customized web apps
　creating, for user experience 202-206

D

database credentials
　retrieving 266-273
　saving 266-273

Index

databases
  best security practices 318
  scenarios, using 317-319
  usage 317
DataFrame 51, 52
date and time 57-62
decorations
  adding 79-86
digital signature 254
Disclaimer and Info section
  adding 192-196
Django 8, 9
  features 8
  need for 8

F

file uploader
  app skeleton, building 237-239
  creating, for web apps 243-249
  features 236
  radio button, creating for app menu 239-243
  virtual environment, creating 236, 237
Flask 8
  features 8
forms 299

G

GitHub 148
  disadvantages 149
  features 148
  Streamlit Share 149

H

hash 252
HTML color codes 286

I

Image Enhancement section
  adding, with Pillow library 184-186
  brightness feature 188, 189
  contrast feature 186, 187
  original feature 190, 191
information
  basic functions, adding 99-104
  columns, adding 95-99
  displaying 95
  expanders, adding 95-99
  hiding 95
  text box, adding 95-99
  wordcloud, adding 105, 106
integrated development environment (IDE) 13, 20, 21

L

language translation 122
  text area, adding 122, 123
  translation task, performing 124-128
learning-by-doing approach 67
lemmas 110
libraries
  managing 224-228
local-based web application
  versus cloud-based web application 7
login and signup page 252, 253

M

machine learning (ML) 10, 199
  predictions, utilizing 206-215
machine translation (MT) 121
Markdown syntax 193

menu
  building 79-86
multi-pages
  creating 287-292
  exploring 286, 287
  variable, passing from one page
      to another 292-298

N

**National Institute of Standards
    and Technology (NIST)** 253
National Security Agency (NSA) 253
natural language processing (NLP) 67, 119
neural machine translation (NMT) 121
NLP concepts 107
  lemmas 110
  summarization function, adding 107-109
  text-analysis function, using 112-118
  tokens 110
NLP techniques 120, 121
  sentiment analysis 122
  translation 121

O

object-relational mapper (ORM) 8
open-cv
  reference link 204
opinion mining 122
OS setup 14-19

P

Pillow library
  used, for adding Image
      Enhancement section 184

pipenv 13
plots 53-56
poetry tool 24
pretrained ML models
  benefits 200, 201
  examples 201
prototype
  benefits 11
Python 6
  reference link 19
Python Imaging Library 184
Python libraries for web application
  Django 8, 9
  Flask 8
  overview 8
Python packages
  importing 70-73
  installing 70-73
Python web framework 5, 6
  application programming interfaces (APIs) 6
  containerization 6
  deployment 6
  JavaScript 6
  server-side language 6
  version control 6
  web framework 5

R

relational database
  connecting 257-259
  graphical user interface, adding 264-266
  interacting with 257-259
  Login menu, creating 259-261
  Sign Up menu, creating 261, 262
  web application, running 262, 263

S

Secure Hash Algorithm 256 (SHA-256) 251, 253
  need for 254-256
sentiment analysis 122-135
sessions 306
Session State 299-311
  capabilities 307
  in code 308
  scenarios, using 307
  working 308
spaCy 71
SQLite3 database 251, 257
statistical machine translation (SMT) 121
Streamlit 6
  installing 32-35
  launching 32-35
  reference link 33
Streamlit capabilities
  examples 10
Streamlit Cloud 148
  app, deploying 228-231
Streamlit features and widgets 36-38
  audio 40-46
  balloons 51
  colored text boxes 39
  images 40-46
  inputting text and numbers 47-50
  slider 50, 51
  video 40-46
Streamlit forms 300, 301
  classic approach 305, 306
  context manager approach 30-304
  need for 300
  scenarios, using 300

Streamlit, Python libraries for web application
  cloud deployment 9
  community and support 9
  convenience and ease of use 9
  interactive dashboards 9
  Python integration 9
  rapid prototyping 9
  reusable components 9
Streamlit Share 148
  service 150-161
Streamlit features
  customized pages 318
  forms 319
  multiple pages 318
  subdomains 319
  themes pages 318
Sublime Text 13
  reference link 20

T

text analysis
  adding 90
  Analyze button, adding 91, 92
  basic functions, adding 93, 94
  Blob object, creating 92, 93
  function, using 112-118
  text area, adding 91
theming 285, 286
tokens 110, 111
translation 121

U

Ubuntu
  reference link 14
user experience 236

V

venv module 22
virtual environment (virtualenv) 22-29
  benefits 23
  configuring 68-70
  reference link 22
virtual private servers (VPS) 6
visualization 57

W

web app content
  arranging 88
  decorations, adding 89, 90
  organizing 88
  text analysis, adding 90
web application 135-144
  benefits 5
  deploying, on cloud 319, 320
  simplifying, with smart components 250
  used, for creating file uploader 243-249
web application deployment 146
  additional benefits 147
  best practices 147
  Streamlit Cloud 148
  Streamlit Share 148
web app working template
  scenarios, using 316, 317
web browser 5

‹packt›

Packtpub.com

Subscribe to our online digital library for full access to over 7,000 books and videos, as well as industry leading tools to help you plan your personal development and advance your career. For more information, please visit our website.

Why subscribe?

- Spend less time learning and more time coding with practical eBooks and Videos from over 4,000 industry professionals.
- Improve your learning with Skill Plans built especially for you.
- Get a free eBook or video every month.
- Fully searchable for easy access to vital information
- Copy and paste, print, and bookmark content.

Did you know that Packt offers eBook versions of every book published, with PDF and ePub files available? You can upgrade to the eBook version at Packtpub.com and as a print book customer, you are entitled to a discount on the eBook copy. Get in touch with us at customercare@packtpub.com for more details.

At www.packtpub.com, you can also read a collection of free technical articles, sign up for a range of free newsletters, and receive exclusive discounts and offers on Packt books and eBooks.

Other Books You May Enjoy

If you enjoyed this book, you may be interested in these other books by Packt:

Streamlit for Data Science

Tyler Richards

ISBN: 978-1-80324-822-6

- Set up your first development environment and create a basic Streamlit app from scratch
- Create dynamic visualizations using built-in and imported Python libraries
- Discover strategies for creating and deploying machine learning models in Streamlit
- Deploy Streamlit apps with Streamlit Community Cloud, Hugging Face Spaces, and Heroku
- Integrate Streamlit with Hugging Face, OpenAI, and Snowflake
- Beautify Streamlit apps using themes and components
- Implement best practices for prototyping your data science work with Streamlit

Packt is searching for authors like you

If you're interested in becoming an author for Packt, please visit `authors.packtpub.com` and apply today. We have worked with thousands of developers and tech professionals, just like you, to help them share their insight with the global tech community. You can make a general application, apply for a specific hot topic that we are recruiting an author for, or submit your own idea.

Hi!

I'm Rosario Moscato, the author of Web App Development Made Simple with Streamlit. I really hope you enjoyed reading this book and found it useful for increasing your productivity and efficiency in Web App Development with Streamlit.

It would really help me (and other potential readers!) if you could leave a review on Amazon sharing your thoughts on Web App Development Made Simple with Streamlit here.

Go to the link below or scan the QR code to leave your review:

`https://packt.link/r/1835086314`

Your review will help me to understand what's worked well in this book, and what could be improved upon for future editions, so it really is appreciated.

Best Wishes,

Rosario Moscato

Download a free PDF copy of this book

Thanks for purchasing this book!

Do you like to read on the go but are unable to carry your print books everywhere?

Is your eBook purchase not compatible with the device of your choice?

Don't worry, now with every Packt book you get a DRM-free PDF version of that book at no cost.

Read anywhere, any place, on any device. Search, copy, and paste code from your favorite technical books directly into your application.

The perks don't stop there, you can get exclusive access to discounts, newsletters, and great free content in your inbox daily

Follow these simple steps to get the benefits:

1. Scan the QR code or visit the link below

   `https://packt.link/free-ebook/9781835086315`

2. Submit your proof of purchase
3. That's it! We'll send your free PDF and other benefits to your email directly

www.ingramcontent.com/pod-product-compliance
Ingram Content Group UK Ltd.
Pitfield, Milton Keynes, MK11 3LW, UK
UKHW052224170425
457560UK00003B/8